SENECA MYTHS AND FOLK TALES

THE ATMOSPHERE IN WHICH LEGENDS WERE TOLD.

FROM A PAINTING SHOWING THE INTERIOR OF A BARK LONG-HOUSE, BY RICHARD J. TUCKER.

SENECA MYTHS AND FOLK TALES

BY

ARTHUR C. PARKER, M.S.

Introduction by William N. Fenton

University of Nebraska Press
Lincoln and London

Introduction copyright © 1989 by the University of Nebraska Press
Manufactured in the United States of America

First Bison Book printing: 1989
Most recent printing indicated by the last digit below:
10 9 8 7 6 5 4 3 2 1

Library of Congress Cataloging-in-Publication Data
Parker, Arthur Caswell, 1881–1955.
  Seneca myths and folk tales / by Arthur C. Parker: introduction
by William N. Fenton.
     p. cm.
"Reprinted from the 1923 edition published by the Buffalo Histori-
cal Society"—CIP verso t.p.
     Bibliography: p.
     Includes index.
     ISBN 0-8032-8723-2 (alk. paper)
     1. Seneca Indians—Legends. 2. Indians of North America—
New York (State)—Legends. I. Title.
E99.S3P27 1989   89-4869 CIP
398.2′089975—dc20

Reprinted from the 1923 edition published by the Buffalo Historical
Society, Buffalo, New York. It was issued as volume 27 of the Society's publications.

The paper used in this publication meets the minimum require-
ments of American National Standard for Information Sciences—
Permanence of Paper for Printed Library Materials, ANSI Z39.48–
1984.

TO

FRANK H. SEVERANCE, L.H.D., LL.D.

Secretary, The Buffalo Historical Society
President, The New York State Historical Association

WHOSE NUMEROUS ESSAYS AND HISTORI-
CAL WRITINGS HAVE BEEN A SOURCE OF
INSPIRATION AND ENLIGHTENMENT, AND
WHOSE INTEREST IN THE SENECA INDIANS
AND THEIR HISTORY HAS NEVER WANED,
THIS VOLUME OF

SENECA FOLK TALES

IS DEDICATED IN TESTIMONY OF THE
AUTHOR'S SINCERE ADMIRATION AND
ESTEEM.

CONTENTS

ILLUSTRATIONS

INTRODUCTION TO THE BISON BOOK EDITION

BY WILLIAM N. FENTON

Some fifty years ago during a visit to Rochester, Arthur Parker, then the eminent director of the Rochester Museum of Science, presented me with a copy of his scarce *Seneca Myths and Folk Tales* (1923) to assist me in my research among his people. The volume carries the marginalia entered during my field interviews with native informants; it has been read and reread and is badly worn and coming apart at the binding. It is high time that this treasure was reprinted and made available in a paperback edition to scholars, the native Iroquois, and the general reader. I am glad to examine it once more and share my knowledge of the author and of Iroquoian folklore.

Arthur Caswell Parker (1881–1955) was a man of two worlds and two cultures. Genetically of Seneca sires through his father and father's father, both of whom had married New England missionaries and teachers of Anglo-Saxon descent, he was not more than one-quarter Seneca by "blood." Yet early and late in life he identified readily with Iroquoian culture and values, even while he rose through the ranks of American society by sheer achievement as ethnologist, folklorist, archaeologist, and museologist (a term he invented). In appearance and in photographs, Parker looked as much Indian as his Seneca contemporaries, although well-tailored, and his English speech retained the resonance of Iroquoian languages. But, with the rule of matrilineal descent, politically he was an "outsider" and not an enrolled Seneca.

The men who carried the English name of Parker in the third ascending generation—principally Nicholson, who was

Arthur's father's father, and Ely S.—were sons of William Parker and his wife of the Tonawanda Reservation, themselves of lineages bearing sachemships, and they were related to the Seneca prophet, Handsome Lake. The William Parker family took in Lewis Henry Morgan of Rochester and hosted the first scientific ethnography in America.[1] Morgan dedicated his pioneer work to Ely, who went on to become Sachem, engineer, and aide-de-camp to Gen. U. S. Grant. Nicholson ("Nick") attended Albany Normal School, forerunner of the University at Albany; removed to Cattaraugus Reservation, where he farmed; engineered; served as U.S. Interpreter; acted as lay reader in the Mission Church; and read aloud from classics to his grandson, Arthur. As a young lad Arthur spent much of his boyhood in the Parker menage near the Mission Church; but the pull of traditional culture created an ambivalence in him, as it did for his grandfather, who was nominally a Protestant.

English was a second language to Cattaraugus Senecas in the 1880s; grandfather "Nick" had mastered it, but it was Arthur Parker's first language. Arthur's father, Frederick Parker, a graduate of Fredonia Normal School and a station agent for the New York Central Railroad, and his mother, Geneva Griswold Parker, a reservation school teacher, spoke English at home. But Arthur's boyhood playmates who accompanied him on forays the length of Cattaraugus Creek spoke a variety of Seneca sprinkled with English nouns but adhering to the Iroquoian syntax that Arthur learned and remembered years later in collecting and interpreting folktales. His vocabulary of Seneca terms and expressions was extraordinary; he understood but did not control the language. This background and perception made his folklore unique and original, as will appear momentarily.

Parker wrote brief autobiographical sketches at various stages in his career to satisfy interests just then, and his correspondence in the New York State Museum documents his term in Albany. His Rochester period is covered by Thomas.[2]

During his first decade, Parker attended Indian district school, on the Cattaraugus Reservation, and after school engaged in bow-and-arrow hunts and similar activities. Especially, his group called on "old warriors in the woods," who entertained them with tales of past glories. And there were senior Senecas who visited his grandfather, stayed a day, a week, or a winter, performing chores for keep. There were lengthy "Indian conversations" that a curious lad could listen to, and there were storytelling sessions to keep him awake, which he describes in this book (pp. xxxi–xxxiii).

By his ninth year he had begun a lifelong interest in natural history with a collection of birds' eggs. And he was fascinated with Devonian fossils that abound in the rocky gorges of Cattaraugus Creek (where the Senecas said the Little People abide). He developed a remarkable knowledge of plants and became an avid mushroom seeker in later life.

He was age eleven when the New York Central transferred his father to New York City. The family followed him to White Plains, where Arthur and his sister entered public schools. Graduating from White Plains High School in 1897, Arthur earned the recommendation of the local Presbyterian minister to study for the ministry. But the reservation and Seneca life exerted a strong pull, and the Parkers returned to Cattaraugus frequently with free passes, I presume, on the railroad. He became fascinated with "pagan dances" and the semisecret medicine societies that he would later study. He never shook the ambivalence between the cultural distance of White Plains and native Cattaraugus. Like his grandfather, he was always aware of the conflict.[3]

It took him three years after 1900 to discover his life's work. He enrolled at Williamsport Dickenson Seminary in Pennsylvania but dropped out. Always keen on writing, he worked for a time as a newspaper reporter, learning how to "write it quick and short" and soon mastering the elements of style. Indeed, he brought to writing some of the native eloquence of his people. During this period of discovery, while still a student and afterward, he haunted the ranges of the American Museum of Natural History. He was befriended by Professor F. W. Putnam of Harvard, who was to museums what Boas became to academic anthropology, and by Mark Raymond Harrington, who was to be his colleague and relative by marriage. At Professor Putnam's suggestion, Harrington introduced Parker to field archeology on the shell heaps of Oyster Bay.

When not at the American Museum, "Putnam's Boys"—Parker, Harrington, Alanson Skinner, Frank G. Speck—and other Indian buffs frequented the soirees of Harriet Maxwell Converse, impressario to the Iroquois and amateur folklorist.[4] Mrs. Converse had developed, notably at Cattaraugus, a remarkable rapport with Seneca traditionalists, who admitted her to ceremonies, entrusted her with tribal relics, and from whom she heard explanatory myths, origin legends, and stories. These she wrote up in an imaginative fashion. On her death in 1903, Parker was named literary executor, and one of his first projects on going to Albany as archeologist at the New York State Museum was to edit and supplement the Converse oeuvre for publication.[5]

Parker's collection of folktales was incidental to his developing career as a professional archaeologist. He had declined to go the academic route to the Ph.D. under Boas at Columbia University and found more congenial a museum career under the tutelage of Professor Putnam. This decision markedly affected his later life when people insisted on addressing him as "Doctor Parker" and he knew he had not earned the title, unlike his professional contemporaries. His interest in the oral literature of his people was rekindled when Putnam sent him with Harrington to explore sites in southwestern New York, notably on his native Cattaraugus Creek. He tells us in the foreword to this book how Seneca annalists, whom he names (p. xx), soon visited the dig and related tales and oral history of the old people. It was then that Parker began to note the plots and incidents in their narratives from which he would construct his own versions. He knew that Jeremiah Curtin and J. N. B. Hewitt had preceded him, but he decided not to use previous collections for comparative purposes and to preserve the literary integrity of his own materials.[6]

Mrs. Converse and Professor Putnam were behind Parker's

appointment as archaeologist at the New York State Museum, and it was in this position that Parker pursued ethnological inquiries and collected folktales and ethnographic art among the Senecas after 1903. He operated on a contract basis at first, submitting manuscript reports for hire, before attaining full civil service status. He rapidly gained the confidence of the native people, was adopted into the Bear Clan, and was given a clan name, *Gawasowaneh,* or "Big Snowsnake," a game he described in the *Anthropologist.*[7] He was now a socially acceptable Seneca.

Parker soon found a job constraining. He wrote a plan for a full-blown department of anthropology at the State Museum that included folklore, but he never succeeded in getting the director, John M. Clarke, a palaeontologist, to see the broad picture, and was ordered to concentrate on exhibits.[8] But Parker found a way to get back to the field. He convinced Clarke that the authenticity of the new Indian Groups, the famous diaramas of Iroquois life then in preparation, for which Clarke had secured private funds, depended on further ethnological research. Parker's field trips to Tonawanda, Cattaraugus, and the Six Nations Reserve in Canada produced a steady stream of publications and greatly increased the ethnological collections of the State Museum. He enlisted key people to collect for him, and he commissioned Jesse Cornplanter, son of his principal informant Edward, to make a series of drawings illustrating various activities and themes in the traditional culture.[9] Several of these appear in the present volume. His most important achievement just then was a systematic paper on the medicine societies, written at a time when such sodalities were a top priority with ethnologists (see Traditions, numbers 69 and 70, and Appendix E in this book).[10]

Colleagues who had gone the professional route were urging Parker to get his Seneca texts in publishable form because J. N. B. Hewitt at the Smithsonian was about to launch the Curtin collection.[11] But Parker was already heavily committed, which explains the delay in publishing *Seneca Myths and Folk Tales.* He was also most likely aware that his method and materials might not stand up to the standards being set by Boas's insistence on native texts, and by Boas's students. It was the literary aspects of the tales that interested Parker as a writer.

In the Introduction to the Converse bulletin, and again in this volume, he relates how stories were told and the expected response of listeners. He contrasted the rigorous accuracy of taking native texts in phonetics, and translating them literally (and analyzing the tales for plot, motifs, and borrowed elements) with Converse's (and his own) more "interpretive" approach to the material, which he thought preserved its "natural beauty." Parker used interpreters, found the result but a caricature of the original, and then, resorting to another extreme, recast the material "in the author's [Parker's] own mold." This, too, was unsatisfactory. He finally resorted to making his own version of the material, a method he thought had more merit than defects. He wrote:

> By this method the transcriber attempts to assimilate the ideas of the myth tale as he hears it, seeks to become imbued with the spirit of its characters, and, shutting out from his mind all thought of his own culture, and momentarily transforming himself into the culture of the myth teller, records his impressions as he recalls the story. His object is to produce the same emotions in the mind of civilized man which is produced in the primitive mind, which entertains the myth, without destroying the native style or warping the facts of the narrative.[12]

Parker was attempting to assume the role of the mythtellers in Seneca society, to learn the tales as he heard them, and to reproduce them in part like native storytellers while interpreting them for a wider audience. He was more faithful to originals than Converse, less precise than Curtin and Hewitt, but he produced works of real literary merit at several levels. His children's books, notably *Skunny Wundy*, were real successes.[13]

It would be unfair to say that Parker was not analytical.

His chapter on "Basic Premises" isolates themes, motifs, incidents, and personages. His foreword hints at distinctions between "tales" (ka?ka:?), legends, and true myths. His chapter on the "Gods, etc" covers cosmology and religion aptly. He then treats "themes" systematically, as well as "incidents" and "objects." The components of the cosmological myth have since been overhauled. [14] His classification of Seneca folklore is best seen in the table of contents. The bibliography reveals important works that he sought to emulate. And bless him for the index.

Such material can no longer be had on the reservations. Television has completely supplanted cycles of tales such as *Skanawundi* and Turtle's War Party. This entire genre of oral literature was already disappearing in the 1930s which I began field work and it has since gone the long trail.

Slingerlands, New York
26 January 1989 (in the moon of Niskowakneh)

NOTES

1. Lewis Henry Morgan, *The League of the Ho-de-no-sau-nee, or Iroquois* (Rochester, N.Y.: Sage, 1851).

2. William N. Fenton, Introduction to *Parker on the Iroquois* (Syracuse University Press, 1968), p. 6; W. Stephen Thomas, "Arthur Caswell Parker: 1881–1955," *Rochester History,* vol. 17 (July, 1955): 1–20. For Parker's place in the intellectual history of his day, see Hazel W. Hertzberg, "Arthur C. Parker, Seneca," in *American Indian Intellectuals,* ed. Margot Liberty, *1976 Proceedings of the American Ethnological Society* (St. Paul: West Publishing Co.), pp. 129–38. William A. Ritchie, Emeritus New York State Archaeologist, who began his career under Parker at Rochester, contributed the biography to *Dictionary of American Biography,* supplement, vol. 5 (1951–1955): 533–34.

3. Parker wrote about his grandfather's several roles in *The Life of General Ely S. Parker* (Buffalo, N.Y.: Buffalo Historical Society, 1919), p. 198.

4. Fenton, Introduction to *Parker on the Iroquois*, p. 9; See Fenton, "Harriet Maxwell Converse," in *Notable American Women*, vol. 1 (Harvard University Press, 1971), pp. 375–77.

5. Harriet Maxwell Converse (Ya-ie-wa-noh), *Myths and Legends of the New York State Iroquois*, edited and annotated by Arthur C. Parker (Ga-wa-so-wa-neh), *New York State Museum Bulletin 125* (Albany, 1908).

6. *Seneca Fiction, Legends and Myths*, collected by Jeremiah Curtin and J. N. B. Hewitt, edited by J. N. B. Hewitt, Thirty-Second Annual Report of the Bureau of American Ethnology, 1910–1911, Washington, D.C., 1918, pp. 37–814.

7. "Snow-Snake as played by the Senecas," *American Anthropologist* 11, no. 2 (1909): 250–56.

8. Fenton, Introduction to *Parker on the Iroquois*, p. 18.

9. Fenton, " 'Aboriginally Yours,' Jesse J. Cornplanter, Hah-yonh-wonh-ish, the Snipe, Seneca, 1889–1957," in *American Indian Intellectuals*, ed. Margot Liberty, *1976 Proceedings of the American Ethnological Society* (St. Paul: West Publishing Co., 1978), pp. 177–95.

10. Arthur C. Parker, "Secret Medicine Societies of the Seneca," *American Anthropologist* 11, no. 2 (1909): 161–85.

11. Speck and Skinner both wrote to him in 1908. See Arthur Parker Papers, New York State Museum, Albany.

12. Parker, Introduction to Converse, *Myths and Legends*, p. 12.

13. *Skunny Wundy and Other Indian Tales* (New York: Doran, 1927).

14. Fenton, "This Island, the World on the Turtle's Back," *Journal of American Folklore*, 75, no. 298: (1962) 283–300. For an overview of Iroquois Folklore Research at the midcentury, see "Iroquois Indian Folklore" in "Folklore Research in North America," *Journal of American Folklore* (October–December 1947): 60.

FOREWORD

The author of this collection of Seneca folk-tales cannot remember when he first began to hear the wonder stories of the ancient days. His earliest recollections are of hearing the wise old men relate these tales of the mysterious past. They were called Kă'kāā, or Gă'kāā, and when this word was uttered, as a signal that the marvels of old were about to be unfolded, all the children grew silent,—and listened. In those days, back on the Cattaraugus reservation, it was a part of a child's initial training to learn why the bear lost its tail, why the chipmunk has a striped back and why meteors flash in the sky.

Many years later,—it was in 1903,—the writer of this manuscript returned to the Cattaraugus reservation bringing with him his friend Mr. Raymond Harrington, for the purpose of making an archæological survey of the Cattaraugus valley for the Peabody Museum of Archæology, of Harvard University. Our base camp was on the old Silverheels farm, which occupies the site of one of the early Seneca villages of the period after the Erie war of 1654. Here also is the site of the original Lower Cattaraugus of pre-Revolutionary days.

To our camp came many Indian friends who sought to instruct Mr. Harrington and myself in the lore of the ancients. We were regaled with stories of the false-faces, of the whirl-winds, of the creation of man, of the death panther, and of the legends of the great bear, but in particular we were blessed with an ample store of tales of vampire skeletons, of witches and of folk-beasts, all of whom had a special appetite for young men who dug in the ground for the buried relics of the "old-time folks."

To us came Tahadondeh (whom the Christian people called George Jimerson), Bill Snyder, Gahweh Seneca, a lame man from Tonawanda, Frank Pierce and several others versed in folklore. I filled my note-books with sketches and outlines of folk-fiction, and after our return to New York, I began to transcribe some of the stories.

The following winter was spent on the reservation among the non-Christian element in a serious attempt to record folk tales, ceremonial prayers, rituals, songs and customs. A large amount of information and many stories were collected. Some of this material was published by the State Museum, the rest perished in the Capitol fire at Albany, in 1911.

Later I was able to go over my original notes with Edward Cornplanter, the local authority on Seneca religion, rites and folk-ways, and to write out the material here presented. Cornplanter's son Jesse assisted by way of making drawings under his father's direction. I also had the help of Skidmore Lay, Ward B. Snow, Delos B. Kittle, Mrs. John Kittle, James Crow and others. My informants from the lower reservation, the Christian district, were Aurelia Jones Miller, Fred Kennedy, George D. Jimerson, Julia Crouse, Moses Shongo, Mrs. Moses Shongo, David George, William Parker, Job King, and Chester C. Lay; and Laura Doctor and Otto Parker of the Tonawanda Reservation.

In the preparation of these versions of old Seneca tales the writer used no other texts for comparative purposes. It was thought best to rest content with the version given by the Indian informant, and to wait until a time of greater leisure came before attempting to annotate the collection. Leisure has never seemed to be the privilege of the writer, and one busy year has crowded upon another, until eighteen have passed since the tales were written down. It may be best, after all, to present the text just as it was prepared, and merely correct the spelling of a name or two. It was not until after this text was in the hands of the Buffalo Historical Society that the Curtin-Hewitt collection of Seneca folk tales appeared, and though differences will be found between our texts and those of Curtin, it must be remembered that variations are bound to occur. All versions of folk tales recorded by different individuals at different or even identical times will vary in certain particulars, as is explained hereinafter.

In the preparation of this volume the writer wishes to record his indebtedness to Mr. George Kelley Staples, Senator Henry W. Hill, Mr. George L. Tucker and Dr. Frank H. Severance, all members of the Buffalo Historical Society, for the advice and encouragement given.

ARTHUR C. PARKER.

Buffalo Consistory,
A. A. S. R.
Nov. 26, 1922.

INTRODUCTION

In presenting this collection of Seneca myths and legends, the collator feels that he should explain to the general reader that he does not offer a series of tales that can be judged by present day literary standards. These Indian stories are not published for the mere entertainment of general readers, though there is much that is entertaining in them, neither are they designed as childrens' fables, or for supplementary reading in schools, though it is true that some of the material may be suited for the child mind. It must be understood that if readings from this book are to be made for children, a wise selection must be made.

This collection is presented as an exposition of the unwritten literature of the Seneca Indians who still live in their ancestral domain in western New York. It is primarily a collection of folk-lore and is to be looked at in no other light. The professional anthropologist and historian will not need to be reminded of this. He will study these tales for their ethnological significance, and use them in making comparisons with similar collections from other tribes and stocks. In this manner he will determine the similarities or differences in theme, in episode and character. He will trace myth diffusion thereby and be able to chart the elements of the Seneca story.

There is an amazing lack of authentic material on Iroquois folk-lore, though much that arrogates this name to itself has been written. The writers, however, have in general so glossed the native themes with poetic and literary interpretations that the material has shrunken in value and can scarcely be considered without many reservations.

We do not pretend to have made a complete collection of all available material, but we have given a fairly representative series of myths, legends, fiction and traditions.

One may examine this collection and find representative types of nearly every class of Seneca folk-lore. Multiplication is scarcely necessary.

The value of this collection is not a literary one but a scientific one. It reveals the type of tale that held the interest and attention of the Seneca; it reveals certain mental traits and tendencies; it reveals many customs and incidents in native life, and finally, it serves as an index of native psychology.

The enlightened mind will not be arrogant in its judgment of this material, but will see in it the attempts of a race still in mental childhood to give play to imagination and to explain by symbols what it otherwise could not express.

While there is much value in this collection explaining indirectly the folk-ways and the folk-thought of the Seneca and their allied kinsmen, the whole life of the people may not be judged from these legends. Much more must be presented before such a judgment is formed. Just as we gain some knowledge of present day religions, governmental methods, social organization and political economy from the general literature of the day, but only a portion, and this unsystematized, so do we catch only a glimpse of the life story of the Seneca from their folk-tales.

To complete our knowledge we must have before us works on Seneca history, ethnology, archæology, religion, government and language. Finally, we must personally know the descendents of the mighty Seneca nation of old. We must enter into the life of the people in a sympathetic way, for only then can we get at the soul of the race.

While all this is true, these folk-tales are not to be despised, for they conserve many references to themes and things that otherwise would be forgotten. Folklore is one of the most important mines of information that the ethnologist and historian may tap. We can never understand a race until we understand what it is thinking about, and we can never know this until we know its literature, written or unwritten. The folk-tale therefore has a special value and significance, if honestly recorded.

METHODS EMPLOYED IN RECORDING FOLK TALES.

There are several methods which may be employed in recording folklore, and the method used depends largely upon the purpose in mind. A poet may use one method, and grasping the plot of a tale, recast it in a verbiage entirely unsuitable and foreign to it; a fiction writer may use another plan, a school boy another, a student of philology another, a missionary another, and finally a student of folk lore still another.

The poet will see only the inherent beauty of the story, and perhaps failing to find any beauty, will invent it and produce a tale that no Indian would ever recognize. Plot and detail will be changed, fine flowery language will be used, and perhaps the whole given the swing and meter of blank verse. This is all very well for the poet, but he has buried the personality of the folk tale, albeit in petals of roses,—instead of allowing it nakedly to appear the living thing it is.

The fiction writer will take the original Indian tale and tear it apart with keen eyed professional discrimination. He will recast the plot, expand here and there, explain here and prune down there. He will invent names and new situations to make the story "go," then, as a rule, he sells it to a magazine or makes a collection of tales for "a supplementary reader for children." But are these Indian tales?

The amateur, finding good material in the Indian story will do as the fiction writer does, but he will work in foreign allusions and inconsistent elements and in other ways betray his unfamiliarity with his material. Like the fiction writer he is primarily after a story that he can dress as he pleases.

The sectarian enthusiast, recording folklore, will frequently seek to show the absurdity of the Indian tale, and point out the foolishness of peoples who are unacquainted with biblical teachings, but it is fortunate that all missionaries have not done this. Many have recorded folk-tales with great conscienciousness, and some of our best sources are from the notes of well informed missionaries.

The philologist will seek to make literal transcripts of every Indian word in painstaking phonetic spelling, and then secure an analytical interlinear translation. This is an accurate but awkward way of securing the tale, for readers who are accustomed to reading only straight English. It makes it a most tedious and laborious thing to read, and totally deprives the text of all literary life.

The student of folk lore starts in with a purpose. This is to secure the tale in such a manner, that without unnecessarily colored verbiage, it may be consistently dressed, and set forth in fluent English (or other modern language) in such a manner that it may be understood by an ordinary reader. The folk-lore student has still another motive and purpose, which is to so present his legend that it will awaken in the mind of his reader sensations similar to those aroused in the mind of the Indian auditor hearing it from the native raconteur. The recorder of the tale seeks to assimilate its characteristics, to become imbued with its spirit, to understand its details, to follow its language,—its sentences,—one by one, as they follow in sequence, and then he seeks to present it consistently. He adds nothing not in the original,—despite the temptation to improve the plot,—he presents the same arrangement as in the original, he uses similar idioms and exclamations, similar introductory words and phrases, and presents an honestly constructed free translation. This is far from an easy thing to do, for it frequently lays the recorder open to the charge of being a clumsy story teller. The temptation is ever present to tell a good story, and let the legend become the skeleton over which the words are woven. Needless to say, this is not an honest thing to do, and the folk-lore student resists this temptation, and gives his product a genuine presentation, regardless of what literary critics may think. He strives only to be the medium by which a native tale is transformed from its original language to that of another tongue. The thought, the form and the sequence of the story he insists must remain exactly as it was, though the verbal dress is European and not Indian.[1]

Perhaps actual illustrations of these methods will serve to convey the thought we are attempting to explain. Examples follow:

TEXT IN SENECA WITH INTERLINEAR TRANSLATION.

Ne" gwā', gi"o^n, hadi'noñge' ne" sgäoñ'iädï" ne"
There it seems / they dwell / the / other side / the
it is said / / / of the sky

hěñ'noñgwe'. Da', s'hă'degano'ndāě^n' ne"ho' ni'hono^n'sō't
they (M) man / So / just in the center / there / just his
beings / / of the village / / lodge stands

ne" hă'sěñnowā'ně^n', ne"ho' hādjwadä'iě^n', ne" ne'io'
the / he Chief / there / his family / the / his
/ (great name) / / lies / / wife

ne" kho" ne" sgā't hodiksă'dā'iě^n', ie'o^n' ne" ieksă"ă'.
that / and / the / one / they child have / she / the / child.
/ / / (it is) / / female is /

Waādiěñgwă"s'hoñ' o'ně^n' ho' wă"săwě^n' ne" hăgweñdä"s.
He was surprised / now / it / that / he became lonesome.

O'ně^n' dï'q we'so' ho'něñ'iathěñ' ne" Hagě^n'tcï; ne"
Now / moreover much / his bones are dry / the / He Ancient / that
/ / (he is very lean) / / One

gai'ioñnǐ t'hě^n"ě^n' deo'nigoñ"iiō' he" odiksă'dā'iě^n'āiěñ"
it causes / not (it is) / his mind happy / because / they child one would
/ / is / / have think

ně" noñ" heniio"děn' ne" ne" hosheie'o^n.
that / perhaps / so it is in / that / the / he is jealous.
/ / state

---

[1] This is important in order to preserve every folk-motive and element by which the tale may be compared in detail with those of other tribes and stocks.

LITERAL TRANSLATION.

There were, it seems, so it is said, man-beings dwelling on the other side of the sky. So just in the center of their village the lodge of the chief stood, wherein lived his family, consisting of his wife and one child, that they two had. He was surprised that then he began to become lonesome. Now furthermore, he the Ancient was very lean, his bones having become dried, and the cause of this condition was that they two had the child, and one would think, judging from the circumstances that he was jealous.

Such is the beginning of the Seneca version of Iroquoian cosmology as given by J. N. B. Hewitt in the 21st Report of the Bureau of Ethnology. This faithful record of a native text and its translation is literally a most painstaking work involving the closest attention to the minor sounds in the language, in order that each word may be phonetically recorded. To wade through this literal translation from the beginning to the end of the myth would be too tedious for anyone but an enthusiastic student of native tongues. To the majority of readers it would be a forbidding task. Even to follow the involved language and grammatical forms of the close literal translation would tire the mind of anyone whose mother tongue was not that of the text.

A free translation, therefore becomes a prime necessity, but this must not disturb the original thought. Just how to make such a translation honestly becomes a problem beset with difficulty. Our plan is to smooth out the language, divest it of its awkward arrangement, and allow the thought to flow on. Let us attempt this in the following:

FREE TRANSLATION.

In ancient times a race of transcendent men dwelt on the other side of the sky. In the center of a village in that land stood the lodge of Ancient One, the chief, and there he lived with his wife and one child. To his astonishment, though he had these companions, he began to feel lonely and neglected. His form grew emaciated and his "bones became dry," for he longed for the attentions his wife now gave to his child.

Just how the poet would handle this version we hesitate to conjecture but we may easily imagine that he would make the most of the land above the sky, the celestial lodge, the age of the Ancient One, his initial joy at the birth of his child, and his gradual discovery that his wife's affection had been transferred from him to their offspring, of the agony of soul that wilted his heroic form and caused his very bones to wither and lose their marrow, and of the final madness of the Ancient One, who (to follow the myth in its fullness), had a tormenting dream which caused him to tear up the celestial tree and cast his wife into the cavernous hole that dropped down into chaos.

The plot of this myth-tale has elements that make it excellent material for the fiction writer who would recast it entirely and weave it into the thrilling story of celestial tragedy. We have seen such attempts and have been astonished at the audacity of the writer who thus presents his product as a "genuine Indian myth." Yet, most popular versions of Indian legends are recast to such an extent that the Indian who supplied the bones would never recognize the creature the white man "teller-of-tales" has clothed with civilized flesh. As an example of such fabrication, witness the speech of Hiawatha to the assembled tribes as presented by J. V. H. Clark in his "Onondaga." (Vol. 1, p. 28 ff.) This famous speech has been passed down as Hiawatha's own words and has been the inspiration of more than one poet, though Clark admitted in later years that he invented the entire address, basing it upon some obscure references in the original tradition. In many a work on "Indian fables for children" the so-called fable is merely an invention, and the only Indian thing about it is the dash of Indian flavor used to give the story plausibility. Indians who have never seen or read the text of such stories of course might easily be induced in various ways to sign statements vouching for them, thus contributing to the intensification of error.

It is well to analyze the folk-tale or myth for its theme and to check it against others, thereby determining whether or not it is actually authentic. If it appears unusual and unlike anything other informants have given, it may be placed in the class of doubtful fiction, and especially so if the "fable" has a "moral" attached to it.

OBTAINING CORRECT VERSIONS.

It might be supposed that myths and folk-tales which are orally transmitted would suffer great changes as they pass from one story teller to another, and that in time a given tale would become utterly corrupted, and indeed so changed that it would bear faint resemblance to the "original." Yet, an examination of the myths and legends recorded by early observers, as the early missionaries, show that the modern versions have suffered no essential change. An excellent example is the Iroquoian creation myth, as recorded by the Jesuit fathers in the *Relations*.

Religious traditions, ceremonies and myths, being of a "sacred" character, must be related with a certain fidelity which forbids any real change in the content. To a lesser degree, perhaps, but not much less, the "gă′gāā" legends of the Iroquois are protected from violent alteration. The legend is a thing, to the Indian mind, and it has a certain personality. In certain instances the legend is a personal or group possession and its form and content are religiously guarded from change. With tales told for mere amusement, tales belonging to the class of mere fiction, greater liberties may be taken.

Notwithstanding all this, it is certain that there are several versions of each legend. Certain groups tell the myth or legend in different ways. There are short versions and long versions and there are Seneca versions and Mohawk versions. In order to ascertain the "correct version" we must examine several versions as related by different narrators, and then after making an outline of the episodes, the characters and the motives, determine what the central theme of all is. We can in this manner judge what is essential and what is non-essential.

There is a wide variation in the language used in the narration of some legends, just as there is in the relation of modern stories told over the banquet table. A better example of variation, is to consider the innumerable versions of common nursery stories, as Puss in Boots, Cinderella, or Aladdin's Lamp. Yet the theme of the story and the episodes, to say nothing of the characters, remain unchanged. Just so with most Iroquois folklore, much depends upon the author-raconteur. Some will add explanatory matter, some will add picturesque descriptions, some will add an abundance of conversation, and some will expand on the emotions of the characters. There is a wide individual variation in these matters, and much depends upon the training and education of the narrator, as well as upon his temperament. Language may differ somewhat, but the theme must remain,—the real story must never suffer essential change.

STORY-TELLING CUSTOMS OF THE SENECA.

Among the Seneca, in common with other Iroquois tribes, each settlement had its official story tellers whose predecessors had carefully taught them the legends and traditions of the mysterious past.

According to ancient traditions, no fable, myth-tale, or story of ancient adventure might be told during the months of summer. Such practice was forbidden by "the little people" (djogĕ'oⁿ), the wood fairies. Should their law be violated some djogĕ'oⁿ flying about in the form of a beetle or bird might discover the offender and report him to their chief. Upon this an omen would warn the forgetful Indian. Failing to observe the sign some evil would befall the culprit. Bees might sting his lips or his tongue would swell and fill his mouth, snakes might crawl in his bed and choke him while he slept, and so on, until he was punished and forced to desist from forbidden talk.

Certain spirits were reputed to enforce this law for two purposes; first, that no animal should become offended by man's boasting of his triumph over beasts, or at the same time learn too much of human cunning, and fly forever the haunts of mankind; and second, that no animal, who listening to tales of wonder, adventure or humor, should become so interested as to forget its place in nature, and pondering over the mysteries of man's words, wander dazed and aimless through the forest. To listen to stories in the summer time made trees and plants as well as animals and men lazy, and therefore scanty crops, lean game and shiftless people resulted. To listen to stories made the birds forget to fly to the south when winter came, it made the animals neglect to store up winter coats of fur. All the world stops work when a good story is told and afterwards forgets its wonted duty in marveling. Thus the modern Iroquois, following the old time custom, reserves his tales of adventures, myth and fable for winter when the year's work is over and all nature slumbers.

The story teller (Hage'otă') when he finds an audience about him or wishes to call one, announces his intention to recite a folk tale, (gă'gāā, or in the plural, gägä"shoⁿ"o') by exclaiming "I"newa'eñgegĕ'odĕⁿ, Hau"nio" djadaoⁿ "diïⁿus!" The auditors eagerly reply "Hĕⁿ" " which is the assenting to the proposed relation of the folk tale.

At intervals during the relation of a story the auditors must exclaim "hĕⁿ"." This is the sign that they were listening. If there was no frequent response of "he," the story teller would stop and inquire what fault was found with him or his story.

It was not only considered a breach of courtesy for a listener to fall asleep, but also a positive omen of evil to the guilty party.   If any one for any reason wished to sleep or to leave the room, he must request the narrator to "tie the story, "eⁿsĕgägha"a."   Failing to say this and afterwards desiring to hear the remainder of the tale, the narrator would refuse, for if he related it at all it must be from the beginning through, unless "tied."   Thus "ĕⁿsĕgäha"a" was the magic word by which a legend might be told as a serial (from ĕⁿsege'odĕ).

A story teller was known as "Hage'otă' " and his stock of tales called "ganondas'hägoⁿ".   Each listener gave the story teller a small gift, as a bead, small round brooch, beads, tobacco, or other trinket.   To tell stories was called "ĕⁿsege'odĕⁿ", and the gift was termed "dagwa'niatcis," now an obsolete word.

PHONETIC KEY.

a as in father
ā preceding sound, prolonged
ă as in what
ä as in hat
â as in all
ai as in aisle
au as *ou* in out
c as *sh* in shall
ç as *th* in wealth
d pronounced with the tip of the tongue touching the upper teeth , as in enunciating English *th* in with; the only sound of *d* employed in writing native words
e as in they
ĕ as in met
f as in waif
g as in gig
h as in hot
i as in pique
ĭ as in pit
k as in kick
n as in run
ñ as *ng* in ring
o as in note
q as *ch* in German ich
r slightly trilled; this is its only sound
s as in sop
t pronounced with the tip of the tongue touching the upper teeth, as in enunciating the English *th* in with; this is its only sound
u as in rule
ŭ as in rut
w as in wit
y as in ye
dj as *j* in judge
hw as *wh* in what
tc as *ch* in church
ⁿ marks nasalized vowels, thus eⁿ, oⁿ, aiⁿ, ĕⁿ, äⁿ, âⁿ
' indicates an aspiration or soft emission of breath
' marks the glottal stop, ä', ĕⁿ'
t'h In this combination *t* and *h* are separately uttered, as *th* in the English words hothouse, foothold

FUNDAMENTAL FACTORS IN SENECA FOLK-LORE

I

SENECA MYTHS AND FOLK-TALES

BASIC PREMISES OF SENECA FOLK-LORE

The myths and legends of the Seneca are built upon certain well recognized and deeply rooted postulates. Each bit of folk-lore must have its consistency adjudged by these elements in order to be credible. Any myth or legend that offended the standards so set would immediately be rejected by the Seneca as spurious. To a large extent the premises of folk-lore are founded on folk-thought, and woe to the innovator who sought to direct his theme from the accepted thought patterns.

Among the basic beliefs upon which the folk-tale is built are the following:

Unseen spirits. Spirits pervade all nature and affect man for good or evil. Their desires and plans must be satisfied by man. There are both good and evil spirits. Spirits may inhabit anything in nature.

Conflict of good and evil spirits. Good spirits are constantly making war upon evil spirits.

Magical power. There is such a thing as orenda or magical power. Such power makes its possessor the master over the natural order of things. This orenda may be acquired in various ways. It may be residual, and therefore an attribute of the individual, or it may be inherent in some charm or fetish. Virtuous persons may be given a good orenda, which is always more powerful in the end than the evil orenda which is possessed by witches and sorcerers.

Transformation. Any being possessing orenda may transform himself into any form,—animate or inanimate, as his orenda gives power. Anything seen in nature may be a temporary or a permanent transformation of a being having

3

orenda. Transformation may be by command or by entering the skin of the creature whose form one desires to
assume. Animals having orenda may assume human form
and mingle with human beings. A group of people, therefore, may in reality be a transformed group of animals,
and likewise with individuals.

All nature is conscious. Everything in the Seneca phil-
osophy lives and is conscious. It is a being and in commun-
ication with other parts of nature. Anything in nature may
be spoken to and it will hear what one has said. It may
be induced to act in one's behalf.

All living creatures have souls. The Seneca believes that
animals have souls that are alike in their nature to the souls
of human beings. The hunter, therefore, propitiates the
soul of the animal he kills, and explains why he killed it.
The souls of friendly animals help man, if man has been
courteous, and has properly propitiated them. Souls of
evil animals injure men and must be "bought off." The
souls of all creatures return to the Maker of Souls just as
man's does.

Master of souls. There is in the heaven world a Master
of life and soul. He allows his subordinate spirits to rule
the earth-world and concerns himself generally with his
own realm. Souls that return to him are taken apart and
readjusted that they may function properly in the immortal
realm. Evil is therefore conceived in a measure as a mal-
adjustment of the soul's parts.

Ghosts. The manes of departed men and animals wander
over their familiar haunts and startle men by their "ma-
terializations." Wandering ghosts generally want something and must have their desires satisfied. The evil of the
living person is intensified in the ghost. A ghost is the
body spirit and not the real psychic personality.

Dreams. Dreams are experiences of the soul as it leaves
the body during sleep. The dream god guides the soul to
its dream experience. Dreams that prompt the individual

EDWARD CORNPLANTER—SOSONDOWA

Leading chief of the Cattaraugus Wolf Clan and High Priest of
the Ganiodaiu religion. Mr. Cornplanter was probably the last
of the New York Iroquois who knew by heart every one of the
ancient ceremonial rituals. He died in June, 1918, aged 67,
and was buried near the Newtown Long House.

to certain desires must be interpreted by a chosen person or by volunteer guessers, and the desire must be satisfied, or calamity will befall the dreamer as well as the unsuccessful guesser. Prophetic dreams must guide action and dream demands must not be lightly set aside.

Monsters. There are monsters that men seldom see. These affect the welfare and the destiny of man. They are generally evil and seek to destroy and sometimes to eat human beings.

Wizards. There are such beings as wizards, witches and sorcerers. These beings possess an evil orenda and seek to destroy innocent people.

GODS, MAJOR SPIRITS AND FOLK-BEASTS OF THE SENECA

1. BEINGS OF THE PRIMAL ORDER.

The first of the God Being was Te'haoⁿ'hwĕñdjaiwă"-khoⁿ' or Earth Holder. It was he who ruled the sky world and lived in the great celestial lodge beneath the celestial tree. As the result of a dream this chief, who also bears the title, Ancient One, was moved to take to himself as a wife a certain maiden, known as Awĕⁿhā'i', Mature Flower (Fertile Earth). Mature Flower consented to the betrothal, but due to the embrace of her lover inhaled his breath, and was given a child. The attention she gave this child caused the Ancient One to be moved to jealousy, this emotion being aroused in him through the machinations of the Fire Beast, whose invisibility rendered his work the more subtle. Little is known through mythology of Ancient One, since his field is a celestial one, and he seldom interferes with the doings of men of our present order. Of his unhappy wife, who was cast through the hole made by the uprooting of the celestial tree we learn more.[1]

The wife of the Ancient One was Iageⁿ"tciʻ, also meaning Ancient One (Body). We recognize her in the Huron myths as recorded or mentioned in the Jesuit *Relations* as Ataentsic (Ataaentsik). In Onondaga this would be Eiă'tăgĕⁿ"tciʻ. Her story is given in all versions of the creation myth.

Her personal name seldom appears, but Hewitt gives it as Awĕⁿʻhā'iʻ, this referring to her maturity, or ability to bring forth seed. In some versions the Chief casts his wife into the abyss made by uprooting the celestial tree, Gaiⁿiă"tgä"heiʻ; in others her own curiosity is responsible. The tree in such versions is uprooted as a dream demand and her enraged husband pushes her into the hole made thereby through the crust of the heaven-world. After the completion of the earth-world the sky mother returned by way of an etherial path that plainly was visible to her, this having been made by her daughter, the first born and the first to die of earth creatures.

Fire Beast (Gaăsʻioñdie't'hă'), appears to have been one of the important primal beings, and to have exercised a malign influence even upon the inhabitants of the celestial world. He is described as of "sky color" or invisible, and he is only detected at all when he emits streams and flashes of light from his head. When a meteor flashes the Iroquois recognizes the Fire Beast. His appearance is counted as a sign of direful calamity and death.

Whirlwind (Sʻhagodiiweⁿ"gōwā or Hadu"i'), was also a primal power of great importance. He is the controller of the violent winds, and he takes his name, He-who-defends-us, from his promise to help mankind when threatened by

---

[1] Consult Hewitt in Handbook of the American Indians, under his article Teharonhiawagon. We have re-edited some of our notes in accord with his findings.

calamity. His symbol is the crooked-mouthed false-face. There is also the concept of the four defenders, one for each of the cardinal directions. It was Whirlwind who boasted his power to the Good Mind (Iouskeha) and who had the contest with him of mountain moving. The face became mutilated by the mountain coming too quickly against it, at the command of the Good Mind. Agreeing

THE THUNDER SPIRIT

This is the powerful Hihnon, one of the principal spirits in the Seneca pantheon. Drawing by Jesse Cornplanter.

that he was now a subordinate he agreed furthermore, to drive away disease and pestilence and to defend men-beings, who should be thereafter created, from malign influences. His face carved in wood, after certain propitiatory and invocatory ceremonies, was and still is used by the conservative Iroquois in their ceremonial events, particularly at the mid-winter thanksgiving, when parties of masked figures go from house to house, singing the magical songs deemed potent for this purpose. The common name is Hadu"i', but in all ceremonies the full Seneca appelation is given, (Shagodiiwĕⁿ"gōwā).

The Thunderer, Hĭ"noⁿ', was another of the great beings, but he appears in the second order of mythology, as a servant to Iouskeha. He occupies a high place in the category of Iroquois gods, so high a place that it is an open question whether or not the Great Being whom the Iroquois now address as Hawĕñi'o' is not identical with the Thunderer, though there is also a recognition of the Thunderer as a separate being. The name Hawĕñi'o', apparently is derived from owĕñ'nă', (voice) and i'o' (good, great, majestic or beautiful). The initial *Ha* is the masculine sign. The name thus means, He-great-voice. This alludes to the thunder. The Thunderer is a mighty being, the maker of rains. He wrinkles his brow and the thunder rolls, he winks his eyes and lightnings flash like arrows of fire. The Thunderer hates all evil spirits, and he is charged with terrorizing the *otgont* or malicious dwellers of the under world to return to their cave. He seeks to slay the under water serpent and all folk-beasts that would use evil magic.

The benificient earth-god was T'hahoⁿ'hiawă"koⁿ, the light or elder twin of the Sky Woman's daughter. He is variously called Iouskeha (Huron), Hă'ni'go"io', Good Mind, Elder Brother, and Sky Holder. It was he who watched at the grave of his mother, and discovered the food plants. It was he who set forth on the journey "to the

East" and obtained from his father the power to rule. He made the earth habitable for man, obtained the mastery over the Thunderer and the Whirlwind, and even made his grandmother, Eiä'tägĕⁿ'tci' (Awĕⁿ'hä'i') play the game of plum stones, the result of which should determine who should rule the earth. He animated his plum stone dice and gave them understanding, ordered them to arrange themselves as he directed, and thereby won the highest count in a single throw. This gave him mastery over his evil brother Tawis'karoⁿ (the icy or flinty one), for the grandmother sympathised with this ugly twin brother of his. In the heaven world, T'hahoⁿ'hiawă''koⁿ, now lives with his grandmother, in the reunited family of celestial beings, and though he grows very old he has the power of renewing himself at will, and exercises this power over good souls that come into the heaven world. He created man after observing his own reflection in a pool of water, after which he made miniature figures in clay and commanded them to live.

Tawis'karoⁿ, was the second born of the daughter of the Sky Woman. He was of destructive nature, and found his way to life through the axilla of his mother, killing her at birth. His heart was made of ice or of flint (the words are similar). His delight is in destroying living things, especially by freezing. He created all the evil beasts, serpents, insects and birds. He invented thorns, briars, and by kicking at the earth made cliffs and precipices. During his career he stole all the good animals and hid them in a cave; he drove all the birds away. His great feat was in stealing the sun and hiding it in the far southwest. Aided by the fires which his brother, T'hahoⁿ'hiwă''koⁿ, and his cohorts secured, the birds and animals were found and the sun was released. This of course typifies the annual triumph of summer over winter, the return of the migrating birds, and the return of the heat of the sun. Tawis'karoⁿ is then confined to his cavern, hence his name Hanis'he'onoⁿ, meaning He who dwells in the earth. With the coming of the Christian missionaries, Tawiskaro was identified with the Christian devil, (Hă'nigoiĕt'gä', bad mind).[2] Strangely, about this time it was the Thunder god, instead of the good-minded Sky Holder, who was metamorphosed into the Great Spirit, Hawĕñi'o', this name being the Seneca equivalent for Jehovah (God).[3]

Lesser known gods were Ai'koⁿ' the Dream god, Haskotă'hiāhāks, the Head Opener, and Deiodă'sondäi'koⁿ', Thick Night. Aikon, caused the dreams which demanded interpretation, and Haskotahiahaks, opened the heads of soul-bodies as they passed over the sky-trail (Milky Way), and examined them for good and evil thoughts, after which he ate the brains.

Cosmic trees. There is a marvelous tree in the center of the heaven world. It bears all manner of fruits and flowers. (See cosmological myth, p. 59.)

There is a great tree in the center of the earth. Its top touches the sky. It grew in the world of the first order and it bore flowers-of-light. To touch this tree is to acquire great magical power. The Whirlwinds rub their rattles against it and become full of orenda.

2. NATURE BEINGS

The Sun, among the nature gods, is recognized by the Seneca as a powerful being. Yet, unlike the gods in other theogenies, the Sun is a creation made after the formation of the world,—at least so it would appear from the common cosmogeny. Sun was created from the face of the earth-mother, yet it may be that her face was the sacrifice that

---

[2] S'hagoewat'ha, also meaning He-punishes-them.
[3] Oddly enough, the original Hebrew concept of Yahweh, (Jehovah) was of a God of elements, particularly the storms. He manifested himself in the thunder's roar and by the lightning's flash, and blew like a great wind from the Ark of the Covenant, terrifying the Philistines.

THE SPIRIT OF DIONHEKON

In this drawing the spirit of the food plants is shown touching the shoulder of Handsome Lake, the Seneca Prophet. Drawing by Jesse Cornplanter.

brought the Sun into evidence. There is evidence of attempts to conceal the origin of the sun in several of the myths. He appears as the messenger of the Sky Chief and as the special god of war, Ho'sgĕⁿ'age"dăgōwā. He also appears as existing before the birth of the primal twins, and it appears that he is the being who sat on the mountain "to the east across the sea," and who gave power to the Good Mind, or T'hahoⁿhiawă"koⁿ. It thus appears there is an imperfect assimilation of conflicting myths, probably from different sources.

Each day the Sun starts from his resting place in the branches of the celestial tree, takes his path under the lifted east sky, rolls up the dome and commences his unerring watch of the movements of men. Wherever there is light, there is the messenger of the Sky Chief watching human behaviour. Returning at night, he recites all that he has observed on earth.

He bears the name Endĕ'ka Gää"kwă, Diurnal Orb of Light.

The Moon is Soi"ka Gää"kwă, Nocturnal Orb of Light, and she is hailed as "Our Grandmother." In each of her several phases she has a different name and function. She is watched by the females as a sign of health, and by the men as a sign of hunting luck. By the Moon time is regulated, and each monthly moon has a special name. Of all heavenly bodies she is the most mysterious, though not the most powerful.

Morning Star, Gĕndeñ'wit'hă, is one of the great beings of the sky and her appearance is watched as an omen. It appears that once Morning Star was an important celestial personage, but the Iroquois have drifted away from giving her special honors. She appears in several rolls, sometimes as a siren who lures hunters into a luckless marriage, mysteriously leaving them to wander the world over in search of her. She appears to have charmed an elk into loving her, and also as a rescuer of starving villages in time of famine. She is called Gadjĭ'son'dă' gĕndeñ'wit'hă'.

Storm Wind, Dagwanoeient, (Dagwano'ĕñ'iĕn) is a being of great activity, and he has a whole tribe of subordinates bearing his name. He appears to men as a Flying

THE FLYING HEAD OF THE WIND
This is the whirlwind or Dagwanoeient.   Drawing by Jesse Cornplanter.

Head, with long streaming hair, and his exploits are generally discreditable. He is a great wizard and takes delight in destroying things. His friends are generally sorcerers and otgont (evilly potent) beasts. Many legends are related about Dagwanoeient in his various forms, for he has several transformations.

Gä'ha', the zephyr, is a softer wind than the stormy Dagwanoeient, and appears to be of a kindlier disposition. While Gä'ha' may have done magical things, it was not malign, and there are legends that tell how Gaha wooed some fair forest maid and married her. Gaha helps plant grow and is associated with the warm season when fruits ripen and mature.

The Frost god is known as Hă"tho', and he is described as a fierce and relentless old man who lives where frosts and ice abound the year around. His home in the north is called Othowege. It is he who brings the frost and who causes the snows to sweep over the earth. His clothing is ice and he carries a maul with which he pounds the ice

THE SPIRIT OF THE FROST

This is Haht'ho, the spirit of the frost who signals by knocking on the trees in winter. Drawing by Jesse Cornplanter.

on rivers and lakes, making them crack with a resounding boom. He also causes that peculiar knocking sound on trees when the weather is very cold. He has one great enemy, it is the spirit of Spring, who assisted by Thaw drives him from the region that he has invaded and sends him grumbling back to the northland. The Frost god has as his friends Dagwanoeient, the Storm Wind, and Falling Hail.

The Hail spirit is called Owisondyon. He loves to startle people by coming unexpectedly in the warm months of early summer and to pelt the growing crops with his icy missles. Sometimes he is given the name, Dehodyadgaowen, meaning Divided Body.

The Spring god is Dedio's'hwineq'do^n, and he is young and very muscular. He loves to wrestle with the winter winds and even enters Ha"tho's lodge and teases him to desperation while his faithful ally, Thaw, plays havoc with the ice and the drifts outside. Spring tortures the Winter god with a medicine made of blackberry juice, for Winter god knows that when blackberries grow winter is beyond the power of injuring the world. At last Spring and Winter have a wrestling match in which Winter is overcome and his bodily form melts upon the ground, while his spirit whines away, driven north by the south winds. Spring lives in Onē'na^n'ge', Sunshine land.

The Thaw god is Dăgā'ĕ^n"dă, the faithful ally of Spring. When he comes, in midwinter he appears suddenly and begins to wreck the icy blankets that winter has placed over the earth. Winter then knows that Spring is coming and exerts all his magic to freeze the world again and to make his reign even more terrible. Time passes and Thaw comes again bringing his master, Spring, and then there is a fight to the finish, and Spring is supreme, while Thaw pursues ever to torment Hă"tho', on his frontiers.

The spirits of sustenance are knownw as Dio^n'he'ko^n, and they are represented as the inseparable spirits of the corn, the bean and the squash. They are sometimes referred to as "the three sisters." The ceremonial dance in their honor is called Goñdă'goñwi'sas. There are many legends of these spirits of sustenance and the wise men and women of ancient times tell of hearing them talk together in the fields where they grow together.

Tide spirit is known as S'hagowe'not'ha, and it is he who controls the rising and falling of the great waters, twice in each day. It is said that he controls the lifting of the sky's rim in the land of Gaenhyakdondye (the horizon), which allows the sun to emerge in the morning and depart at night. Sometimes he tempts canoemen far out to sea and then crushes them under the edge of the sky's rim. He sometimes lures disobedient boys to lonely islands where witches and wizards live on human flesh. Altogether, aside from certain functions, he is an evil monster.

Will-o'-the-wisp, or Gahai", is known as the witch's torch. It is not a spirit of the first order, but merely a flying light which directs sorcerers and witches to their victims. Sometimes it guides them to the spots where they may find their charms. Sorcerers have been detected by the frequent appearance of their Gahai", which leaves their smoke hole and guides them as they ride in mid air on their evil journeys.

3. MAGIC BEASTS AND BIRDS.

Chief among all the creatures that inhabit the air is the wonderful O's'hă'dă'geă', the Cloudland Eagle. He seems ever to watch over mankind, especially the Iroquois, and to come to earth when great calamities threaten. Living above the clouds he collects the dews in his feathers, and some say that he has a pool of dew on his back between his shoulders. The Iroquois regard him with great reverence, for he is connected with many a worthy exploit.

Horned Snake, Gas'hais'dowăne^n, has several names among which are Doonă"gaes and Djo^{n}di"gwado^n. He is a monster serpent of the underwaters and his head is adorned with antlers of great spread, though he is also said to have monster horns shaped like a buffalo's. He is capable of transforming himself to the appearance of a man, and as such delights in luring maidens to his abode. In a few instances he appears as the gallant rescuer of women marooned on bewitched islands. Like other monsters he has a brood of his kind, he having females as well. These sometimes lure men under water and seek to transform them by inducing them to put on the garments they wear. Horned Snake is hated by the Thunderer, who spares no energy to kill him before he can dive.

Monster Bear, Niă"gwai'he'gōwā, is the most feared of magic beasts and one of the most frequent among them to enter in to the fortunes of men. He loves to race and in various forms which he assumes, seeks to get men, and particularly boys, to bet their lives on the race, which generally lasts from sunrise to sunset. He has a vulnerable spot on the bottom of one of his feet and unless some hero hits this the monster does not die. His bones form important parts of "magic medicine" and the dust from one of his leg bones if taken as a medicine is reputed to make a runner invincible.

White Beaver, Na"ga"niă"go", is an otgont beast who lives in magic waters. He seldom appears, but when he does he means disaster. Usually he is represented as the transformed son of a great witch. He is sometimes called Diat'dagwŭt.

Blue Otter, is another magic beast whose home is in the water. His function is to poison springs. He has another function, that of inflicting disease by his magic, and in this way he secures offerings of tobacco.

Blue Lizard, Djai'nosgōwa, seems to be a beast looking something like an allegator. He lives in pools and is the servant of wizards and witches.

4. MAGICAL MAN-LIKE BEINGS.

The Stone Giants, or Stone Coats, Gĕⁿnoⁿ'sgwā', are commonly described in Seneca folk-tales. They are beings like unto men, but of gigantic size and covered with coats of flint. They are not gods and are vulnerable to the assaults of celestial powers, though the arrows of men harm them not at all. The early Iroquois are reputed to have had many wars with them, and the last one is said to have been killed in a cave.

Pygmies, Djogĕ'oⁿ, are little people who live in caves. They are a tribe by themselves and live in houses as men do. They frequent deep gulches and the borders of streams. In some ways they are tricky, but in general do not injure men. They are not successful hunters and are grateful for the fingernail parings of human beings. These are saved by the thoughtful and tied in little bundles which are thrown over cliffs for the Djogeon to gather as "hunting medicine." They also require tobacco and when they require it they will tap their water drums in their meeting places. The observant then make up little packages of tobacco which they throw to them. Out of gratitude for favors they frequently warn men of danger or assist them to fortune.

Mischief Maker, S'hodi'oⁿsko, is a trickster, and sometimes is called the "brother of death." He delights in playing practical jokes, regardless of how they result. He possesses a store of magic and is able to transform himself into many forms. It is related in one legend that in the end he repented and returned to the sky-world in a column of smoke. This appears however, to be an allusion to the Algonkin trickster.

Ghostly Legs, Ganos'has'ho'oⁿ', are beings composed only of a pair of legs, having a face directly in front, though the face is seldom seen. They appear only in the dark and no one has ever made a complete examination of one. They have no arms or bodies, but are like the lower bodies of men, cut off at the waist, and on either loin gleams a faintly glowing eye. Some have only one eye which protrudes and draws in as it observes an intended victim. The Ghostly Legs are always, or nearly always running rapidly when seen. They usually betoken death and disaster. No one knows from whence they come or whither they go. Indians of today on some of the reservations claim to have seen these creatures. While they have never been known to injure anyone they are at the same time as greatly feared as ghosts.

Sago^{n}"dada"kwŭs, (Sagodadahkwus) is a grotesque being with a lean, hungry looking body, and an insatiable appetite. He seeks out gluttons, and catching them in the dark, takes a long spoon which he inserts into their vitals and spoons out his food. For fear anything may be lost he carries a kettle into which he places everything he cannot immediately eat. He is the spirit of gluttony, and is the terror of all who gorge themselves unduly. It is well for a man who overeats to stay indoors at night, lest He-who-eats-inwards devour everything within him. So, with his kettle and spoon, Sagodadahkwus wanders over the earth looking for the gluttons.

Gonoñk'goĕs, the Big Breast, is a gigantic woman whose breasts hang down like pillows. She roams the earth looking for lovers who sit close together in the dark. If they make one remark that seems to be improper in their love making, or if they stay at their love making too long, she leans over them, catching their faces beneath her breasts and smothering them. Then she stands upright, still holding the smothered lovers to her bosom, and walking to a cliff, leans over and drops them into the dark depths below.

O"nia'tä^{n}, the Dry Hand, is a mysterious mummified arm that flies about to bewitch those who pry into the affairs of others by asking too many questions. It will thrust its fingers in he eyes of the peeper who tries to watch others out of idle curiosity. Generally the touch of this hand means death.

THEMES AND MATERIALS

II

THEMES AND MATERIALS

There are certain characteristic types of action to be found in Seneca folk-tales, and these are closely followed in all tales. However rambling a tale may be it never departs from certain stereotyped themes, expressing as they do the accepted idea patterns over which the story is woven. Among these themes we mention the following:

1. *Transformation.* Characters in the story are able to transform themselves into any person, animal or object, as their orenda or magical power gives them power. The Seneca believed in transformation to such an extent that he was never sure that a rolling stone, a vagrant leaf fluttering along, a scolding bird or a curious animal, might not be some "powered" person in a transformation stage.

2. *Magically acquired power.* The hero of a tale finds himself in a predicament and through his effort to extricate himself is endowed with magical power by which he overcomes enemies and difficulties.

3. *Overcoming monsters.* The journey of the hero is beset with magical monsters that seek to destroy him. The hero uses his wits and his orenda and subdues them.

4. *Precocious twins.* Twins are born of a romantic marriage, particularly where the hero or heroine has lost a relative. The twins rapidly grow to maturity and set forth to conquer.

5. *Contest with sorcerers.* The hero is placed in opposition to a sorcerer and matches his power against him, finally killing the sorcerer.

6. *Son-in-law put to tests.* The hero is allowed to retain his place, possessions or mate providing he procures certain magical objects for the sorcerer. In some stories an evil

mother-in-law demands such objects as the magical beaver, white otter, or blue lizzard. The hero obtains them very quickly and sometimes calls a feast to eat them. The mother-in-law is angry because these beasts are her brothers.

This is a widely diffused theme and is found from one coast to another.

7. *Dream animal rescues hero.* The hero finds himself in a predicament and remembering that a helper appeared to him in a dream, calls upon it for rescue. A rescue is made.

8. *Race with monster.* A monster, generally a monster bear, becomes enraged at or jealous of the hero. The monster challenges the hero to a race, the winner to kill the loser. The hero wins, generally by aid of some fetish given by his uncle or grandfather.

9. *Boaster makes good.* The hero boasts his power to do certain things, as to run faster than any living creature. He is warned to stop before the spirits of swift-running beings hear him. He continues to boast and a monster comes to the door to make the challenge. See 8, *supra*, for a continuation of this theme.

10. *Imposter fails.* A jealous rival overcomes the hero and strips him of his clothing. Hero becomes weak and old while Imposter becomes youthful. Imposter now assumes the character and rights of the hero. Finally he endeavors to perform the magical tricks of the hero and fails miserably.[1]

11. *Thrown away boy.* A child is thrown away because it seems too small to live, or it is lost in a blood clot and cast into a hollow stump. Thrown-away lives and becomes a powerful being that achieves wonders.

12. *Hidden lodge child.* A child born with a caul is

---

[1] Skinner in *J. A. F. L.* 27-29, cites this as a central Algonkin theme.

concealed in a lodge, generally under an enclosed bed. It is cared for by some elderly person, generally an uncle or aunt. A normal brother endeavors to rescue it, being told of its existance by some magical being; or, the child is hidden to protect it from an evil sorcerer who wants to steal it. Hero overcomes sorcerer.

13. *Double deceives sister.* A youth lives in a secluded cabin with his sister. The youth's double comes to the lodge when the hero is absent, endeavoring to seduce the sister. Double is repulsed. Sister will not believe brother has not insulted her. Brother finally makes a sudden return from a hunting trip and apprehends the double, killing him.[2]

14. *Uncle and Nephew.* An uncle and nephew live together in a secluded lodge. Uncle generally becomes jealous of youth's ability and desires the woman predestined for the nephew. In other cases uncle assists nephew to find lost parents. Generally the uncle guards the nephew and forbids him to go in a certain direction. Nephew disobeys orders.

15. *Evil step-father.* Step-father endeavors to rid himself of an unpromising step-son. Hides the boy in a cave or hole which he stones up. Boy is rescued and taught by animals, and finally returns a powerful being and confronts step-father.

16. *Witch mother-in-law.* A youth marries the daughter of a witch who endeavors to cause his death through conflict with monsters.[3]

17. *Animal foster-parents.* Animals find an abandoned boy. They discuss which one will care for him. A mother bear generally succeeds in securing him and takes him to a hollow tree where he is protected and educated in animal lore.

---

2 Skinner in *Anthrop.* P. of A. M. N. H. XIII, 528, cites this as a Menomini theme.
3 See 6, *supra,* for continuation of motif.

18. *Bewitched parents.* A boy finds that he has no parents. Asks his uncle or grandfather where they are. Is told that they are under some evil enchantment and secured in a place beset with magical monsters. Boy overcomes obstacles and rescues parents.

19. *Obstacles produced magically.* The hero is beset by a witch or monster and flees. Upon being pressed the hero creates obstacles by dropping a stone and causing it to become an unsurmountable cliff. He casts pigeon feathers and conjures them into a great flock that makes a slime that is impassable, or he finds "uncles" who interpose barriers for him, as webs, nets, holes, pits, etc. Hero finally escapes to lodge of a waiting mother-in-law.

20. *Lover wins mate.* Young man marries girl of his choice in spite of tricks of older rival and enmity of sorcerers. This must have been a popular theme in a society where the old were married to the young.

21. *Jealous sister-in-law.* Sister-in-law offended at hero's choice seeks to harm bride or to kill hero.

22. *Magical monster marries girl.* The monster may be the horned snake or the Thunderer.

23. *Thunderer wars upon horned snake.* The Thunder god hates the horned serpent and fights it.

24. *Turtle's war party.* Turtle gathers a company of offensive and loyal warriors. All are killed in action save turtle who begs not to be placed in water when captured. He is thrust in river and escapes.

25. *Bungling Guest.* An evilly inclined trickster plays practical jokes. Performs magical acts and induces a guest to imitate. Success attends in presence of Trickster and perhaps once in a private rehearsal, but miserable failure attends demonstration before others.

26. *Sorcerer's Island.* Sorcerer lures hero to enchanted island. Sorcerer has control of the tides and currents of water.

27. *Restoring Skeletons.* Hero finds bones of persons slain by sorcery. Commands them to arise quickly, "before I kick over a hickory tree," and skeletons rise so quickly that bones are mismated. Popular ending of stories.

28. *Vampire Corpse.* Body of dead sorcerer revives and procures hearts of living victims which it eats at leisure in its grave.

29. *Dream Demand.* Hero guesses the meaning of a fabricated dream and satisfies it, thereby thwarting intentions of the witch who pretended to dream.

30. *Sky Journey.* Brothers journey to rim of horizon and seek to go under it and enter the sky-world. All succeed but one who is so cautious that he makes a late start. Sky comes down and crushes him. His spirit speeds ahead and greets living brothers when they arrive. Regeneration by Master of Life.

STEREOTYPED OBJECTS AND INCIDENTS

INCIDENTS.

1. Lonely bark lodge. Hero and associates live in secluded hut.

2. Twins play in ground. Twins find an underground world in which they live and play.

3. Hero spies upon associate through hole in his blanket. Discovers the secret of associate's power. Tries this in associate's absence.

4. Monster is shot in vulnerable spot in bottom of foot and is killed.

5. Hero in contest kills magical animal. He alone is able to pull out the arrow, thereby establishing his claim to power or reward.

6. Hero's double buried in fireplace speaks through fire and reveals his murder to his mother.

7. Burning witch's head explode's sending forth cloud of owls.

8. Sorcerer controls flow of waters. Almost captures hero fleeing in a canoe by drawing the current of the water toward himself. Hero reverses current and escapes.

9. Magical objects are concealed under a bed. Hero dreams he wants them in retaliation for his "uncle's" evil desires.

10. Pursuing or sentinel monsters are pacified by gifts of meat.

11. Youth not yet able to hunt practices shooting at an animal's paw, hung on lodge rafter.

12. Sorcerers' hearts or livers are concealed in a safe place in their lodges, guarded by conjured dogs or ducks. Hero finds hearts and destroys sorcerers.

13. Hero obtains hearts of enemies and squeezes them, causing enemies to faint. He dashes them on rocks and kills enemies.

14. Hero conjures lodge of witches into flint. Orders it to become red hot and so destroys enemies.

15. Hero learns how to jump through the air.

16. Hero reduces sister to miniature and places her in a conical arrow tip, shooting her away to safety. Hero follows by magic flight creating obstacles as he goes.

17. Corn rains down into empty bins of starving people. Corn maiden comes to marry hero whose younger brother is ungrateful for food, casting it in fire thereby burning Corn Maiden's body. She departs.

18. Powered man throws flint chips calling upon them to kill animals.

19. Hero violates taboo. Calamity impends but hero overcomes.

20. Heroine kills pursuing monster by throwing boiling oil into its face.

21. Hero kicks over tree and causes skeletons to rise in flesh. Bones are mismated through haste. Origin of cripples.

22. Hero or twin heroes walk into the ground and disappear.

23. Lonely bird sings for a mate. Various creatures seek to comfort lonely bird but all are rejected until a natural mate calls and is found injured or trapped. Released by lonely bird who flies away with him.

24. Animals talk to men. Some animal warns hero of impending danger and plans escape.

OBJECTS.

1. *Dream helpers.* These are animals or persons that have come to the hero in a dream and promised to assist him in times of peril.

2. *Astral body.* The hero has an astral self that appears in times of great danger and points out a way of escape.

3. *Hollow log regeneration.* Hero who has been abused or conjured is regenerated by passing through a hollow log.

4. *Talking flute.* The flute kept in a "bundle" talks to hero's friend and informs him of condition, or it tells hero where he may find game.

5. *Running moccasins.* Hero pursued takes off moccasins and orders them to run ahead and make tracks that baffle pursuer.

6. *Magic Arrow.* An invincible arrow that kills whatever it is aimed at. It may be shot permiscuously into the air and game will return with it, falling dead at hero's feet. No one but hero can withdraw arrow.

7. *Forbidden chamber.* A certain walled-off part of the

lodge is forbidden to the hero, who in older relative's absence explores it, causing anger of magical beings.

8. *Door-flap action.* Sorcerer commands hero to perform dream demand by going out of door and consummating demand before the door curtain flaps back.

9. *Magic fish-line.* Sorcerer hooks hero's fleeing canoe with a magical fish-line. Hero burns off line by emptying pipe upon it.

10. *Hero ties his hair to earth.* When hero suspects he is in the hands of a sorceress he ties a hair to a root before he sleeps. Sorceress makes off with him but cannot go beyond the stretching length of the hair and is compelled to return.

11. *Lice hunting.* Sorceress hunts lice in hero's head, lulling him to sleep.

12. *Saliva gives power.* If a powered being touches any object or weapon with his saliva it takes some of his power.

13. *Wampum tears.* Captured hero or heroine when tortured sheds wampum tears which enemies greedily take.

14. *Magical animal skins.* Hero or sorcerer has enchanted skins which he can conjure to living animals. He may enter a skin and assume the characteristics of its original owner.

15. *Magic pouch.* The pouch of animal skin holds the hero's utensils, tobacco and pipe. It may be conjured to a living thing.

16. *Magic suit.* A self-cleaning suit that gives power to wearer.

17. *Magic canoe.* A canoe that has unusual speed and may be paddled into the air.

18. *Inexhaustible kettle.* Hero's friend puts scrapings of corn or nut into it and it expends enormously supplying enough food. Hero tries the experiment and expands kettle too greatly bursting the lodge.

19. *Magical springs.* Springs that have been enchanted by sorcerers are the dwelling places of monsters that lure the unwary to drink. The monster then drags in his victim and eats him.

20. *Enchanted clearings.* Clearings guarded by monsters who prevent hero from visiting sorcerer living in a lodge within.

21. *Bark dagger.* Hero incapacitated by thrust of bark dagger piercing his back. Villain steals hero's clothing and impersonates him. See Imposter.

22. *Sweat lodge regeneration.* Hero recovers through a sweat of bear's grease. Lodge covered with a fat bear pelt.

23. *Powered finger.* Hero has power to kill animals by pointing his finger at them.

24. *Animated finger.* Hero obtains a magic finger that stands in his palm, pointing out the location of anything he desires.

25. *Sharpened legs.* A character is able to whittle his legs to points and use them as spears.

25. *Borrowed skin.* Hero borrows skin (coat) of deer, mole, or other animal, and entering it moves about without exciting suspicion of enemy.

26. *Borrowed eyes.* Hero borrows eyes of deer or owl for a blind uncle enabling him to recover his own eyes or to see for a few moments a long lost relative, generally a brother.

27. *Stolen eyes.* Sorceresses rob young men of their eyes.

28. *Quilt of eyes.* Quilt made of winking eyes stolen from young men who have looked at the witches who continually sew upon such a quilt.

29. *Girls in box.* Enchanted girls hidden in a bark box come forth upon demand of conjurer. The enchantment is not of an evil nature.

30. *Enchanted feathers.* These placed upon hero's hat give him great power, particularly for running.

31. *Enchanted birds.* Hero has enchanted birds upon his hat that bring coals to light his pipe.

32. *Bark dolls.* Dolls are enchanted so that they speak for their maker, deceiving evil pursuer of hero.

33. *Talking moccasins.* Moccasins placed in lodge talk to evil pursuer, setting him or her astray.

34. *Reducable dog.* A tiny dog that is kept in a pouch. It may be enlarged to a size sufficient to carry the hero or his fleeing sister. Upon being patted with the hand or magic rod it becomes reduced to a size almost invisible.

35. *Talking skull.* Hero finds the skull of his uncle. It asks him for tobacco and then directs him how to overcome sorcery.

36. *Flayed skin.* A human skin is the slave of sorcerers and guards their lodge, clearing or path, screaming out the presence of intruders. It may be revived by hero who removes the enchantment.

37. *Wampum eagle.* An eagle covered with wampum. Many people shoot at this eagle trying to kill it. Only the hero can with his magic arrow.

38. *White beaver.* A magical beaver, generally the "brother" of a witch, is killed by hero who invites in friends to help eat the beast.

39. *Blue lizard.* Lives in a magic spring and lures the unwary to death by pulling them into the water.

40. *Flying heads.* These are spirits of the storm winds. They are generally evil characters in stories.

41. *Pygmies.* There are tribes of "little people" living under ground or in rocky places. They have valuable charms and can be forced to give them to men. They have a ceremony in which they delight. If men beings perform

this ceremony favor is gained. They like tobacco and nail parings.

42. *Buffalo one-rib.* A magically endowed buffalo kills men. It cannot be injured by arrows because it has only one rib, a bony plate protecting its entire body. Vulnerable in the bottom of one foot.

43. *Fast-growing snake.* A boy finds a pretty snake and feeds it. It grows enormously and soon eats a deer. Game is exhausted and snake goes after human beings.

44. *White pebble.* A white stone is given magical power and when thrown at a magical monster hits and kills it.

45. *Flesh-eating water.* The water of a magical lake eats the flesh from the bones of the unwary. Monsters living in it are immune.

46. *Sudden friend.* Hero in predicament sees a strange person before him who announces that he is a friend and will help the hero escape. Tells hero what to do.

COMPONENTS OF THE COSMOLOGICAL MYTH

1. *Sky world.* A world above the clouds inhabited by transcendent beings.

2. *Celestial tree.* A wonderful tree in the center of the sky-world.

3. *Sky woman.* Falls through hole made by uprooted sky-tree and brings a promised child with her.

4. *Primal turtle.* Rises from sea to receive sky-woman.

5. *Earth diver.* Animals dive to secure earth for turtle's back.

6. *World tree.* Springs up from root of sky tree brought down by sky-woman. Grows in the "middle of the world." Flowers of light.

7. *Female first born.* A daughter soon born to the sky woman. Grows to quick maturity.

8. *Immaculate conception.* Daughter conceives in mysterious manner.

9. *Rival twins.* Twins born to daughter. Warty, flint hearted one, kills mother at birth. Fair one, the elder, watches her grave and finds corn, beans, squashes, potatoes and tobacco springing from it. Elder twin is constructive, younger is destructive.

10. *Hoarded water.* Evil twin causes a great frog to drink all the water of the earth. Good twin hits it with a stone causing it to disgorge.

11. *Father search.* Good Minded twin searches for father and finds him on a great mountain to east.

12. *Son testing.* Good Minded's father tests him with wind, water, fire and rock. Good Minded proves sonship and returns to earth island with bags of animals.

13. *Man making.* Good Minded molds man from clay after reflections seen in water.

14. *Primal beings return.* Good Minded and grandmother return to sky.

15. *Evil banished.* Evil Minded placed in underground cavern.

THE ATMOSPHERE IN WHICH THE LEGENDS WERE TOLD

III

THE ATMOSPHERE IN WHICH THE LEGENDS WERE TOLD

Let us journey backward into the forgotten yesterday; let us catch a fleeting glimpse of a little village along the creek of Doshowey.

It is during the closing year of the Eighteenth Century. The time is in the moon Nïsha (January), and the whole earth is covered by a thick blanket of heavy snow.

There is a deeply worn trail along the bank of the creek, but nobody walks in the trail, for it is as deeply rutted as it is deeply trodden. It is not now a road but a trench floored with rough ice and carpeted with broken patches of snow. Along the sides of the trail, over the white way, are supplementary and parallel trails that in places spread wide with the tell-tale mark of snowshoes. Here and there are deep dents where boys have wrestled and thrown each other into the drifts.

About us are great trees. Back from the creek are areas covered with tall pines and hemlocks; toward the creek are great deciduous trees looking gnarled and weather-worn. In the more open spaces are groves of nut trees, the hickory, the butternut and the walnut. Even in the depth of winter the region is inviting and suggests happiness and opportunity.

We continue our journey until we come within sight of a little village of log huts and bark lodges. The huts are rather small and primitive looking and the lodges for the most part look battered and smoky. Here and there, however, is a log cabin more sumptuous than the rest, and there are even bark houses that look comfortable. There seem to be no streets in this village, for the houses are set in any spot, seemingly, where the builder chose to erect his dwelling. Stretching in every direction are little corn-fields, stripped of their ears and standing like ragged wrecks in the wind.

Before we reach the village there is an open space occupying a level area. Here and there are a score of boys and as many men shouting and playing games. In an icy trough, made by dragging a log through the snow for a quarter of a mile or more, the older boys are playing a game of snowsnake. We find that there are two rival teams, each with twenty-four long flat pieces of polished wood called "gawasa," or snowsnakes. The idea of the game seems to be to find out who can throw a gawasa the greatest distance.

There is a great shout as one contestant rushes forward holding his gawasa by the tip and throws it with all his might into the trough. On it speeds like a living thing, gliding ahead with a slight side to side movement like a serpent springing forward. At the entrance of the trough a band of opponents is crying out discouraging remarks, while his own cheer squad is shouting its confidence and praises. A hundred feet down the trough an opponent waves his feathered cap over the gawasa as it speeds by, calling it "a fat woodchuck that cannot run," while just a bit beyond, a friend also waves his cap and shouts a cabalistic word of magic. Finally the gawasa slows down and stops. Two trail markers rush to the spot and plunge colored sticks into the snow to mark the distance it has traveled. There is a referee from each team to insure absolute accuracy. In another moment another gawasa comes darting ahead, its leaden nose striking the tail of the first, nosing under it and throwing it out of the track, then speeding onward a score of paces ahead. The trail markers rush forward with other sticks and there is a great shout from the winning side.

Each team keeps its gawasa in leathern cases. A special "snowsnake doctor" draws out each as it is wanted and

Drawn by
J.J.Cornplanter The Snow Snake Game —
1905

THE SNOW SNAKE GAME.—From a drawing by Jesse Cornplanter.

carefully wipes it with a soft fawn-skin, then waxes or oils the snake with some secret compound designed to make it slip with less friction over the icy path. These formulae are great secrets and a successful "doctor" is in great demand, and receives big fees.

We glance over into the square where boys are playing a game of javelins and hoops. The object, we soon discover, is to pierce the hoop with the javelins, thus stopping its progress as it rolls onward between the lines of contestants to its goal. This is also a popular game with the dogs, especially the puppies, who every now and again dash after the hoop, much to the disgust of the team throwing it. We hear the cry of "Sigwah, ahsteh, sigwah!" meaning *get out, go away,* and then hear the yelp of the poor pup as it is struck with a javelin, and whimpers away from this maddened crowd of humans.

In another portion of the field we see a group of large girls playing football with a small ball stuffed with deer hair. There is a grand melee as the two "centers" come together and kick at the ball, missing and striking each other's shins. There is a peal of laughter as each falls in the snow from the impact, and rolls over upon the ball which other eager players strive to extricate with their feet, for their hands must not touch the ball. The game is a rough-and-tumble one, but no one is injured, for the kicking feet that fly about so nimbly are clad in soft-nosed moccasins.

We pass on and leave this scene of winter fun for a more sober group sitting on logs beneath the pines at the creek bank. It is a group of older men waiting for the return of a hunting party, and we learn that soon there is to be a great feast,—in fact a nine-day celebration in which all the people will participate. Out on the creek we also see little clusters of men fishing through the ice, and, judging by the shouts, fishing is good.

It may be well to pause here and carefully note the

appearance of the men. It is not difficult to see that they are Indians. Their coppery red skins and raven black hair indicate this. Moreover, their dress and language permits no mistake in our conclusion. One man, more aged than the rest, is garbed in buckskin from head to foot. His shirt is long and of a beautiful white tan. About the neck, the chest, the shoulders, the sides and upon the cuffs there is a rich adornment of porcupine quill embroidery in various tasteful colors,—red, yellow and white being predominant. The leggings are of the same soft velvet tan, and embroidered at the bottoms in a deep cuff of quill work, which extends up the front in a thin line. Just below each knee is a garter embroidered with a finer appliqué than the rather coarse quill work. Close inspection shows it to be long hair from the "bell" of the moose. It is so flexible that, unlike quill work, it allows the garter to be tied snugly without stiffness. Beneath the shirt, though it hangs down nearly to the knees, the edge of a loin cloth is just seen. Looking down at his feet you will observe a pair of beautiful moccasins. They are of the puckered toe type, with a single seam up the center of the foot, the leather being drawn up in neat puckers to conform to the shape of the foot. The flaps of the moccasins are also embroidered with quill work, in a running pattern looking like half circles and above which rise tendril designs,—looking like the zodiacal sign of Aries. It is the old man's cap, however, which interests us most. It is not at all like the conventional war-bonnet which we have seen in picture and pageant. Instead it is like a closely fitting cap of fine fur, apparently beaver. It has a wide band about it, holding it tightly to the head. On the upper part of this band are close rows of dangling silver cones that jingle against one another as the old man moves his head. From the center of the hat rises a spool-like socket into which is inserted a fine eagle plume, that turns on a spindle within the socket. Around the spool and fastened to it are clusters of smaller feathers that fluff over the top of the cap in gay abandon. Across the old man's breast is a worsted belt, red in color, and decorated with beads in a most interesting fashion. About the old man's waist is a stouter belt of buckskin, into which is thrust a tomahawk, and from which dangles a pipe-bag. Stooping over, he picks up a pair of overshoes made of woven cornhusk stuffed with pads of oiled rags and buffalo hair. Looking at the other men you observe that all have on similar crude looking over-moccasins, but that most of them are of thick oil-tanned buckskin leather, instead of cornhusk.

The old man walks away toward the village and we linger a moment to learn that his name is Jack Berry,[1] and that he is considered an old-fashioned fellow, but that he commands great respect. We find, in fact, that the village just ahead is named after him, "Jack Berry's Town," and that it is one of the eight villages of Indians scattered over the Buffalo Creek tract.

It is now late in the afternoon and the sun is sinking over the forest to the west. Men and boys, and now and then a small group of women, walk swiftly toward the village. Some of the men are bending low under heavy loads of game, trussed up in burden-frames. Several men have strings of fish and a few men and women have long strings of white corn upon their shoulders.

Naturally we are hungry after our long journey through the brisk winter afternoon. We are also ready to sit down by the fire and dry our damp feet. Where shall we go, who will know us?

Everybody seems to know us, for everybody speaks, saying, "Nyahweh skanoh, Gyahdasey," ("I am thankful to see you strong of body, my friend.") We stop and talk

---

1   There is an interesting anecdote concerning Major Jack Berry in the first Annual Report of the Buffalo Historical Society, page 175. Jack Berry Town was on the present site of Gardenville. He was born in Little Beard Town in the Genesee country and had his home on Squawkie Hill until he removed to the Buffalo tract. He was an ardent admirer of Red Jacket.

with one group after another and tell them that we are strangers, rather tired and very hungry. Everybody smiles and says, "Yes, that's so," but not a soul invites us to supper and lodging. Our guide smiles at us and finally says, "You may go to any cabin here, walk in and sit down." You may take off your shoes and put on any warm pair of moccasins you find hanging on the wall, you may pretend that you are dumb, and say nothing. No one will ask you a question, but every want that you have will be anticipated and every comfort of the lodge given to you, though it is the only bed as your couch, the only buffalo robe your cover, and your food the last bowl of soup. Among the Seneca you are welcome. No matter who you are, you are an honored guest and welcome to any home you chose to enter. It is for you to invite yourself to a home and honor it with your presence.

We look about with some concern, for most of the houses are small and look overcrowded. Finally, since we are in search of knowledge, as well as amusement and adventure, we choose a very commodious bark long-house, from whose roof we see six fires sending up columns of black smoke. This place looks as if it might afford us company enough to satisfy our social inclinations and room enough to stow us away for the night. If we hesitated a moment we were soon convinced of our good judgment by the tempting odors of steaming maize puddings and hull-corn hominy, together with the appetizing smell of venison roasting over hot stones.

We pause at the entry of the lodge and note the wooden effigy of a bear's head hanging in the gable of the building. This is a symbol that clansfolk of the Bear dwell within and that all "Bears" are welcome. However, as we know that neither Turtles nor Hawks, nor any other clansman or stranger will be denied admission, we push aside the buffalo robe that curtains the doorway and enter.

Before us is a vast hall some twenty-four feet wide and

eighty feet long. On either side are low platforms, scarcely more than knee high from the earthen floor. Above are other platforms, but these are six or seven feet above and form a roof over the lower platforms. On the latter we see people lounging, sitting or reclining, as suits their inclination.

An elderly woman comes forward and greets us, and as she does so, several men also come forward. Some, dressed in trader's cloth clothing grasp our hands in welcome, while an old man, evidently a relic of an older day, places his hands on our chests and says, "Strength be within you." This we learn is the old Indian way of greeting, in the days before hand-shaking came into vogue.

Some one points out an unoccupied seat filled with robes and we are invited to place our luggage on the platform above. From a long pole, hanging from the beams that form the roof supports, hang braids of corn, forming a curtain that nearly makes our loft inaccessible. As we push our pack basket well toward the center of the platform we hear a squeal, and a seven-year-old boy who has been sleeping there on a pile of pelts darts over the corn pole and swings himself to the floor.

The whole building is replete with stores of food, and besides the corn, we see large quantities of smoked meat, dried fish, dried pumpkins and squashes and dried herbs of various kinds. The center of the lodge is a broad aisle and at every eight paces there is a fire-place on the floor, the smoke from which rises to the roof and escapes through large rectangular holes made by leaving off the bark roofing.

We join a group of men and learn from their conversation that they are discussing the great war of the white men, in which the Thirteen Fires overcame the British King. Alas, these Indians had fought for the King and as a punishment a mighty general had come against them with a cannon, burning their villages on the Genesee and sending them terror-stricken to their red-coated allies at Fort

Niagara. Here they had endured a terrible winter of privation during which time hundreds died of disease, starvation and freezing. The British King had not done well by them and his agents had deceived them. It was Town Destroyer (Washington) who was their real friend, for it was he who said they might remain in their ancient seats. So here they were on Buffalo Creek, in the land of the Wenroe and the Neutral, peoples whom they had conquered a century and a half ago. Here was their refuge, but the contrast between this and their former secure position on the Genesee had disheartened them. The war and the flight had disorganized them, their old ideals had been broken, and the only safety seemed to be to avoid the white man. He brought all this trouble and his traders brought the fire water that made the young men crazy. He had brought a new religion too, and many of the villagers of the Buffalo tract had been converted to it and were trying to live in accordance with its teachings. Some of the men thought that this spoke the doom of the Indian race, while others thought it would be better to offset this movement by embracing the religion of Handsome Lake, a sachem from Allegany who was now preaching temperance and morality among the Indians at Allegany. Most of the men, however, thought that it was best to avoid all new schemes and philosophies. "The old way is the best," we hear them say. "In the old way we know just where we stand. We are familiar with the methods of the old way: the new way has not been tried."

Then someone says, "Jack Berry is going to go over to Handsome Lake. Maybe this is the right way. He is an intelligent man and his father was a white man, though he is more Indian than any of us in his manners and speech."

Long the discussion goes on, and embraces one topic after another. There is nothing to do but to talk and this soon grows tiresome, for the same old topics are worn threadbare. Brains that are hungry for new ideas and for facts

find no food. The mental life of the people, we quickly discover, is circumscribed. The people crave stimulation; of
physical stimulation they have plenty, but of mental stimulation there is little indeed. This is one of the reasons why
in the old days the men went on long tedious hunts, sought
adventure, went on war parties, and played the game of
death. "Better to die in the hurricane like a young oak that
has been broken in the gale," said they, "than to die because
rot has set in and eaten up the heart."

Here among the discouraged and broken people of the
Buffalo tract, bitterness gnawed at every heart, and there
was a sense of having been overwhelmed by some irresist-
ible force. The people craved amusement, excitement, and
the stimulation of the imagination. It was because of the
lack of healthful means to procure these things that the
men gambled so much, and drank the traders' rum.

The evening meal is now ready and we find that the
matron of our fire is dipping our hull-corn hominy. Everybody grabs a bark dish and some take out neatly carved
wooden bowls. These are filled with the hominy and the
group begins to eat, dipping the steaming corn with wooden
spoons of large size. Now comes the meat portion, and
each person is given from one to three pounds of roasted
venison. This we eat with boiled corn bread, dipping the
bread into a bowl of grease that is passed about among us.
We have no forks, and the only thing that resembles one
is a sharpened splinter of bone. We have our knives, however, and the meat is cut by holding it with the hands. If
our greasy fingers bother us we have a box of corn husks
upon which to wipe them. We then cast our "napkins" into
the fire. At the close of the meal we receive bowls of
"onegadaiyeh," or hot fluid, which we find to be a fragrant
tea made from the tips of hemlock boughs mixed with a
dash of sassafras. Those who do not like this drink are
given wintergreen "tea" sweetened with maple sugar. As
we drink our tea a bright-eyed maiden brings us a bark tray

A BARK COMMUNAL HOUSE

From a drawing by Jesse Cornplanter, son of Chief Edward Cornplanter. There were houses similar to this along Buffalo Creek as late as 1838.

with generous slices of sugar-nut bread, made by molding white corn flour with pulverized maple sugar into which is mixed hickory and hazel-nut meats, the whole being molded into a cake held into shape by husks, and then boiled until done. Everyone exclaims, "Oguhoh," meaning "Delicious."

The house is full of men, women and children. To each child there is a dog,—and a mighty well-behaved dog. Though they sit on their haunches looking hungry indeed, not one ventures near the mat or bench where the food is placed. Patiently they await a scrap of meat or a bone as it is thrown to them.

One is impressed with the various costumes of the throng. Some are dressed in military coats, some wear red flannel shirts made in coat style, with the flaps worn outside, some wear leather leggings, and some have cloth or buckskin trousers. Some of the women, as well as the men, wear tall beaver hats with silver bands around them. Everybody wears a blanket. Some are red, some are green or yellow, but nearly all wear gray or blue blankets. The women have especially fine blankets of blue broadcloth, beautifully beaded in floral patterns at the corners, and having geometrical designs around the borders. Only a few of the men wear boots, the majority wearing the ancestral moccasin. The skirts of the women are of broadcloth, beaded like the blankets, though several of the matrons have skirts of buckskin. The women wear pantalets, with beaded or quilled bottoms. They also wear small head shawls, and their hair is neatly braided. The maidens wear two braids, but the married women wear one, looped up behind and tied with a ribbon or a quilled strip of soft doeskin.

The house looks gloomy inside, for it is rather smoky, but the liveliness of the children and the puppies makes up for the darkened interior. If one does not wish to be walked over he had better crawl up on his bed and make himself comfortable in a buffalo robe. At best the lodge only shuts out the wind, and the fires add but little warmth.

With the abundance of fresh air one does not feel oppressed by the numerous people on every hand. No one in this dwelling has that unhappy disease that infects the dwellers in the tight and warm log houses,—the disease that eats the lungs and makes people fade away like ghosts of their real selves. The abundance of fresh air and the creosote from the smoke, together with exercise out of doors in the sunshine, makes these dwellers in the long bark house lively and healthy.

Again the men fall into groups about the fire, and again they talk of the events about them. One tells of a British agent who wants the Indians to come over to Canada and dwell with their brethren who followed Chief Brant to the Grand River after the war. A Mohawk Sachem had been with the British agent and had confirmed his description of the beautiful land on the other side of the Niagara, where the Iroquois Confederacy might once more rise from its ashes and become a great power. They had found but few followers, however, for the Buffalo Seneca were loyal to the memory of Washington, the great White Father, who just a month ago had died. "We are now the children of Town Destroyer," the British agent had been told. "We shall abide here where our fathers fought. This is their land and though we have been hurt in this conflict we will not run away, like dogs whipped, and who scamper whimpering to a hollow log. We shall stay here and be men." It was in vain that the agent had appealed to their natural desire for revenge.

As the night grows darker, a shout is heard outside and all the children run to the door. "Dajoh, dajoh!" they exclaim, and rushing out surround a tall man of middle age, one taking his hand and leading him in. We can hear the shout of "Hoskwisäonh, the story teller,—the story teller has come!"

He is a jovial-looking fellow, this story teller, and his entrance to the lodge puts the young people in a state of

suppressed excitement. Even the older people are pleasantly disposed toward him, and one matron draws forth
a bench which she sets before the central fire. Several cornhusk mats are then placed around on the floor and the company draws into a circle, at least such a circle as the building
will permit.

The story teller wears a long white flannel toga, or over-
shirt bound with blue ribbon. It is embroidered richly with
colored moose hair. His gustoweh or cap is of soft doeskin
quilled in herringbone patterns, and the feathers that droop
from the crest spindle are the white down feathers of the
heron. The spinning feather at the tip is from the tail of
a young eagle and from its tip rises a little tassel of red
moose hair held on by a bit of fish glue. He has two bags,
one containing his pipe and tobacco, and the other filled with
mysterious lumps. Just what these are everyone waits
patiently to see, for they are the trophies that "remind" him
of his stories,—bear teeth, shells, bark dolls, strings of
wampum, bunches of feathers, bits of bark with hieroglyphs
upon them, and the claws of animals.

He takes his seat and after smoking a pipeful of sacred
tobacco throws some of this fragrant herb upon the fire, at
the same time saying a ritualistic prayer to the unseen
powers, about whom he is soon to discourse. Finally he
exclaims, "Hauh, oneh djadaondyus," and all the people
respond, "Hauh oneh!" He plunges his hand into his mystery bag and draws forth a bear's tusk. "Hoh!" he says.
"The bear! This is a tale of nyagwai". Do you all now
listen!" And then comes the story of the orphaned boy
who lived with his wicked uncle and how he was rescued
from burial in a fox hole and cared for by a mother bear.
Another trinket comes forth, and again another, as a new
tale unfolds. When the night has grown old, and the
youngsters show signs of weariness by falling asleep, the
story teller closes his bag, carefully ties it and then starts
to smoke again.

The listeners have been thrilled by his dramatic recitation, they have been moved to uproarious laughter or made to shudder with awe. They have been profoundly stirred and their eyes glisten with pleasurable excitement. Everyone files past the story teller with a small gift,—a brooch, a carved nut, a small bag of tobacco or a strand of sinew for thread. No gift is large and most gifts are pinches of native tobacco. The story teller then finds a comfortable bed.

The children climb into their lofts by aid of notched ladders, the old people repair to their compartments, pull down the robe curtains, and soon all but a watcher or two are asleep, dreaming of the folk-beasts and the heroes of the story teller's tales. The more imaginative continue the adventures that have been told, and journey into dreamland to meet the myth-beings and learn of the mysteries that only slumberland can reveal.

Such is the setting of the story teller and the atmosphere in which the legends of the Seneca were told, in the days of early Buffalo. These old-time tales can scarcely be appreciated unless one knows and *feels* the circumstances under which they were related. Then, too, we may dream as the Seneca dreamed and know why he loved the story teller.

In the morning we are awakened by the noise of the corn pounders. "Ka-doom, ka-doom, ka-doom!" they sound as the pestle strikes the corn in the mortar and crushes it into hominy or meal, as the case may be. Children then begin to tumble out of bed and run about the lodge, but most of them are sent back to their warm robes until the morning meal has been prepared.

As we open our eyes we see little light, for we are within one of the bed compartments, over the front of which hangs long buffalo robe curtains, shutting out the light and securing us from the sight of others. The head and the foot of our sleeping quarters likewise are partitioned off by screens of bark, strengthened by upright poles. At our feet are little cupboards where we have stored our clothing and valuables. Over our heads hang uncertain bundles, attached to the parallel poles that form the platform above us. These contain the treasures and personal possessions of our host, whose bed we occupy. As we dress and emerge from our compartment, we feel the cool air of the great hallway and smell the smoke of the lodge fires. We look at the underside of the bed and find it walled up by bark over a layer of parallel poles. Beneath this bed are the greater treasures of our host, treasures that no one may touch or see save himself. He reaches them by lifting up the floor of the bed, a floor made of slats laced together. No person, not the owner of the compartment, would ever dare pry beneath that bed. It is a crime as black as calumny and worse than murder, for it is a violation of fundamental laws. As the women come from their compartments, and throw back their curtains upon the platform above, we catch a glimpse of "bed rooms" neatly kept and hung with furs and pelts. Some are embroidered and some are painted with signs and symbols. We note also their neat bundles and quilled bark boxes at the foot of the bed or over their heads. We long to pry into these secrets and to discover just what is in this mysterious boudoir, but modesty forbids anything more than a fleeting glance. Each compartment is its occupant's "castle" and must not be violated by so much as a curious look.

As we make ready for a bit of corn bread and a large bowl of soup, the liquor in which the bread has been boiled, we note the ascending smoke from the fireplaces on the earthen floor. The drafts are regulated by opening one door-flap or the other. The great ridgepole and the rafters of the lodge are black with soot. The roof is pitched, and the gable is made by a pole placed above and resting upon the plate-poles, across the front and rear of the building. These support the inner ridge pole upon which rests the tops of the roof supports or rafters. These are stiffened by inner poles that run parallel with the ridge pole and rest upon the end gable rafters. All are tied in place with ropes of bark or fastened with pegs, some of them spikes of deer antler. On either side of the door are the major roof supports which being securely driven in the ground rise to the gable rafter, giving a stronger support than could possibly be given by a central post. The building is absolutely rigid. The triple plaiting with bark, most of it elm, placed the long way of the grain, instead of up and down, makes the building wind-proof and comfortable enough to people inured to the weather.

We note with a great deal of interest the long rows of corn placed along the roof poles that rest just above the edge of the upper platforms. These braids of corn form curtains that screen off the upper platforms except in places where there are small openings into which the lodge matrons may thrust their possessions. It is there that they keep their bowls of bark and wood, also stores of dried food. We are told that there are barrels of bark up there filled with dried and smoked meats of various kinds, also stores of vegetable foods and herbs.

The shed of the house interests us greatly. It is an entry way attached to the lodge and has a slightly sloping roof. It is large and roomy and here on one side is piled a great quantity of wood and on the other are boxes and barrels of shelled corn.

We are impressed by the neatness of everything and by the compact manner in which food and clothing is stowed away. Of course, in a modern sense, the things we see are not clean, by any means, for dust and soot cover everything not within arm's reach. The place reeks of smoke, but we have grown so accustomed to this that we scarcely notice it, save when the wind changes direction and the smoke fills our eyes.

Around the fires are mats woven of corn husk, over a

warp of twisted elm bark fiber. Upon these we sit as we
are given wooden bowls which are filled with soup. The
big ladle which we see used to dispense our portion holds
a bowlful. It is carved from curly maple and has a dove
carved on the upper part of the handle. Our smaller spoons
are carved in a similar manner but they hold only a white
man's half cupful. There is nothing formal or full about
this breakfast and we note the frugality of the people. The
second meal will be the hearty one.

As we sit on the mat before the fire we note how conservative some of the older people are. One or two have
bowls or pots of baked clay, rare relics of the earlier day
before the white man's brass kettles made the fragile clay
pot an obsolete thing. We note that one pot has a serrated
rim which flares out, while the other has a tall collar decorated with parallel lines arranged in triangular plats. Very
gently do these old folk handle their clay pots which they
call "gadjĕⁿ". Several of the old men take from their
pouches ancient clay pipes, relics of the days when they
lived beyond the Genesee. These are molded with bowls
in the shape of raccoons and have copper eyes. The stems
are rather short, not more than eight inches, and the pipe is
not held in the mouth continually but lifted to the lips to
allow an inhalation, and then taken down. These relics we
learn are sacred things and are to be buried with the old
men when they die.

Breakfast is over and there is little for the men to do.
Their autumnal hunt has filled the larder with game. There
is plenty of corn, and the younger men supply the fresh
meat and fish needed. Winter is a time when everyone
clings to the hearth fire, save upon ceremonial occasion, or
for the usual winter sports. But even these become tiresome, and the minds of the people crave stimulation. Even
the gambling games do not supply the right sort of awakening. The minds of the people are hungry and demand a
feeding even upon husks. They demand that their imag-

inations be kindled and that from sordid life they be lifted to the fairylands of pure imagination. The story teller who can lift the individual out of self and transport him to the land of magic, where he may picture himself a super-man performing mighty feats, is in great demand. Absurdity counts for nothing; what though the myth or legend is impossible,—this does not matter. It gives the hungry mind and yearning soul wings upon which it may fly away from a real earth to the land of "I-wish-I-could." In a world where reliable facts are few and where critical investigation is impossible, the imagination must be fed. The story teller of the lodge supplies that food. He is the storehouse of all knowledge, the repository of ancestral lore. To the untutored mind of the aborigine he supplies what is almost as necessary as food itself, for while man is a combination of body and mind, mind must have its sustenance no less than body; it must have its sweets and its stimulants no less than the physical nature. And so the story teller weaves the spell, with all his rhetoric and oratory,—and hungry minds gather round to feast. . . . . .

Time goes by and the world has changed. There is a different order of things. The power of the Seneca has gone, and the pale invader has taken over all the land, save tiny areas in out-of-the-way places. Still the Seneca has not relinquished his hold entirely; in various bands he still lives in tribal estate. But how different is the Seneca today! His life is that of the surrounding white man, in an economic sense. Little remains to distinguish him as of another cultural order, but there is still enough to mark him as aboriginal. He still preserves his rites and ceremonies, and on the reservations at Cattaraugus, Allegany and Tonawanda he still tells the folk-tales that his ancestors loved, and *these remain unaltered to this very day.*

WHEN THE WORLD WAS NEW

DELOS BIG KITTLE—SAINOWA.

A leading chief of the Wolf Clan of the Cattaraugus Seneca. Chief Kittle was a man of great influence and numbered many devoted friends among the citizens of Buffalo and vicinity. He died in the Buffalo City Hospital, Dec. 30, 1923.

Photo by E. C. Winnegar.

IV.

1. HOW THE WORLD BEGAN

Beyond the dome we call the sky there is another world. There in the most ancient of times was a fair country where lived the great chief of the up-above-world and his people, the celestial beings. This chief had a wife who was very aged in body, having survived many seasons.

In that upper world there were many things of which men of today know nothing. This world floated like a great cloud and journeyed where the great chief wished it to go. The crust of that world was not thick, but none of these men beings knew what was under the crust.

In the center of that world there grew a great tree which bore flowers and fruits and all the people lived from the fruits of the tree and were satisfied. Now, moreover, the tree bore a great blossom at its top, and it was luminous and lighted the world above, and wonderful perfume filled the air which the people breathed. The rarest perfume of all was that which resembled the smoke of sacred tobacco and this was the incense greatly loved by the great chief. It grew from the leaves that sprouted from the roots of the tree.

The roots of the tree were white and ran in four directions. Far through the earth they ran, giving firm support to the tree. Around this tree the people gathered daily, for here the Great Chief had his lodge where he dwelt. Now, in a dream he was given a desire to take as his wife a certain maiden who was very fair to look upon.[1] So, he took

1 In another version this chief was killed and his body hidden in the trunk of the celestial tree. Another chief, a rival, desired to marry the daughter of the deceased one and indeed took her in the manner here related. In this version it was the bride who desired to have the tree uprooted in order that she might hunt for her father's body. The concealing of the body of the celestial father in the body of a tree reminds one of the legend of Osiris.

her as his wife for when he had embraced her he found her most pleasing. When he had eaten the marriage bread he took her to his lodge, and to his surprise found that she was with child. This caused him great anger and he felt himself deceived, but the woman loved the child, which had been conceived by the potent breath of her lover when he had embraced her. He was greatly distressed, for this fair Awĕⁿʻhā'i' was of the noblest family. It is she who is customarily called Iagĕⁿ'ʻtci'.

He, the Ancient One, fell into a troubled sleep and a dream commanded him to have the celestial tree uprooted as a punishment to his wife, and as a relief of his troubled spirit. So on the morrow he announced to his wife that he had a dream and could not be satisfied until it had been divined. Thereupon she "discovered his word," and it was that the tree should be uprooted.

"Truly you have spoken," said Ancient One, "and now my mind shall be satisfied." And the woman, his wife, saw that there was trouble ahead for the sky world, but she too found pleasure in the uprooting of the tree, wishing to know what was beneath it. Yet did she know that to uproot the tree meant disaster for her, through the anger of Ancient One against her.

It so happened that the chief called all his people together and they endeavored to uproot the tree, it being deep-rooted and firm. Then did the chief grow even more angry for Iagĕⁿ'ʻtci had cried out that calamity threatened and nobody would avert it. Then did the chief, himself embrace the tree and with a mighty effort uprooted it, throwing it far away. His effort was tremendous, and in uprooting the tree he shook down fruits and leaves. Thereafter he went into his lodge and entered into the apartment where his wife, Iagĕⁿ'ʻtci, lay moaning that she too must be satisfied by a look into the hole. So the chief led her to the hole made by uprooting the tree.

He caused her to seat herself on the edge of the hole

and peer downward. Again his anger returned against her, for she said nothing to indicate that she had been satisfied. Long she sat looking into the hole until the chief in rage drew her blanket over her head and pushed her with his foot, seeking to thrust her into the hole, and be rid of her. As he did this she grasped the earth at her side and gathered in her fingers all manner of seeds that had fallen from the shaken tree. In her right hand she held the leaves of the plant that smelled like burning tobacco, for it grew from a root that had been broken off. Again the chief pushed the woman, whose curiosity had caused the destruction of the greatest blessing of the up-above-world. It was a mighty push, and despite her hold upon the plant and upon the ground, she fell into the hole.

Now, this hole had penetrated the crust of the upper world and when Iagĕⁿ"tci fell she went far down out of sight and the chief could not see her in the depths of the darkness below. As she fell she beheld a beast that emitted fire from its head whom she called Gaăs'ioñdie't'hă', (Gahashondietoh). It is said that as she passed by him he took out a small pot, a corn mortar, a pestle, a marrow bone and an ear of corn and presented them to her, saying, "Because thou has thus done, thou shalt eat by these things, for there is nothing below, and all who eat shall see me once and it will be the last."

Now it is difficult to know how this Fire Beast can be seen for he is of the color of the wind and is of the color of anything that surrounds it, though some say he is pure white.

Hovering over the troubled waters below were other creatures, some like and some unlike those that were created afterward. It is said by the old people that in those times lived the spirit of Gä'ha' and of S'hagodiioweⁿ"gōwä, of Hĭ"noⁿ' and of Deiodasondaiko, (The Wind, the Defending Face, the Thunder and the Heavy Night.) There were also what seemed to be ducks upon the water and these also saw the descending figure.

The creature-beings knew that a new body was coming to them and that here below there was no abiding place for her. They took council together and sought to devise a way to provide for her.

It was agreed that the duck-creatures should receive her on their interknit wings and lower her gently to the surface below. The great turtle from the under-world was to arise and make his broad back a resting-place. It was as has been agreed and the woman came down upon the floating island.

Then did the creatures seek to make a world for the woman and one by one they dove to the bottom of the water seeking to find earth to plant upon the turtle's back. A duck dived but went so far that it breathed the water and came up dead. A pickerel went down and came back dead. Many creatures sought to find the bottom of the water but could not. At last the creature called Muskrat made the attempt and only succeeded in touching the bottom with his nose but this was sufficient for he was enabled to smear it upon the shell and the earth immediately grew, and as the earth-substance increased so did the size of the turtle.

After a time the woman, who lay prone, aroused herself and released what was in her hands, dropping many seeds into the folds of her garment. Likewise she spread out the earth from the heaven world which she had grasped and thus caused the seeds to spring into germination as they dropped from her dress.

The root of the tree which she had grasped she sunk into the soil where she had fallen and this too began to grow until it formed a tree with all manner of fruits and flowers and bore a luminous orb at its top by which the new world became illuminated.

Now in due season the Sky-Woman[2] lay beneath the tree and to her a daughter was born. She was then happy for she had a companion. Rapidly the girl child grew until very soon she could run about. It was then the custom of Ancient One to say: "My daughter, run about the island and return telling me what you have seen."

Day by day the girl ran around the island and each time it became larger, making her trips longer and longer. She observed that the earth was carpeted with grass and that shrubs and trees were springing up everywhere. This she reported to her mother, who sat beneath the centrally situated great tree.

In one part of the island there was a tree on which grew a long vine and upon this vine the girl was accustomed to swing for amusement and her body moved to and fro giving her great delight. Then did her mother say, "My daughter, you laugh as if being embraced by a lover. Have you seen a man?"

"I have seen no one but you, my mother," answered the girl, "but when I swing I know someone is close to me and I feel my body embraced as if with strong arms. I feel thrilled and I tingle, which causes me to laugh."

Then did the Sky-Woman look sad, and she said, "My daughter, I know not now what will befall us. You are married to Gä'ha', and he will be the father of your children. There will be two boys."

In due season the voices of two boys were heard speaking, eiä'da'goñ', and the words of one were kind and he gave no trouble, but the words of the other were harsh and he desired to kill his mother. His skin was covered with warts and boils and he was inclined to cause great pain.

When the two boys were born, Elder One made his mother happy but when Warty One was born he pierced her through the arm pit and stood upon her dead body.

---

2 We use this name for convenience only.

So did the mother perish, and because of this the Sky Woman wept.

The boys required little care but instantly became able to care for themselves. After the mother's body had been arranged for burial, the Sky Woman saw the Elder One whom she called Good Mind, approach, and he said, "Grandmother, I wish to help you prepare the grave." So he helped his grandmother who continually wept, and deposited the body of his mother in a grave. Thereupon did the grandmother speak to her daughter:

"Oh, my daughter," she said. "You have departed and made the first path to the world from which I came bringing your life. When you reach that homeland make ready to receive many beings from this place below, for I think the path will be trodden by many."

Good Mind watched at the grave of his mother and watered the earth above it until the grass grew. He continued to watch until he saw strange buds coming out of the ground.

Where the feet were the earth sprouted with a plant that became the stringed-potato, (onĕñno$^{n'}$dă'o$^{n'}$wĕ') where her fingers lay sprang the beans, where her abdomen lay sprang the squash, where her breasts lay sprang the corn plant, and from the spot above her forehead sprang the tobacco plant.

Now the warty one was named Evil Mind, and he neglected his mother's grave and spent his time tearing up the land and seeking to do evil.

When the grandmother saw the plants springing from the grave of her daughter and cared for by Good Mind she was thankful and said, "By these things we shall hereafter live, and they shall be cooked in pots with fire, and the corn shall be your milk and sustain you. You shall make the corn grow in hills like breasts, for from the corn shall flow our living."

Then the Grandmother, the Sky Woman, took Good Mind about the island and instructed him how to produce plants and trees. So he spoke to the earth and said, "Let a willow here come forth," and it came. In a like manner he made the oak, the chestnut, the beech, the hemlock, the spruce, the pine, the maple, the button-ball, the tulip, the elm and many other trees that should become useful.

With a jealous stomach the Evil Mind followed behind and sought to destroy the good things but could not, so he spoke to the earth and said: "Briars come forth," and they came forth. Likewise he created poisonous plants and thorns upon bushes.

Upon a certain occasion Good Mind made inquiries of his Grandmother, asking where his father dwelt. Then did the Sky Woman say: "You shall now seek your father. He lives to the uttermost east and you shall go to the far eastern end of the island and go over the water until you behold a mountain rising from the sea. You shall walk up the mountain and there you will find your father seated upon the top."

Good Mind made the pilgrimage and came to the mountain. At the foot of the mountain he looked upward and called, "My father, where art thou?" And a great voice sounded the word: "A son of mine shall cast the cliff from the mountain's edge to the summit of this peak." Good Mind grasped the cliff and with a mighty effort flung it to the mountain top. Again he cried, "My father, where art thou?" The answer came, "A son of mine shall swim the cataract from the pool below to the top." Good Mind leaped into the falls and swam upward to the top where the water poured over. He stood there and cried again, "My father, where art thou?" The voice answered, "A son of mine shall wrestle with the wind." So, there at the edge of a terrifying precipice Good Mind grappled with Wind and the two wrestled, each endeavoring to throw the other over. It was a terrible battle and Wind tore great rocks from the mountain side and lashed the water below, but Good Mind overcame Wind, and he departed moaning in defeat. Once more Good Mind called, "My father, where art thou?" In awesome tones the voice replied, "A son of mine shall endure the flame," and immediately a flame sprang out of the mountain side and enveloped Good Mind. It blinded him and tortured him with its cruel heat, but he threw aside its entwining arms and ran to the mountain top where he beheld a being sitting in the midst of a blaze of light.

"I am thy father," said the voice. "Thou art my son."

"I have come to receive power," said the son. "I wish to rule all things on the earth."

"You have power," answered the father. "You have conquered. I give to you the bags of life, the containers of living creatures that will bless the earth."

Thus did the father and son counsel together and the son learned many things that he should do. He learned how to avoid the attractive path that descended to the place of the cave where Hanishe′onoⁿ′ dwells.

Now the father said, "How did you come to find me, seeing I am secluded by many elements?"

The Good Mind answered, "When I was about to start my journey Sky Woman, my grandmother, gave me a flute and I blew upon it, making music. Now, when the music ceased the flute spoke to me, saying, 'This way shalt thou go,' and I continued to make music and the voice of the flute spoke to me."

Then did the father say, "Make music by the flute and listen, then shalt thou continue to know the right direction."

In course of time Good Mind went down the mountain and he waded the sea, taking with him the bags with which he had been presented. As he drew near the shore he became curious to know what was within, and he pinched one bag hoping to feel its contents. He felt a movement inside which increased until it became violent. The bag began to roll about on his back until he could scarcely hold it and a portion of the mouth of the bag slipped from his hand.

Immediately the things inside began to jump out and fall into the water with a great splash, and they were water animals of different kinds. The other bag began to roll around on his back but he held on tightly until he could do so no more, when a portion of the mouth slipped and out flew many kinds of birds, some flying seaward and others inland toward the trees. Then as before the third bag began to roll about but he held on very tight, but it slipped and fell into the water and many kinds of swimming creatures rushed forth, fishes, crabs and eels. The fourth bag then began to roll about, but he held on until he reached the land when he threw it down, and out rushed all the good land animals, of kinds he did not know. From the bird bag had come good insects, and from the fish bag had also come little turtles and clams.

When Good Mind came to his grandmother beneath the tree she asked what he had brought, for she heard music in the trees and saw creatures scampering about. Thereupon Good Mind related what had happened, and Sky Woman said, "We must now call all the animals and discover their names, and moreover we must so treat them that they will have fat."

So then she spoke, "Cavity be in the ground and be filled with oil." The pool of oil came, for Sky Woman had the power of creating what she desired.

Good Mind then caught the animals one by one and brought them to his grandmother. She took a large furry animal and cast it into the pool and it swam very slowly across, licking up much oil. "This animal shall hereafter be known as niagwaih, (bear) and you shall be very fat." Next came another animal with much fur and it swam across and licked up the oil, and it was named degiiă"go^n, (buffalo). So in turn were named the elk, the moose, the badger, the woodchuck, and the raccoon, and all received much fat. Then came the beaver (na^{n}ga^{n}niă'go^n'), the porcupine and the skunk. Now Good Mind wished the deer to enter but it was shy and bounded away, whereupon he took a small arrow and pierced its front leg, his aim being good. Then the deer came and swam across the pool and oil entered the wound and healed it. This oil of the deer's leg is a medicine for wounds to this day and if the eyes are anointed with it one may shoot straight.

Again other animals came and one by one they were named weasel, mink, otter, fisher, panther, lynx, wild cat, fox, wolf, big wolf, squirrel, chipmunk, mole, and many others.

And many animals that were not desired plunged into the pool of oil, and these Good Mind seized as they came out and he stripped them of their fat and pulled out their bodies long. So he did to the otter, fisher, weasel and mink. So he did to the panther, wolf, big wolf, and fox, the lynx and the wildcat. Of these the fat to this day is not good tasting. But after a time Evil Mind secured a bag of creatures from the road to the Cave and unloosed it, and evil things crawled into the pool and grew fat. So did the rattlesnake and great bugs and loathly worms.

Thus did Evil Mind secure many evil monsters and insects, and he enticed good animals into his traps and perverted them and gave them appetites for men-beings. He was delighted to see how fierce he could make the animals, and set them to quarreling.

He roamed about visiting the streams of pure water made by Good Mind and filling them with mud and slime, and he kicked rocks in the rivers and creeks to make passage difficult, and he planted nettles and thorns in the paths. Thus did he do to cause annoyance.

Now Good Mind sat with his grandmother beneath the tree of light and he spoke to her of the world and how he might improve it. "Alas," said she, "I believe that only one more task awaits me and then I shall go upon my path and follow your mother back to the world beyond the sky.

It remains for me to call into being certain lights in the blackness above where Heavy Night presides."

So saying she threw the contents of a bag into the sky and it quickly became sprinkled with stars. And thus there came into being constellations (haditgwă"dā'), and of these we see the bear chase, the dancing brothers, the seated woman, the beaver skin, the belt, and many others.

Now it seems that Good Mind knew that there should be a luminous orb and, so it is said, he took his mother's face and flung it skyward and made the sun, and took his mother's breast and flinging it into the sky made the moon. So it is said, but there are other accounts of the creation of these lights. It is said that the first beings made them by going into the sky.

Shortly after the creation of the stars (gadjĭ"so"dă'), the grandmother said unto Good Mind, "I believe that the time has come when I should depart, for nearly all is finished here. There is a road from my feet and I have a song which I shall sing by which I shall know the path. There is one more matter that troubles me for I see that your brother is jealous and will seek to kill you. Use great care that you overcome him and when you have done so confine him in the cave and send with him the evil spirit beasts, lest they injure men."

When morning came the Sky Woman had departed and her journey was toward the sky world.

Good Mind felt lonely and believed that his own mission was about at end. He had been in conflict with his brother, Evil Mind, and had sought, moreover, to overcome and to teach the Whirlwind and Wind, and the Fire Beast.

Soon Evil Mind came proposing a hunting trip and Good Mind went with him on the journey. When they had gone a certain distance the Evil Mind said, "My elder brother, I perceive that you are about to call forth men-beings who shall live on the island that we here have inhabited. I propose to afflict them with disease and to make life difficult, for this is not their world but mine, and I shall do as I please to spoil it."

Then did Good Mind answer and say, "Verily, I am about to make man-beings who shall live here when I depart, for I am going to follow the road skyward made first by my mother."

"This is good news," answered Evil Mind. "I propose that you then reveal unto me the word that has power over your life, that I may possess it and have power when you are gone."

Good Mind now saw that his brother wished to destroy him, and so he said, "It may happen that you will employ the cat-tail flag, whose sharp leaves will pierce me."

Good Mind then lay down and slumbered, but soon was awakened by Evil Mind who was lashing him with cat-tail flags, and yelling loudly, "Thou shalt die." Good Mind arose and asked his brother what he meant by lashing him and he answered, "I was seeking to awaken you from a dream, for you were speaking."

So, soon again the brother, Evil Mind, asked, "My brother, I wish to know the word that has power over you." And Good Mind perceiving his intention answered, "It may be that deer-horns will have power over me; they are sharp and hard."

Soon Good Mind slept again and was awakened by Evil Mind beating him with deer-horns, seeking to destroy him. They rushed inland to the foot of the tree and fought each other about it. Evil Mind was very fierce and rushed at his brother thrusting the horns at him and trying to pierce his chest, his face or tear his abdomen. Finally, Good Mind disarmed him, saying, "Look what you have done to the tree where Ancient One was wont to care for us, and whose branches have supplied us with food. See how you have torn this tree and stripped it of its valuable products. This tree was designed to support the life of men-beings and now you have injured it. I must banish you to the region of the great cave and you shall have the name of Destroyer."

So saying he used his good power to overcome Evil Mind's otgont (evil power) and thrust him into the mouth of the cave, and with him all manner of enchanted beasts. There he placed the white buffalo, the poison beaver, the poison otter, snakes and many bewitched things that were otgont. So there to this day abides Evil Mind seeking to emerge, and his voice is heard giving orders.

Then Good Mind went back to the tree and soon saw a being walking about. He walked over to the place where the being was pacing to and fro. He saw that it was S'hagodiiweⁿ"gōwā, who was a giant with a grotesque face. "I am master of the earth," roared this being (called also Great Defender), for he was the whirlwind. "If you are master," said Good Mind, "prove your power."

Defender said, "What shall be our test?"

"Let this be the test," said Good Mind, "that the mountain yonder shall approach us at your bidding."

So Defender spoke saying, "Mountain, come hither." And they turned their backs that they might not see it coming until it stood at their backs. Soon they turned about again and the mountain had not moved.

"So now, I shall command," said Good Mind, and he spoke saying, "Mountain, come hither," and they turned their backs. There was a rushing of air and Defender turned to see what was behind him and fell against the onrushing mountain, and it bent his nose and twisted his mouth, and from this he never recovered.

Then did Defender say, "I do now acknowledge you to be master. Command me and I will obey."

"Since you love to wander," said Good Mind, "it shall be your duty to move about over the earth and stir up things. You shall abandon your evil intentions and seek to overcome your otgont nature, changing it to be of benefit to man-beings, whom I am about to create."

"Then," said Defender, "shall man-beings offer incense tobacco to me and make a song that is pleasing to me, and they shall carve my likeness from the substance of trees, and my orenda will enter the likeness of my face and it shall be a help to men-beings and they shall use the face as I shall direct. Then shall all the diseases that I may cause depart and I shall be satisfied."

Again Good Mind wandered, being melancholy. Looking up he saw another being approaching.

"I am Thunder," said the being.

"What can you do to be a help to me?" asked Good Mind.

"I can wash the earth and make drink for the trees and grass," said Thunder.

"What can you do to be a benefit to the men-beings I am about to create?" asked Good Mind.

"I shall slay evil monsters when they escape from the under-world," said Thunder. "I shall have scouts who will notify me and I shall shoot all otgont beings."

Then was Good Mind satisfied, and he pulled up a tree and saw the water fill the cavity where the roots had been. Long he gazed into the water until he saw a reflection of his own image. "Like unto that will I make men-beings," he thought. So then he took clay and molded it into small images of men and women. These he placed on the ground and when they were dry he spoke to them and they sprang up and lived.

When he saw them he said unto them, "All this world I give unto you. It is from me that you shall say you are descended and you are the children of the first-born of earth, and you shall say that you are the flesh of Iagĕⁿʷtci, she the Ancient Bodied One.

When he had acquainted them with the other first beings, and shown them how to hunt and fish and to eat of the fruits of the land, he told them that they should seek to live together as friends and brothers and that they should treat each other well.

He told them how to give incense of tobacco, for Awĕⁿʻhā'i', Ancient Bodied One, had stripped the heaven world of tobacco when she fell, and thus its incense should be a pleasing one into which men-beings might speak their words when addressing him hereafter. These and many other things did he tell them.

Soon he vanished from the sight of created men beings, and he took all the first beings with him upon the sky road.

Soon men-beings began to increase and they covered the earth, and from them we are descended. Many things have happened since those days, so much that all can never be told.

2. THE BROTHERS WHO CLIMBED TO THE SKY.

There were once three brothers who had spent their lives as hunters. At last one growing tired of the chase suggested that, as a break in the monotony of existence, they would walk to the end of the earth where the sky touched the water of the great seas. This proposition met with favor with all and together they set out on their long journey. Many years of adventure were spent, when at last they reached the spot where the sky bends down to earth (gaenhyakdondye).

For two changes of the moon they camped near this spot and watched the mysterious things that happened about the blue dome's rim. Each day it rose high from the earth and fell back upon the sea. When it rose the water would recede and when it fell the water would rise high on the shore. Finally two brothers desired to run upon the sand beneath the rim of the bowl but the third brother hung back and was afraid, but seeing the others afar off he ran beneath the rim and hastened to overtake them but just as the two stepped out from the farther side of the blue wall it came down and the third was crushed; but his spirit sped forward like the wind on its journey. The two mourned the loss of their brother in this summary way but continued their adventure.

Now on the other side of the sky all things seemed turned around. Before them was a high rounded hill and when they ascended it they found a large village in the distance. A man came running toward them. It was their brother.

"How came you here, brother?" they asked. "We did not see you pass us," but all the other brother would say was, "Never hesitate, never delay!" and passed on.

They saw an old man approaching. His youthful vigor and strong, well-proportioned body surprised them. No earthly symptoms of old age had he. His white hair alone betokened that.

Coming near he greeted them. "I am the Father of All," he said, "and my son is T'haho^n'hiawä"ko^n, the Great Spirit. He is the ruler of all below. Now let me advise you. When you see him call him quickly and say 'Nya'wĕ"skäno' '! If you fail to speak first he will say, 'you are mine,' and you will no more be men but spirits as your brother is."

The brothers went their way and came to a high white lodge. As they walked up the path a tall handsome man stepped out.

"Nyawĕ"skäno'!" shouted the brothers in chorus.

"Dogĕ^{n}s!" responded the being. "Come in. I have been watching you a long time."

The brothers entered the lodge.

"How are your bodies, men?" asked the being.

"Good indeed!" replied the brothers.

"Untrue," said the great being. "I am the Master of Life and know! One of you must lie down and I will purify him first, and then the other."

One brother placed himself upon the ground. Master of Life took a small shell, placed it to his lips, tapped him upon the neck, and then carefully sealed the shell with a lump of clay. He now began to skin the prostrate man. He stripped every muscle from its fastenings, took out the organs, and separated the bones. He cleansed each fibre from corruption and disease with a fluid from his mouth and then put the man together again. The same process was repeated with the second brother. Then, placing the shells upon their mouths, he loosened the clay and tapped the necks of the men. Sitting up they said, "It seems as if we have slept."

Every power of your bodies is renewed," said the Master of Life. "How would you like to test your skill now?" And, leading the way, he entered a beautiful forest surrounded by a hedge. The borders of the grove were lined with beds of vegetables and flowers.

"Come into the inner part of my garden," said the Master of Life, "and see my droves of deer."

A stalwart buck with proud branching antlers came bounding toward them.

"He is the swiftest of all my runners," said the Master of Life. "Try to catch him."

The men followed after and easily overtook the fleeing deer.

"He has given us good speed," said the brothers, nor was this the only power. For long they tried their skill in every way and found it equal to any task that creatures could perform.

Returning to the great white lodge the brothers saw a messenger of wondrous swiftness come speeding toward them. Upon his wide expanded chest was suspended a brilliant ball of light. In some unknown tongue he shouted as he dashed by on his journey.

"Do you understand his words, or do you even know him?" asked the Master. "He is Sun, my messenger, Ho'sĕⁿ"äge"dagōwā. Each day he brings me news. Nothing from east to west escapes his eyes. He has just told me of a war raging even now between your people and another nation, so come, let us look down upon the earth."

Going to a high hill the men looked down through a hole in the sky and saw the struggling bands of men, saw the flaming lodges, and even the cries of anguish and rage.

"Such things men will ever do," said the Master of Life as he led them away.

The brothers lived long in the upper world and learned much that their tongues never could tell. They saw untennanted villages awaiting the coming of tribes yet to be born and saw their own lodges where they should be when they came again as spirits. Many good things the great Master of Life told them, and our preachers proclaim them now.

At last the Master told them they must depart, and, guided by two messengers, they descended to the earth by night and slept on the ground.

In the morning they discovered that their native village was overgrown with trees, and following a path through the woods came to another settlement. In a council they told their story and no one knew them except a sister, aged and on the verge of the grave.

"The war of which you speak," said they, "took place fifty years ago."

The men did not love earth now but longed for their lodges in the sky world. They were men of wonderful physical power and neither pestilence nor enchantments could kill them but two fiery shafts of the sky did. They then journeyed back to the great white lodge, but this time could not return.[1]

---

1 This was because the Creator had first spoken. To have resisted death by the hand of a mysterious power one must salute it with its own greeting.

3. THE DEATH PANTHER.[1]

Now the old folk say this is true.

Two boys were fast friends and always were seen together. Their favorite sport was to play in the waters of a deep lake that washed the feet of a tall white-headed mountain that lay a distance from the village.

One day as they splashed in the water, swimming, diving, and sporting as boys do, one suggested that they both dive at the same instant and see which could remain below the surface the longer. This suggestion was at once acted upon and each time they dove they remained below a greater time.

In the course of the game one of the boys, Oohoosha, by name, discovered a flat projecting rock to which he could cling. As he lay holding fast to the rock after a dive he saw a hazy indistinct object approaching him and when it neared him he saw that it was a tall warrior whose smooth glistening body was the color of the sky or the color of clear water when the clouds pass over.

"Come with me," said the man, in a friendly manner and although he had never heard this language before, Oohoosha strangely understood it now. So, marveling, he followed.

The dark green water began to clear and in the distance, he thought he saw a number of boys playing ball. The guide led Oohoosha into a large moss-covered council hall where a stout preacher, with a yellow and pink face, swaying body and large round eyes was declaiming to the people.

"God created all good things and made men as well as fish!" he shouted, as the bubbles floated up from his mouth. "The earth people are his children as well as we, so why should not we who know and foreknow many things, notify them that trouble is coming and warn them to avoid it?"

---

1 Related by Edward Cornplanter, Jan., 1905, at Newtown, Cattaraugus reservation.

"I will go," said the boy's friend, as he pulled his cap. "It is my office."

The preacher rolled his eyes and looked at the speaker, with a shudder and then called out, "Gaă'sioñdie't'hă' has promised to go. May he succeed!"

The preacher sat down and the dances began, and long and solemnly the people danced. After these ceremonies the boy's friend told him that he must go up to the earth-world and warn men of disaster. He took him to his lodge and bade him care for it during his absence. He was to have free access to everything save the back room of the lodge which he must shun. With a few general instructions he departed, leaving Oohoosha to care for his interests.

For four moons the boy kept watch, over the lodge and dwelt there but no one came near him, and when at last the friend returned Oohoosha asked how he had fared.

"Ah!" sighed the man, "do not ask me. You must not stay here longer, for in my madness you may see me as I am. I am the messenger of death. He is Sondowekowa, I am Gahachendietoh. I am in disguise but should you see me you would soon die, so depart and preach what I whisper that henceforth mankind may profit."

With trembling limbs and blanched face the boy listened to the whispered words of his friend and when he had learned all, he shot upward to the surface of the lake. Striking out he swam to the shore and searching beneath a rock shelter he found his clothing as fresh as when he had doffed them. Dressing, he set out to find his comrade. He came to the village but found on its site only charred and blackened frames. A deep-trodden trail bordered with the bones of dogs and fragments of kettles led away to the west, and following it Oohoosha saw a new village, but only a few houses were there. The people who moved like ghosts silently about were gaunt and scarred.

Suddenly a lodge door opened and out rushed his old comrade, who seeing Oohoosha, drew back with a cry of fear and surprise; but Oohosha calling, he came forward timidly and took his hand. Looking at him doubtfully he spoke.

"Oh, Oohoosha!" he cried. "How came you back from death! I thought you drowned four moons ago when we dived in the lake."

"While I clung to a rock," answered Oohoosha," a man came to me and said 'follow!' I did not drown but lived this while in the under-water world. Now, tell me, why is the village so altered and why do the people stalk silently about, with dull eyes?"

"Ah me!" said the comrade. "A devastating war has been waged and we are reduced in number; a terrible famine has swept away the game and crops; a pestilence carried away all but a handful of our people, then to add to our trouble a marauding band came and burned our village while we slept."

"And did no warning sign appear?" asked Oohoosha.

"Yes, but we knew it not as such until it was long too late and then we noticed a blue panther floating high in the trees. He had no visible face but from his tail shot flames of fire."[2]

"That creature," exclaimed Oohoosha, "is the herald of disaster. His name is Gaä'sioñdie't'hä' and when he is seen all men must burn tobacco. Tobacco incense is the sign that disaster is not wanted and when he has breathed it he will go away satisfied with the offering and turn aside the impending evil. But come, I must call a council and tell the people."

---

[2] A comet or shooting star is considered a sign of the death panther.

4. THE GREAT BEAR CONSTELLATION.

In the days of the first people, before the creation of our kind of man-beings, there were seven brothers. All were hunters, but one was not as skillful as the others, and he was called the Lazy One.

The brothers on a certain occasion had failed to find any game though they had hunted many moons. They became very hungry and their minds were charged with magic because of their long fast. When their hunger semed unendurable they resolved to go out and make one last effort to find game. One brother was reluctant to go and clung to his bed, but the others wrestled with him and forced him to go with them, but he assumed to be so weak that they had to make a burden litter upon which they carried him. Four brothers carried this burden, one went before with a torch and one behind with a kettle, hoping for food.

When they had gone a long way in this manner the leading brother said: "By aid of my torch I see the tracks of a large bear. I believe that we shall soon overtake him." When he had said this the lazy brother in the litter said, "I am very weak and you must bathe me with your salivary fluid."[1] They paused to do this though the brothers did not like to delay their hunt.

After a time the bear tracks appeared to be fresh before them and all five brothers made ready for the hunt. The rear brother commenced to gather firewood for the feast. Thus they traveled for three days more until the bear appeared just ahead. "We must now abandon you, brother," said the litter-bearers, for we are weak and all of us shall have to assist in killing him before he overpowers us. Now, we shall leave you here alone and we hope you may recover."

---

1 In this manner he hoped to absorb the power or strength of his brothers.

When the lazy brother found himself abandoned he leaped up and ran ahead. Being full of power from the bath he had received and from his rest, he quickly engaged the bear and killed it with an axe.

When his brothers came up he had skinned the bear and had cut off some meat. Soon the brother who bore the torch made a fire and the brother with the kettle had placed the meat therein.

When all were satisfied they looked about them and discovered that they were far up in the air and that the earth was a good ways below them. They looked down and saw that the blood and oil from the bear had stained the leaves of the trees and made them red, orange and yellow. This is how the autumn leaves became colored.

After a time they went on their journey and soon found that the bear had revived, though they had killed and eaten him. So they again pursued him, being hungry, and when they killed him it was autumn again.

This bear chase keeps up all the time,—year after year, and has been so since the first people came. If you will look into the sky where the bear-chase cluster is seen to the north, you will find the man with the torch at the end of the group (big dipper or great bear constellation), and will see the man with the pot in the middle of the handle.

It seems also that there is a cave in which the bear hides and out of which he comes at the time the brothers are very hungry. Then he is pursued until killed by the brother who has saved his strength. This keeps on forever. So we call those stars Nia'gwai' hadês'he' (Bear they pursuing are).

THE SEVEN DANCING BROTHERS.
From a painting by Richard J. Tucker.

5. THE SEVEN BROTHERS OF THE STAR CLUSTER.[1]

Seven brothers[2] had been trained as young warriors. each day they practised in front of their mother's lodge, but this did not please the mother. With the boys was an uncle whose custom it was to sit outside the lodge door and drum upon a water drum, that the boys might learn to dance correctly.

In time the boys became perfect in their dancing, and then announced that they were about to depart on an expedition to test their skill. The seven assembled about the war post and began their dance. They then went into their mother's lodge and asked her to supply them with dried meat and parched corn for their journey but she sent them away, scoffing at their presumptions.

Again they danced and again returned for food. "I will not give you so much as a small cake of corn bread," said the mother hoping to restrain them. But they went back to their dance. A third time they returned but again were repulsed.

The fourth dance started and the oldest youth changed his tune to the song of Djihaya. With great enthusiasm he sang compelling his brothers to dance a dance of magic.

Hearing the wierd music the mother rushed out of the lodge and saw her sons dancing in the air over the trees. This greatly startled her and she cried, "Return, my sons! What manner of departure is this?" But the song continued and the boys danced higher and higher.

Again the mother cried, "Oh, my eldest son, will you not return?" But the eldest son would not listen, though his heart was touched. Then the mother screamed, "Oh my eldest son, will you not hear your mother's voice? Only look down to me!" Then was the oldest son's heart touched

---

1   Related by Edward Cornplanter.
2   Cf. Barbeau, Origin of Seven Stars, Huron Mythology, p. 59.

very deeply, but he did not respond, for fear of making his brothers weak.

"Oh my brothers," he called. "Heed no sounds from the earth but continue dacing. If you look down you shall fall and never more be able to dance."

The mother now gave a heart-broken cry and called, "Oh my first born son, give your mother one look,—one last look or I die!" This weakened the heart of the oldest son and he looked down toward the figure of his mother with outstretched arms, weeping for him.

As he looked he lost his power to master the air, and began to fall. With great rapidity he fell until he struck the earth and penetrated it, leaving only a scar where the soil came together again.

The mother rushed to the spot and swept aside the rubbish, but no trace of her son could she find. Finally looking up she saw her other boys dancing far up in the sky. They had become the "dancing stars."

In deep sorrow the mother with covered head sat beside the spot where her first born had fallen. For a whole year she wept as she watched.

Winter came and her dancing boys appeared over the council house and each night were observed overhead, but no sign of her eldest could be seen.

Came springtime and the time of budding plants. From the spot where the eldest had disappeared a tiny green shoot appeared. This the mother watched with great solicitude. It grew into a tall tree and became the first pine. This tree was guarded by the melancholy old woman and she would allow no man to touch it; she knew that it was her son and would sometime speak to her.

The winds blew and the tree swayed, it began to speak, and the mother heard. Only she could interpret the sounds that came from the waving branches, only she could see the face of the young warrior with his plumes.

A careless hunter slashed at the tree and blood flowed,

but the mother bound up the wound and drove other intruders away. In time the tree bore small short feathers (cones), and more trees grew. These the hunters slashed in order to get pitch for canoes and ropes.

Every winter the pine tree talked to its dancing brothers in the sky and the mother knew that her eldest son should be her comfort while she rested on this earth.

GENERAL NOTES. This legend I had from Edward Cornplanter but being so familiar with it I made only a few rough notes which I have transcribed. This myth is similar to the Huron and Wyandot forms recounting the origin of "the cluster."

6. THE SEVEN STAR DANCERS.[1]

Now this even happened a long time ago in the days when the whole world was new. Our Creator it was (S'hoñgwadiĕnnu'k'dăon), had finished his work. One of the first men beings lived with his nephew in a lodge near a river. The river was broad and had a wide sandy shore. The nephew received the name Djinaĕñ"dă' and his uncle sent him away to dream on the shore of the river, there to stay and dream until his dream-helpers appeared. For a long time he did not eat, but drank water and sweat himself in a sweat lodge.

One night he thought that he saw a light upon the water and he looked and saw lights moving toward him. Hiding in the reeds on the shore he watched. Soon he saw seven shining young women dancing[2] in the water against the shore and they made no splashing but went up and down. He heard them speak but could not understand what they said. He observed them all intently, for all were without clothing and were very beautiful of body. The youngest appeared the most beautiful of all. The young man watched her and thought that she would do for a wife.

Hoping to catch her he rushed out from his hiding place but the maidens were alarmed and leaped into a great corn basket and were drawn rapidly up into the sky and he looked and said, "They are dancing," (De'hoñnont'gwĕⁿ').

Djinaĕñ"dă' (Elk) continued his vigil and the next night he saw the dancers swing back over the water in their basket. Soon they came to the shore and alighted. Again he heard their voices and again they began their bewitching dance. Djinaenda's eyes were upon the youngest dancer and she appeared more beautiful than ever. He waited until she danced very near to him and away from the

---

1   The Pleiades.
2   Cf. Barbeau, C. M., Huron and Wyandot Mythology, p. 56.

basket, then he rushed out from his hiding-place and pursued the maidens, at length grasping the youngest before she touched the basket, but she gave a leap, and the youth holding to her was drawn upward as she fell into the basket. She looked to see who held her so tightly and immediately both fell to the earth.

The maiden gazed upon Djinaenda and asked him what he wanted. "I want to marry you," he said. "You have caused me to love you."

"Then we shall be married," said the maiden, but we must return to the sky and prepare for living upon the earth." So the basket came down and drew them into the sky.

Djinaenda was taken to the lodge of the dancing sisters and then led to the lodge of a great chief who caused him to recline upon the ground. The chief then took him apart, joint by joint and removed all his organs. After cleansing them he replaced them and Djinaenda was regenerated. He now felt very strong and able to do mighty things.

His bride now came to him and said that she would now return to the earth with him and live as his wife. The sisters then placed the couple in the basket and lowered them to the earth. They came down on the beach of the river but it was changed and there was a great village of men beings there.

Djinaenda inquired where his uncle lived but no one knew. Finally an old man said, "An old man such as you describe lived in the woods with his nephew near this place more than a hundred years ago."

The couple now tried to live contentedly but could not understand the ways of the people, and so, in time the two returned to the sky. The wife rejoined her sisters but she had lost her brightness, and Djinaenda roamed the sky world hunting game which he captured by running it down.

My grandmother told me that they are up there yet.

7. THE COMING OF SPRING.[1]

In the ancient times when this world was new an old man wandered over the land in search of a suitable camping spot. He was a fierce old man and had long white flowing hair. The ground grew hard like flint where his footsteps fell, and when he breathed the leaves and grasses dropped and dried up red, and fell. When he splashed through the rivers the water stopped running and stood solid.

On and on the old man journeyed until at last on the shores of a great lake by a high mountain he halted. He gathered the trees that had been uprooted by hurricanes and made a framework for a dwelling. He built the walls of ice and plastered the crevices with branches and snow. Then, to guard his lodge against the intruder, he placed uprooted stumps about on every side. Not even bad animals cared to enter this house. Everything living passed by it at a distance. It was like a magician's house.

The old man had but one friend. It was North Wind, and it was he alone who might enter the door of the stronghold and sit by the fire. Very wonderful was this fire and it gave flames and light but no heat! But even North Wind found little time to enter and smoke with the old man, for he took greater pleasure in piling high the snow and driving hail, like flints, against the shivering deer or hungry storm bound hunter. He liked to kill them. There came times, however, when North Wind needed new tricks and so he sought the advice of the old man,—how he might pile up the snow banks higher, how he might cause famine or make great snow-slides to bury Indian villages.

One very dismal night both North Wind and the old man sat smoking, half awake and half dreaming. North Wind could think of nothing new and the old man could give no more advice. So, sitting before the fire, both fell

---

1   Related by Aurelia Miller, Jan., 1905.

asleep. Towards morning each sprang to his feet with a cry. Not their usual cries, either, were their startled yells, for instead of a shrill "agēē! agēē! agēē!" the North Wind only gasped hoarsely and the old man's jaw opened with a smack and his tongue, thick and swollen rolled out on his chin. Then spoke the North Wind:

"What warm thing has bewitched me? The drifts are sinking, the rivers breaking, the ice is steaming, the snow is smoking!"

The old man was silent, too sleepy to speak. He only thought "My house is strong, very strong." Still the North Wind called loudly:

"See, the rivers are swelling full, the drifts are getting smaller."

Then he rushed from the lodge, and he flew to the mountain top where snow made him brave again. So he was happy and sang a war song as he danced on snow crust.

At the lodge of the old man a stranger struck the doorpost. The old man did not move, but dozing, thought, "oh some prank of North Wind." The knocking continued and the old man grew more sleepy. The door rattled on its fastenings but the old man's head did not raise to listen but dropped on his chest and his pipe fell down to his feet.

The logs of the lodge frame shook,—one fell from the roof. The old man jumped to his feet with a war yell.

"Who is it that dares come to my house in this way? Only my friend North Wind enters here. Go away, no loafers here!"

In answer the door fell down and a stranger stood in the opening. He entered and hung the door upright again. His face was smiling and as he stirred the fire, it grew warmer inside. The old man looked at the stranger but did not answer his pleasant words, but his heart was very angry. Finally when he could no longer keep silent he burst forth:

"You are a stranger to me and have entered my lodge,

breaking down my door. Why have you broken down my
door? Why have your eyes a fire? Why does light shine
from your skin? Why do you go about without skins
when the wind is sharp? Why do you stir up my fire
when you are young and need no warmth? Why do you
not fall on my wolf skins and sleep? Did not North Wind
blow the sun far away? Go away now before he returns,
and blows you against the mountains. I do not know you.
You do not belong in my lodge!"

The young stranger laughed and said, "Oh why not let
me stay a little longer and smoke my pipe?"

"Then listen to me," yelled the old man in anger. "I
am mighty! All snows and ice and frosts are my making.
I tell the North Wind to cut the skins of men to let the
blood through to make war paint on the drifts. I tell him
to freeze things that are food. Birds and animals run away
from the North Wind. I pile the drifts on the rocks on the
mountains and when it gets very high the North Wind
knocks it off to crush the villages beneath."

Listlessly the stranger viewed the raving old man, and
only smiled and said, "I like to be sociable, let me stay a
little longer and we will smoke together."

So, shaking with fear, the old man took the pipe and
drew a breath of smoke and then the warrior sang.

"Continue to smoke for me, I am young and warm, I
am not afraid of boasting, I am young and strong. Better
wrap up, you are old. I am here. I am here, keep on
smoking. I am Dedio's'nwineq'do^n, the Spring. Look at
your hair it is falling out, look at the drifts, they are melt-
ing. My hair is long and glossy, see—the grasses are sprout-
ing! I want to smoke with you. I like smoking. See—
the ground is smoking! My friend Dăgā'ĕⁿ'dă, the South
Wind, is coming. I guess your friend is dead. You had
better wrap up and go away. There is a place. You
cannot own all things always. See—the sun is shining.
Look out now!"

As the young warrior sang the old man shrank very small and shriveled up smaller until his voice only whispered, "I don't know you!"

And so the young warrior sang, "I am the Spring, I am the chief now. The South Wind is coming. Don't be late. You can go yet while I sing."

A rushing wind made the lodge tremble, the door fell in and an eagle swooped down and carried Hä"t'howä'ne' away toward the north.

The lodge fire was out and where it had burned a plant was growing and where the provisions were buried in a hole a tree was starting to have buds.

The sun was shining and it was warm. The swollen rivers carried away the ice. So the winter went away and in the morning it was spring time.

8. THE COMING OF DEATH.

When the world was first made men-beings did not know that they must die sometime.

In those days everyone was happy and neither men and women nor children were afraid of anything. They did not think of anything but doing what pleased them. At one time, in those days, a prominent man was found prone upon the grass. He was limp and had no breath. He did not breathe. The men-beings that saw him did not know what had happened. The man was not asleep because he did not awaken. When they placed him on his feet he fell like a tanned skin. He was limp. They tried many days to make him stand but he would not. After a number of days he became offensive.

A female man-being said that the man must be wrapped up and put in the limbs of a tree. So the men did so and after a while the flesh dropped from the bones and some dried on. No one knew what had happened to cause such a thing.

Soon afterward a child was found in the same condition. It had no breath. It could not stand. It was not asleep, so they said. The men-beings thought it was strange that a girl man-being should act this way. So she was laid in a tree.

Now many others did these things and no one knew why. No one thought that he himself would do such a thing.

There was one wise man who thought much about these things and he had a dream. When he slept the Good Minded Spirit came to him and spoke. He slept a long time but the other men-beings noticed that he breathed slowly. He breathed (nevertheless). Now after a time this man rose up and his face was very solemn. He called the people together in a council and addressed the people. The head men all sat around with the people.

The wise man spoke and he said, "The Good Minded spirit made every good thing and prepared the earth for men-beings. Now it appears that strange events have happened. A good word has come to me from the Good Minded spirit. He says that every person must do as you have seen the other persons do. They have died. They do not breathe. It will be the same with all of you. Your minds are strong. The Good Minded spirit made them that way so that you could endure everything that happened. So then do not be downcast when I tell you all must die. Listen further to what I say. The name of the one that steals away your breath is Shondowekowa. He has no face and does not see anyone. You cannot see him until he grasps you. He comes sometimes for a visit and sometimes he stays with us until many are dead. Sometimes he takes away the best men and women and passes by the lesser ones. I was not told why he does this thing. He wants to destroy every person. He will continue to work forever. Every one who hears me and every one not yet born will die. There is more about you than living. Any moment you may be snatched by Shondowekowa, he who works in the thick darkness.

"You must now divide yourselves into nine bands, five to sit on one side of the fire and four on the other and these bands shall care for its members. You must seek out all good things and instruct one another, and those who do good things will see the place where the Maker of all things lives when their breath goes out of their body".

BOYS WHO DEFIED MAGIC AND OVERCAME IT

V

9. ORIGIN OF FOLK STORIES

There was once a boy who had no home. His parents were dead and his uncles would not care for him. In order to live this boy, whose name was Gaqka, or Crow, made a bower of branches for an abiding place and hunted birds and squirrels for food.

He had almost no clothing but was very ragged and dirty. When the people from the village saw him they called him Filth-Covered-One, and laughed as they passed by, holding their noses. No one thought he would ever amount to anything, which made him feel heavy-hearted. He resolved to go away from his tormentors and become a great hunter.

One night Gaqka found a canoe. He had never seen this canoe before, so he took it. Stepping in he grasped the paddle, when the canoe immediately shot into the air, and he paddled above the clouds and under the moon. For a long time he went always southward. Finally the canoe dropped into a river and then Gaqka paddled for shore.

On the other side of the river was a great cliff that had a face that looked like a man. It was at the forks of the river where this cliff stood. The boy resolved to make his home on the top of the cliff and so climbed it and built a bark cabin.

The first night he sat on the edge of the cliff he heard a voice saying, "Give me some tobacco." Looking around the boy, seeing no one, replied, "Why should I give tobacco?"

There was no answer and the boy began to fix his arrows for the next day's hunt. After a while the voice spoke again, "Give me some tobacco."

Gaqka now took out some tobacco and threw it over the cliff. The voice spoke again: "Now I will tell you a story."

Feeling greatly awed the boy listened to a story that seemed to come directly out of the rock upon which he was sitting. Finally the voice paused, for the story had ended. Then it spoke again saying, "It shall be the custom hereafter to present me with a small gift for my stories." So the boy gave the rock a few bone beads. Then the rock said, "Hereafter when I speak, announcing that I shall tell a story you must say, 'Nio,' and as I speak you must say 'Hĕⁿ",' that I may know that you are listening. You must never fall asleep but continue to listen until I say 'Dā'neho nigagā'is.' (So thus finished is the length of my story). Then you shall give me presents and I shall be satisfied."

The next day the boy hunted and killed a great many birds. These he made into soup and roasts. He skinned the birds and saved the skins, keeping them in a bag.

That evening the boy sat on the rock again and looked westward at the sinking sun. He wondered if his friend would speak again. While waiting he chipped some new arrow-points, and made them very small so that he could use them in a blow gun. Suddenly, as he worked, he heard the voice again. "Give me some tobacco to smoke," it said. Gaqka threw a pinch of tobacco over the cliff and the voice said, "Hau'nio",'" and commenced a story. Long into the night one wonderful tale after another flowed from the rock, until it called out, "So thus finished is the length of my story." Gaqka was sorry to have the stories ended but he gave the rock an awl made from a bird's leg and a pinch of tobacco.

The next day the boy hunted far to the east and there found a village. Nobody knew who he was but he soon found many friends. There were some hunters who offered to teach him how to kill big game, and these went with him to his own camp on the high rock. At night he allowed them to listen to the stories that came forth from the rock, but it would speak only when Gaqka was present. He therefore had many friends with whom to hunt.

Now after a time Gaqka made a new suit of clothing from deer skin and desired to obtain a decorated pouch. He, therefore, went to the village and found one house where there were two daughters living with an old mother. He asked that a pouch be made and the youngest daughter spoke up and said, "It is now finished. I have been waiting for you to come it." So she gave him a handsome pouch.

Then the old mother spoke, saying, "I now perceive that my future son-in-low has passed through the door and is here." Soon thereafter, the younger woman brought Gaqka a basket of bread and said, "My mother greatly desires that you should marry me." Gaqka looked at the girl and was satisfied, and ate the bread. The older daughter was greatly displeased and frowned in an evil manner.

That night the bride said to her husband, "We must now go away. My older sister will kill you for she is jealous." So Gaqka arose and took his bride to his own lodge. Soon the rock spoke and began to relate wonder stories of things that happened in the old days. The bride was not surprised, but said, "This standing rock, indeed, is my grandfather. I will now present you with a pouch into which you must put a trophy for every tale related."

All winter long the young couple stayed in the lodge on the great rock and heard all the wonder tales of the old days. Gaqka's bag was full of stories and he knew all the lore of former times.

As springtime came the bride said, "We must now go north to your own people and you shall become a great man." But Gaqka was sad and said, "Alas, in my own country I am an outcast and called by an unpleasant name."

The bride only laughed, saying, "Nevertheless we shall go north."

Taking their pelts and birdskins, the young couple descended the cliff and seated themselves in the canoe. "This is my canoe," said the bride. "I sent it through the air to you."

The bride seated herself in the bow of the canoe and Gaqka in the stern. Grasping a paddle he swept it through the water, but soon the canoe arose and went through the air. Meanwhile the bride was singing all kinds of songs, which Gaqka learned as he paddled.

When they reached the north, the bride said, "Now I shall remove your clothing and take all the scars from your face and body. She then caused him to pass through a hollow log, and when Gaqka emerged from the other end he was dressed in the finest clothing and was a handsome man.

Together the two walked to the village where the people came out to see them. After a while Gaqka said, "I am the boy whom you once were accustomed to call 'Cia"dŏdǎ'.' I have now returned." That night the people of the village gathered around and listened to the tales he told, and he instructed them to give him small presents and tobacco. He would plunge his hand in his pouch and take out a trophy, saying, "Ho ho'! So here is another one!" and then looking at his trophy would relate an ancient tale.

Everybody now thought Gaqka a great man and listened to his stories. He was the first man to find out all about the adventures of the old-time people. That is why there are so many legends now.

10. THE FORBIDDEN ARROW AND THE QUILT OF MEN'S EYES.[1]

Now (it seems), there were twin brothers one named Younger and the other Driven. The brothers were accustomed to play about two hills. Driven would go up one hill and jump to the summit of the other. Younger would stay in the valley between and amuse himself by shooting arrows at him as he jumped. Now as Driven jumped Younger sang a song:

"Ha–do–wi, Ha–do–wi, Ha–do–wi, Ha–do–wi,
O–ne–di–no–o–ha–ga–gon Ha–do–wi!"

Now their grandmother always forbade them to use a certain arrow. This arrow belonged to their father who used it. They played day after day in this manner. After some time they began to discuss among themselves why it was that their grandmother had forbidden them to use the arrow. Then they decided notwithstanding to use the arrow. So Driven ascended the hill and made ready to jump. Then Younger fixed his arrow ready to shoot. Then Driven jumped and Younger shot the arrow. Now an arrow never before had struck Driven as he jumped but this forbidden arrow pierced his body and carried him in a northward direction. Now as he flew with the arrow the arrow sang,

"Gwent–gwe–o, gwent–gwe–o, gwent–gwe–o!"

because it was feathered with the feathers of a wild duck. When Younger saw what calamity his arrow had wrought he gave a scream of alarm and started off in the direction of the arrow. He ran a long distance and after some time found the body of his brother transfixed to the earth with the arrow. He was not dead so he lifted him up and placed him on his back. Then Driven directed him to follow a northward road.

---

1 Related by Edward Cornplanter (Great Night) and recorded as translated by William Bluesky, Ganosho.

"There is a house a certain distance away," said Driven, "where a number of women are gathered dancing. We must pass this house but we must not look upon them. Oh brother, cast not your eyes upon one of them!"

Now as they passed along they heard the women singing. They heard the echo of the songs and the sound of dancing. Soon they came near the house and the women saw them and called out inviting them to look up and see them. "Oh what have you on your back? Look up and behold us!" Now Younger did not look up nor did he make reply for he knew that the women were witches and that one glance of their eyes would be fatal to him. So when he passed by he kept his eyes directed to the ground and stooped over. So then they were safe.

Now again the brother spoke and said, "There is yet one more danger and it is the last. It may be fatal. A company of women is making a quilt of young men's eyes. They gouge out the eyes of young men and sew them into a blanket (quilt). Now the eyes live and wink as in life for the skin of the eyelids are with the eyes. Now we must pass through their lodge and if we can do so without looking at the awful quilt we will be safe then."

Now the lodge was a long one and when the two brothers entered the women saw them and said, "Bend not so low. Look up and see the beautiful quilt we are making. It is beautiful. What is it that you have upon your back? Look up!" Younger gave no heed to the words of the women but continued through the room. They were about to emerge from the door at the back when one woman held the quilt before the eyes of Younger. She held it where he saw it. Then Younger saw no more. He was blind and he had no eyes in his eye sockets; they had jumped out and into the quilt. Driven leaped from his back and jumped out of the door. He did not know where Driven went.

Now Younger could not see, so he crept on his hands

and knees. He crept a long ways and after a time he came to a place where corn was planted. There he halted for he thought that some one would surely notice him when they came to examine the corn. So he lay down there, and there he lay day after day. After a long time he heard the sound of a woman's voice singing. And soon the woman saw him and was surprised to find a man in the field. She ran home to her sister and told her that a man was in the field and that he had no eyes in his eye sockets. He was a human being, blind and alive. His eye sockets were hollow. Then the older sister said, "We must not leave a human being in distress. We must take him into our house and nurse him to health. He will be a companion for us. We are alone." So they went and found him and brought him to their house. They cleansed him and fed him on bear's oil, for he had not eaten for a long time. Afterwards he was given stronger food. They gave him nourishment until he was stronger. After a time he grew strong and then they asked him how he came to be in so bad a condition. So he related how it happened.

"I was passing through a house," he said, "and there were women within making a quilt of young men's eyes. They put the quilt under my face and I saw and then I became blind. My brother was on my back for an arrow was through him. He disappeared. I know not where my brother is. So did the accident happen."

Now Younger recovered his strength and then the older sister said, "You must marry my younger sister and live here as our companion." So he consented and married the younger sister.

Now it appeared that after a certain time his wife gave birth to twins, boys. The older one they named Hanonni-da, meaning, he is a thistle, and the younger one they called Ho-da-da-o meaning, he cries. At the time of their birth the older sister called out their names and tossed them into the adjoining room. Then she told the husband that he was the father of twins and he gave thanks. Now the children seemed to be wizards. They did not suckle but played alone together in the room. No one talked to them but they talked. After a time they asked for a net ball that they might play lacrosse. So a net, a net-club and ball were brought to them. Then they played lacrosse in the room. Then they went out doors and played and again they went into the ground under the house and played. After a time they asked for bows and arrows. Then they went away for long periods of time, no one knew where. After a time the older sister brought them into the living room and said, "It is time for you to see your father." So they said, "We will see our father." Then the father felt over them for the first time and touched them. They climbed over his lap and played with him. After a time they began to laugh at him and the Last said, "How can he be my father since he has no eyes? I believe that he is not my father." Then he asked his father, "Where are your eyes?" Then the father answered him, "In a certain place there are women making a quilt from young men's eyes. Once I had to pass through their house and I would not look upon the quilt but they forced it under my face and that was the last that I saw. My brother was on my back and he jumped. Now I know not where my brother is. He has gone from me." The Last replied, "Father, we will go there and get back your eyes." But the older folk said, "Do not try, the women are horrible witches and we would lose you. We forbid you to go. So do not go." So the boys went out and played together.

The two sisters went out after a time to get provisions and the father was left alone with the boys. He heard them talking together. It was strange and he did not understand them. "Hang on, hang on," they were saying. "Hang on and after a time we will reach where father is and he will help us." So they talked and pulled and called out each other's names. Now it happened that they took their father by the hand and placed upon him the body of a human being. They had pulled it up through the ground. Now the body of the man they had, had an arrow in his chest. Also he had no eyes in his eye-sockets and he was nearly dead. The man was the father's brother. Then the children said, "We will go and borrow some eyes for you that you may look upon each other." So they went into the forest and when they had found a fawn they asked if she would give her consent if they should ask for her eyes to put in their father's eye sockets. The fawn consented when she heard their story and gave them her eyes. So they gave her moss to eat while they were gone. They went home with the fawn's eyes and placed them in the father's eye-sockets. Then he saw how his children looked and he was glad. So, moreover, they saw how he appeared when he had eyes in his eye-sockets. And they said, "Father, how long your eyelashes are!" for the fawn's eyelashes were long. Now also the father saw his brother and was glad that it was he. Then said the boys, "We are now going in search of both of your eyes and you will have a joyous time." Then they took the eyes of the fawn and carried them back to her and thanked her for their use.

Now they went on their journey to the place where there father had told them the house of the women quilting was. After a time they found it. Now on their way they had been discussing their plans. They decided to hide at the spring. Last was to transform himself into a duck and Thistle-like was to wait in hiding. They reached the spring and the younger brother changed himself into a duck and swam upon the surface of the spring. The older brother hid himself. Now after a time the youngest sister from the house came down to the spring for water and saw a duck swimming in the spring. So she tried to catch him but the duck dodged whenever she tried to grasp him. Then as she jumped over the spring the duck entered her body. Then she went home and the old woman of the house said,

"Daughter you look as if you would soon have a child. It must be by the Creator for no man has passed this way. So after a short time the daughter gave birth to a boy and the mother said, "It must be the gift of the Creator for no man has passed by." Now the child would cry and would only be pacified when some valuable object was shown him. But soon again he would cry and they would show him another treasure. Now he began to cry very hard and nothing would pacify him, not even all their valued treasures. So the old woman said, perhaps the quilt of human eyes would please him, so the quilt was brought and he ceased crying and played with the quilt. Then the women all went out to work in the field. Now when they were gone he took the quilt and folded it and ran out of the house. The women discovered him and pursued him with hammers. They closed about him endeavoring to strike him but he dodged and they struck each other and killed each other, all but one and he killed her. Then he went and found his brother.

Now they returned home and greeted their father. They asked him what kind of eyes he had had and the father answered, "Oh they were peculiar eyes. They had a reddish cast." Now the Last found the eyes and took them off the quilt and placed them back in his father's eye-sockets. And when the father had his own eyes he said, "There are the eyes of my brother." So the boys took them from the quilt and placed them in their uncle's eye-sockets. And they saw each other and were very glad. Then the younger twin said, "We must now go and find the bones of the dead and restore them their eyes." So they went and found the graves of the dead and gathered together all their skeletons,—half as many as there were eyes. And a voice from the pile spoke and said, "We are under the cover of a white bear." So the boys found a white bear and skinned it and built a lodge like a sweat-lodge and covered it over with the skin of the white bear. In the lodge they placed the bones of the dead men. In a short time the wigwam began to quiver and then the younger brother ran to an elm tree and began to kick it and it fell over and as it was falling he cried, "The tree is falling upon you. Flee for your lives."

Now as they heard his warning the skeletons arose and ran out of the wigwam and into the woods. Now the eyes had been placed upon the skulls and the people had time to select their own, but Last was too hasty in kicking over the tree and they had little time to find their own bones. Thus when they came together in the woods they found themselves in a mixed condition. Some had legs too short, some had long arms and short legs,—their limbs, ribs, feet and finer bones were mismated. Then Last was sorry he had been so hasty. So he asked them all where they lived and some knew but some did not. He told all that knew to go to their homes and he told all that did not to come home with him. Now they went home with him but the house was too small to contain all. Then Last paced out the dimensions of a large house and his footprints outlining it were on the ground. Then he commanded a house to spring up and it did and was large enough to hold all the men and they lived there. Now these were cripples and deformed people and from them sprang the deformed and ugly people of today. Now the uncle recovered his health and the older sister married him so there were two couples in the house. So everything came out well and everyone was happy. So the legend ends.

NOTE.—The legend of the magic arrow and the quilt of eyes is a typical Seneca transformation myth. Its characteristic elements are, the orenda of twins, the magic arrow which they were forbidden to use, the transfixing of one party with an arrow and the tests of magic. The conception of the quilt of young men's eyes appears in other stories, as also does that of borrowing eyes from animals to assist persons who had lost their eyeballs. The theme of the magical twins who grew to immediate maturity and played under the ground is also one employed elsewhere. The idea of conception through entering into a female to be born of her, also is a more or less frequent episode. As in other legends, the hero who acquires great orenda ends his career by restoring the bones of the magically slain and hastening their resurrection to such an extent that they appear with mismated limbs, thereby being the first monsters and cripples.

This legend was related in the Seneca tongue by Edward Cornplanter, and translated by William Bluesky, whose language forms the bulk of the version here presented. Certain corrections were made after reading the recorded account to Cornplanter.

11. CORN GRINDER, THE GRANDSON.[1]

In a clearing in a thick pine forest there lived an old man and woman. Their lodge was far away from any Indian village, for they had no liking for the company of other people. They were a strange couple and often talked with trees, and the trees would answer them.

With the old folk lived a boy, their grandson, but he found no pleasure in the society of his grandparents, for they would never speak to him except to admonish him not to wander beyond certain limits.

"Go east, go west, go north," they said, "but not away from the sound of the corn grinder. We have named you Corn Grinder so that you remember. Listen, never go south. Remember!"

Each morning after breakfast Corn Grinder would run into the woods with his bow and pass his time hunting birds. He became an expert marksman and could bring down a bird as far as his arrow could fly. By the time he was twelve years old he was familiar with the woods, to the east, the west and the north as far as the sound of his grandmother's corn grinder reached. As he grew older he began to wonder why it was that daily the old people repeated the same old charge. "Go east, go west, go north, but not away from the sound of the grinder. Never go south!"

"Ho!" he exclaimed, "I will go south as far as I please."

Taking his bow and quiver he ran from the lodge, skirted the clearing and came around to the southern border. With arrow fixed for instant use he skulked from tree to tree. He was going toward the forbidden south! Surely there must be some hideous monsters, poisonous reptiles or terrible witches here, that made his grandparents enjoin him to shun the south woods. They would not tell him what

---

1 Related by Guy Miller, a Tuscarora, Jan., 1905.

it was and because of this he was determined to find out at
any cost. He listened at every footstep and glanced anxiously in every direction. His fears began to subside, however, when he saw nothing unusual. The same kind of
birds flew in the trees and fell when his arrows pierced
them. Plainly there were no witches here. He strode on
bolder than before nor halted until in the distance he heard
the sound of a corn mortar. He was on the alert in an
instant, dropped on his hands and knees and crawled forward, covering his approach by the trunks of the pines.
Presently he saw a few paces ahead an opening and drawing nearer saw an immense bark lodge in the clearing. A
gigantic woman was standing beneath a tall tree cooking
corn soup in a huge kettle. An extraordinarily large baby
board leaned against the tree but no baby was in sight.
Crawling, serpent-like, he wriggled his way through the
high grass to the lodge. Entering it he saw a large fat
baby, tall as a warrior and as fat as an old woman. The
day was hot and the baby was without clothing as it lay
on a couch of skins. Peering stealthily from the door he
saw that the giantess was coming toward the lodge. Trembling yet determined to learn all he could of the strange folk,
he concealed himself under the hemlock branches beneath
the bed.

The woman came in and stretched herself out on the
floor for a nap. The baby commenced to cry and then
nearly crushed Corn Grinder by rolling over the very spot
beneath which he lay. This made Corn Grinder angry
indeed, and crawling out as best he could he ran from the
lodge, skimmed a ladle full of scalding grease from the
soup and running in threw it upon the baby's abdomen and
fled to the edge of the woods.

The infant awoke with a piercing shriek and began
rubbing its stomach in frenzy, howling like a stricken wolf
with agony. This awoke the mother who did her best to

soothe her child and discover how it had been so mysteriously injured.

Meanwhile little Corn Grinder had thrown a bunch of pungent weeds into the soup and hastily concealed himself in a thicket.

Soon the gigantic woman emerged from the lodge and began stirring the soup. She drew a deep breath as its appetizing vapors reached her nostrils and said, "Age-wiu, how good!" Presently she began to sneeze. Again she sneezed and again and again, until she could scarcely stand, tears streaming from her eyes, water from her nose and saliva from her mouth. "Agē! Agē!" she gasped, "Some witch must be near."

Little Corn Grinder chuckled with glee and rolled over and over, his sides quaking with merriment, to think how his weeds were destroying the giantess.

The fire died down, the steam ceased rising and the strangely affected woman stopped sneezing. The soup was done by this time and going back to the house the woman strapped the baby to the board and grasping a basket of bread and meat in one hand and the kettle of soup in the other, started off in a southerly direction. Corn Grinder followed close behind and saw her stop at a huge dead tree.

"Luk–ste, luk–ste, da–ja–jent!
Luk–ste, luk–ste, da–ja–jent!"

sang the woman in a low voice. The ground beneath them rumbled and in a moment the tree opened and out stepped a tall giant saying "Onĕk to-ha!" He greeted the woman with a friendly slap, patted the baby and then poured a laddle-full of soup down his throat. The pungent weeds burned the giant's mouth. Wildly he danced around the tree tearing up the sod and holding his mouth open, drew his breath in and out to cool his blistered throat and tongue. When the smarting sensation ceased he ran toward the offending dish, and gave the kettle a kick that sent it flying over the trees and spilling the soup over the frightened woman and baby. The angered giant then began to berate the giantess for the mean trick she had played on him and kept grumbling until he had devoured the bread and meat and disappeared into the tree.

Corn Grinder's eyes bulged from his head and he shuddered as, ear to the ground, he heard strange subterranean roarings. "Wah!" he exclaimed, "why can not I say 'Luk-ste, luk-ste'?"

Gliding through the grass and bushes he followed the woman back to the lodge where she began to wash corn previous to preparing another meal for the giant in the tree.

"When the sun stands high she'll be ready again," said Corn Grinder to himself. "Then I will say 'Luk-ste, luk-ste!'—that's fun."

With this determination he crawled back and hid behind a tree facing the mysterious dead trunk.

When the sun had risen to the mid-heavens Corn Grinder arose from his hiding-place and walking cautiously to the mysterious tree struck it sharply with his bow, singing in a low tone the woman's song, then jumped quickly back and fixed his arrow for instant use.

The ground trembled, the tree shook, then opened and the giant came forth. He looked around in all directions and growled in rage when he failed to discover any one: "More tricks," he yelled.

Corn Grinder watched his chance and when the giant's back was turned, he let fly an arrow piercing him through the stomach. Without a groan the giant fell. Corn Grinder looked down the path, saw the woman coming and fled with all haste back through the forest to his grand-parents' lodge. Bursting in the door he exclaimed breathlessly, "Oh grandmother! I killed him, I killed him!"

"Hold on," said his grandmother, "who did you kill? Tell me all about it."

Corn Grinder obeyed, omitting no detail of the adventure.

"Agē!" wailed the old woman. "You have killed your father, my own son. You must go on a long journey to a high mountain and obtain certain magical roots to restore him! You must go immediately! O grandson, why did you disobey us? How often did we tell you never to go south. All your family are wizards and witches and we hoped to save you! Agē, Agē!"

"I went, grandmother," replied the boy, "because you told me not to go. If you had told me everything I should never have gone. Now hurry and get food for our journey,—two are going."

As he was speaking the giantess and the baby came running down the path and rushed into the lodge.

"Corn Grinder has killed his father!" screamed the giantess.

"Where is he, where is he? We are going to kill him!"

"All right," said Corn Grinder, popping out from under a bed, "kill me if you can."

The furious giantess seized a corn mortar, the baby a pestle, and each strove to hit the boy with these weapons.

Corn Grinder dodged around in glee,—the excitement was exhilarating. The possibility of receiving a blow from the pestle or being smashed with a mortar made his feet nimble as never before. Finally when he had been hit and his doom seemed sealed he said to himself, "If I belong to the family of witches, I must be a witch as well," and bounding into the air he jumped down the giantess' mouth, slid down her throat, wrenched her heart from its fastenings and when she had fallen dead, he crawled out again, grabbed the pestle from the baby's hands, cried "Da, da, da, da, da, da!" and killed the infant with a blow.

Without the least sign of excitement he said, "Now

grandmother, hurry with my lunch. It will soon be dark and my friend and I wish to go early."

"What friend?" asked the grandmother. "Why Da-ga-ga-we-so-da-de (Standing cob is coming)," replied Corn Grinder, "but you can't see him. We have been companions since we were babies. Hurry, grandmother."

Mutely the old woman obeyed and soon had a basket of food prepared for the journey.

Corn Grinder started on and entered the north woods where he must meet his friend Cob.

For a day they tramped through unknown forests, crossed mirey swamps and struggled through windfalls and at night lay down beneath a sheltering rock. The next day passed as the first, but the third presented increased obstacles. Wild beasts growled all around them. Toward noon, as Corn Grinder was munching a slice of corn bread, a monstrous dog rushed toward them. Ever prepared to ward off danger, Corn Grinder threw down his slice and spat out the morsel he was masticating. The dog bent his head to eat and the two boys ran out of sight, but not into safety, as they had imagined, for before them was a gigantic wild cat with wide open mouth. Without pausing in his flight Corn Grinder flung a chunk of meat into its jaws and ran faster than before. Exhausted, he sat down a moment to rest but as he did so a big bear rushed at him with a growl. Corn Grinder jumped form his seat, flung a dish of honey into its eyes and summing up all energy hurried on once more. Cob ran at his side and kept encouraging him to keep a stout heart.

At length they reached a clearing near the base of a mountain. Some one high in the air seemed singing a song over and over. They halted a moment and then pushed aside the underbrush, pausing again to listen to the song, which seemed growing louder. They were startled when they caught the words.

"Some strange thing is heralding our approach," said

Corn Grinder, and pushing aside the bushes he came out into the open.

A great multitude of people were assembled about a tall pine, shooting at something in the topmost branches of a tall pine. The two boys came nearer and noticed that whenever an arrow struck the tree near the creature in the branches, drops of water would run from its eyes and striking the ground become wampum. Corn Grinder was about to pull his bow when Cob struck his arm and said, "Stop! That is your father up there. Hurry on and let us get the medicine. If you do not soon his tears will cease to flow and they will kill him."

The two boys ran panting through the crowd. Cob was invisible and Corn Grinder might as well have been for no one noticed him. They labored up a mountain, crossed great rocks and chasms and at sunset, in a deep rift in the mountain side, at the foot of a cataract found a wonderful plant.

"Grab it!" whispered Cob. "It is the medicine!"

Corn Grinder snatched at the plant, which flew from the ground and eluding his grasp soared upward but wary Cob with a high leap caught it by the roots before it was entirely beyond his grasp.

Cob instructed Corn Grinder to chew the roots of the plant and then rub his saliva over his body, his clothing, his bow and his arrows. This he did and felt new vigor thrilling every fiber. The journey down the mountain seemed easy and his feet were lighter than ever before.

Toward nightfall they reached the great pine again and saw people busy as before, shooting at the creature in the tree, but the tears were fewer and the wampum less.

"Hurry," cried Cob. "Unless you shoot him before the next man's arrow strikes he will truly be dead."

Grinder spat on his arrows, rubbed the roots in his hair and then shot. The arrow struck the creature and it instantly vanished. Simultaneously, both Corn Grinder and Cob were pulled from their feet by some unseen force and sped through the air like the wind. High into the sky they went and when the moon began to shine they dropped down to earth again at the doorway of a new lodge, which they entered.

A woman was chanting a song to a baby. Corn Grinder looked closely and saw that it was the same woman and baby that he had killed but each had now become smaller. He looked back and saw the giant he had shot. He, too, had become smaller.

"I am your brother," said the baby.

"I am your father," said the man.

"I am your mother," said the woman, "come, let us eat!"

GENERAL NOTES.—The story of Corn Grinder is another tale of an enchanted family. Corn Grinder is cared for by his grandparents who wish to shield him from his parents who are evilly magic people. He is told that he may venture from his grandmother's lodge but to the south at no greater distance than the sound of the corn pounder, though in other directions he might go as far as he liked. The time comes when Corn Grinder resolves to disobey and travel south, where he discovers a lodge of giants and a gigantic infant. By craft he disturbs the giants, annoying them without being discovered, finally shooting the male giant. Rushing home he tells his grandmother who reveals to him that the giant is his father, and orders him to make haste to procure medicine roots to effect a restoration. When the giantess and infant pursue him to the lodge he escapes them and jumping down the giantess' throat tears out her heart, soon afterward killing the infant.

He then reveals that he has an "unseen friend" who will aid him in his search for the medicine roots. After overcoming great dangers they obtain the roots and fly through the air to a new lodge where Corn Grinder discovers his parents restored to normal form. The injection of the beast in the tree wailing and transforming its tears into wampum brings into the story a common theme, that of a being excreting wampum. The songs and magical words used in this tale are not Seneca.

12. HE-GOES-TO-LISTEN.[1]

In the old days when the Senecas were strong on the Genesee there lived near a large hill that rose from a river, a boy and his uncle.

When the boy was born he was named Hatondas, meaning *He goes to listen.* This name was bestowed because just before his birth his mother had dreamed that when he should arrive at a marriageable age two singing women would come from afar to be his wives. The mother also dreamed that she would die. In order to prepare him for his marriage she therefore sewed three bags that were *witched.* She filled one with great quantities of wampum, the second with beautiful clothing but the third was left empty. Though the bags were scarcely the size of a man's hand they could hold things hundreds of times their own size.

When Hatondas was yet young his mother as her dream had foretold became mysteriously sick and shortly died, leaving her baby son to the care of his grandfather. The uncle knew the prediction of the mother's vision concerning the coming of the women for the child, and, being a widower of many years and unable to secure a wife by fair means, resolved to disfigure the boy and claim the women destined for him. And so it was that when the boy reached the age of fourteen the old man each morning and evening would send him up the hill to listen.

"Listen nephew," he commanded, "go up the hill, stop in the pines near the trail and listen. When you hear a strange sound hurry back and tell me. Be sure you sound it exactly."

The boy would thereupon run as fast as possible to the hill top and secrete himself in the pine woods. The old

---

[1] This legend is related almost verbatim as it came from the lips of Gohweh Seneca, an old Tonawanda Seneca.

man had used every artifice to make the boy cowardly and so when he heard an owl hooting in the darkness of the wood he trembled and ran in wild terror down the hill and rushed into the lodge.

"O O O—uncle, I've, I've—I've heard—"

"Now wait a bit my son, wait 'till I smoke." And when the old man had finished his pipe he asked, "Well, what did you hear?"

"Noise like this,—O-O-O-Owah! o-o-o-owah!"

"Ugh, that's nothing," said the old man. "You are no good." So saying he thrust a ladle into the fire and drew it out full of embers and bidding the boy stand fast threw them on his legs. Maddened by the pain the boy rushed from the lodge with cries of agony.

The next day Hatondas was again sent on the same errand and again terrified by a strange sound ran back to the old man and reported.

"Stop, stop!" the old fellow yelled. "Let me smoke first!" And when the last curl of blue vapor had been drawn from the old stone pipe he spoke, "Now tell me!"

"It was gak-gaw-gak-gaw-gak-gaw! O grandfather!"

"Chisnah! That was nothing," the old man replied, and again threw hot ashes on the boy.

Day after day the same procedure continued and after a year the boy, once handsome and lithe, was scarred and crippled. The grandfather now devised new schemes. When he had sent He-goes-to-listen up the hill he stretched a deer tendon across the door way, and returning, the boy tripped and fell, severely bruising his face. The old schemer laughed and said, "Good joke, good joke, I'll never do it again." But each day as he sent the boy up the hill he would break his promise and the youth would be frightfully cut by the fall over the thong. However, after a while in spite of the old man's promises the youth became wary in his pell-mell rush into the lodge and would step over the cord.

One autumn in the seventeenth year of He-goes-to-lisen he returned from the hill in unusual haste and in great excitement. "O grandfather!" he exclaimed, and before the old man had time to smoke he cried out, "I heard noise, singing, like this: (SONG).

"Well, that all?" said the grandfather in a voice that revealed his suppressed excitement, "Well, I will thrash you hard for that." Thereupon Hatondas received a most brutal beating and was thrown into the roaring fire. The next day the boy was bidden listen to every word in the song he should hear and report immediately.

The old man rubbed his face with oil and painted it with streaks of vermillion. He tied sinews to his flabby cheeks and pulling the wrinkles back, tied the strings behind his neck and let down his long black hair to hide the ruse. His sole idea in abusing and disfiguring the boy was to make him such a horrible sight that the mysterious women would refuse to marry him. He wanted them himself, and thus on the night after the singing, decked himself in his best, hoping to gain their favor. Hatondas had set out early in the morning but entranced by the singing did not return. On came the voices until he saw the singers themselves and saw them pass down the hill and enter the lodge.

The old man decked in his feathers and paint arose to meet them. "Welcome, welcome, my women," he said. "Come in, the house is yours."

But the women only said, "Where is Hatondas?"

"Oh I am he!" ejaculated the old reprobate.

But the women again asked, "Where is Hatondas?"

"Oh he? He is lying around somewhere with the dogs in the garbage,—but never mind him,—come sit by me."

The women did not obey but sat on the low bench that belonged to Hatondas, and the would-be-youthful old man with all his smooth cheeks and decorations could not get them to converse with him.

"Come, come, better stay with me,—marry me," he

pleaded. "I am handsome,—Hatondas is crippled and ugly. Say 'yes,' you will marry me. Of course, say so."

"Where is Hatondas?" was the resolute question.

The old man shuffled up and touched one of the women in a pleading way and she promptly knocked him down.

Hatondas returned. He had suddenly become bold. All his former fear of his grandfather had flown, likewise his fear of sounds and moving things. Courageously he entered the door and saluted the women. Seating himself on his grandfather's bench he spent the entire afternoon chatting with them. As evening came on the women cooked his supper, leaving the old man to fare the best he could.

Night came and the time for sleeping. Hatondas threw himself upon his husk mats and rolled up in his skins. The two women lay on either side.

The old man frowned fiercely and the strings slipping from their fastenings let fall his skinny jowls, now more wrinkled than before.

"Ugh!" he exclaimed. "I say, two women don't want one husband!" But as the women did not stir the frustrated old fellow lay down with a disgusted groan.

That night as he slept his heart changed and the next morning he awoke without any ill feeling toward Hatondas.

"Now, my boy," he said after breakfast, "you must go away from here. Long time ago your mother left three bags for your journey. One bag is empty,—I will fill it."

Bringing out a bag the size of a man's hand he filled it with a basket of parched corn mixed with maple sugar, put in a bow and a bundle of arrows and last of all a buckskin suit and then charged Hatondas not to speak to a living creature other than his wives while on his journey, and warned him that if he should it would cause the loss of a bag.

Hatondas with his wives set out on the trail that led to the far country. Reaching the top of the hill that he had so often climbed one of the women said, "Oh here is a hollow log. There is an animal in it! You are ugly, Hatondas,—crawl in and see if you can scare it out." The husband obeyed and wriggled through the log. He felt strange and when his head emerged from the other end of the log he felt like a different person. Looking in the next spring he saw that his face was smooth and handsome. He lifted his legging and saw a limb clean and unscarred. More than this, he noticed that instead of his filthy clothes he was clad in a new suit of white skin.

His delight was so great that he immediately forgot all warnings and talked without fear to two strangers whom he met, while his wives strode on ahead. Having satisfied their curiosity the strangers started on. Hatondas ran with great strides and after some time overtook his wives who immediately asked, "Where is your magic bag?" Alas, it was gone with all the wampum that it contained. This meant that when Hatondas should enter the strange country, it should be without honor and that he should be as a common man.

For several years Hatondas dwelt in the land of his wives and so well did he fight in battle and so brave was he in all things that by deeds he gained great fame. However, he tired of the strange land and longed to return and visit his own old home. After preparation he set out on the return journey, each of his wives bearing a large bundle of presents for the old uncle.

After a weary journey and after many days he reached the old lodge by the hill but found it tied fast.

"Kway!" he cried.

"Kway!" came the answer in a cracked voice. "Who are you?"

"Hatondas and my two wives."

"Well, how do I know that?" asked the same cracked voice.

"Let me in and see."

"Don't you dare come in! If you try I'll shoot you through the door-hole."

"Well, I am going to go in so tell me how."

"Well put your hands through the peek-hole and I will tie them to the post. I will come out and see and if it is real Hatondas you may come in."

Hatondas did as bidden and some one inside tied his hands around the post. Then a decrepit old man came out with a hatchet.

"Aha! You were deceiving me just as I thought. You are not my nephew! Aha! I will kill you. So!"

"I am your nephew but my face is changed. Look and see if you don't recognize my women."

"No, I don't know any of them. You must be killed now." (Uncle sings death chant.)

"Hold on, old uncle, can't we come to a bargain?" asked Hatondas.

"Ugh!" exclaimed the old fellow. "Bargain? Yes, guess so. Let me see. Yes, give me one of the women."

"Truly, truly, if she will take you."

In haste the grandfather cut the thongs that bound Hatondas and bade the entire party enter the lodge. When all were seated he said, slyly, "Well, I guess I like this one best."

"What do you mean, uncle?"

"I mean I like this one for cutting you loose."

"Ha! ha! ha! ha!" laughed Hatondas. "She won't have you!"

Then the uncle laughed too and said it was all just for fun and that he knew them all the time.

As Hatondas looked about him he saw that the elm bark house had grown old and moss covered and in one place a tree had commenced to grow, but before another moon had come all things were as new again, but the old man grew older.

13. HATONDAS, THE LISTENER, FINDS A WIFE.[1]

Hatondas was a poor orphan boy who lived with his uncle, an old man who was very wrinkled. They lived in a lodge far removed from any settlement, so that the boy grew up not knowing how other people acted.

The old uncle became more and more abusive and threw hot coals on Hatondas seeking to mutilate him. The boy never lifted his hand to strike his uncle but received his wounds without murmuring.

After a time the uncle said, "Now is the time when you must go up the hill and listen to all kinds of sounds. When you hear one that you never heard before, return to me."

Soon Hatondas returned and imitated the notes of a chickadee. "No, no, that is not anything different!" exclaimed the old man, and straightway fell to abusing the boy.

Day by day Hatondas listened, hearing an owl, a hawk, a woodpecker, a deer and a bear. With each report his uncle threw coals of fire down his shirt or beat him on the face with a paddle.

One morning he heard a song, and listening, heard his own name called out.

Listening with strained ears he caught the words, "Hatondas, Hatondas, I am coming to marry you now. You hear this song so make ready."

Quickly Hatondas ran to his uncle and reported what he had heard. The uncle now became greatly enraged and threw all manner of filth at Hatondas, then fell to beating his face with brands from the fire. When he had finished scolding the boy, the uncle washed his own face and put on his best clothing. Then he greased his hair

---

1 Related by George D. Jimerson. This version is apparently a mixture of two distinct legends.

and tied his cheeks back with a string, tying the string behind his head under his braid, to give the appearance of
smooth cheeks.

Hatondas could not sleep that night for his bed was
infested with vermin his uncle had put into it, and it was
foul with refuse that his uncle customarily threw there to
make Hatondas an unsavory person.

Morning came, and all kinds of birds began to sing.
Hatondas listened as before, and at sunrise he arose and
went up the hill where he was accustommed to wait listening for the sounds which his uncle ordered him to report.

Again he heard the sound of distant singing, and it was
a woman's voice. Now Hatondas began to feel very sad,
for his appearance bothered him. He was dirty beyond all
measure and his hair was encrusted with dried refuse. So
he felt very lonely and without friends.

Soon again he heard the song and saw a woman a long
ways off. She seemed calling his name, so he listened more
intently. Then he saw a fine-looking young woman running
toward him. As she neared him he saw that she had a
basket of marriage bread. She looked at him in great pity
and asked him to lead her to his lodge.

When they entered the lodge the young woman greeted
the uncle, and said, "I have been sent by my mother to
find a man here."

"Oh I am the man you are looking for," said the uncle,
at the same time ordering Hatondas to leave the lodge. "I
am so sorry my nephew is filthy," said the uncle, in his most
gracious language. "He is very dirty and utterly no good."

"He is the man I have come to marry," said the young
woman.

Then the young woman took out a pot of oil and heated
it, and calling Hatondas to her cleaned his head, lifting of
a great mass of filthy crusts. At this the uncle was furious,
and demanded that the young woman leave the boy alone.
She continued her work until she had cleansed him when

she said, "Oh, he will make a good husband when I clean him!"

"You must marry me," cried out the uncle. "I have been waiting for you many years. See, my side of the lodge is very clean, and you could never sleep where Hatondas is accustomed to lie." But the young woman repulsed him and went out into the woods with Hatondas, whereupon the old man burst into great rage, breaking his cheek-strings and making himself look hideous. "Oh, I knew it would come," he screeched, "but I did not think so soon."

When the young woman had found a hollow log she required Hatondas to crawl into it and then through to the other end. When he emerged he was clean and healed of his scars.

That night they were married, but at midnight a queer sound awoke Hatondas. He rose up and listened. Then the young wife awoke.

"He is upon us!" she cried, and leaping up, she called upon Hatondas to flee with her. Jumping upon the fireplace she scattered the glowing embers about the room and in a moment the lodge was in flames.

Together the two ran to the top of the hill to the rear of the lodge. The young wife drew from her garment a small bundle and dropped it upon the ground. Taking the whip she struck the bundle a smart blow. A tiny growl issued from the skin wrappings and grew louder as she continued to ply her switch. Presently a dog burst from the bundle and stood wagging his tail at her feet. She continued to lash it and with each stroke the dog grew larger and finally so large that both she and Hatondas were able to mount its back and sent it dashing onward at great speed.

After some time they arrived on the shores of a vast expanse of water. The wife patted the dog back into its bundle and dropped it in her pouch and with her husband leaped into a large canoe that lay moored to the shore.

Untying the line, each grasped a paddle and swept the canoe out into the lake. They had gone but a short distance when a loud snort caused them to look back and there on the shore was a gigantic bear in the act of casting a long fish line, and even as they looked it fell, wrapping around the stern of the canoe. The craft stopped in its course with a sudden jerk and then began to speed backward to the shore.

"Quick, Hatondas," exclaimed his wife, "empty your pipe on the line," and Hatondas obeyed with surprising alacrity. The line snapped and with a sweep of the paddle this wife sent the canoe back into its track.

Foiled in his attempt to capture the pair the enraged monster pawed up the sand and pebbles. Swelling to an enormous size he thrust his mouth into the water and gulped it down in such immense quantities that the lake changed its current and flowed toward the mouth of the monster. Death seemed certain to the young couple for the canoe was drawn with great rapidity toward the beast, but ever resourceful, the young woman steadied herself, aimed and threw a round white stone directly at the creature's belly. It struck him with great force causing him to jerk up his head with a roar of pain and then belch the waters back into the lake. In the swiftly outflowing stream, spurred on by the paddles, the canoe shot back to its former course.

The great bear was furious with disappointment and roared, "You cannot escape me, soon I will catch you. I am Nia-gwa-he!" and then began to blow his icy breath upon the water. Ice commenced to form and when he judged it sufficiently thick he galloped out over the surface of the lake. "You cannot escape me!" he bellowed, "I am Nia-gwa-he!"

The canoe stood fast in the ice and doom seemed certain to its inmates.

"Don't be downcast, Hatondas," said the wife, "only trust me."

The wife knelt in the bottom of the canoe where she had a little fire burning and a pot of water.[2] She was apparently resigned to the fate from which there seemed no escape. Then when the bear was almost upon them she stood upright and flung a kettle of steaming water at his feet. The beast stopped with a sudden jerk as the clay pot broke into fragments and the water splashed upon the ice. This momentary halt was fatal, for the water softened the ice and the monster sank beneath the waters and disappeared. The ice vanished and the canoe sped on once again.

Late in the day the canoe grated against the base of a high cliff that rose perpendicularly from the water. The wife called up to the top. A woman leaned over the edge far above and seeing the couple below dropped down two pairs of claw mittens. These Hatondas and his wife fastened to their hands, and, with their aid, made their way slowly and cautiously to the summit.

The wife's sister greeted the bridal pair, and lead the way to a spacious lodge where a savory supper awaited them.

The wife told the story of her adventure expressing great joy at her escape from the monster bear.

After the evening meal the time for sleeping came and together the happy couple lay down upon a new bed of spruce boughs and wrapped themselves in soft newly-tanned skins.

A year passed and to the wife came twin baby boys. And so precocious were they that at their very birth they felled to the floor two curious men who had intruded into their mother's lodge. They grew so rapidly that in a few hours they had become mature men of prodigious strength and great agility. The old woman provided them with warrior costumes and gave them presents of bows and

---

2 Fires were kindled in large wooden dugouts. A mat or pan of clay prevented the embers from injuring the canoe.

ing brought a bear and a deer for the larder. A half starved settlement now feasted. New houses were reared, and new canoes built by these wonderful boys and great riches came to the family.

The mother was happy in her offspring and proud, but in the midst of her joy she began to contrast her present fortune with the unhappy days of her girlhood. She fell to brooding, and, as she lay upon the ground, the roar of a monster echoed through the forest. The twins rushed to her side exclaiming,

"Oh mother, here comes Nia-gwa-he looking like a buffalo!"

The boys stood guarding their mother as toward them rushed the huge beast. It dashed full upon them. The boys sank to their knees, and stabbed it on the bottom of its foot. When they arose their arms were wrapped around the creature and in a moment it was thrown through the air into a grove of oaks and there they buried it.

14. THE ORIGIN OF THE CHESTNUT TREE.

In a lodge that stood alone in a land of hills lived Dadjedondji with his older brother Hawiyas. Dadjedondji busied himself each day in the forests hunting game, catching fish, gathering fruits, berries, roots and nuts and studying the wonders of the woods. He prepared his own meals in the lodge and always ate them alone, for, strange to relate, his brother steadfastly refused to eat with him or, indeed, to eat in the presence of anyone. He never hunted or cooked, but sat all day smoking moodily.

The boy often pondered over the strange difference between his brother and himself and at length resolved to pretend to start on his daily hunt, then turn back and secretly watch his bother. He did as he had planned but failed to discover his brother, Hawiyas, eating or at any extraordinary practice. Night came and the two boys lay side by side with their feet toward the fire. Dadjedondji remained awake in order to continue his watch and toward midnight heard his brother stir. In his anxiety to spy upon him Dadjedondji sat upright and his brother seeing him dropped back upon his couch. Dadjedondji chided himself for his impulsiveness and when, some time later, Hawiyas asked in an undertone, "Are you awake now?" he remained quiet and did not reply.

Later Hawiyas arose cautiously believing himself unobserved and crept to the side of the lodge. Dadjedondji was peeping through a hole in the skin that covered him. Hawiyas pushed aside a sheet of bark and drew forth a small kettle and a tiny bag. From the bag he took a small nut from which he scraped a few shavings with a flint. Casting them into the kettle he poured in a quantity of water and shaking the kettle placed it over the fire. The water soon began to heat, and as it did so, the kettle increased in size until a pudding was cooked, when he dipped it out, cleaned the kettle, shook it and stored it away with the bag. Then he began to eat greedily, and, having satisfied his hunger, lay down and slumbered again.

The next night Dadjedondji concluded to try the experiment and while his brother slept crept to the hiding place, found the kettle and bag, and did exactly as his brother had done. He ate the pudding and found it most delicious. Wishing more, he threw the entire contents of the bag into the kettle and set it on to boil again. It was not long before the kettle began to expand so much so that it filled half the house. Moreover the pudding began to boil over in enormous quantities.

With a cry of dismay the brother awoke.

"Oh what have you done?" cried he, "Oh! I am dead, you have killed your own brother. Oh!"

"What troubles you, brother?" asked Dadjedondji as he skipped out from the lodge, "You do not look very much like a dead man."

"Oh!" exclaimed the brother, "you have used all my food. It is all I eat and can eat. No one can obtain more of its kind for it is far away and charmed, so you have killed me!"

Scarcely had he spoken when the walls bulged and the building collapsed.

"Oh, do not worry brother," said Dadjedondji, "'there is more where this grew."

"Ah yes, but no man can get it, use what magic he may."

The brother raved throughout the remainder of the night but Dadjedondji slept unmoved.

When the morning came Dadjedondji sprang from the ground and expressed his surprise at his brother's sober countenance. "Tell me the full history of your magical food," he commanded.

Moodily the brother answered, "To the east is a great gap in the earth. Beyond it is a monstrous serpent whose poisonous breath kills all that comes where it blows. Should a man by chance, escape him, beyond are two panthers. Should some cunning magician creep by unobserved, beyond, high in the tree that bears the wonderful nuts, is a witch whose very look makes men fall apart, and her six sisters devour their meat. So boast not my brother, you cannot reach the tree. Know only this,—you have killed your brother."

Dadjedondji thought about it and said to himself, "All these things are strange. They are not right, neither are they in according with the ways I know about, and, therefore, I can conquer all these obstacles."

Boldly he set out with his face toward the rising sun. After a day's journey he came to a chasm that extended far beyond the eye's reach. "This is not right," thought the boy, so whittling a doll from a soft chunk of decayed log, he threw it across the chasm and followed it with a running jump. He landed safely on the other side and immediately resumed his journey. For a time he hurried onward and then nearly rushed into the yawning jaws of a big snake that leaped from a hidden cavern.

"Oh, get out of my way," said Dadjedondji flinging a wooden doll into its mouth.

Presently from a thicket appeared two panthers. Dadjedondji drew two more dolls from his pouch and cast one into the mouth of each beast. Then, without looking behind hurried onward again. A song came floating through the air and following the direction Dadjedondji came to a large branching tree. In its topmost branches hung the singer,— a flayed human skin,—but her charm song had no effect upon the boy for he said, "It is all wrong and I am right, therefore evil cannot befall me."

The skin-woman lifted her voice and sang with increased vigor, "An intruder comes to our clearing."

"Come down here," called Dadjedondji, "I have a present for you, gaswe"da, wampum. Promise you will be kind."

The skin-woman seeing the handsome purple quills descended and accepted the gift with many grimances and then drew back into the tree.

Now wampum is the emblem of truth and the skin-woman was entirely controlled by evil. Holding the beautiful necklace in her hand she sang, "I have been bribed by a present of wampum not to tell of a stranger's approach."

While she sang she threw the beads over her head and around her neck and the beads grew tight and choked her into silence.

Out rushed the six sisters that had been called ravenous cannibals, but their shouts were not those of anger or of gluttons, but glad cries of joy. Coming up to Dadjedondji they saluted him and with extravagant flattery thanked him for coming to rescue them from their evil sister.

The gave him a great bag of brown nuts and sent him back on his journey. The great witch had now no food and perished.

On his return the panthers angry at the deception he had practiced on them, pounced from the bushes.

"Go away, you are not doing right. I never heard of panthers acting as you are. Are you not ashamed? Go now and never dare trouble men again! You are now free!"

The panthers, surprised at their intended victim's words, rushed off in fright. Dadjedondji continued his journey and rebuked the serpent and sent it wriggling to the nearest lake. Then he addressed the chasm.

"Oh, Earth, why are you rent? This is not the way of doing things. I have never seen such fissures in my life before. Close up once again and let men enjoy themselves!" And the earth closed with a loud crash.

Walking safely across the solid earth where once the breach had been, he persevered until he reached the ruins of his home. His brother was sitting mournfully on a log still lamenting, but Dadjedondji bade him cheer up, and showed him the large bag of nuts. He gave him enough for several meals and then sent him on to the lodge of the six sisters where he could find a good wife to cook for him. Then he went upon the side hills and scattered the nuts over the ground and in time beautiful trees grew and now all the world has chestnuts. When they were confined to one tree they were magical but now their powers have gone and they neither spread nor burst kettles.

———

GENERAL NOTES.—There are a number of stories similar to this. In some the hero is a nephew living with his uncle. The adventures of the hero in overcoming the magic beasts that guard the paths to the chestnut tree are various and recited in greater or less detail. In some stories the youth pacifies the hunger of the monsters by flinging chipmunks at them which increase in size and afford them a full meal. In one version the last guard of the tree is the skin of the boy's sister, dried and hanging over the path. The skin is alive but held by sorcery as the slave of the wicked witch sisters. When the hero presents the wampum to her she sings out: "I cannot tell you now that a stranger is about to assail us, for he has stopped my mouth with wampum." The six sisters thereupon rush forth and finding no enemy beat the skin and tell it to tell the truth hereafter and not give false alarms. In similar stories the hero projects himself into the body of one of the witches, as is done in the story of the magic arrow and the quilt of men's eyes. He is then born and cries incessantly for power over the tree and the witch, yielding, he becomes master of the chestnuts. He is also the deliverer of the dried skin which he conjures back to its normal self, when he finds it to be his own sister. The mole is the hero's dream animal and it aids him to perform his deeds of magic.

15. DIVIDED BODY RESCUES A GIRL FROM A WIZARD'S ISLAND.

A brother and younger sister dwelt in a lodge together. The sister cooked the meals and the brother did the hunting. The brother, whose name was Crow, never allowed his sister to leave the lodge. "Oh my sister," he would say. "Do not even venture to the spring." When the young man went on a hunting trip he would set his dog as guard over his sister and caution him to prevent her from leaving the lodge.

On a certain morning the girl began to debate with herself the reasons why she should be kept within the lodge. Soon she decided that it was wrong to keep her from seeing the world outside. So she pushed aside the curtain, exclaiming, "Now I shall see!" Being thirsty she had taken a bark water vessel and made ready to dip water from the spring. As she sank her bowl beneath the surface of the water something grabbed her by the hair and whisked her through the air. She did not know where she was going but when she again felt the ground beneath her feet she looked about and saw that she was on an island in a large lake. Soon an old man came to her and said, "This is where you are going to stay," at the same time pointing to a great lodge.

All about the lodge were human bones from which the flesh had been gnawed, and the place was most filthy. The girl then knew that she had been abducted by a cannibal wizard, Oñgwe Iās. She knew that there was no easy way of escape but she resolved not to give up hope. Each morning Oñgwe Iās would come to the lodge with human flesh which he would demand that she prepare as food for him. Then he would demand that she bring him water from the spring, carrying it in a bark container that hung on the center pole of the lodge.

133

One morning while she was at the spring she saw a young man standing before her. He looked very pleasant and soon spoke to her. "Oñgwe Iās has not been successful today," he said. "Tomorrow morning when he asks you to bring him water he will hit you with his club, seeking to kill you. Be ready and when you reach for the bowl jump around behind the post and Oñgwe Iās will hit the pole and break his arm. Then run to the spring here and I will give you assistance. My name is Sgagedi, the Other Side."

The next morning Oñgwe Iās was very ferocious and roared at the girl, ordering her to bring him water from the spring. Cautiously she reached up for the water bowl and then slipped around the pole. With a crash a great club swung against the spot where the girl had been but in a moment she had fled from the lodge, while the monster was bellowing with the pain of a broken arm.

Quickly the girl reached the spring where she found the young man looking very pleasant. "Be ready now," he called. "My canoe is on the shore."

She stepped into the canoe and sat in the center while Sgagedi with a jerk shoved it from the beach, throwing one half of his body to the bow of the canoe and leaving one-half at the stern. He paddled from both ends and went very rapidly.

Oñgwe Iās soon restored his broken arm and began to sing a charm song, calling upon the winds to blow the canoe back to him. A strong wind began to blow and presently the canoe was swept back to the island, where Oñgwe Iās was waiting on shore. It seemed as though they were doomed but just as they were about to ground, Sgagedi threw tobacco on the water and called upon the wind to blow the other way, which it did. Sgagedi now did not cease to paddle but kept up his effort until the canoe was safe on the opposite shore.

With a great bump the canoe struck the beach, sliding

up onto the sand. As it did so the body of Sgagedi came together with a snap and he became reunited.

From the beach, inland there was a path, and by this the couple ran on into the forest. Presently the path divided and as it did so Sgagedi's body was cloven and each half ran on, the girl following the left side. The path reunited and so did the body of the man. Still the two ran on until they saw an elderly woman on the path ahead. She approached and took the girl into a lodge. "I am glad you came," she said. "I have been waiting for you to become my daughter-in-law."

After a while the young woman and Sgagedi were married, but the bride could not be happy for she continually was saying, "Oh where is my brother?"

Now when the brother returned to his lodge and found his sister gone he had scolded the dog and forced it to tell what had happened. "I tried to grasp the sister as the monster seized her," he asserted, but the brother called him an unfaithful friend, whereupon the dog turned into a smooth stone. The brother grieved the loss of his sister and sat with his head down before the ashes of his lodge fire.

In due season the sister bore two sons who were twins, and they quickly grew to be large boys. Every day they would run down to the shore to see their father scouring the lake after witches and monsters, seeking to slay them. At last they, too, wished to explore the lake and so took a canoe and paddled across it to the opposite shore. "Now we will search for our uncle, for whom our mother continually cries," said they to one another.

They noticed an old streak in the sky and followed it far inland until they came to a clearing overgrown with bushes. Looking carefully into this opening, one twin said to the other, "A bark lodge appears to have fallen down here." So they went forward and examined the ruined lodge and in pulling aside the bark and poles they felt a body and it was breathing. They pulled it out of the rubbish and found it to be a man. They brushed him off and restored him to his wonted self. Then one said, "This appears to be our uncle."

"I am your uncle," said the old man. "My dog is a stone. Oh, will you restore my dog to life!" So the twins restored the dog and then all went back to the lake and entered the canoe.

By rapid paddling they reached home that day and when the sister saw her brother she knew him and was very glad.

16. THE ORIGIN OF THE BUFFALO SOCIETY.

A youth who had wandered out into the plains of the West in search of game, lost the trail, and though he searched with all diligence he was unable to find it again. Throwing himself upon the ground he brooded over his ill fortune and longed with all the intenseness of his soul that he might be again back in his native village.

It was sunset and in the gloaming the youth saw a company of people gathered about a fire, evidently in earnest council. Cautiously he advanced, hoping to learn who the people were. For several minutes he lay concealed in the tall rank grass and creeping nearer was surprised to learn that it was he, himself, who formed the subject of the discussion. Much greater was his amazement when an old lady arose, and walking directly to his hiding place lifted him to his feet and said, "Come, I have adopted you."

"Oh is that it!" exclaimed the boy in disapppointment, "I was hoping you would guide me home."

"No, not yet," said the old lady, "you must learn first."

Marveling at her words, the youth followed the old woman to her lodge and dwelt there.

It seemed strange to him that the people of the village never hunted but traveled together in bands over the prairies. He wondered at the shaggy heads of the men and their dark hairy leggings. He seemed as in a dream and yet all he saw and did seemed real. He learned much of the wondrous tribe with which his lot had been cast, and as the months went by he learned more and more. Often he danced in the ceremonies of the tribe, often he sang and often he made medicine in the council lodges on the prairies until he knew almost everything that a tribesman knew. Although his sojourn was one full of incidents and adventures he never ceased to mourn for his own home and people and often plead to be shown the trail, but his foster mother would only say, "No, not yet, for you have not learned all." What this meant he did not know and pined as before for home.

One night he was awakened by the far-away sound of a drum. Its slow dull note made the youth more melancholy than before. His heart seemed to stop in its natural course and beat slow to the tap of the drum. Greatly depressed, he crept to the bedside of his foster mother and pleaded for a guide to his home trail.

"No not yet, my son," said the old woman, "but perhaps very soon. Listen to the sound of that far distant drum. Now let me tell you that which you have not known. Far away to the west beneath a great hill lives the great chief of all buffaloes and an evil chief is he. When he drums it is a sign he wishes all to gather around his mound for he is anxious for a race. He has an evil plan. Being a mighty runner he often calls us to his lodge and he whom the chief selects must race until death strikes away his life from the unequal chase. The terrible race continues until the evil chief has satisfied his insane fancy and dismissed the assembled throngs. Soon you will hear the chief sing and when he does all of us must answer his call by starting immediately on the journey."

"How is it that a buffalo is your chief?" asked the youth.

"Because we are all buffaloes," was the answer.

The youth bit his lip and felt much chagrined to think he had not known this before. Surely he had had sufficient evidence.

Supplementing the note of the drum came a song. Simultaneously there was a great stamping. Everyone was rushing at a furious pace in the direction of the song. The youth ran with his mother. For ten days and ten nights the wild rush continued, ever led on by the song.

On the evening of the tenth day the rushing multitude reached the hill from whence the song issued and rested.

That night the old lady came to the youth and said: "This has been a terrible rush and many have died from exhaustion, many from wounds and many have been trampled to death. Many children have been left behind to die. Oh that this may be the last mad stampede! Now listen, he will challenge you to a race. Do not fear, but take this medicine and when he calls you, race him to death. Shoot him in the red spot on his hand. When you awake tomorrow I will give you a bow and arrow.

The youth awoke late the next morning and to his amazement saw a great herd of buffaloes gathered around the hill. From the summit of the hill came a great roar. It was the chief buffalo speaking.

"There is a human boy among us," it said, "I command him to race me."

Trembling, the youth walked toward the hill and as he did so a shaggy buffalo came sauntering slowly up to him. On her neck was a bow and arrow.

"I am your mother," said the buffalo. "Remember if you run swiftly you may overcome the evil chief. Remember his body is, under the skin, covered with a bony plate. His ribs have all grown together so that no arrow can pierce to his heart. No matter what is said, shoot only at the spot on his hand, for as a human he runs."

"Come boy, it is time to run," roared the buffalo chief.

Around the great hill-like mound stretched two circles of animals. Between them was a path over which the contestants must run. The buffalo chief started the race by shouting, "Catch me or at sunset I will trample you to the dust."

Undaunted, the boy leapt to the course and ran his best. Toward noon the chief, surprised at the endurance of his intended victim, yet believing himself safe, sat down for rest, but the youth strode faster the longer he ran and doubly fast when the buffalo lagged.

Springing toward the chief the youth shouted, "I'll catch you, yow! yow!"

Up leaped the buffalo and panting, ran around the course at the top of his speed. Close behind him was the youth, disconcerting him with his cries of derision, and his calls of "Yow! Yow!" Calling up all his energy the buffalo sprinted ahead and sat down for rest, but hardly had he touched the grass when the youth with his aggravating "Yow Yow!" sped toward him shouting, "I'll catch you soon. You have not seen me run yet." So, fearing defeat, the buffalo chief ran as fast as his magic could send him but to his intense annoyance the boy stuck close to his heels.

The sun was sinking low and as it sank large and red to the level of the western prairie the buffalo chief fell with a groan and moaned. "Oh I am worsted, I am disgraced! Shoot me, boy, shoot me, your one arrow will transfix my heart, oh I am beaten!" The crafty beast was endeavoring to deceive the boy but the human boy saw through the beast's subtilty.

"Arise!" commanded the boy, "I am ready to shoot you!"

"Oh my heart," moaned the defeated chief as he arose.

"Throw up your hands!" and quicker than thought the boy sent an arrow speeding into the red spot on his hand.

A great shout rent the air. The buffalo chief had fallen, had perished. The glad cry of the assembled herds floated far over the plains and rumbled like the echoing voice of the thunder gods. Long did the stamping herds roar their shout of thanksgiving and afterward heaped upon him honor and praise and called him their deliverer. They promised him all the power that the race of the buffaloes could bestow.

"When you wish health and fortune, when you wish a balm for fear and a panacea for trouble, and a cure for disease burn tobacco and call upon the spirits of the buffalo," was the instruction of the new chief who was chosen.

The throngs of animals dispersed in bands, each led to its range by its chief.

The youth accompanied the old woman back to her lodge ten days journey away and listened attentively when she imparted to him all the secrets the buffaloes knew.

"You know our dances, our songs and our mysteries. Preserve these things forever in a society of human creatures," said the buffalo woman. "Now you may go to your home among the man animals. Now I bid you adieu, my son, I am sorry you must go. A guide will lead you to the trail."

The youth bade the people farewell and last of all his good foster mother and followed the guide to the trail that lead to the land of the human.

After many days the youth came to a village of his people and calling a council told his adventures. To all but the old folk he was a stranger, but when he made friends he selected a company and to them he imparted the secret of the buffaloes.

Thus originated the Society of Buffaloes, which today exists as a power among the Seneca.

17. THE BOY WHO COULD NOT UNDERSTAND.

A Study in Seneca Idioms. Related by Edward Cornplanter, 1906.

There was a boy who had been reared in the woods by
an old woman who never thought it worth while to teach
him oratory[1] or rhetoric[2]. He had never attended a council
or listened to a sachem's speech and so he never learned the
use of words. When the old woman died the boy's grandfather came and took him home with him hoping to make
him useful. The boy was very obedient and obeyed every
word commanded. His grandfather began to have confidence in him and one day sent him out to locate a bear
tree. "Now when you discover the tree wade"ode", (*leave
your nails on it*)," said the grandfather.

Now the boy thought this strange advice but hastened
to obey his old protector. After some wandering he found a
bear tree and then remembering that he must leave his nails
upon it tore off his finger nails and stuck them in the bark
of the tree. This caused him most excruciating pain and
he was hardly able to get home. However, he thought that
this was to make him brave and he was confident that his
grandfather knew best how to educate a warrior. He went
to his grandfather and proudly displayed his bleeding
fingers. "See, grandfather," he said, "I have found a bear
tree and have left my finger nails upon it."

The old man looked at the boy in wonder. "What have
you done?" he asked.

"Left my nails upon the tree," answered the boy.

"Oh, you poor ignoramus," laughed the old warrior, "I
did not mean that you should tear out your nails by the
roots and stick them in the bark. I meant that you should
put your eyes on the tree when you saw one. When I said

---

1   Oratory—hai'wanotä'.
2   Rhetoric—haya'dushäiendï.

142

'put your nails on it' I meant that you should remember the tree so that you could take it at any time you wished. Go now and put your eyes on the tree (ĕⁿse″ganeiondĕⁿ')."

"Oh, grandfather," moaned the boy, "why did you not say what you meant!" and ran out to put his eyes on the tree. He found the tree again, and began pulling at his eyelids and eyes. Having no nails he could not get a good hold and the operation was most painful. Finally he gouged out one eye with a stick and hung it on the bear tree. Going back to his grandfather's lodge he greeted him.

"I have left one eye on the tree, grandfather," he said. "I kept the other so that I could find my way home."

The old man looked at his grandson and was angry. "You are most foolish!" he said. "When I say, 'leave your eyes on a thing' I mean that you must be able to recognize it instantly when you see it again."

"Oh, grandfather," wailed the boy, "why do you never say what you mean?"

"I do," said the grandfather, "but you do not easily understand my meaning."

Now when the boy was recovered from his bruises the old man asked that the boy take him to the bear tree that they might kill a bear. Each had a bow and quiver of arrows. When they reached the tree the old hunter climbed up the trunk and lighted a torch and threw smoke wood down the hollow to smoke out the bear. "Now, grandson," he said, "shoot him *here* when he comes out," and the old man patted his heart.

The bear came out on a run and as he did the boy lifted up his bow and aimed at the old man's heart. It was the place that he had been instructed to shoot, so he thought.

The old man was exceedingly angry and yelled out, "You shoot the bear, not me." The boy shot the bear and the old man slid down the tree. "You fool," he yelled, "so you were going to shoot me!"

"You told me to shoot right *there*, grandfather," pleaded

the boy, "and I wanted to obey for I thought you knew best."

"No, I meant the bear," retorted the old hunter. "Now we will cut him up." So they dressed the bear.

Now it is customary to call the pancreas, the oskwi'sont (tomahawk); the diaphragm the o'kăā (skirt); the fat around the kidneys the face (ogo^n"sa'), and the ventral portion (oho'a), door. So the old man said, "I have placed the door, the tomahawk, the false face and the skirt aside. Go home and cook them for me and I will return. Split a stick and put the tomahawk in it and put it in the fire. When it snaps yell 'Hai-ie' and I will come."

Now the grandfather busied himself cutting up the bear and cutting its meat into strips and chunks. He also prepared its skin. Then he was ready to go home. He glanced at the log where he had laid the organs and found them still there. "I wonder what blunder the boy has made now," he mused and took them with him to the lodge. When he arrived there he found that the stupid orphan had torn the door from its fastenings and had split it into pieces. Moreover the boy was running around the lodge yelling, "Hai-ie!" Inside the old man saw his best stone tomahawk in the fire. It was read hot and when a draft of air struck it it would snap and every time it did the boy would whoop, "Hai-ie!" In a cauldron a false face, a breech skirt and the splinters of the door were boiling.

"It is too hot within!" explained the boy. "Hai-ie!" he paused to say as the tomahawk snapped. "It's too hot, so I am watching outside and—hai-ie!"

The patience of the long suffering grandfather was exhausted and he said some things that the boy thought himself much aggrieved for he said, "Why did you not tell me what you meant?"

The grandfather took matters in his own hand and cooked the meal. The time was at hand also when he must notify his charge that by right of birth he was a chief and that on the morrow he must commence his duties as a runner. The next day the old man with due solemnity told the boy that he was a secondary chief. "We will have a great feast," he said. "I want you to run and notify all the tall trees (Gai'eso^{n}s), all the rough places (Ain'djatgi), all the swamps (Gai^n'dago^n), and all the high hills (Gai'nonde). When you return do not fail to 'jounce your uncle on your knee' (esĕ^n'sĕnt'o')."

Now the young chief thought this peculiar but he found tall trees in plenty and invited them all to the feast, likewise he invited the mountains and the swamps and returning gave his uncle a kick that knocked him down. The uncle immediately did the same thing to the impudent boy who ran rather lamely back to his grandfather. The old man listened to the tale with impatience and then explained that the 'tall trees' were the sachems, the 'mountains' the war chiefs, and the 'swamps' the common warriors. By 'uncle' he meant the relatives of the family and by 'jouncing with his knee' simply to notify them. "Oh," gasped the boy, "why do you never say what you mean!" Of course he had the work to do all over and the feast came in due season. When it was over the boy said, "Grandfather, there is meat left and soup also."

"Well," said the grandfather, "give each one half a spoon."[3]

The lad did not see what good that would do but he instantly obeyed, going to the shed and chopping twenty wooden spoons in halves and then giving each guest a piece.

"Here you," some one objected, "What are these things for?"

The boy was about to say that he had but obeyed his grandfather when the old man himself looked up and saw that the stock of finely carved spoons had been destroyed by his stupid ward. "Shawĕn'noiwĭs!" roared the old fellow. (Sha-wen-noi-wis means incurable fool.) "Why have you ruined my good spoons?"

---

[3] This may be a modern interpolation.

"I did just as you said," was the meek answer. Then he answered, "There is yet meat left, Haksot!"

"De sa di wa o gwut, tie it on your head and let it hang," commanded the grandfather, meaning that it should be distributed to the particular friends of the family.

The boy took an elm bark rope and tied the juicy meat on his forehead.

"It is disagreeable, grandfather," he complained, "for the juice and oil drip into my eyes."

The old man explained, and the boy feeling much abused answered, "Oh why can you never say what you mean?"

The time came when the boy chief must marry. The grandfather told the boy where a family of lovely girls lived. "Go shove your legs in the door," (Satci'nondăt—show your leg), said he, meaning that the boy should go visiting.

The young chief stuck his legs under the door and sat there all night. The next morning the old woman within gave him a blow with a corn pounder and he ran limping to his advisor to discover the trouble. "Oh you fool," said the old man, "I meant that you should 'shake the old lady's skirt'," meaning that he should seek a daughter. When he did this however he was kicked and pounded until he could hardly crawl. Now he had a very difficult time courting for it is hard to describe in direct words how to court and to marry, so when he followed his grandfather's words he found much trouble. Now when he married his wife made him understand and he learned many new things. Now this is all that I can tell.

GENERAL NOTES.—The Boy Who Could Not Understand is the only tale of its kind secured by the writer among the Seneca. It is related as a humorous commentary on the literal meanings of certain idioms of the Seneca that are so well understood that they never cause confusion. The author of this tale must have deliberately analyzed each term and sought to give it a literal application. One might suppose that a captive Algonkin invented it to explain his own plight in learning the Seneca tongue.

This tale was related by Edward Cornplanter and it has been recorded essentially in his own language, except where better grammar or a better word straightens out the English. I am sure that Cornplanter might have expanded his story considerably, but he hastened it to a conclusion to give me the Seneca equivalents of some obscure bits of slang frequently heard in English. His own literal translations of American slang into Seneca made him wax merry, and he concluded by saying, "So you see it don't make any sense at all."

18. THE BOY WHO LIVED WITH THE BEARS.

Hono' was an unloved stepson. His foster father never had a kind word for him and begrudged the very food that little Hono' ate.

"You eat like a wolf," the harsh man would snap. "It is a nuisance to feed you."

"Agē'," sighed little Hono', "when I am a man and can hunt and fight I will repay you. Then will you like me?" implored the boy, but his evil guardian only growled.

At length the stepfather began to cast about how he might rid himself of the child and after some meditation decided to feign friendliness and lure Hono' away on a hunting excursion. So it happened that one day he said pleasantly, "Come now Hono', it is time for you to learn to hunt. How would you like to go on a journey with me?"

Hono' was delighted and promptly replied he would go.

The two traveled for some time through the bush lands and Hono' thinking this strange said, "I always thought hunters went to the deep woods and not in the bushes."

"Don't worry," the stepfather replied, "I am an old hunter and know my business. Come hurry along, I will show you a wonderful place."

"Well where is my bow and my quiver of arrows?" asked Hono' anxiously. "I ought to have one."

"Oh after a while," was the retort. "Now hurry along."

"And when I am a great hunter will you be good to me always?" asked Hono', dreaming of the success he hoped to achieve, but the only answer was a grunt.

After a journey of several miles the stepfather stopped abruptly and simulating surprise said excitedly, "See, look, look! There is a hole. Hurry Hono', crawl in and catch the game. Oh you will be a big hunter now!"

Little Hono' was happy that he could be of service and in imagination saw glorious days ahead. Dropping upon his hands and knees he crawled into the hole in the ground and ran down the tunnel until he could no longer see, because of the darkness. Then, as he was about to return he saw the round opening ahead suddenly grow dark and with it the entire cavern. Guided by the walls he ran forward with speed born of terror and crashed his head into the stone that obstructed the opening.

Outside the evil man laughed in savage glee as he thought how easily he had shaken off the untaught Hono'.

"He will never push that boulder away," said he, as he strolled back to his lodge.

The blow had stunned the boy but after some time he was awakened by the sound of voices. Listening he discovered that on the earth outside a council was in session and his name was being frequently used. He had not long marvelled over the matter when he heard someone endeavoring to remove the stone. Finally it rolled down the hill and a voice called down the hole.

"Come out upon the earth if yet you are living," it said.

Shyly the boy emerged from the hole and sat down upon the grass. About him on every hand were animals.

"The boy is rescued," said a porcupine, who seemed to be the spokesman. "Who will care for him?"

Instantly there was a prolonged medley of cries. Each animal about him was either barking, yelping, grunting or screaching. Everyone was shouting "I'll care for him!"

"Hold!" cried the porcupine. "Do not volunteer without reason. You must be fit for the task. Let each tell his temper and his habits and most of all what he eats, then the boy may choose his own guardian."

Acting upon the suggestion each one extolled its own merits to the boy, but all in turn were rejected until a bear woman said, "I am old and rather surly, but I have a warm heart. I live happily in summer and sleep much in winter. I eat honey, nuts and berries."

"Oh you will do," interrupted Hono', shouting as loudly as he could. "I can stand that all right!"

To Hono' the strange part of the proceedings was that all the animals seemed human creatures and yet like beasts. They all spoke in one language and acted as friends although Hono' believed many mortal enemies.

The council adjourned and Hono' followed his bear mother down a trail that led to a thick wood.

On the way the bear spoke. "I wished you to become my grandson," she said, "because I have lost one and wish you to take his place and drive away my sorrow."

The two soon arrived at a great hollow stub and the bear taking the boy by the neck like a cub drew him into the hollow. Hono' looked about and found his quarters very comfortable. He was greatly pleased when the grandmother introduced him to two young bears, her grandsons, and told him they were his playmates.

When Hono' was hungry the grandmother bear gave him a honey-comb and some dried berries. When he was thirsty she gave him her paw to suck.

Hono' found his playmates boisterous fellows and many a time he received hard knocks but gave back as many as he received.

"Have care, Hono'," his grandmother warned him. "Wherever you get scratched hair will grow. So take caution, for unless you do you will look like a cub."

Summer came and the berries ripened. The bear grandmother suggested that it might be sport for the boys to go with her and gather the winter store of berries. The boys were delighted and consented instantly. . Then the old bear said: "Now, Hono', we always have much trouble while gathering berries. Bad animals and bad men and bad birds swarm to the berry patches and seek to harm us. Now you are a warrior and I wish to dress you in skins, to paint your face and to give you a bow and a quiver of arrows. Run around the hill and shout and whoop as loud as you can, and if enemies appear, shoot without mercy. This done we will have a prosperous season."

Hono' did as was asked and returning reported that he had shot many birds but nothing else. The bears, therefore, went upon the hillside fearlessly and gathered great baskets full of berries.

The summer season grew into autumn and nutting time came.

"This is a dangerous time," said the old bear, "and I feel that evil will befall us. Hunters swarm the woods now after autumn fruits, roots and game."

It was cautiously, indeed, that the bears gathered up the winter's store of nuts but for some time no human hunter was seen. One day, however, the old bear exclaimed, "Ah, here he comes. Now Hono', I will show you the classes of hunters you humans have. I do not fear this one for he is a Do-sko-a-o, or brush-in-the-mouth-hunter. See, he is chewing a pine twig. This gives us the scent and we can flee long before he reaches us, for this 'brush-mouth' is too careless."

The bears were hiding in a large hollow tree, and, true to the mother bear's prophecy, the hunter did not see them but plodded along trailing his bow and chewing the pine. When he had passed by the bears scampered back to the chestnut tree and climbing it shook down the delicious brown nuts.

On the morrow, as Hono' and the bears were starting out, the old bear exclaimed in a whisper, "A hunter is coming, but fear not, he is a blind man. See, he is eating and holds his bowl so far over his eyes that he cannot see anything before him. When he walks through the forest he looks neither right nor left but walks unconcerned, yet strangely hopes for game. Look again, for another hunter will shortly appear. He is 'heavy stepper' and warns before he comes. Still another hunter comes," continued the

THE BEAR DANCE

In this drawing, by Jesse Cornplanter, the ceremonial dance in honor of the spirits of the bears is represented.

bear woman, "He is 'swinging mouth'; keep away from his chin and you are safe. Notice, he appears to be singing loudly, but in reality he is only humming very low or even only thinking of his song. Listen to me Hono', bears can hear singing if only thought and sung in the mind."

On their homeward journey the old bear putting her nose to the ground said: "Alas, alas! We must hurry now and hide for real evil is coming." The bears hastened their steps and soon were safely concealed in their tree. Then the wise old bear looking through her window in a frightened tone said: "At last, a true hunter has come. He is of the class we call four eyes. He has a dog with him and no sign escapes their eyes. See even now he is approaching this tree. Ah, he is a great hunter and is your own evil foster-father. When he cuts down the tree let me run first, and, last of all, Hono' you follow."

Scarcely had she spoken when the hunter approached the tree and surveyed it critically. Gathering some dry leaves and twigs he built a fire around the dry old stub and as the flames ate in he cut out the coals leaving a fresh surface for the fire. In a few minutes it crashed and fell. The old woman bear rushed out and began to run towards the west but had only taken a few leaps when an arrow pierced her heart, but her ghost-body ran on. The two cubs emerging met death in a similar way, then Hono' crawling out cried, "Father, are you going to shoot me, too?"

"Agē'!" exclaimed the hunter in surprise. "How came you here," and Hono' told his story.

The stepfather was greatly impressed, and taking the boy by the hand, said, "I am sorry, my boy, I was ever unkind. I am sorry I killed your friends. If you had only called me I should have hearkened and all would have been well, but now Agē'! I shall always have bad luck!"

The hunter looked upon his stepson with great awe and invited him back to his home, for he was afraid of the bear ghosts.

"And am I useful now?" asked the boy, "and will you like me?"

The hunter said, "truly."

He never dared hunt again but Hono' did.

GENERAL NOTES.—In this legend an unloved stepson is lured to a hole in the ground by his foster father and caused to enter it on the pretense of looking for game. The hole is then closed by a boulder and Hono' left a prisoner. Soon he hears animals talking about his fate and in a few moments the boulder is rolled away and he emerges to hear a lively discussion by the animals as to who can best care for him. A bear mother finally secures him and takes him with her, instructing him in the ways to avoid the human beings who hunt bears. In the end the bear mother gives up her life to save Hono' and he escapes only to find tha this foster father was the hunter. The two become reconciled.

The ideas of the bear mother and of the bear wife of a human man are common Seneca concepts.

This legend was related during the winter of 1904-1905 by Edward Cornplanter. Later I secured versions from Mrs. Aurelia J. Miller and David George. From the notes of all these versions this present version has been compiled. I am aware that it is in my own words rather than in the language of any one of my informants. I have added nothing, however, and have carefully kept the story to its original form.

19. THE SEVENTH SON.[1]

My grandfather used to tell it to go to sleep by.

There were seven brothers two years apart. Their grandparents took care of them. They were all extra hunters. It seems the way my grandfather told it, each one shot an animal and used its skin for a short skirt; one had bear skin and the others different skins.

The grandparents knew of a family of beautiful daughters a good ways east that would make good wives, but had bad habits. Oh my, they were queer folks.

It seems each boy must go out when he was come to manhood and listen for signs of women,—the women to marry. So when the oldest was a man the grandfather said, "Now you must go away and listen, then come back." All right, so he went away and by and by he came back and said: "Oh Grandfather!" "Now wait," said the grandfather, "I must smoke first." So he filled up his pipe hard and took a coal and made big clouds,—smoke, it was. Then by an' by he said, "Now you tell me." So the boy,—man now,—said, "O-whoo-oo-o. Whoo-ho-wa-a!" "All right," grandfather says, "next morning you go off again. Go east and don't stop. You keep right on." So he went on and didn't come back.

By and by the second son said, "I am a man now. Now's my time to go off." All right, so he went off and came back and heard a wren and he said he had heard something. When the grandfather finished smoking he said: "Now you follow that on and keep right east and don't stop 'tall." So he never came back.

So turns came to all and they went too, same way and heard crow, rabbit, deer, cracking sticks, and they followed the sounds.

---

[1] A legend, written verbatim as told in Indian-English by Aurelia Jones Miller, Gah-yoh'wes, whose grandfather, Chief Warrior, told it to her when she was a child.

Then the seventh son came of age and he was a kind of a witch [*sic*] and he dressed up in his best. Now I am going to describe his dress. He had a short skirt to the middle, most to his knees, made of nice spotted deer-skin,—yearling,—and he had nice moccasins and nothing else only a ga-gē-da, (a breast sash). And so he was like a big witch.[2] He went off and he didn't turn round when he heard a noise but kept right on going.

By and by he came to a path and saw one man's tracks, by and by two, three, four, by and by, good many,—regular path. Pretty soon so many that the path, it was good deal dust in it, and he kept on. Then he noticed other tracks and paths coming on,—the big road it is, now, from every direction. Now way off in the distance he saw smoke rising. He kept looking. He thought something was going to happen. He was all alone on the big path in the dusty plain. Path gets wider the more he goes along. By and by he thinks he'd better look nice so he stripped off some bark and rolled it and spit on it to make a nice neck-string. My! it was a nice one and shined where he spit on it. By and by he went along and he saw a bush and a big thing on it— what hornets live in,—hanging down. It was a very big thing, so he went up slow and took some moss and clay in his fingers and made a plug and pasted up the door where hornets came out. Then he picked it off and he was a big witch, and rolled the big,—why, I guess it's nest, you call it,—roll in his hands and got it small like a little bottle and he spit on it. My, it shined! Then he fastened the bottle to his neck on the bark. Oh it looked nice! Then he shook up the bottle hard. Oh! Then he went along and he saw a milk-weed stalk with pods popped open. So he pulled out the white threads and cut the stalk and got his hands sticky —and rubbed it on his long hair. Then he spit on it some more and stuck in the white stuff and worked a long time

---

2 The Seneca seldom use any other word to describe a sorcerer, when relating legends in English.

and it looked nice. You couldn't see his black hair. It looked all white, like a dandelion. So he went along and he thought he would spit on his hands and rub it on his body and he did and it got all colors and they changed. Oh my! And he went on and he began to notice he was going down hill and he went on and the hill got steeper. He saw smoke all the time and now he saw it coming out of a big house and the road went right into the door. And the hill got steeper and by and by very steep and slippery. And he got there and said, "Yo hoh'! I am in for it now!" So he looked sharp and saw a woman in the door and he was all right. Then all of a sudden he looked around and oh my! his foot slipped and he fell right down the hill and didn't stop until he landed right in the middle of the room. Now the old woman there said, "Yes, get the kettle ready. We've been waiting long enough for that animal."

Now there were seven sisters there and the oldest was an old maid and all were except the youngest, and the oldest said, "Go get the knife and we will butcher him." So they tied his body to a post and they were ready to kill him. Then the youngest said, "Oh look, he isn't like the others. He has curious hair and his body shines! His skirt is nice, it is spotted and pretty and has deer's hoofs rattling for a fringe. Let us look at him." So she touched his hair and pulled it and said, "My, it is funny, it won't pull out. Let's not kill him yet." So she looked at him some more. Pretty soon she says, "Oh what a funny bottle," and she pulled out the cork and all of a sudden, out came something, bump, on the floor. Now he was a great witch and when the hornets struck the floor he used his great magic, and oh! it was strong magic! Now when the women looked, Ah-gey! the hornets were warriors! And they kept falling out until the house was full and the hornet captain took out his knife and cut the strings on the post and then he stopped up the bottle.

The old woman called her youngest daughter to her

and said: "I am a big witch but he is a bigger one. If I get beaten you must burn down the house and all things in it. You must burn all the medicine because it will kill you all if you don't. Then have all the ashes of me and everything buried." Then the mother rushed and yelled, "Kill him!" and she tried it but a hornet-man warrior raised his tommahawk and he didn't hit her but she fell down dead. So the oldest sister ran to stick a knife in him and a warrior raised his arm and she fell dead and he didn't hit her. And they were all afraid and stood back and the youngest daughter kind o' cried and said, "I'll give up my way and eat what he eats and I'll take him for my husband." So right away the chief hornet married them.

So there was no more fighting and it was dark and he and the seventh daughter went to bed because they were married and the five sisters planned to kill him as he slept but it was so he had a friend, a guard who was a star. And the star came down and sat on his eye and the witch sisters thought him awake and by and by the star went away, but it was morning then and they couldn't kill him.

So that day he ordered the big lodge to be burned and all the medicine in it and the body of the mother in it. It was a very big fire and hot and after awhile the mother's head burst open and up in the smoke flew all kinds of evil birds that no one eats,—owls and screech owls, and hawks and crows, and big crow buzzards, and black eagles and wild poison animals with feathers. Now the wife said he must not kill those animals but let them fly away. She told him before her mother died that must be the way. So that's how it happened all kinds of mischief got scattered around.

Then the sisters told him that once in a fight all of their men were killed and everybody else only them and they didn't have any men and wanted some now because they had made up their minds that they wouldn't eat any more people. So some of his warriors married the sisters and others he sent out to find wives for some of the hornet men had no hornet wives.   He wanted to make a big village there.

So then he went back and brought his grandparents to the new village and they were surprised and knew he was a big witch then.   Now when all the warriors had returned with wives he said, "You are mine."   Then he uncorked his bottle and let out more warriors for his grandparents. So they went to another village and the warriors built houses and boats and cleared land and made a big town.

Now the youngest daughter told her husband where his brother's bones were hidden.   And she showed him the spot and he dug up the bones and was in a hurry to match them and smoked on them and they came to life again but he had been in too much of a hurry.   He didn't put the bones together the right way they ought to be and that was very bad because when the meat grew on again some had long legs, some long some short, some had broken arms, some too many fingers, some not enough, some had not enough ribs and so were soft and bent over.   Oh they were in an awful fix!   Their bones were not a match and some were missing because they had been chewed up.   Oh!   But the brothers had lots of hornets to work for them and it was easy.   So now that's why crooked and lame people come to be born.   They are the grandchildren,—way down,—of the brothers, and it is awful!

Now that's only how far my Grandfather told us because he said we wouldn't go to sleep if we listened to more and he never finished it but next time began it all over again.

GENERAL NOTES.—This is a characteristic Seneca legend and its elements are not at all unusual.   As a variation I have given it almost exactly in the same language as originally related to me by Mrs. Aurelia Jones Miller.   My informant was a woman of unusual natural intelligence and spoke English fairly well, but she frequently ommitted the articles, "the," "an" and "a," and in other ways her language was picturesquely provincial, but typical of the reservation brogue.

The conclusion of the story copies a common theme, that of restoring the bones of persons slain by witchcraft.   The hero is in too much of a hurry and forces the skeletons to assemble so quickly that the bones are mismated, producing cripples and misshapen people when they are conjured back to living flesh.

20. THE BOY WHO OVERCAME ALL MAGIC BY LAUGHTER.[1]

The world was once visited by a demon of enchantment who scattered all the people and bewitched all the animals, all the trees, all the lakes, all the rivers, all the boys and girls and all the older people. Strange to say, nobody knew that they had been enchanted; they only knew that all their wishes were thwarted and that there was misery everywhere.

Now, Gajihsondis did not know that he had been placed under an evil spell. He was a boy and was filled with all the ambitions of a boy, but all his desires were curbed by his queer-looking old grandfather. The boy did not even know that it was strange to live in a hole in the ground under his grandfather's bed or to be whipped with burning switches.[2] He only knew that he wanted to do things,— to play down by the spring and to go hunting. After a while he grew curious to know the reason of things and so asked many questions.

One day when he had grown to the age of twelve years he asked: "My grandfather, where are my parents? Why have you never taken me to my father and my mother?"

His grandfather eyed him curiously and refused to give Gajihsondis any satisfaction. But the boy kept questioning until the old man growled like a bear and said: "My grandson, you should not ask questions. You have forced me to speak and you must not blame me for the trouble that you have now brought upon the world. You shall now die because I am about to answer you. There is a spring near the path that leads from this lodge into the deep forest. I have never let you go there because in that spring is a terrible monster that is filled with great magic. His orenda

---
1   Related by Edward Cornplanter.
2   Or, a burning brand from the fireplace.

(magical potence) is more powerful than anything else in the world. If you go far from this lodge the beast will reach out with his long claws and devour you. You have never been allowed to stray from the doorway because of this. But now that you know this circumstance you must learn to use a bow and arrow. You must become a hunter, for what I have told you has made me very old and I shall soon be unable to hunt."

The old man, looking more ugly than ever, went to his hunting pouch and took out a small bow and a quiver of arrows. "Now, take these, my grandson. Go and hunt. Find your first prey on a tree."

Gajihsondis went out of the lodge very happy. "I am now a hunter," thought he. "I shall soon bring in all the meat." He watched carefully for signs of game. Then he spied what he thought a great bird upon the trunk of a tree. He lifted up his bow and shot but missed his quarry. Thereupon he ran back to the lodge and cried: "Oh grandfather, I have been unable to kill my prey." Then he wept with disappointment.

"I thought you would fail," said the grandfather. "You have never had practice. I will hang up the foot of a raccoon and you must shoot this wherever I hang it. When you hit it every time without missing once you may go on a hunt again." He then hung the coon's foot by a cord to the roof-pole and allowed it to dangle over the fire. "I am going on a hunt now but it will be my last. If you are unable to hit the raccoon's foot by the time I return we are lost."

Thereupon the grandfather took his hunting equipment and departed. This gave Gajihsondis his chance. After many failures he hit the foot and when he became proficient he tried other things.

After many days the grandfather returned. "We are lost now," said he. "The beast is coming to devour us.

Only four days remain for us to live. "I'll shoot it," exclaimed Gajihsondis. "I am a good marksman now!"

The old man laughed. "Oh no," said he. "I gave you an arrow that can never hit its mark. You cannot shoot." "But my grandfather," contradicted the boy, "I never miss the mark." The granfather grounted, "Wha-a-a-ah."

Gajihsondis then shot the raccoon's foot. This made the old man look up. "It is only a chance," he said. "You had power with you but for a moment. Never more can you do it. I will place the foot elsewhere. Thereupon he threw it to the top of a tall tree. "Now you cannot hit it," he said.

Gajihsondis took easy aim and hit the foot knocking it from its hanging to another tree much higher and with a second arrow he knocked it again, bringing it to the ground.

Instead of being pleased the old man was very angry and said: "Who has been here to guide you? There is some evil thing lurking about. Well, never mind this, you can not kill real game. You have no arrows to hit anything."

Gajihsondis then went out and saw the bird he first had aimed at. Again he shot, and killed it this time. Taking it up he ran in great glee to his grandfather. "Oh contempt!" exclaimed the old man. "You have killed nothing but a chickadee." But even so, the old man worried, for he knew that his grandson had killed the first creature which by custom a child is permitted to kill when he learns to hunt.

Again the boy went out and soon returned with a raccoon. It was a fine fat animal and made a good meal for the two, but the grandfather ridiculed the boy and said it was only temporary luck, for the boy possessed no orenda (magical power). Again the boy tried his skill and killed a fine turkey which the old man dressed and cooked, at the same time sneering as before. On his fourth excursion Gajihsondis killed a deer and brought it in. This time the old man angrily exclaimed, "It is not right that you should become proficient as a hunter but it seems that you have. Oh now we shall all die for you will consider yourself able to leave this lodge and to follow the path."

Now, this is just what Gajihsondis wanted to do. He had only one desire,—to overcome the monster that barred him from his father and mother. "Now I am going," said he, without further ado. "I shall slay the monster."

The old man scolded and wept, but Gajihsondis was soon out of sight down the well-beaten path that led from the lodge into the deep forest. After a day's journey he found a gigantic frog crying out terrible threats. "Whoso comes near this spring," he croaked, "shall die. I eat whoever comes near this spring."

Gajihsondis was not a bit frightened; he simply drew his bow and shot the frog, and though it was larger than he, he tied its feet together and hung it to his carrying frame and returned to his grandfather's lodge. The old man was very angry but the boy only laughed. Now he had learned a new trick, that of laughing. He had never done this before and to have him laugh made his grandfather even more angry.

The grandson went out a second time and found a gigantic duck guarding the spring. It cried out threats and proclaimed its great power. This did not daunt Gajihsondis who merely fixed his bow and shot it. Again he returned to his grandfather who became even more angry. "How could you do this?" he asked. "By magic the path was changed, but you found the spring again. You shall not find it again."

For a third time the boy went out on his hunt for the spring and easily found it, for as plain as day he could see a path leading directly to it. (Now this was strange for it was not a path that ordinary eyes could see, which made the grandfather believe that it could not be discovered.) When he neared the spring he heard the cries of a great beaver threatening to gnaw anyone in twain who approached the pool. It was a very terrifying beaver but

Gajihsondis found it an easy mark for his arrows. He laughed as he trussed it in his carrying frame and laughed as three days later he flung it down at his grandfather's doorway. The old man roused himself in furious anger and flung his "bundles"[3] in the fire. He pawed the earth like a beast and shouted until his throat bled, but Gajihsondis only laughed again and went away, saying, "Oh it is very easy!"

Now when he went down the path Gajihsondis knew that it had been changed. First he had gone north, then west, then south, and now he was going east over the path, that while invisible to common eyes, was visible to him, yet he did not know how he could see it. For if he tried to look he could see nothing, and when he did not try he could see everything. He also knew something that he would not tell.

For a fourth time he drew near to the mysterious pool. It was most beautiful and the trees about it were very tall. There were rocks looking like enchanted beasts asleep about it. The water, itself, was very clear and sparkled as if the sun were upon it, even when it was night. Gajihsondis went right up to the spring and flung in a fishing-line. In an instant he had a bite and some terrifying thing began to pull him into the water, but though he was sore pressed and saw himself falling over the edge of the pool he laughed, and when he did he gave a great pull, staggered backward, and pulled out a lizard four times his own length. It was the blue Dagwĕⁿ'nigoⁿ'ge. Though he had hooked it the creature was not dead, but as Gajihsondis looked at it, it sprang toward him with a cry and bit off both his legs. This made Gajihsondis laugh with all his might and he laughed so hard that the beast grew weak. The creature then despairing of killing the boy stabbed him in the breast with its tail, crying, "Put me back in the spring."

Again the boy laughed. "Oh how can I put you back in

---

[3] His charm bundles, because he believed them to have lost potency.

the spring," said he, "seeing that I have no legs wherewith to walk? Replace my legs and I will put you back." Then he laughed again.

Now the lizard was a creature of great magic and it conjured a man and a woman who came forth from the water and made Gajihsondis's legs whole again and smoothed up the wound where the incision had been. The boy laughed and instead of thanking them caught them with his fish line and cut off the heads of each. "I know you," said he. "You are the evil servants of Lizard." So saying he cast them in a fire and burned them to ashes. When the heads were consumed they burst with a loud explosion and out flew a great flock of screech-owls. He then threw the lizard back into the pool, saying, "I despise you for your lack of magic."

Laughing as he went, Gajihsondis followed the path until he came to a clearing. Though he greatly wondered what was in the clearing, for he heard human voices, he could not proceed, for there, hovering over the path, were many white owls, screaming at him and swooping down to pluck out his eyes.

Gajihsondis now thought of a plan to overcome the owls. It seems best to be truthful, he thought, and so he determined what to say. So he called out, "I claim this land. It is mine and I shall possess it, but I am willing to make one of you owls chief with me." The owls then began to quarrel among themselves as to who would be chief. They made a great noise and soon had clawed each other to death. None remained to rule with Gajihsondis, so he went forward. As he proceeded he found that the path had changed and that instead of entering the clearing from the north he was entering from the west. Soon he paused for the path was guarded by powerful panthers.

Again he resolved to declare his intentions. "I claim this land," he cried. "It is mine, I shall possess it, but am willing to make one of you panthers chief to govern with me." The two panthers then began to quarrel and soon were engaged in murderous combat. In a few moments both were dead. Gajihsondis then went on, but noticed that the path had changed and that he was entering the clearing from the south.

He paused as he was about to enter the clearing for there, guarding the path with lowered antlers, were two elk. He saluted them calling out, "This is my land. I shall possess it, but I shall make one of you chief to help me govern." As before, the creatures fought themselves to death, each one desiring to be chief. Gajihsondis then journeyed on, finding as before that the path had changed. This time he approached from the east.

As he was about to enter the clearing two enormous serpents rose up and hissed at him. As before he loudly proclaimed: "I claim this land. It is mine and I shall possess it, but I am willing to make one of you rattlesnakes chief with me." Then did the great serpents begin to fight and after a fierce struggle both bit one another and both died.

Gajihsondis strode on into the clearing and found a great lodge within. It was strongly built and large enough to hold a great company of people. Entering the lodge, he found an old man cooking corn mush. The old man said nothing until the food was cooked when he said, "Come eat; it is ready." The two finished the meal for Gajihsondis was very hungry and was especially fond of corn pudding. "We will now sleep here," said the old man pointing to mats on the floor.

Both lay down on the mats instead of upon the long shelf-like beds that were on either side of the lodge. As the old man lay down with all his clothing, his pouch leaped from him and went to a peg on the center pole; his leggings drew from him and rolled up in a corner; his moccasins leaped to a bench, and his breech-cloth came off and hung itself over a pole. Then all the supper dishes leaped about, the pot emptying itself and then jumping to the upper shelf of the lodge. After a while the old man went to sleep, and as he did a white deer emerged from his breast, leaped into the air and sailed away through the smoke hole. Gajihsondis watched far into the night. He could not sleep for the utensils in the lodge moved about and talked to each other.

Gajihsondis conceived the idea of robbing the house of its magical objects and finally decided it might be better to escape without a burden. Carefully he crawled out from his skin coverings and made haste to withdraw. He did this with entire success, and ran a long way into the night. Soon, however, he saw a white deer dart down from the sky and enter the smoke-hole of the lodge. He knew then that the old man would awake and pursue him. Nor was he mistaken, for soon he could hear the old man running after him. On and on he came until when just behind Gajihsondis he waved his war club and struck the boy on the head.

"I have killed another," shrieked the old man, as he sawed a knick in his war club with his flint knife. "No man escapes me."

The old man then went about the forest and restored all the animals slain or dead through the craft of Gajihsondis. At length he found the lizard in the pool and told it all concerning his work of restoration. "It must be Gajihsondis who has done all this," said the lizard after he had been restored to his own magical power. "Only Gajihsondis could have slain all these helpers. I greatly fear that he has acquired sufficient magic to slay us all."

"But I have slain him and he will trouble us no more," said the old man.

"Oh, no," replied the lizard. "Gajihsondis will revive. Then let us beware."

The old man returned to his lodge and passed the body of Gajihsondis and to his great satisfaction saw the great crows picking at it. "He is dead," he thought, and went straightway to sleep.

The boy soon recovered consciousness and, completely restored, he crept into the old man's lodge. "I will now be truthful," he thought. "I will address the war club."

"War club," he commanded. "Stand up," and the club stood erect. "Now war club, in you is power. I want you to be my friend and assist me in slaying my enemy. I am a man and will not be denied."

The war club then pointed to a bed far away from the door and Gajihsondis went to the bed and saw a pile of soft tanned pelts. Removing these he saw a sleeping maiden. He took a brand from the fire and held it over the girl. "I have now come for you,' he said. "I am going to rob this house and take you with me. This is my land and I shall rule it." The girl looked at Gajihsondis and was pleased. She liked the looks of Gajihsondis. "I will go," she said, "but first you must slay my uncle. It is because he fears you will find me that we are all bewitched."

The boy then went over to the old man and awakened him. His clothing flew upon him, a white deer entered his body and then he sat up. "What do you want?" he inquired.

"I want to fight with you," said Gajihsondis.

"Now just wait," said the old man. "I must get my war paint ready." So saying he threw charcoal from the fire in the corn mortar and made a black paste. Then he took red paint from a box. He applied black to one side of his face and red to the other.

"Now I am ready," he announced. "Why do you wish to fight me?"

"I want all your things and I am going to take your niece," said the boy.

At this the old man became very angry and whooped. He then sang a magic song and grasped his war club, and rushed upon Gajihsondis. The young man grasped his war club and then the two began to fight. In a short time the old man was overcome and exhausted. Gajihsondis bound up the old man and put him in his carrying frame. Then he took the girl by the hand and led her away to his own lodge.

Reaching his grandfather's lodge he noticed for the first time that it was identical with the one in which he had had his fight. His grandfather and the old man looked the same. There was no difference.

When the old man, his grandfather, saw that Gajihsondis had brought home the old man bound and also the girl, he was very angry but said nothing. He made up his mind to kill the boy and to marry the girl. Now when the boy slept and the girl had crawled into her robes afar from the door, the old man grasped his war club and sang to it. Now the prisoner sat up and did likewise, and both did exactly as the other did. "I will kill the boy now," said the old man, and so saying, he shot three arrows into his back.

In a short time the boy awakened, being in great pain. He arose and went out of the lodge. Near the creek he found a sweat lodge and as he stood near it a voice spoke: "Go in," it said. "I will help you." He looked and there saw another person exactly like himself, only very white and clear. "I have always known you were my friend," said Gajihsondis. "But this time I see you."

Gajihsondis went into the lodge and took a sweat, and when the arrows had come out he took an emetic. After a while he saw clearly in the dark. He saw his friend walk toward him and enter his body. The two became one. "This is the power that has guided me," he thought. "But I will never tell anyone I have seen him, until the day I am about to die."

Thereupon he returned to the lodge and awoke his grandfather. "Come and fight me, grandfather," he exclaimed. "I believe that you have done me a great wrong."

The old man sprang from his bed and as he did so the prisoner became as a mist and floated into him. Then the grandfather grasped his war club but it was no longer strong like good hickory, but soft like wet rawhide. He could not fight.

He began to whimper. "Oh, my grandson," he moaned. "Do not kill your granfather. My strength is gone. I will confess. I have been a great wizard and have created many evil monsters and slain many people by magic. Now I am undone. Oh restore my nature and make me human again. Do not kill me."

"Then tell me everything," demanded Gajihsondis, and the old man told him of his conjuring. The girl, he said, was fore-ordained as Gajihsondis' wife, his parents were in the ground back of the lodge in the clearing. He had exercised his magic in order to claim the girl. He and the old man in the house in the clearing were one and the same person, though dual by magic. The path was well trodden because he had traveled over it so many times.

"I must now go out and kill all the monsters," said Gajihsondis. He did so and killed all the magically evil creatures. He dug up the ground back of the lodge in the clearing and there found a bark house hidden by the roots of the trees. There he found his mother, his father and his sister. All were very happy that Gajihsondis had released them and together they made their journey back to the grandfather's lodge. When he saw them returning he died and turned into a shriveled human skin. This Gajihsondis rolled into a bundle and hid it in the rafters. Then he called to the girl and she came out of the blankets from the bed at the far side of the lodge. She was a beautiful young woman and dressed in fine garments.

"Who is this?" askekd Gajihsondis's father and mother.

"This is my wife," he replied. "We shall all live in a new house."

So he took them all away and he showed them a new lodge of bark he had built. So this is the story of Gajihsondis.

GENERAL NOTES—The introductory paragraph of this legend is not a part of the story but is the answer which Cornplanter gave me in response to my inquiry how it happened that so many stories began with a recital of unnatural conditions.

There are interesting allusions in this tale, and many of them are characteristic. These include the theme of the orphaned boy living with an uncle or grandfather, cruel beatings or punishment by fire, living in the ground, the boy suddenly becoming self-confident through the reception of orenda or magical power, overcoming all obstacles and destroying the source of evil enchantment.

There are other elements, which while characteristic in a measure, are so striking as to be worthy of comment. In this story the cycle of *four attempts* emphasizes the importance of the number four in Seneca folk-thought. Gajihsondis kills four animals in his attempts to learn to become a hunter, he overcomes four beasts at the spring, he finds four paths, each in one of the prime cardinal directions, he overcomes four magical guards of the trail. When he finally enters the clearing and discovers the bark lodge he discovers a new obstacle.

The unusual elements now follow. These are the discovery that the lodge in the clearing is after all only a replica of the one in which his grandfather and he had lived together (although the story does not at first make this clear) ; the strange conception of clothing flying from the body of the wearer, completely undressing him, and returning to him when he awakens ; the idea of the man's name-genius (the white deer), leaving his body when he sleeps, the talking war club (which seems somewhat symbolic), and finally the concept of a double personality, one portion or unit being unseen. Gajihsondis had a soul-self which materialized and guarded his life, gave him information and pointed out his means of restoration. The grandfather also had a double in the person of the evil wizard in the identical lodge.

This legend has another element which seems quite unique ; it is the power of laughter over wizardry. Gajihsondis had only to laugh at a monster to overcome it, though he did not always do this.

I cannot help but feel that in the form here presented this tale of the occult and mysterious is only a portion of a fuller story, the details of which are only partially developed in this version. This comment may apply to many of the legends, for inquiry about certain points always brings forth additional information and frequently other episodes.

TALES OF LOVE AND MARRIAGE

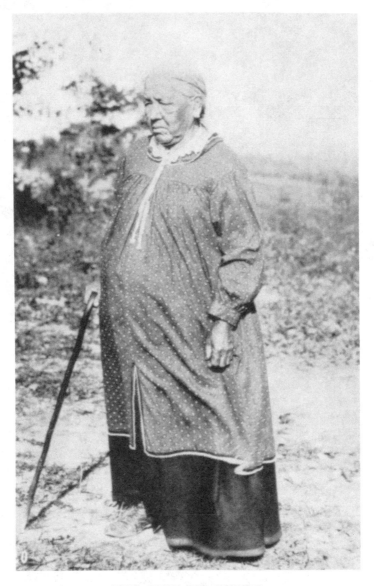

MRS. JOHN BIG KITTLE.

Chief matron of the Cattaraugus Seneca Wolf Clan. Mrs. Kittle was born on Buffalo Creek Reservation in 1822.

Photo by E. C. Winnegar.

VI

21. TWO FEATHERS AND TURKEY BROTHER

Long ago a whole tribe had been exterminated by powerful sorcerers. Of all the tribe only three persons remained. These were an old uncle and his two nephews, one very young and the other on the borderline of manhood.

The older boy was known as Two Feathers (Doä'danē'gĕⁿ'), and the younger received the name Turkey (Osoon), because he wore a robe made of a turkey skin. It was a magic skin and the little fellow was able to fly to the tops of trees, which gave him great pleasure.

There came a time when the uncle after watching the older nephew for some days, said, "My nephew it is my opinion that you should prepare yourself for your manhood. It is customary to depart from your abode and fast until your protecting friends appear unto you. Go forth to the river and build a sweat lodge, and when you have purified yourself, await the coming of your protectors."

In obedience to his uncle's directions Two Feathers departed and built himself a sweat lodge where he purified himself and fasted. On the tenth day he saw a great spider dropping down from the tops of the trees, and it spoke to him saying, "When you are in great distress I will be your protector." Again he saw a great black snake rising from the ground and when it had reached the tops of the trees it spoke saying, "When you are in great distress and need a strong friend, I will be your protector."

When Two Feathers returned to his uncle's lodge he was a man and he knew that unseen powers were his friends. His uncle looked at him carefully and said, "My nephew, it is my opinion that you have become a man. Now it is customary for a man to seek a wife. It would make our lodge pleasant to have a young woman cook for us. Now, far away from here in a country to the east is a great man who has two daughters. It is my wish that you prepare for the journey and bring back a wife. It will take you several years,—how many I do not know."

Two Feathers prepared for his journey and as he made his weapons his uncle watched him. "Come here," said the uncle. "I would like to inspect your clothing." So saying he looked at his nephew and then told him to disrobe. "You are not in the condition to make a woman receive you," he said. "I will find a better costume for you."

Opening his treasure chest, which he kept under his bed, the old man took out a fine fur robe made of raccoon skin. It was most beautiful and the fur was long and glossy. "Put this on, my nephew," he said. Two Feathers donned the new costume and advanced for inspection. The uncle looked at him to discern any imperfection. This robe is not good enough," he said. "You are still not in condition to seek your wife. Disrobe and I will seek further among my treasures."

The uncle now drew forth a robe of wildcat skin. It had short hair and was made so that it hung down like a long shirt with many tails. There were ears sewed around the neck and there were eyes on the sleeves. After looking at this shirt for a moment, the old man said, "Now, my nephew, this is a very old shirt and the wearer becomes very powerful in magic. It has eyes and ears and will guard the wearer when he sleeps. Put it on and let me see how you look."

Two Feathers put on the shirt which just fitted him. It was very fine and he greatly admired it and wished to keep it as his shirt. The Uncle, however, surveyed it with a critical eye. Finally he said, "This shirt is not good enough. You are still in no condition to seek a wife and to overcome all the obstacles that lie in your trail from this lodge to

where she resides. Disrobe, I must find something different."

This time Two Feathers disrobed with reluctance. He
wanted to keep that beautiful shirt. But as he watched his
uncle he saw that another fine outfit was forthcoming. At
the bottom of the treasure chest was a bundle done up in a
deer skin folded into a case. This was opened and the uncle
took out a panther-skin shirt, a pair of leggings, a pair of
moccasins, a bow and quiver, a fisher skin pocket (pouch),
a warclub and a pipe. "Now put these things on, my
nephew," said the uncle.

Two Feathers dressed and found that the panther shirt
had the head of the panther as a cap and that the cap had
two heron feathers above it. The whole costume was wonderful to see and Two Feathers now felt that there could
be none better in all the world.

"Now, my nephew," said the uncle. "I will show you
what can be done with your clothing and accoutrements.
The heron feathers on your hood will watch out for you
and when you are in danger they will speak. Your fisher
skin bag is alive and should anyone seek to harm you when
asleep it will bite him. Your pipe and medicine root are in
the bag. The medicine will give you power to spit wampum.
The black end of the root will make dark wampum and the
white end will make white wampum. Your pipe has the
head of a bear upon it and it will growl when an enemy
touches it, while the snakes on the bowl will hiss when you
light your tobacco. Your bow looks old and useless, but
it is filled with powerful magic and will guide your arrows
straight."

The uncle continued his instructions. "Now as you
journey from here you will find three enchanted spots, and
all must be avoided. You will pass a certain tree where
there will be a boy playing about. He will ask you to lift
him from the ground and place him in the long branch
where he would like to swing up and down. Do not touch

the boy for a sorcerer lives in the tree and when you lift up the boy the sorcerer will grasp you by the hair and tie you to his arrow and shoot you far away, and you will fall through the smoke hole of a witch's lodge and will be eaten by her. She is the sorcerer's wife. Further along the trail is a deep spring where there is sparkling water. Oh nephew, do not drink this water for there are monsters living in it who will draw you in and drown you. Further along and near the settlement where you are to go is a grove of very tall trees. Here you will see an old man who will hop around strangely. He will ask you to shoot a raccoon. Oh my nephew, do not pay any attention to him. He will be the cause of your ruin if you heed his pleas."

Two Feathers now understood how to proceed and was about to start when Turkey, his younger brother, began to cry that he also wanted to go. Neither the uncle nor Two Feathers could dissuade him, and so he, too, made ready for departure.

Off they went on the journey. Turkey flew ahead in short flights and called back from the tree tops the condition of the trail, for it was very early in the morning and it was still quite dark. Very rapidly they traveled, until by noon they had traveled a distance that takes ordinary people three years to go. This was because Turkey flew and Two Feathers wore magic moccasins which made him take very long strides. They now saw a trail lodge and sat down to rest. Soon they espied a small boy playing about a large oak. As he played he came nearer in a friendly manner and asked to be placed in the long branch of the tree that he might swing up and down. Two Feathers placed the boy on a stump and put this under the tree. As he did this there was a great roar as if the wind were moving through the forest, and two gigantic arms came down and grabbed the stump, at the same time fixing it to the tip of a large arrow, and soon the stump flew through the air and into the witch's lodge and knocked her into the fire.

Two Feathers and Turkey now went on their journey and in a short time came to a clearing where there was a fine spring of bubbling water continually outflowing. "Oh brother, do not drink," said Turkey. "Remember what our uncle told us." Two Feathers went on, but being very thirsty turned back and knelt by the spring to drink. As he leaned over a horrible creature leaped from the water and endeavored to pull him in. Two Feathers gave a pull and jumped back, throwing the monster into the clearing. "Oh put me back," it cried. Two Feathers asked Turkey to watch it, then he went back to the spring to drink, but as he did so another monster covered with hair leaped at him and hung onto his head. Two Feathers pulled again and dragged the monster out, placing it in the care of Turkey. A third time this was repeated, after which both boys drank from the spring. The clearing was a spot where had once been a prosperous village, but sorcerers had poisoned the spring and killed all the people by dragging them into the depths of the water.

Two Feathers and Turkey made a fire and burned the monsters, and their heads bursting with shrieks, there flew away a flock of screech-owls.

The journey continued until it was near sunset. The boys sat down again and soon observed that they were in a grove of very tall trees. Presently they noticed an old man dancing about and shouting, "Hai', hai', hai', hai'." In a moment he approached and said, "Oh my nephews, there is a raccoon on that branch and I have no bow or arrow. I wish you would shoot it for me."

Two Feathers would not listen to Turkey, who flew about gobbling, in order to draw his attention to the warning their uncle had given.

"Most truly, my uncle," said Two Feathers. "I will shoot that raccoon for you. It is a very easy matter." So saying, he took out an arrow, strung his bow and shot.

"Hiñg," went the arrow and hit the raccoon, piercing its heart.

Now in an altogether unexpected way the raccoon ran from the limb to the trunk of the tree and down a large hole at the top where the tree was broken off.

"Oh my nephew," cried the old man in distress. "I am too old and weak from lack of food to climb after the raccoon, which has gone into its hole to die. Oh my nephew, climb after it for me."

"That will be easy uncle," said Two Feathers. "I will climb now."

"Oh no, no, no! Do not spoil your clothing which I see is very nice. Take it off beneath the tree and I will watch it for you." So Two Feathers took off all his clothing and climbed the tree.

Up he went like a squirrel and soon was at the top, but as he stood looking down into the hole he heard a noise behind him and caught a glimpse of the old man who shoved him into the hole. Down went Two Feathers into the hollow of the tree, and down into a pit beneath the roots where he smelt the flesh of victims and felt their bones beneath his feet. He knew that he had been trapped. Outside he could hear Turkey calling with a gobbling call, and he knew that something evil was in progress.

The old man descended the tree by a route known to himself by long familiarity, and then he went to the clothing which Two Feathers had left behind. "I have been looking for nephew's clothing for I expected that he would pass this way. Now I shall be able to cross the river and take the great man's daughter as my wife. Now I shall possess great magical power."

Off went the old man, looking renewed in body and becoming more and more handsome with every step. Soon he reached the river and standing upon the bank he gave a loud clear call that could be heard for a long ways. On the other side of the river was a long house and the voice penetrated it.. The elder of two sisters, ran out and taking her canoe paddled it across the stream.

When the imposter was in the canoe he said, "I have come a long ways to reach this place. I am a great hunter and am looking for a wife."

"I think I would like to have you for my husband," said the girl. "I will take you to our lodge and show you where we live."

When the imposter came to the lodge he met the chief, and said he had come as a son-in-law. "You will do," said the Chief. "Go in and see where we live."

Going into the lodge the Chief's wife gave him food and then the young woman showed him her bed. It was a fine bed wtih many soft robes of skin and a curtain made of fox skins sewed together. "Here is where you will lodge, as my husband," said the girl. So that night Imposter ate wedding bread and was married.

When Two Feathers awoke the next morning he was very sick and could scarcely stand. His bed had been a place of filth and terror. His head felt light and he could see lights before his eyes. He began to think how he might escape, and then remembered that he had dreamed of the spider. "Come, my friend Spider," he called, "release me, for you promised to be my protector."

In a moment a great spider appeared above the opening and let down a braided strand of web. Two Feathers grasped it and was drawn up nearly to the top, when the web broke and he fell into the tree. He was greatly disappointed, but determined to call upon the black snake. "Come, my friend Black Snake," he called, "release me, for you promised to deliver me from trouble." In another moment a great serpent had climbed the tree and let down its tail, which coiled about Two Feathers and drew him forth. It then vanished.

Turkey was happpy to see his brother and helped him put on the dirty clothing left by the old man. Two Feathers

dressed with great difficulty and when he had put on the
stiff worn-out moccasins and scabby looking cap, he looked
like a very old man who was very sick. Slowly Turkey and
he walked down the trail to the river. At length they
reached the bank, and Two Feathers called, but his voice
was so weak it could not be heard. It was like a whisper.
Turkey then called and when he did so a young woman
went down to the river and leaped in a canoe. Imposter
saw her. "O do not go across," he said. "It is only a dirty
old man with a turkey."

The young woman did not like Imposter, and gave him
no heed. Across the river she went and took Two Feathers
and Turkey in her canoe. When they were part way over
the river Two Feathers said, "I have come a long ways to
this place. My name is Two Feathers and I am a young
man seeking a wife."

"It is apparent that you are an old man," said the girl.
"I am the only girl whom you can marry, but how can you
who look so old and filthy expect to secure a wife?"

"I met with trouble as I approached the river," answered
Two Feathers. "I helped an old man who wanted me to
kill a raccoon but it was only a wizardly creation of his and
he required that I should take off my clothing and climb
after it. I removed my clothing, which had great power,
and climbed the tree. When I was looking into the hole
he pushed me in, and there were bones beneath."

"Alas," said the girl, "I am of the opinion that my
brothers are among the victims."

When they landed on the opposite side, the girl led the
lame old man to the lodge and told him to look in. "I have
brought my husband," said she. Thereupon Imposter spoke
to the Chief and asked if he would allow his daughter to
marry a diseased old man. The Chief looked at Two
Feathers and answered, "I am of the opinion that my
daughter knows her own mind in this matter."

So the girl took Two Feathers into the lodge and showed

him her bed. It was a most beautiful bed and its robes
were of the softest doe skin, with a mattress of deer hair
beneath. The walls and top were covered with porcupine
quill embroidery like a box, and the curtain was of martin
skins sewed together, and the apartment had sweet herbs
hung within, to make it pleasant. The platform over the
bed was arranged as a sleeping place for Turkey.

At supper Two Feathers ate marriage bread, but nobody spoke to him but his wife, for he was not attractive
in appearance and added nothing to the strength of the
lodge, only providing another mouth to feed, when famine
was almost upon them. When all had eaten Imposter took
off his pouch of fisher skin and said that he would now
smoke. He placed his hand in the mouth to reach for
the pipe, and gave a wild cry, for the fisher bit his wrist
and caused him great pain. In dropping the bag the magic
medicine fell out, and being only like a withered root it was
not noticed, so Two Feathers grabbed it and hid it in his
bosom.

The time for sleep came and all retired. Imposter would
not lay off his garments, much to the disgust of his wife.
He was afraid that Two Feathers would steal them, and he
knew that though he slept Turkey was watching.

Many days passed and Two Feathers looked more sick
than ever, while Imposter grew more bold. Yet he never
went on a hunt for he had no bow and arrows; these he had
failed to pick up from Two Feather's outfit, for they had
looked so old and ill made. One night Two Feathers told
his wife that he must have a large bowl when he awoke,
for he had eaten an herb. So the next morning he called
for the bark bowl, and taking it opened his mouth and blew
into it, filling it with dark wampum, to the brim. "Present
this to your father," said Two Feathers, and the young
woman did so to the great delight of the old man, who
said, "Ah, I knew that he was a great man."

Now when Imposter saw what had been done he felt

that he had lost favor, so he asked his wife for a bowl and taking an emetic filled the bowl with all manner of foul lizards, toads and worms that he had eaten. Ordering his wife to take this to the Chief, he strutted about proudly. When the Chief saw the malodorous mess he roared in great anger and drove his son-in-law from the lodge.

The next night Two Feathers ate of the root again and called for the bowl. This time he filled it with white wampum to the delight and gratification of the Chief, who again said, "I am of the opinion that we entertain a great man." Imposter tried to imitate Two Feathers once more but only produced little round worms that so fouled the bark bowl that the Chief ordered the wife to scrub it all day to clean it.

That night there was a great feast and Imposter ate so much that he was forced to remove his clothing, and he was so sleepy that he threw it at the foot of the bed and on the floor. Long he slept, and failed to awaken in the morning. Two Feathers was up very early and before anyone else. He took his bow and magic arrows and killed a great quantity of deer which he dragged to the lodge. Then he took his own fine clothing, which had become frayed and soiled and put it on. Immediately it became bright and new. Two Feathers also began to grow more and more youthful until he entirely recovered. His wife was very happy. The Chief, moreover, was glad and called all the people to a council.

Two Feathers was the central figure in this council and exhibited the powers of his costume. He pointed his pouch toward a woman and she fell down dead; he sprinkled her with medicine and she rose to her feet. He smoked his pipe and the bear upon it blinked its eyes and opened its mouth, while the snakes on the stem wriggled as if alive. The eyes of the panther hood glowed and the feathers spoke. Then again Two Feathers made wampum. Everybody was satisfied, most of all the Chief and his daughter.

After a while Imposter awoke and found his wife looking at him in disgust. "You are a filthy old man," she said. "I will have no more to do with you." She kicked him out of bed and made him put on his old clothes. "You lied to me," she said and led him to a hole where the women customarily threw their garbage and thrust him in. Then she went away from him and nobody ever saw him again.

The Chief then said that it was his wish that all the people follow Two Feathers back to his home, for he was a great man and had slain all the wizards and monsters that infested the path. So they went and it took them a good many years to return. Turkey was now a man and took off his turkey clothes and dressed like a warrior. He, too, found a good-looking girl and married her.

After a long time the people all came to the uncle's lodge and he was a very old man. Two Feathers told what he had done and the uncle was happy. He now had women to cook for him, and he felt that the world was rid of sorcerers. Then the old lodge was repaired and all the people dwelt there, and if you can find it you will find the people dwelling there to this day.

22. TWO FEATHERS AND WOODCHUCK LEGGINGS.[1]

Now this is a Two Feathers story. All the old people of the old time knew about this; and it happened a long time ago.

Do'cioweⁿ' was the place where they lived,—an old uncle and his nephew. The young man was called Two Feathers and the uncle was known by name as Woodchuck Leggings.

Two Feathers was a hunter and never feared to hunt any animal, but he was kind to the animals and could talk to them, so they became his friends. He had a pet bear in a small yard and he had a wolf that he had tamed. He said that it was the same as a man.

Now you ought to know that he had fine clothes. They were made of white buckskin and embroidered all over with porcupine quills. He had also a tobacco pouch made of a spotted fawn's skin with the feet and head on and in this he kept a pipe having a bear's head carved on it, and eyes that rolled when the jaws of the bear chewed the tobacco inside. He had a gŭstoñ'we' (feathered hat), with two feathers in front, and on the hat there were two chirping birds.

Two Feathers acquired magic and became very strong, but he did not let anyone know that he was Hotci'noⁿ'ga', (a charm holder).

One day when Two Feathers was hunting in the woods he saw an old bark house. Cautiously approaching it he found an old man inside; though at first he thought it was a wolf. The old man was very hungry and so Two Feathers gave him meat to eat. "I have been looking for you a long time," said the old man. "You have been merciful to me and I am going to give you my arrow. It does not look

1   Related by George D. Jimerson (Tahadondeh), 1903.

like a good arrow, but most truly it has great power." So saying he drew forth from a bundle in which he kept many kinds of war charms, an arrow and handed it to Two Feathers. Two Feathers was glad and leaving the old man some dried meat, departed.

After a while he came to another village across a river where he slept overnight. He noticed two girls, one older and one younger, named Drooping Flower. He looked at the younger girl and she looked at him, and something went out of his eyes into her eyes, and something went out of her eyes into his. He said to himself, "That's the one." One of the villagers saw this and told Two Feathers that he was now under the spell of a very evil witch, the mother of the girl.

After a time Two Feathers saw the girl again and said to her, "I am coming for you by and by." Then he went home to his uncle who all this time had been living on woodchuck meat, because he was an unskillful hunter. The old man was angry at Two Feathers for his long absence, and upbraided him.

After a time a runner came to the village near which Two Feathers and his uncle dwelt. He called the people together and told them that all the people in the valley across the river were starving. Hunters had been unable to secure game and the corn harvest had failed.

Now Woodchuck Leggings thought this a good time to find a wife, who weakened with famine, he could overcome and drag back to his lodge. Two Feathers thought about the young girl whose eyes' light had gone into his own. He thus prepared to take the trail along a creek having rapids and falls, and to go by a short but difficult route. Off he went in great haste, taking all his bundles and charms with him. Woodchuck Leggings noticed this and was angry for he had resolved to steal them when he had an opportunity. He now resolved to follow his nephew and slay him if he could.

When Two Feathers reached the valley village he found
the people starving. Drooping Flower was too weak to
stand up. Two Feathers now asked all the women who
could to gather about their doorways and play the plum-
stone game and to sing:

"Ganio daweeni, the game is coming."

He then went into the woods at the edge of the clearing
and sang a magic song, at the same time taking out four
arrows which had lain close to the arrow the old man had
given him.

One by one he shot the arrows into the air, each in a
different direction, at the same time calling, "Bring me meat
from different animals."

Returning to the lodge of Drooping Flower he sat in the
doorway and waited. Soon high overhead he heard a song.
The people rushed out of doors and listened, and sure
enough, there was a song in the air. The words were: "The
wild animals are coming." In a moment the song had
reached the ground and four animals came running to the
doorway where Two Feathers sat waiting. Each animal
had an arrow sticking in its heart. On they came to the lodge
and then dropped dead at Two Feathers' feet. There was
a deer, a moose, an elk and a bear.

The starving village then had food and Drooping Flower
recovered. Then a council was called and all the people sat
around to see Two Feathers, who sat in the middle of the
hall on a bench. He took from his pouch his bear-bowled
pipe and put a pinch of tobacco into it.

"My friends and cousins," he said. "I must have an
ember for my pipe. How shall I get it? Ho yo ho! Fly
birds, fly!" As he spoke the chipping-birds on his hat began
to flutter and then to fly. They flew to the fire and took
coals from it which they placed in his pipe, after which the
birds sat on his hat. Oh the fragrance of the smoke was
pleasing, and the bear on the bowl rolled its eyes and chewed
the tobacco. "Oh you like my tobacco?" asked Two Feath-

ers. "So does my pouch. Dance pouch, dance!" What was happening? The spotted pouch detached itself from his belt and scampered over the floor a living fawn. Then he called it back to its strap.

"It is now getting late," observed Two Feathers. "Now bring me a good deer-skin, well tanned. I will give all of you good presents." Drooping Flower brought a skin and placed it before him. He began, then, to make a noise like "*tsŭt, tsŭt, tsŭt*." Opening his mouth wide he blew out a great stream of wampum beads. Immediately there was a scramble for the beads and nearly everybody grabbed a handful.

As Two Feathers left the house he saw the jealous, blazing eyes of his uncle, Woodchuck Leggings. The old man had never dreamed that his nephew had powers like these. He then began to spread mischief by saying that Two Feathers was an evil sorcerer and that he would soon become Oñgwe Iās and eat up everybody.

Now Drooping Flower's mother was a witch and hated anybody with power. So she called Woodchuck Leggings and talked to him. He told her how to proceed to overcome Two Feathers.

That night Two Feathers and Woodchuck Leggings slept on one side of the witch's lodge. Midnight came and the old woman began to have a bad dream. She began to throw fire upon Two Feathers but the chipping-birds chirped so loudly they awakened him, and he saw the old woman on her knees at the fire grunting, as if in a dream, "ĕⁿ', ĕⁿ', ĕⁿ'!" Leaping up he hit her with a corn pounder, exclaiming, "What is it, my aunt?" Pretending to awaken she answered, "It is now finished. . I have had a dream and must be satisfied. Oh I must have the antlers of two large buck elk that live in a cold lake. I must have them by morning or direful things will happen."

Two Feathers immediately set out to satisfy the old woman's dream demand. Now no one had ever seen these elk, which were known by their splashing only, and all persons who went into the lake were devoured by the horned serpent. Two Feathers jumped into the water saying, "I know that I can do this thing." Long he swam into the darkness, for there was no starlight or moon. After a time he heard splashing and a noise like heavy breathing. Taking his arrow from an oiled skin bag he spoke to it and then shot. There was a great flash of light in the sky and the mysterious lake elk were revealed. The arrow had pierced both of them. Mounting one of the elks he ordered them to swim ashore. "What do you want?" they asked when they stood upon the homeward beach. "I want your horns," he answered. "Oh that is all right, nephew," they said and shed their antlers. "I am sorry I had to kill you, but the woman desired it in satisfaction of a dream." The elks spoke again, "The woman has deceived you." Then they disappeared.

The gift of the great antlers only increased the old woman's anger and the next night she dreamed that she must have the pelts of the wampum-coated deer. They had no hair but curled shells on their skins. If they saw anyone they would trample them to death. So then, Two Feathers set forth to catch the wampum deer. He made a sweat house by the lick where the deer came in the night. He threw tobacco all around it and then waited. Soon two does came and Two Feathers shot his magic arrow, killing both. Then he lighted his pipe and began to sing. Instantly a great drove of bucks came rushing to the sweat lodge but they could not touch it, so powerful was the magic of Two Feathers. After a while he heard them stamping away and he arose and went out and skinned the deer.

The beautiful pelts covered with shells only made the old woman more angry, as Two Feathers presented them at daybreak. She screeched and scolded and called him an evil sorcerer. But the next night she again asked satisfaction of a dream.

On this occasion she demanded that Two Feathers go
to a hot lake and bring back two white beavers, reputed
to be of great magical potency. "Oh that is very easy, my
aunt," answered Two Feathers, "I will bring them at daylight." Setting forth he reached the lake and taking out his
arrow spoke to it. "Speed on and find the game that I
desire," he commanded.

The arrow sped forth and soon it struck a beaver which
came swimming toward him, bringing another with it on a
wave. This he struck with a small white stone and both
were dead. Taking them to the old woman's lodge he threw
them at her feet. "You may have the meat," he said, "but
I will keep the skins." This made the old woman angry for
the beavers were her brothers. So then again she dreamed
and commanded him to satisfy her by dangerous tasks, but
his magic power always won. At length, dispairing of causing him harm in this manner, the mother announced that her
right mind had returned. She resolved upon a new plan,
and became very kind to Two Feathers. When Two Feathers found that the mother was no longer the oracle of the
spirits he started home where he might provide for his own
father and mother.

The Do'ciowe[n] people listened with great sorrow to
Two Feathers' story of the distressed tribesmen of Ganun
dasēy and rejoiced when he told them how his luck had
delivered them. But he was restless and could not bear
separation from Drooping Flower, thus he announced that
he was going again to the Valley of the Pleasant River to
get a wife.

Woodchuck Leggings had seen Drooping Flower and
he wanted her, and hearing that his nephew was to visit
her, resolved to accompany him, kill him on the journey,
put on his clothing, gain the magic articles, and then steal
Drooping Flower. The mother of the girl had given Woodchuck Leggings a death charm and he made up his mind to

use it upon his nephew. Moreover the woman asked him to do so.

"May I go with you?" he asked Two Feathers, when he saw his nephew ready.

"No, Uncle," was the reply.

"But I am going nevertheless!"

"Then not with me,—never!" was Two Feather's answer.

Two Feathers set out the next morning and when he had travelled three days he met Woodchuck Leggings, who had a day's start on the journey. He saw him sitting on a stump with his back toward the trail.

"Niawĕ"skäno'!" shouted Two Feathers.

"Dogĕ's!" was the startled reply.

"How came you here, Uncle?"

"I am on my journey."

"Then if it is your journey you must not expect to go with me, for I will not allow it." Two Feathers ran on ahead leaving his uncle still sitting on the stump. When night came he set up camp and kindled a fire for cooking a supper. As he lay down for sleeping he heard the night birds scream and listening he heard the crackling of sticks. Lifting his bow, he prepared for the enemy, whatever it might be. In the dim light of the dying camp fire, he saw the shadow of a ragged old man, limping along the trail. It was Woodchuck Leggings.

"Niawĕ"skäno", Uncle!" said Two Feathers in greeting.

"Doge's! Agī! dodŭs'ha ä'kwa!" (Truly, O give me to eat)!" gasped the hungry uncle.

Two Feathers spoke to his arrows, shot into the tree tops and a large turkey fell to the ground at the feet of the uncle, who was too frightened to move.

"Pull the arrow out and cook the bird," commanded the nephew. But his uncle was too frightened, for the arrow was magic. (Beyond this, it was not right to touch the arrows of another hunter when they were sticking in dead game.) Woodchuck Leggings was too exhausted to prepare his own meal and fell to the earth from weakness. So the faithful and unsuspicious nephew roasted the bird and shaking the dozing man exclaimed, "Sĕdekonĭ (Come eat)!"

So he devoured the bird and ate his fill of parched corn and maple sugar. He begged that his nephew should not turn him away in the darkness, for he was afraid of the flying heads. He pleaded for a little space on one side of the fire by his nephew's side. Two Feathers did not relish the idea but pitied the old coward, and gave him a place in which to sleep.

The crafty old scoundrel watched his opportunity. When Two Feathers was fast asleep, he made his way, stealthily to the other side of the fire and drew from his shirt a long sharp point of hickory bark. It was the death charm. Two Feathers was lying on his side. Kneeling at his back he lifted the bark high above his head and brought it down with all his strength, plunging it into the back of his victim just between the shoulders. Removing his own dirty garments. Woodchuck Leggings replaced them with the beautiful white clothes of Two Feathers. He felt for the magic pipe and pouch and found both safe, but he had forgotten the magic arrow in his haste.

In the morning he continued his journey and at sunset came to the village. A scout noted his arrival and cried, "Here comes Two Feathers!" As false Two Feathers passed by the fires between the lodges, the people noticed with wonder that the beautiful white deer skin clothing had become soiled and torn. The tobacco pouch had caught in a bush and half the quill-work had been ripped off.

He entered Drooping Flower's lodge. "Come, we can get married now," he said.

Drooping Flower did not need to look at him a second time. "You are not real Two Feathers," she exclaimed. "Where is Two Feathers?"

"I am he!"

"Sonohweh! You are a liar!"

"We shall see," answered the pretender.

The next day he called a council and when all had taken their seats he strode through the door with great pomp and took his position on the singer's bench. Grasping a rattle he began to sing, but his voice was cracked. He stopped suddenly, as he caught the gaze of the men. "I have a cold, brothers," he apologized. "But now I will smoke, and the sweetness of my tobacco will please you; but where shall I get my fire,—Ho, ho! Fly little birds!" But his commands were in vain and he was compelled to get his own light. "My birds are bashful," he explained. He lighted his pipe and began to blow the smoke into the air. The foul fumes filled the lodge and nearly stifled the people. Women held their breaths or breathed through their shawls; the men coughed and the babies cried. "My tobacco is damp tonight," he said, "but you shall see my pouch dance for me,—dance pouch, dance!" The pouch clung to his side limper than ever. In spite of his commands and threats it would not move a finger's breadth. "My pouch," he explained, "is bashful and now as I am tired, if Drooping Flower will bring me a skin I will speak out wampum. Drooping Flower refused to obey and whispered, "He is a liar!" Drooping Flower's older sister, Wïäso^n', took pity on the unsuccessful conjurer, and hoping to win a man, took down a skin from the wall behind her and placed it on the singer's bench.

"Now since all my things are bashful, I will pay you for the trouble in coming here, see—I blow out wampum when I breathe!" Sure enough, from his mouth flew a quantity of small white cylinders. The people bent over to pick up the valued wampum beads, but were again disappointed, for instead of wampum were clusters of loathly worms. With a shamed face Wïäso^n' returned the skin to the peg and the council was dismissed by the head sachem.

False Two Feathers felt that he must do something to

redeem himself, so going to the woods the next morning he shot all his arrows and called for game, but failing to get any, in desperation clubbed two woodchucks to death and brought them back. No one would touch them.

The people looked at him as one who had lost power by displeasing his own charms and paid more attention to him. No one would now associate with him save Wīāso^{n}' who asked him to marry her, and he did.

Two Feathers awoke after several days unconsciousness and found a great herd of forest animals about him.

"Our brother, you have been sick," said the wolf, the spokesman. "You were stabbed by Woodchuck Leggings as you were sleeping. But as you were kind, so we are not ungrateful and our blood has kept you nourished while you slept. The animal spirits are crafty and know their friends and foes. You are about to undergo misfortune but do not faint,—keep up courage and listen to what we tell you."

Two Feathers was weak and dizzy, and it took him a long time to reach the Valley village. Painfully he crept along the sunken trail until he reached a corn field where he heard women singing as they cut the blighted corn stalks. He called, and Drooping Flower hearing his voice, found him wounded and exhausted. She stooped down and he whispered something in her ear. The crowd of women was now about him. "Where is Woodchuck Leggings?" he inquired. "You are Woodchuck Leggings; don't you know yourself?" cried all women. Two Feathers said no more.

For nearly a year Two Feathers lived in an old bark house which hardly sheltered him from the snow or kept away the springtime rain. He looked like, and was, a sickly old man. Every one knew him by his cough and pitied him.

In those days there was a great white eagle, a magic bird. The people of the village had erected two high poles with cross-pieces, upon which the eagle was wont to alight as it passed over the settlement.

The mother of Drooping Flower worried because her

daughter would not take a husband and asked her why she would not marry. To such inquiries the girl replied, "I shall never marry until the white eagle shall be shot. The man who sends an arrow through him shall be my husband!" These words pleased the mother and she told everybody about it and gave it out in council.

A day for the tournament was set and when it came a hundred young men from the entire nation gathered on the council grounds, eagerly awaiting the signal. The great white eagle, with whistling wings, flew from pole to pole, pausing now and then to give a scream. The signal was given, and a hundred arrows struck its feathers, broke, and fell to the earth below. Through all the day the contesting warriors shot their arrows upon the magic eagle, but he shook them off like snow flakes and mocked their efforts by his screaming.

Two Feathers, dressed in the tattered skins of Woodchuck Leggings, watched the flight of arrows from his doorway. The young men laughed at him and asked him if he were going to try his skill, but to no one would he reply. At length when no one was watching, the ugly, lame, coughing old man made his way to a corner of the council grounds. He had no bow, but in his hand he carried an arrow. Drooping Flower's mother saw him, and recognized who he was, but kept her secret. She looked him in the eyes and contemptuously exclaimed "Chisna!" While she was still looking this despised old man made a pantomine motion as if grasping a bow, pulled his arrow and let fly. He hobbled back to his lodge, coughing violently.

There was a great shout followed by an excited hum of voices. "It was my arrow—no mine—liars, it was my arrow —wrong, I know my arrow by the painted shaft—mine— mine—no mine—my arrow, I know it by the red quill!" The din grew louder and wilder. Blows were exchanged and some struck with clubs. The older men rushed out and surrounded the excited throng and said they would shoot them with their arrows and commanded the riot to cease. When quiet had been restored the old sachem cried out, "That man killed the bird who can draw the arrow out!"

Man after man tried very hard but all failed. False Two Feathers made his boast and kneeling, prepared to pull it. He faltered;—his eyes filled with water. It was the same arrow that had killed the turkey for his supper on the night when he had plunged the death charm into Two Feathers! He arose and went to his house. "The eagle is shot," said he to his wife. "No one can draw the arrow out."

There was a great discussion and every one was asked for his opinion, but no one had any idea who the marksman was, save the mother of Drooping Flower, and Woodchuck Leggings. Then a stranger who had not hitherto ventured to speak, stepped upon a stump and shouted, "You have not asked the old man with a cough!" The people laughed at the stranger's suggestion and watched him curiously as he ran to the abode of Two Feathers. The stranger grasped Two Feathers by the hand, by both hands, and whispered in his ear. The stranger was the wolf whom he had befriended in the lonely cabin.

Two Feathers limped to the slain bird and all the people shouted "Hōa'ho"! Old-Bones-with-a-cough is going to try, yo-a-hoh!"

"Old Bones-with-a-cough" touched the arrow, it clung to his finger and followed his hand into the air. All the people shouted "Whoei'!"

The sachem took his stand and proclaimed Drooping Flower the wife of the old man with a cough, and the mother frowned as she was compelled to say, "Nio'!"

"A medicine man quick!" shouted Two Feathers. "Give me him whom you call fallen Two Feathers!"

Woodchuck Leggings hurried forward, ever ready to be where there was a chance of being looked at.

"Build a sweat lodge of fat bear skins, bring large lumps

of fat and them heat fire-stones and bring them in," directed Two Feathers.

Woodchuck Leggings built a little dome-shaped lodge by sticking the ends of flexible poles into the ground and bending them over, and after a hunter had skinned a fat bear, he covered the lodge frame with the skin, hair-side out. When the hot stones were brought in they heated the interior to such a degree that the fat on the skins melted and ran down in streams. After Two Feathers' body was drenched with the oil, he asked that his "doctor" rub him until it had been well absorbed by the skin. He then requested the famous "medicine man" to pack a lump of fat between his shoulders, cover it with a small skin and place a hot stone over it. A cold one was selected. "Hotter, Uncle!" said Two Feathers, for the first time calling him by this name. The second stone was only slightly warmer, "Hotter yet, Uncle!" Another stone was placed on the skin but Two Feathers still shouted, "Hotter yet, Uncle." The next stone was dull red and Woodchuck Leggings slapped it on with a thud. "Doge^n's wi' o!" shouted Two Feathers and putting his hands to the back of his neck he threw off the poultice. He grasped the bark which had worked partly out. He gave it a hard pull. Woodchuck Leggings grew suspicious and began to tremble with fear. With a loud cry Two Feathers pulled the bark point from his neck and before the cringing man before him had time to utter a sound, Two Feathers struck him a heavy blow over the neck. The death charm sank into the flesh, passed between the bones in his back and Woodchuck Leggings lay dead.

"The sick one has recovered!" shouted Two Feathers. "Every one go away while I dress." The wondering throng which had sat chanting about the lodge during the ceremony, went to their lodges, curious to know what had happened, for the voice which they had heard commanding them was one which in itself compelled obedience and awe, and seemed to come from neither of the men whom they had seen enter the lodge.

Two Feathers washed his body in ashes, put on his old suit which Woodchuck Leggings had ruined, but which was restored as it touched his body, and ran out into the council grounds. The people looked at him in astonishment. Who could it be? The handsome man seemed like someone whom they had known before, and yet no one ventured to say who it was.

"I shall call a council for tonight; I bring news!" shouted Two Feathers.

Two Feathers took the speaker's seat and addressed the people. "Brothers! I am Two Feathers, the same who once delivered you from the famine, by the power of my charms, I delivered you from the two grim sisters that breathed into your faces and almost stopped your breath. So soon have you forgotten me, but remember, I am not blaming you, for I know the reason, and you are not to be blamed."

"Brothers! I was stricken in the forest by the treachery of Woodchuck Leggings, who thought that by taking my life he could take my power, but he was mistaken, for he has taken neither. For a long time I have suffered, alone, neglected and despised by all the people, but now that I have recovered, he who designed my misfortune himself has met it. I have killed him with his own charm."

The gestures of Two Feathers, his face and his voice thrilled the people and with one accord they shouted, "Nio"!"

"Now friends and brothers, let us rejoice in my restored life and power. See, I smoke! Fly birds, fly and bring me a light." The birds flew from his hat with chirps of joy. They fluttered up and down and flew through the council house from end to end. They went into the fire, pulled out a brand and placed it in his pipe. They brushed against his face again and again singing. Two Feathers caught them in his hands and placed them back on his feather cap. He spoke to his pouch, "Dance, pouch, dance,—be my spotted fawn." The pouch leaped from his side and danced better than it had before. It danced in a circle around him as he stood on the floor, it jumped over his head, rolled and tumbled, rubbed against his legs, leaped and gave every sign of life. "Enough!" exclaimed Two Feathers, and reluctantly it ran back to his belt, nothing but a limp skin pouch. "Now brothers, bring a skin." Someone brought him the pelt which Woodchuck Leggins had used. "What, spoiled by worms? See, I smoke." A puff of smoke purified the skin. "See, I breathe. Now look." Wampum dropped from the frost of his breath and piled up in a heap on the skin.

The sachems and head men now began to speak. Never did a man receive a better welcome. The people were glad, the women sang a welcome song and then all rushed to put friendly hands on him,—all but two. These slunk from the room, one with eyes briming with angry tears and the other with a face drawn into a horrible frown. This one ground her teeth in rage, she ran her claw fingers down her cheeks until the blood flowed in streams. She tore her hair, and with shrieks ran into the darkness.

The council was over and there was a commotion in the lodge of Drooping Flower. The mother lay on her couch screeching as she tore her clothing into shreds, chewed the flesh from her fingers and bit them off at the joints. Then she suddenly sprang up and shook her hands before her face. The sinews dangled over the white bones and blood spurted from the meat. Suddenly the lodge became darkened,—a rush of air was felt and a yelp was heard, like that of a dog pierced with an arrow. When a torch was lighted the mother had gone. She could not be found though the people searched in forest and in open. Only tracks of a big dog could be seen leading from the lodge. They were traced to a pond which had neither inlet nor outlet, and there they stopped. It was found out she had been a witch.

GENERAL NOTES.—The story of Two Feathers and his jealous uncle, Woodchuck Leggings is one of the favorite tales of the Seneca. It is related in several forms but always has the same general plot. The version here given was secured during the summer of 1903 during my stay on the Silverheels' farm, and was related by George D. Jimerson, comments being made by Fred Kennedy, a half-blood, and Peter Snyder. As auditors who nodded their approval we had Gahweh Seneca and Fred Pierce.

As here recorded this bit of Seneca fiction is an example of a folk tale taken down in note form and rewritten in the language of the transcriber. It is not an exact translation by any means. It does give, however, all the essential ideas conveyed by the narators. The plot is followed exactly in all the peculiar turns and in some cases we have used the same expressions of the story tellers who gave the tale.

The plot is a love theme in which a hero is thwarted by a jealous uncle. Magic plays its usual part but magic is employed by the hero to bring about his own recovery in due time. The heroine's mother turns out to be in league with the villain, and after the villain's exposure the hero is compelled to perform certain tasks thought to be impossible. He succeeds and the evil woman stands revealed an odious witch.

When I had written out this tale substantially as here presented I read it to Edward Cornplanter. He criticized it by saying that I had received it from Christian Indians who had given locations not in the original tale and that my informants had tried to explain too much. "It is all right, though," he said. "I do not object at all because white folks will understand it better the way you have it. Only one big mistake you have made. Now, when Two Feathers went away from that big bark house where the girl lived he made up his mind to take the girl with him to his own village. So, he grabbed her and jumped up through the smoke hole. He had his snow-shoes hidden on the roof. He put on his snow-shoes, grabbed the girl around the waist and then slid down the slippery roof. He was magic and sailed away right in the air for a mile and then came down on the snow as nice as you please. It was great to see it.

"Now, soon, Woodchuck Leggings missed the girl. All the time he still wants her, which makes his own woman mad. So Woodchuck Leggings tried to jump up through the roof hole but fell back in the fire and burned himself. So he climbed up on the roof with his snowshoes to sail away after Two Feathers. He started down the slippery, icy roof and went fine,—until he came to the edge of the roof. Then he fell head first in a big drift and the only thing anyone could see was a pair of snowshoes on the level with the top of the drift. This made the whole village laugh with a big roar. His wife was madder than ever for she had to dig him out, and I hate to tell you what she did to him when she got him alone. This is the best of the story."

23. HOW TURKEY BOY SQUEEZED THE HEARTS OF A SORCERER AND HIS SEVEN SISTERS.

There was an old woman who lived with her grandson, Osoon (Turkey), in a lonely lodge a long ways from a settlement. The lodge was old and very large, but only the two lived in it, for all others had been killed by sorcerers.

Winter was coming on and the old woman was busily engaged each day in gathering firewood for the winter's store. Every day she would cry as she started on her journey and when she returned she would cry again, for she was old and weak.

After a time the boy, Turkey, asked his grandmother why she wept continually. "Oh my grandson," she answered, "all our people are dead and I am getting old. I have a hard time getting roots and bark for winter food and gathering wood makes me very tired."

Then she took Turkey to the end of the long house and pushed aside a piece of bark. Beyond was another room which Turkey had never seen before. As they entered it Turkey saw that it was filled with all kinds of clothing and weapons and many strange things. "This is where I have placed all the things that belonged to our family when it lived here," said the grandmother. "I will show you this place but you must never enter it or touch anything."

The next day when the grandmother left the lodge to gather wood Turkey pushed aside the bark and entered the room. It was dark but after a time he could see. He found a large drum which pleased him very much. He fell to beating it and it made a sound that he thought delightful. Then he went out and closed the bark over the opening.

When the grandmother returned with her load of wood she wept again. "Why do you always weep?" asked Turkey. And she replied, "All of our people are dead. They have been destroyed by a monster wizard who eats human flesh. His lodge is to the east and near it is a great bed of strawberries. Oh, they are as large as hearts. Once there was a good village of our tribe there, but the people were killed and the houses have now fallen down." Then she fell into a fit of weeping again.

Turkey now said, "My grandmother, now is the time for me to go. I shall shortly go."

The next day when the grandmother was away, Turkey entered the forbidden room and found a net bat and a ball. He removed them and went out and played ball (lacrosse). Then he returned and found the drum, which he beat with great vigor. So loudly did he beat it that his grandmother heard it and returned in great fright. "Do you want the monster to find out where we live and come here and eat us?" she scolded, but Turkey only repplied. "Oh my grandmother, don't scold me. Tell me more about the monster."

"His name is Deadoeñdjadase^n," replied the grandmother, "and he has seven sisters who wait upon him. Oh never go east."

"Make me some moccasins," commanded the boy. "I am going east."

Still forbidding him to go, the grandmother, nevertheless, made the moccasins. In a short time he was ready to start.

Now Turkey was cautious and crept along through the underbrush until he came to a clearing where he saw a dried human skin fastened by a cord to a tall pole. It swung around in the wind and watched the clearing. Turkey noticed that there was a large strawberry patch there with berries as big as hearts. He was very crafty and knew that he could not approach the Hadjoqda (dried skin), without being seen and reported to its masters. Looking about he saw a mole and made a bargain with it to borrow its coat. Shrinking himself by magic he entered the mole skin and then burrowed underground until he was directly under the skin, when he broke a little root into beads and stained them with berry juice. He called to the skin and offered to give it wampum if it would talk for a while. This the skin agreed to do, and told him all the mysteries of the clearing. Turkey learned that the master sorcerer was Deadoeñdjadse[n], and that the seven sisters cooked human flesh for him, grinding it in a corn mortar with white corn meal. Only this would he eat. When the sisters were not cooking they guarded the strawberries from the deer that came into the clearing to graze.

"What more should I learn to be safe?" asked Turkey.

"What will you give to know?" replied Skin Man.

"I will rub my hands on you and make you free," answered Turkey.

Then he learned that the lives of the sorcerer and his sister were secure, for they could not be killed, their hearts being concealed under the wing of a loon that swam in a pool under a bed in the lodge. A dog guarded the hearts and they could only be surrendered upon order of Deadoeñdjadse[n], himself.

Meanwhile the sisters had been calling the skin, and louder and louder did they call. Turkey said, "Tell them that you have been making wampum for them, and that Deadoeñdjadse[n] is about to return spitting blood. Then I will stir up the deer and enter the lodge. Then you will report the deer and the sisters will rush out to save their strawberries. I will find their hearts and kill them. Then I will make you free."

Hadjoqda, the skin man, returned to the lodge, saying that he had been making wampum, and was delayed. He said moreover that he saw their brother returning, being sick. The youngest sister was suspicious of the wampum, but it appeared to be good, and the sisters divided it. Skin Man then returned to his station.

In a short time Turkey had gone back to the mole and returned its coat with a gift in payment. Then he used magic to make himself appear exactly like Deadoeñdjadse[n], and strode boldly into the clearing, chewing a strawberry and spitting the juice. This gave him great power. He drew near the lodge and called for food, but one sister was suspicious and offered him corn, then meat, then fish, but Turkey refused them all and roared that he was Oñgwe Iãs and wanted his accustomed dinner. This they put before him and he ate it all, satisfying the women that he was indeed their brother.

Suddenly Skin Man began to call and the women all ran out of the lodge, for Skin Man was crying that the deer were in the strawberries.

When the sisters were out of sight, Turkey noticed a small dog watching one of the beds. He threw a piece of meat to the dog and then lifted up the bed. Beneath was a pool of water and a loon swimming about. "Give me the hearts," commanded Turkey. The loon lifted up a wing but there were no hearts under it. "You give me those hearts!" commanded Turkey, once more.. This time the loon lifted its right wing and beneath were the eight hearts. Turkey grabbed them and ran out crying, "I am Turkey, and I've got your hearts."

When the sisters saw Turkey with the hearts they began to chase him with the clubs which they used on the deer, but as each assailant approached Turkey squeezed her heart, causing her to faint. One by one he squeezed until they all cried out and fainted but the rest arose as he released his pressure and ran after him, when by giving a hard squeeze they all fell down. By this time the women were at the flat rock where their brother killed his victims. Turkey now threw their hearts one by one on the stone and each cracked open like a flint stone.

Deadoeñdjadse[n], suspecting mischief, now ran to the clearing where he met the Skin Man. Of him he made inquiries as to what the noise was all about. Skin Man was very insolent and called Deadoeñdjadse[n] bad names, enraging him greatly. "Turkey has your heart, Turkey has your heart," sang the Skin Man in derision. The monster sorcerer then rushed into the clearing where he saw Turkey dancing about the flat stone. He rushed upon him, but Turkey threw the heart upon the rock and broke both heart and rock. Then he patted Skin Man all over the body and restored him to his normal form. To his surprise he found him to be his own brother, who had been held by sorcery to obey the commands of the wizard and his sisters.

Together they gathered many bones that were strewn about the flat rock. When all were piled up Turkey kicked over a pig-nut tree and called out, "Disjointed bones, arise before this tree falls upon you!" The tree fell and before it hit the ground a great host of people arose and all were quarreling, for all had portions of the others' bodies. Turkey pacified them and told them to wait. From the throng he picked out his own relatives and with them returned to his grandmother's lodge.

The grandmother was very happy when she saw her relatives,—her children and grandchildren. By her suggestion they all returned to the clearing where the strawberries grew and there they built a new village, and there they live to this day.

24. CORN RAINS INTO EMPTY BARRELS.

At one time there was nothing to eat on all the earth. Nearly all the people had starved to death, and a few that remained gathered together on a high hill. They lived on boiled bark.

There was a certain young man who kept saying all the time, "It will be better after a while." Nobody believed him because things were getting worse each day. His brother used to torture him with sharp stones and say harsh things to him. The young man, however, kept thinking that something would happen soon. After a while he heard footsteps, as if on a clean path. He listened for the span of a moon and then heard them running. He told the people but nobody believed him.

One morning while he sat in the doorway of his lodge with his head down on his knees, a young woman stood before him. He heard her breathe and looked up. She smiled and handed him a basket of bread. "My mother sent me to this lodge to find a young man," she said. "My mother wants me to marry him."

The people came out of the lodge and looked at the young woman and the young man's mother asked from whence she had come. "I have come from the far south," answered the girl. "There is plenty of food there."

So the young man ate the bread and was married to the young woman from the south.

Then the young wife said, "My mother sent me to bring food to you. Let everybody take off the tops of their corn barrels and then enter the lodge and cover their faces."

The sun had now come up and it was hot. The people did not like their faces covered, but soon they heard a sound like corn falling into their barrels. After a time the noise ceased and the young wife said, "It is finished now."

Out into the shed went the people of the lodge and found

the barrels full of shelled corn. Everybody ate and all were satisfied, except the younger brother, who threw his food into the fire and said he wanted game. Now the young wife had cooked the corn the young man threw away, and she was made sad by his action. So she said, "My husband, go to the river and get fish enough for the people." But the younger brother said, "It is foolish to go to the river, for fish have deserted the river. There are none." Nevertheless, the young husband went to the river and drew out enough fish for all the people. The younger brother was very angry.

The next day the husband went hunting and while he was absent the younger brother began to torment the young wife. "Your food is not good," he said. "I cast your food away," and again he threw food into the fire.

When the husband returned he found his wife crying and when he asked her what was troubling her she said, "Your younger brother has spoiled everything. He has rejected my food (speaking thereby the dissatisfaction of all the people). I shall now return to my home."

The husband was very sad and begged her not to go, but his wife told him that her mother instructed her to return if she were abused. During the following night there was a sound of scraping in the corn barrels and in the morning when the women went for their corn it was all gone, and with it the bride had vanished.

After consultation the husband determined to search for his wife, and thus he set out on a long journey. At length he came to a region of great corn fields and after a while saw a high mound covered with corn plants. On this mound he found his wife and her mother. His wife showed him her body and it was burned and scarred. "This is what your brother did to me," she said, "when he threw the corn into the fire. He would have killed me had I remained."

After living in the south for several months the couple returned and found the people again starving. The young wife ordered them to open their corn barrels and hide their faces once again. They did so and shelled corn fell like rain into the barrels filling them to the top.

Then the young wife told the people that corn must never be wasted or thrown away for it is food and if destroyed will cause the crops to be poor and the corn to cease to yield.

25. TWENTGOWA AND THE MISCHIEF MAKER.[1]

There was once a very lazy man named Twentgowa. He had a wife and several children. Twentgowa was always giving excuses to his wife as to why he did not hunt game more often like other men.

Twentgowa often went into the deep woods and had a mossy rock near a river where he would lie and dream of the things he would like to do and how he would kill big game animals if he only had a chance. More and more often he repaired to his favorite spot as his wife scolded him for not bringing home game.

One evening a man came to the lodge where Twentgowa lived. He stood in the doorway and said: "I am your friend. I have visited you before but this is the first time you have seen me. I have known your name for a long time. Now you must come often and see me. I have good things in my place of abode and there is plenty to eat and much game hanging on my rafters." Then he walked away.

Twentgowa did not know where his friend lived but thought he might find him some day. Now on the next day there was nothing to eat in the house, save a few pieces of corn bread, and the wife scolded Twentgowa saying: "Oh you who are always squatting like a duck on a nest, you shall not eat but this food shall be for our children. Begone, and if you have a friend perhaps he will receive you." So that is what she said.

The lazy man arose from his bed and went out of the house. "I will now go and seek my friend," he thought to himself. He went directly to the mossy spot on the rock where he customarily sought refuge and when he arrived there he found his bed very thick with moss, making it a fine spot upon which to recline. When he had lain there a short time he looked up and saw a large bark house, with

1 Related by Edward Cornplanter, 1905.

very fine poles as supports and over the door a head of some animal he could not identify.

He arose and with caution walked toward the door of the house and when he stood before it he saw his friend.

"My friend," said he, "I did not know this house was here. I never saw it before."

"Come in," said his friend, "This is where I live. Oh this house has here stood for many years and I am greatly surprised that you have not seen it. Now it is time to eat. Be seated here on a mat and let us eat together. The first thing we must eat is os'howä, a pudding."

Thereupon the friend went to an upper shelf and took down a bowl into which he placed a loathly mess of substance that had the odor of a fish a long time dead. "Djiskwengo," exclaimed the friend, and the bowl filled up with steaming pudding of most enticing odor.

So the two friends ate the food and relished it greatly. Oh, it was far better than any food that Twentgowa had ever eaten. "It is so delicious," said he, "that I would like to take some home to my family. I would like to borrow a cooking pot to contain it."

"My friend, there is no need of that," said the householder. "I will give you power to do as I have done. You have only to follow my directions and you will have great power to produce delicious food for your family."

So Twentgowa stood at the back of the lodge and his friend threw the pot of food into him right through the wall of his abdomen. It vanished through magic and power was within Twentgowa.

Twentgowa now said he was about to return to his home and he started out on his journey which seemed very much longer than ever before, as if the path had stretched. He kept thinking of his newly acquired power and thought it might be well to test it. So he sat down on a log and used his magical word, "Odjiskwagoh." As he did this a great pile of steaming pumpkin pudding formed on the ground.

"Oh my!" exclaimed Twentgowa. "Power within me is; now I shall eat forever." He was now satisfied that he had a great friend.

Running home he entered his lodge and told his story. He told of his feasting on pumpkin pudding and of the power he had to make it by magic. So he took a jar from the top platform of his lodge and in the manner directed filled it. He placed in it the loathly substance like unto a dead fish and then conjured it until it overflowed into the large bark dish in which the jar was placed. "Ah now," said Twentgowa, "we shall have a feast. Oh, it is so appetizing!"

His wife was very angry and would not touch the food but scolded him, for instead of real food all that was produced was a terrible mess that drove her and the children out of the house. She threw stones into the lodge and called him out, for he was dancing inside.

So the people saw that Twentgowa had lied and could not make food by unnatural means, but made that which was evil. And his wife scolded him and said: "Do not go to the lodge of that man any longer. He is none other than S'hodie'onskon', whom we know as a mischief maker. He will make your mind abnormal and what is bad he will make you think is good. If you persist in visiting him you will suffer and great calamity will befall us all."

Twentgowa was greatly downcast and wondered why he had failed before the people. He determined to go and see his friend again and seek an explanation. So he went as before. "My friend, I was just thinking of you," said his friend when he entered the lodge. "Come we will now eat together. This time we will have the whole pumpkin. Oh it is most delicious."

So when he had said this he sat down on a long bench and laid his war club against his thighs and it became as if alive. It lay upon the bench and it had a round head which was very large. Then the friend said: "Pumpkin come forth. Thou art concealed within the head of my warclub. Burst forth!"

So saying he struck the head of his war club with a long handled maul. Immediately a pumpkin rolled forth from the head of his war club. So they cooked it and ate it. Twentgowa found it most delicious and was continually saying, "Oga"o^n! Oga"o^n! This is so delicious," said he "that I would be most happy to have the power to do the same as you have done, for in this manner I could feed my family."

"I will give you power to so produce twice," said the friend, "but further you must not try for it is not good to always eat pumpkins alone. Now I am ready. Stand, swing your war club until it comes 'whack' against the head of my club. If you can hit mine there will be power within you."

So Twentgowa swung his war club about, spinning on his heel until he came, "squuh" against his friend's club and it made a great whack that nearly broke Twentgowa in twain.

"Now," said Twentgowa, "I will try my power," so he hit his club with a maul and a pumpkin rolled forth. "Now I must go home and make pumpkins," he said. "Now I go."

On his way through the forest he began to wonder if indeed he had power. He thought that by some chance power was within him only so long as he was in the presence of his friend and that his friend had fooled him by magic to make mischief after the fashion of S'hodie^{n}sko$^{n'}$. Thereupon he sat astride a log and laid his war club before him, its round head being at the further end of the log. Then he grasped a stick and reached over and struck the head of the war club. It was as his friend had said, for a pumpkin rolled forth. He did not want to carry the pumpkin home so he made a fire and cooked it. Oh it was a delicious pumpkin and he kept continually saying "Oga"o^n." Then he went home.

He went in his lodge and greeted his wife. "I have new power," he said. "My friend this time has given me good power. I will make pumpkins for you. Get my stake maul with which I am accustomed to drive in the long stakes of the house. Now I seat myself upon this bench and lay my war club before me. This is the right way to proceed. Now I whack my war club with the maul." So saying he hit at the head of his club, but in so doing he lifted up his foot upon the bench and whacked his big toe. It was a terrible and resounding whack, but no pumpkin rolled forth. Instead, Twentgowa fell off the bench like a dead man. He gave one dismal long-drawn-out howl and fainted.

It was a long time before he recovered and when he did he was very sore and limped when he walked. He could not hunt and when his wife scolded him for a lazy man, he sneaked away again and went to the lodge of his friend.

Arriving at the lodge he limped in. "Oh my friend," said the house holder, "I have been awaiting you; come, let us go after fish." So saying he went out and strode down to the creek where he removed his leggings. He took out his knife and passed it through his lips, moistening it. Then he began to whittle the meat off his shins so that the bone stood out sharp like a long knife. "Now, my friend," said he, "I will wade swiftly through the water and strike the fishes before they can move to one side. They will die and float to the top of the water and I will pick them up. After a while we will have enough for a good repast." He then waded in the water very swiftly and soon many fishes were upon the water which he picked up and flung over his shoulder into a basket. Coming ashore he put down his basket and then began to moisten his shins with salivary fluid. They quickly were restored and did not bleed at any time. Thus they made a fire and feasted on fish. Oh it was very delicious and Twentgowa kept saying, "Oga"o^n."

"Now, furthermore," he said, "I would like to have this power of catching fish for if I possessed it I might obtain food for my family."

"You shall possess this power," said his friend, "and when I touch your shins with my tongue you shall have power to twice perform this act of obtaining fish." And it was done.

So Twentgowa tried his new power and caught many fish which he left with his friend. Then he said, "I must go now, I am going home." Then he started home and on the way through the woods came to a stream that looked as if it had no fish in it so that he said, "I will now test my power in order that I may not be laughed at derisively." So he whittled his shins and waded in the water, and it was as predicted,—fish floated upon the surface and when he had eaten them he went on his way.

He went in his lodge and greeted his wife. "I have new power," he said. "My friend has given me new power. I will now go and catch fish for you but you must not mind if they have cuts in them. It is my manner of catching fish." So saying he went to a creek and taking off his leggings whittled his shins. As he cut the flesh blood flowed out and he was in great pain. He tried again and fell down bleeding. He bled very much and began to howl. For a long time he bled until he fainted again.

As night began to draw nigh his wife missed him and went out looking for him along the stream. Soon she saw a red trickle in the creek and going toward it saw her husband bleeding from cuts in his shins. She dragged him to the lodge and then called upon her dog to go and fetch S'hondie'onskon', the magical friend, to come and heal the husband. The dog went and soon the friend returned. When Twentgowa returned to his mind he scolded his friend, but his friend applied salivary fluid to the wounds and they healed. Then said the friend, "I gave you power twice, but further than that I did not give you. You have cheated and wasted your power. I shall go now. Come to see me again."

Then did his wife scold Twentgowa and said, "You must cease your visits to the evil mischief maker. He is only a maker of trouble and you have never profited by his tricks. If you would get busy like a man and hunt like a man you would have food. You are no good, but a bad, lazy man. I forbid you to associate with anyone, not even the dog."

Now when Twentgowa thought about the matter he decided to go once more to his friend and procure power for obtaining food. So he went away by stealth and sought his friend. When he had come to the bark house he found his friend in the doorway.

"I have been waiting for you," said his friend. "I am all ready to go hunting. Come now, I am ready." He then took a skein of twisted elm bark cords each about as long as a man's arm. With these he went to a lake to which Twentgowa followed him. "Where are your arrows?" asked Twentgowa. And his friend replied, "Oh you will never understand my ways. I hunt underwater with strings. I am now going down into the water and hunt ducks."

Away out on the lake were ducks swimming and soon one duck after another disappeared. When all had vanished, after the manner of ducks diving and not returning to the surface, the friend returned to the shore with a large bundle of ducks tied by the feet with the elm bark cord. "Now we may eat," said he. So they ate duck and Twentgowa kept saying, "Ogao." Horeover he said, "Oh I would like this power of catching ducks for if I possess it I might feed my family."

"You shall have this power," said his friend, "but only twice may you try it. I have only to hit your nose with a fish bladder I have held in my mouth and to lick your bark cords with my tongue." So he did the necessary thing, touching Twentgowa's nose with a fish's air-bladder and biting a bundle of cords. Twentgowa was delighted and danced down to the water, into it and under it. Soon he returned with two ducks.

Then he said, "Now I must go home. Now I go." So saying he started homeward, and on his way came to a big pond in which he saw ducks swimming. "I will now use my power," he said and immediately went into the water, returning with the ducks. Thereupon he threw the ducks away and went home.

Again he went into the lodge and greeted his wife. "I have new power," he said. "My friend has given me power this time and I shall bring you many ducks." So then he went into the woods where there was a lake.

Into the lake he went for he saw upon its surface a great flock of ducks swimming closely together. He had trouble this time but as all the ducks were together he tied several together and then poked one of them to scare it.

Upward flew the ducks with such impetus that Twentgowa was drawn up into the air and over the forest. When the ducks had flown a short way the string which he was holding broke and down he fell and into the top of an enormous hollow stub. He stood there stunned until he heard a noise outside. He peeped through a knot-hole and saw a damsel gathering wood. He made a squeaking noise to frighten her and she ran up to the tree and looked into the knot-hole. She saw his head against the hole and immediately thought that there was a bear inside. So Twentgowa rapped on the inside of the tree and it resounded like a drum. Twentgowa then sang "Djii-ha-ha, djii-ha-ha!" many times, and the damsel danced.

After a while she went home and told her sisters that there was a bear tree near by and that a bear within it sang and drummed. So they all went to the bear tree and said, "Oh Bear, make a song for us. We wish to dance." Again Twentgowa sang and they all danced. He found that he could not stop singing, though he was tired, and the damsels found that they could not stop dancing. After a while a man came and stood near them. "There is a bear inside this tree and we are dancing, come dance," they called out to him. He was smiling and after a while began to laugh. "I'll show you what kind of a bear is inside," he said. Then the singing and dancing ceased. He took an axe and chopped down the tree. Where he made the first hole black shaggy hair showed through. It looked like a bear. He kept on chopping and after a time the stub fell over and there inside was a man with his clothes torn off. He had on only his loin-cloth. The damsels ran in fright.

In their place stood the wife and she was very angry. She scolded him for making the damsels dance and for singing so long for them. She scolded him for going to the mischief maker's house and threatened him if he ever went again. Oh, she gave him a terrible scolding and it made him frightened.

Then the friend came out of the bushes where he was hiding and he said, "Now you two who are married, I will speak to you. Twentgowa must not go to the woods any more to the spot where he has been accustomed to recline. He may not come to my house any more. Henceforth he must hunt like other men."

Then his wife said to Twentgowa, "Come along home and be a man like other men. You never will be a magician for you haven't the sense to be one. You must be through with all wizardry."

Twentgowa went home and was a changed man. He never went to the house of the mischief maker again. He became like other men and hunted for his family.

GENERAL NOTES.—This tale of Twentgowa (Big Duck) and the Mischief Maker is related as a humorous story. It is a consistent Seneca folk tale and contains the customary magical elements.

It relates the adventures of a lazy man who would not hunt, and before whom appeared his "unseen friend," the "Mischief Maker." Twentgowa goes to the lodge of Mischief Maker and learns how to produce food by magic. The fact that he is told that he can do it but twice does not impress him. He receives the orenda, or magical ability and immediately demonstrates his power to "the friend." Departing for his own home he grows skeptical and tries again in the woods. Succeeeding, he returns home rejoicing and bragging of his power. When he attempts to demonstrate it, however, he makes a miserable failure and is driven out of the lodge. Again he returns to his friend and obtains magic for another episode, but repeats the experiments and in a final attempt fails. We are reminded, through Twentgowa's experiences, of the man who said he frequently thought he had very funny jokes to relate until he told them to his wife, when he saw how flat they were. Just so, Twentgowa could never satisfy his wife that he possessed any magic.

The various episodes here given are without doubt only a few of the many that the story teller might have given. The final escapade, however, is the one that cured our hero, and the Mischief Maker relents.

26. THE HORNED SERPENT RUNS AWAY WITH A GIRL WHO IS RESCUED BY THE THUNDERER.

There was a Thunderer named Hi"no^n who often hovered about a village where he sought to attract the attention of a certain young woman. He was a very friendly man and would have nothing to do with witches. He hated all kinds of sorcery and his great chief up in the sky whom we call Grandfather Thunder hated all wizardry and sorcery too. All the Thunderers killed witches when they could find them at their evil work.

Now, this Hi"no^n was very sure that he would win the girl he wanted and he visited her lodge at night and took a fire brand from the fire and sat down and talked with her, but she kept saying, "Not yet, perhaps by and by."

Hi"no^n was puzzled and resolved to watch for the coming of a rival. He told the girl's father that he suspected some witch had cast a spell on her or that some wizard was secretly visiting her. So they both watched.

That same night a strange man came. He had a very fine suit of clothing, and the skin had a peculiar tan. It was very clean, as if washed so that it shone with a glitter. Over his back and down the center there was a broad stripe of black porcupine quills with a small diamond-shaped pattern. He had a long neck and small beady eyes, but he was graceful and moved without noise. He went directly to the lodge and taking a light sat at the girl's bedside.

"Are you willing?" he asked her. "Come now, let us depart. I want you for my wife. I will take you to my house."

The girl replied, "Not yet, I think someone is watching, but in three days I will be ready."

The next day the girl worked very hard making a new dress and spent much time putting black porcupine quills

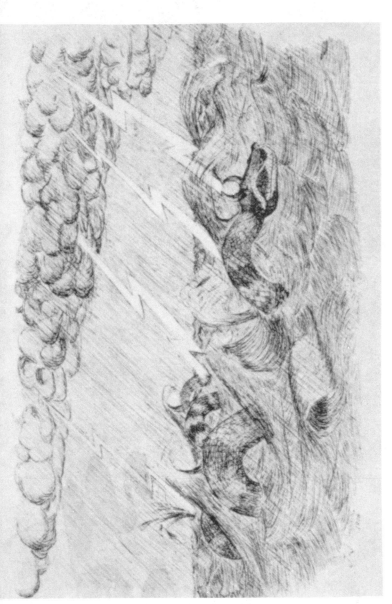

THE HORNED SERPENT.

This is a magical under-water creature with the power to transform itself into the form of a human warrior. The Thunder Spirit wages war against the whole tribe of Horned Serpents and tries to kill them by lightning. This is one of Jesse Cornplanter's finest drawings.

upon it as an ornamentation. It was her plan to have a dress that would match her lover's suit. Upon the third day she finished her work and went to bed early. Her apartment was at the right side of the door and it was covered by a curtain of buffalo skin that hung all the way down.

Hi"no^n again called upon her, taking a light and seating himself back of the curtain. "I am willing to marry you," he said. "When will you become my wife?"

"Not yet," she replied. "I am not ready now to marry."

"I think you are deceiving me," answered Hi"no^n, "for you have on your new dress and have not removed your moccasins."

"You may go," the girl told him, and he went away.

Soon there came the stranger and he too took a little torch and went behind the curtain. Soon the two came out together and ran down the path to the river.

"I shall take you now to my own tribe," said the lover. "We live only a short way from here. We must go over the hill."

So onward they went to their home, at length arriving at the high rocky shores of a lake. They stood on the edge of the cliff and looked down at the water.

"I see no village and no house," complained the girl. "Where shall we go now? I am sure that we are pursued by the Thunderer."

As she said this the Thunderer and the girl's father appeared running toward them.

"It is dark down there," said the lover. "We will now descend and find our house."

So saying he took the girl by the waist and crawled down the cliff, suddenly diving with a splash into the lake. Down they went until they reached the foot of the cliff, when an opening appeared into which he swam with her. Quickly he swam upward and soon they were in a dimly lighted lodge. It was a strange place and filled with numerous fine things. All along the wall there were different suits of clothing.

"Look at all the suits," said the lover, "when you have found one put it on."

That night the couple were married and the next day the husband went away. "I shall return in three days," he announced. "Examine the fine things here, and when you find a dress that you like put it on."

For a long time the girl looked at the things in the lodge, but she was afraid to put on anything for everything had such a fishy smell. There was one dress, however, that attracted the girl and she was tempted to put it on. It was very long and had a train. It was covered all over with decorations that looked like small porcupine quills flattened out. There was a hood fastened to it and to the hood was fastened long branching antlers. She looked at this dress longingly but hung it up again with a sigh, for it smelled like fish and she was afraid.

In due time her husband returned and asked her if she had selected a suit. "I have found one that I admire greatly," said she. "But I am afraid that I will not like it after I put it on. It has a peculiar fishy smell and I am afraid that it may bring evil upon me if I wear it."

"Oh no!" exclaimed her husband, "If you wear that suit I will be greatly pleased. It is the very suit that I hoped you would select. Put it on, my wife, put it on, for then I shall be greatly pleased. When I return from my next trip I hope you will wear it for me."

The next day the husband went away, again promising soon to return. Again the girl busied herself with looking at the trophies hanging in the lodge. She noticed that there were many suits like the one she had admired. Carefully she examined each and then it dawned upon her that these garments were the clothing of great serpents. She was horrified at the discovery and resolved to escape. As she went to the door she was swept back by a wave. She tried the back door but was forced into the lodge again by the water. Finally mustering all her courage she ran out of the door and jumped upward. She knew that she had been in a house under water. Soon she came to the surface but it was dark and there were thunder clouds in the sky. A great storm was coming up. Then she heard a great splashing and through the water she saw a monster serpent plowing his way toward her. Its eyes were fiercely blazing and there were horns upon its head. As it came toward her she scrambled in dismay up the dark slippery rocks to escape it. As the lightning flashed she looked sharply at the creature and saw that its eyes were those of her husband. She noticed in particular a certain mark on his eyes that had before strangely fascinated her. Then she realized that this was her husband and that he was a great horned serpent.

She screamed and sought to scale the cliff with redoubled vigor, but the monster was upon her with a great hiss. His huge bulk coiled to embrace her, when there was a terrific peal of thunder, a blinding flash, and the serpent fell dead, stricken by one of Hi"no"'s arrows.

The girl was about to fall when a strong arm grasped her and bore her away in the darkness. Soon she was back at her father's lodge. The Thunderer had rescued her. "I wanted to save you," he said, "but the great horned serpent kept me away by his magic. He stole you and took you to his home. It is important that you answer me one question: did you ever put on any dress that he gave you? If you did you are no longer a woman but a serpent."

"I resisted the desire to put on the garment," she told him.

"Then," said he, "you must go to a sweat lodge and be purified."

The girl went to the women's sweat lodge and they prepared her for the purification. When she had sweat and been purged with herbs, she gave a scream and all the women screamed for she had expelled two young serpents, and they ran down and slipped off her feet. The Thunderer outside killed them with a loud noise.

After a while the young woman recovered and told all about her adventure, and after a time the Thunderer came to her lodge and said, "I would like to take you now."

"I will give you some bread," she answered, meaning that she wished to marry him. So she gave him some bread which he ate and then they were married.

The people of the village were now all afraid that the lake would be visited by horned serpents seeking revenge but the Thunderer showed them a medicine bag filled with black scales, and he gave every warrior who would learn his song one scale, and it was a scale from the back of the horned serpent. He told them that if they wore this scale, the serpent could not harm them. So, there are those scales in medicine bundles to this day.

27. THE GREAT SERPENT AND THE YOUNG WIFE.

There was a certain young man who married a young woman. Now the young man had three sisters who were very jealous of the young wife, because of her beauty and skill, and because of their brother's affection for her. And so it was that the trio resolved to devise a plot and destroy the young wife.

It was the season when huckleberries are ripe and the sisters had invited the wife to take a canoe trip with them to a small island that arose from the middle of a large lake. Huckleberries were reported to grow there in abundance. Suspecting nothing, the wife mended her baskets and started to prepare food for the excursion.

"Oh no food is needed!" exclaimed the older sister. "We do not need a lunch where so many berries grow. Our baskets will soon be filled and we will return long before our hunger comes, meanwhile we can feast on berries."

The four women entered their canoe and paddled to the island far out in the lake. When at last they had beached their canoe and turned to look about, they found the island covered with bushes laden with berries. The sisters seemed anxious to go farther inland but the wife said that she deemed it wiser to stop where they were and pick, thus making it unnecessary to carry heavy baskets a greater distance to the canoe. So, stooping over she commenced to strip the berries from the bushes. This is exactly what the sisters wished as it gave them an opportunity to leave her behind, and, grumbling at her laziness, they disappeared in the bushes.

The wife worked diligently and soon had her large pack-basket full to the brim. Lifting it to her back and throwing the burden strap (gŭsha'ă') over her forehead, she walked slowly back to the shore expecting to find her sisters-in-law waiting for her. To her horror, however, though she searched in every direction, there was no sign of canoe or women. The situation then dawned upon her, and discouraged beyond all measure, she sat down on the sand and gave vent to her emotions by a burst of tears.

She was alone, a solitary human creature upon a faraway isle. She knew not what evil ghost might be lurking there to transform her to a crow or a wolf. Perhaps he might destroy her in the darkness and feast upon the body. These and other fearful thoughts tortured her mind until at last, as the sun sank low, she lay down exhausted by grieving, and slept. Far into the night she slumbered. Time sped by and she was awakened by a whoop upon the waters. Sitting up she looked out over the lake where she heard a clamor of voices and a multitude of dancing lights. Soon the lights appeared upon the shore and shortly were arranged in a circle on the island.

Creeping up to a log that lay close to the circle of lights, she saw a company of creatures gathered in council. The beings seemed like men and yet more like animals. Sometimes when she looked they were beasts and then again men. One began to speak.

He said, "Now this woman has been deceived by her sisters-in-law and we are met to plan how to save her. She must be taken from this island for the berries are poisoned and if she dies not from them the sĕgowĕnota (singing wizard) will enchant her."

For some time the speaker talked and finally asked, "Who now will carry her basket to the land?"

A large tall being with a deep bass voice answered quickly, "I will!"

"No, you may not, your pride is before your courage," said the chief speaker.

A huge bulky creature arose and called out, "I will save her!"

"No, you are too terrible in form and would frighten her," was the reply.

Several more volunteered but all were rejected until a very tall slender being arose and in a clear ringing voice said he would use his utmost power to save the unfortunate young wife if only permitted.

"You are the chosen one!" exclaimed the chief. "You are one close to the (knowledge of) people."

The council adjourned, the voices gradually died away and the lake was dotted again with flickering lights. The young wife crept back to her bed, half afraid and yet hopeful of the morrow.

Before sunrise a voice called from the water, and, starting up the young woman ran to the beach and saw what at first appeared to be a monstrous canoe, but looking again she saw a great serpent from whose head arose proud curving horns like a buffalo's.

The creature lifted his head from the waters and called.

"I have come to rescue you. Trust me and make your seat upon my head between my 'feathers.' But first break twelve osiers and use them upon me should I lag in my swimming."

The girl took her seat upon the creature's head and laid her whips in her lap. With an undulating motion his long glistening body moved through the ripples but the wife sat high and not a drop of water spattered upon her.

As her mysterious rescuer journeyed his way he told her that he must hasten with all speed as he belonged to the race of underwater people whom the mighty He"no^n hates.[1] Even now the scouts (small black clouds) might have spied him and be scudding through the sky bringing after them a host of thunder clouds. Nor was his an idle surmise, for scarcely had he spoken when a small black cloud appeared and sped with great rapidity toward them. Instantly the

---

1 He"no is the Thunder Spirit.

wind commenced to blow and the great serpent called back to his charge, "Whip me, Oh whip me! He"no[n] has discovered us and is driving onward his warriors!"

The frightened girl lashed the monster with all her strength until nearly all her withes were broken. In the distance the thunder began to roll and soon again in loud claps. The dark clouds piled thicker and came faster. The great serpent in his wild speed was lashing the black waters into a foam that flew through the wind and covered the lake. There was an ear-splitting crash. The Thunder Spirit was coming nearer. The gleaming arrow he had thrown had riven a floating oak tree. The young woman trembled beneath the dark cloud-banked sky and feared. The rumble of thunder was deafening. He"no[n] was casting his javelins faster. A great sheet of fire flashed from the heavens and lit up the lake and the shore. The thunder crashed and cracked and rumbled. In the awful fury of the tempest the great serpent cried in terror: "Oh use your lashes! Oh spur me onward! My strength is failing! Scourge me! I must save you and if I do, oh will you not burn tobacco upon the shore twice each year for me? Oh lash me more!"

A blinding flash of fire shot from the rumbling clouds and buried itself in the water at the side of the serpent.

"Jump now!" cried the creature, "He"no[n] has his range and I must dive."

Hope faded from the young wife's heart. How much better would death have been in the midst of the waters or by the lightning's stroke than within sight of the shore. With a cry of agonized despair she slid from the head of her rescuer and sank into the turbulent waters. The horned monster with a booming sound plunged beneath the lake and disappeared.

The light broke through the clouds and the storm began to retreat. The young woman struggled with the swirling waters. Her esteem for her would-be-deliverer sank to a bitter hatred for he had abandoned her to perish. Her tired limbs could no longer battle with the lake. Her feet sank but to her unspeakable surprise they fell firm on the sand. Wading forward in the semi-darkness she came safely out on the shore. Walking inland she sat down beneath a tree to recover from exhaustion and fright.

The storm sped away growling that it had failed to slay Djodi'kwado' the monster serpent.

The young wife arose, wet and bedraggled, but happy that she was safe again. Now her heart was full of gratitude to her hard-pressed deliverer.

Ahead of her, wandering aimlessly, with hanging head and melancholy mien, was a man. His body was drenched with rain and his spirit with heavy sorrow.

The woman neared him and called, "Husband, Oh husband, is it truly you?"

The man turned with a shout of joy and answered, "Wife, oh wife, returned living, is it you?"

The drenched and storm-bruised couple joyfully turned homeward. The three sisters were there. "Begone now and forever," said the husband.

Then were the couple happy, and envy and jealousy found no place with them. So here the story ends and so it is spoken.

28. BUSHY HEAD THE BEWITCHED WARRIOR RESCUES TWO LOST DAUGHTERS AND WINS THEM AS WIVES.[1]

The daughters of a woman who was a clan matron and name-holder disappeared. She grieved greatly, but her husband who was chief of another clan said nothing. He was a bad man and was chief because he had lied about his brother Donya'dassi.

Now Donya'dassi had once been a skillful hunter but his hunting charms had been stolen, and so with his wife, Gawīsas, he lived away from the village in a poor bark hut.

The mother of the lost daughters, whose children should some day be in the sachemship line, offered large rewards for their recovery and continually urged the young men to hunt for the girls, promising them as wives to the successful finder. They were most beautiful young women and there were many searchers, but when winter came, all returned without news.

Now, it happened that Gawīsas, the poor woman, was boiling corn over the fire in her lodge and thinking very intently about the lost daughters of her sister-in-law. She thought that their father, jealous of them, might have cast a spell over them and hidden them away. While thus thinking she heard a strange sound outside, a sound so unusual that it alarmed her. Her husband was absent on one of his not always profitable hunts. Soon someone knocked at the door, but Gawīsas failing to respond, a strange creature entered, looked into her face, and then advanced to the fire. This being was Bushy Head, a dwarf with an enormous bushy head. Upon its chin was a long white beard that dragged upon the floor. He seemed to be all head. The snow and ice had so caught and frozen in its

---

1   Related by Mrs. Aurelia Jones Miller, Seneca, March, 1905.   Mrs. Miller said that she had heard this story among the Six Nations of Canada and that she thought it might be of Mohawk origin.

beard that as he walked it dragged behind him like a log. Bushy Head stood before the fire, reeled up his beard and thawed out the ice. Gawïsas could not speak because she was so frightened, so she sat on her bed. The monster looked at her and then ran his cane into the fire, stirring up the ashes. The sparks flew upward and fell into the soup. Again the being looked at Gawïsas but she only stared blankly back. Grasping a ladle he filled it with ashes and threw them in the soup, and turning, eyed the frightened woman again but she did not move or speak. He kept looking at the woman until he had filled the kettle with ashes and then departed. After his departure Gawïsas recovered in a measure from her fright and dragging the kettle out of doors emptied and scoured it. To her dismay the creature, whom she had named Sogogo, returned on the next day and for six consecutive days, each time behaving as before and Gawïsas remaining silent to all proceedings. At last on the seventh day her husband, Donya'dassi, returned and she told him of all the strange happenings.

"Well, what did you say to him?" he asked, and when she replied, "Nothing," he bade her speak the next time the Sogogo came. "He wants to tell you something," he said. "So ask him what he wishes." Having given this advice Donya'dassi departed on another hunting excursion, for he had come home empty-handed. He was a chief also, but could not rule, because his wife's uncle was his enemy.

Sogogo returned soon afterward and peered into the face of Gawïsas who could only summon up enough courage to say, "Ä-ä-ä-ä-ä."

"Ä-ä-ä-ä-ä," replied Sogogo, and filled up the kettle with ashes again.

The next day passed with the same results, but on the third day Gawïsas tremblingly asked, "What do you wish, Sogogo?"

"At last," he answered, you have spoken. "I can only speak as I am spoken to, and hoped, since you would not greet me, you would chide me when I spoiled your soup. Now let me tell you that I know where the chief's daughters are and have chosen you and your husband as the ones to claim the reward. You are poor and plenty of wampum will make you powerful. Now tell your husband, and if he is willing to aid me bid him hang half the liver and half the lights of every animal he kills upon a low branch of the nearest tree. For a sign that I am telling the truth, let him chop down the big tree before your lodge and within it will be a bear."

Sogogo departed and when Donya'dassi came back from his hunt, successful this time, he was told the news. He felled the tree as directed by his wife, killed the bear and hung half the liver and half the lights on the branches on the nearest tree.

The wife was cutting some choice pieces of bear meat to cook for the afternoon meal when in walked Sogogo, and greeting Gawïsas and her husband, sat down and began talking to the man. He explained his plan for rescuing the lost daughters of the chief. Donya'dassi was to go to the top of a certain mound and seat himself in a large basket which he found there. This basket would rest on Sogogo's head and would bear him to the inside of the mound, where the chief's daughters had been hidden.

Accordingly the next day Donya'dassi seated himself in the large basket which he found on the mound and sank down under the earth..

Arrived there, Sogogo lifted the basket from his head and proceeded to instruct Donya'dassi how he must rescue the daughters.

"Go to the first lodge on the right hand side of the trail," he said. "There you will see one of the girls. Tell her you are her rescuer. Bid her sweep the floor as soon as she hears her captor approaching and continue to sweep until you depart with her. Her captor, who wishes to become her husband, has seven heads. You must kill the

creature in order to gain the girl. He will ask you to drink
berry juice with him. Poison will be in your cup but when
he winks change the cups. Then he will want to fight.
When you fight him use this short crooked knife, and rushing toward him thrust it between his seven heads and cut off
the middle one. Previously instruct the girl to sweep it in
the fire so that the flames will burn his eyebrows and lashes.
That will destroy his power and all seven heads will die.
When you have done all this return to me with the girl so
you may know what to do next."

Taking the sharp bent knife that Sogogo held toward
him, Donya'dassi thrust it in his pouch and ran down the
trail until he saw a large bark house at the right. Entering
it he saluted the young woman whom he recognized as the
eldest of the chief's stolen daughters. He instructed her,
as bidden, and had scarcely finished when the seven-headed
man entered and spying the stranger he cried, "Kwē! Come,
let us drink a little strawberry juice." He placed two gourd
cups on a bench and said, "Now drink." Just as he winked
Donya'dassi transposed the cups and when the monster
lifted the berry juice to his lips and tasted it he exclaimed,
"Ho ho!" meaning, his power was lessened.

"Come, let us fight now," he cried. "Here are the clubs;
take your choice. How does that fine new one suit you?"

"No, I'll take that old one," said Donya'dassi pointing to
a half decayed stick. "I'll fight you left-handed," he continued, "So ready!"

The daughter began to sweep and the men to fight.
Rushing upon the monster so close that no club could hit
him he thrust his knife between the heads and with a quick
jerk of his arm cut off the middle one. The girl swept it
into the fire and when the eyelashes and brows had been
singed the swaying body and six howling heads crashed to
the floor. The girl dropped her broom and followed
Donya'dassi as he ran out and down the trail.

Sogogo was waiting for them and after listening to the

story of the successful fight said, "On the left hand side, the fourth lodge down, is another lodge. Go there and rescue the other daughter. A seven-headed monster is keeping her prisoner. Instruct the girl as the first. The monster will enter and ask you to eat. When he winks change the spoons, for there is poison in the wood. Then he will challenge you as the first. Chop off his ear with your knife and when the daughter sweeps it into the fire the creature will begin to die."

Donya'dassi obeyed and events occurred exactly as Sogogo had predicted. When in the fight Sogogo had cut off the left ear from the seven-headed man and the ear had been swept into the fire, all seven heads began to whine and the middle one said, "You have plotted to kill me! You have been unfair! The woman has planned it. Oh you wicked woman, you have been a traitor to me."

"It is untrue," shouted Donya'dassi. "Your own rule has been to fight all who enter your door and now you are defeated. Before our fight you boasted you would grind me in your mortar and commanded me to do the same with you and feed your body to the birds."

"Agē, agē, agē!" moaned the monster and died.

"Shall I smash his body?" said Donya'dassi, but the maiden did not know. "Go, then," said he, "and ask Sogogo."

When she returned she told him to grind the body to a pulp in the corn mortar and hasten back to Sogogo who awaited him. Donya'dassi pounded the monster heads and flung the mass to the big crows that already had clustered about the lodge.

Running up the trail, with the girl following him, Donya'dassi found Sogogo waiting. The two girls and Donya'dassi seated themselves in the basket, Sogogo lifted it upon his head and in a short time they emerged from the top of the mound and breathed the outside air once again.

Sogogo led the three to his lodge far back in the forest

where he told all his history and then bade Donya'dassi run to the lodge of the great chief and tell him to call a great council at which important news would be revealed and presents given.

When the chief had listened to Donya'dassi he asked, "What news can you bring and what presents can you give?"

"I have luck now," was the answer.

The feast day came and people flocked from distant villages to hear the news and receive the presents.

Donya'dassi arose and said, "I have come to tell our great chief that his daughters have been found and are now safe and near here and shall be restored on one condition, that he remove his spell from a certain young man whom he has conjured."

The chief was greatly angered that any condition should be given and refused to grant it.

Meanwhile Donya'dassi was arranging long strings of wampum and piles of skins in piles on the council-house floor, one for each person present.

"These cannot be distributed until our chief grants my condition," he said.

The chief remained obdurate. The people were anxious for their feast and gifts. The chief's wife begged him to consent and regain his lost children. So, fearing the anger of his people and fury of his wife, he at last asked that the young man who rested under the spell be brought to him. Sogogo entered. The chief looked ashamed and then frowned in anger. "Come," he said and led the way to a small dome shaped lodge, pushed Sogogo in and then entered himself. Heating some round stones he threw a handful of magical herbs upon them. Then taking his rattle chanted a song. The smoke from the herbs enveloped Sogogo and when the song ended he had become a handsome young warrior. The chief and the transformed Sogogo reëntered the council.

"Where are the daughters!" shouted the people.

Drawing out a red bark box from his pouch he opened it and out fell the two girls. There was a great shout and the chief's wife rushed forward and embraced her children.

Donya'dassi distributed his presents.

Donya'dassi then advanced to the chief who gave him the reward, but so small was it in comparison with Donya'dassi's liberal gifts that it seemed a mere trifle.

The chief soon lost his influence but Donya'dassi, who hod grown rich and successful, succeeded him in the hearts of the people but Sogogo, the transformed, was happy with his two wives, the chief's daughters. He took both, that was all right in those days.

29. THE FLINT CHIP THROWER.

Long ago Tĕg'wandă'[1] married a beautiful maiden and went far away with her to his hunting grounds.

Tĕg'wandă' was famous as a successful hunter but his wife's family had "dry bones",[2] so her elder sister and mother took council together and said, "Come, let us go and live with Tĕg'wandă' and we shall ever be filled." The prospect of a never failing supply of venison and bear was tempting to those who had long subsisted on tubers and maize.

The wife of Tĕg'wandă' was kind and never questioned his actions. He never went long from the house, yet he ever had game in abundance and skins piled high in his stores. This made her marvel, but she never made inquiries. The lodge was divided in two compartments but the couple lived only in one. The other was almost empty, but Tĕg'wandă' often went there. She would hear him singing alone in the room, then there would come a crash like a splintering tree and soon afterward Tĕg'wandă' would bring in a new pelt and the carcass of some beast. This made her marvel but she never questioned.

The young couple lived contentedly and never quarreled. No trouble or sorrow came to mar their happiness until one day, unheralded, came two women to the door of the lodge. These were the wife's mother and sister. When the unbidden guests had eaten their fill of good and mealy nut pudding they began to seek the excuse for complaint. Then, oh the railing, the endless rebukes, the sneers and sarcasm! At last the matters turned from the lodge to the couple themselves.

"How does Tĕg'wandă' obtain his meat? Surely he must be a wizard and likely to eat all of us women when his

---

1 Meaning flint, properly Hot"hagwen"da'.
2 "Dry-bones" is a Seneca idiom meaning "lean from lack of food."

charms fail. He is evil, he is lazy! Let us drive him away."
These and other things the mother said to her daughter.
So it came to pass that the sister insisted she must go with
the husband wherever he went and learn something of his
habits.

"If you must go," said the wife, "obey him implicitly,
else evil will occur."

The husband was downcast but would not yield to his
fear of the woman. Taking a basket of salt he sprinkled
the white crystals upon a flat rock and entered the closed
room with the woman.

"Do not move or touch a thing," he commanded. "Let
no fear, let no surprise cause you to stir!"

Then he commenced to sing. The woman looked about
critically. In one corner was a pile of quarry flakes, beside
them a bench and in a heap before it was a pile of keen
edged flint chips. A sudden sound drew her attention from
the lodge. Tĕg'wandă' ceased singing. Outside some
creature was snorting, "swe-i-i-i-sh, swe-i-i-i-sh!"

Picking up a handful of flint chips the man flung them
with all his strength against the wall nearest the flat rock.
The woman was now curious to find what was outside and
pushed aside the curtain to get a glimpse of the mysterious
things. Instantly the entire door curtain was torn from its
fastenings and a monstrous elk rushed in and trampled
upon Tĕg'wandă'. Then tossing him upon its antlers,
bounded out and fled through the forest. The frightened
woman ran after the elk, but fell back dispairing. Moaning she crept back to the lodge and confessed to the wife.

The wife burst into tears and then bitterly chided her
sister for her meddlesome ways. Throwing on her robes
she hastened to rescue her husband. Carefully she tracked
the elk and after many days journey she heard a low trembling song. She knew her husband was near, so cautiously
advancing she came to a spot where she could see a herd
of elks feeding in an open. A deer was grazing near by.

Gently she whispered. "Come, good brother, lend me your coat. You can do me good service thereby." "Certainly," responded the deer with alacrity, and, walking inconspicuously into the bushes, she removed her coat and threw it upon the woman. In her new habiliments the wife bounded off into the midst of the elks. In the middle and surrounded by the rest was a large reclining elk whose antlers held the emanciated form of Tĕg'wandă'. In a feeble whisper the husband sang.

Walking toward the elk she made a sudden dash and inserting her horns beneath her husband's body lifted him off and dashed away before the astonished animals could remonstrate, and indeed, they were too frightened to do so. Galloping breathlessly into the thicket she set down her husband, removed the deer's skin and gave it back with expressions of gratitude. Then lifting her husband upon her shoulders, she carried him homeward.

On her journey she pondered how she could restore him. He was exhausted and covered with bruises and wounds, his body had wasted away to a skeleton covered with skin and his mind was turned with his sufferings. Sitting down upon a hollow log she pondered. A sudden inspiration came. Quickly she pushed her husband into a hollow log and gave him a shove with her foot that sent him sliding through. When he emerged from the other end he was competely restored.

Together they tramped back home happy to be together once more. Entering the lodge the husband cast out the inquisitive sister and quarrelsome mother and sent them running down the trail.

"One woman is sufficient female company for any man," he said. "More in one house make great trouble."

HORROR TALES OF CANNIBALS
AND SORCERERS

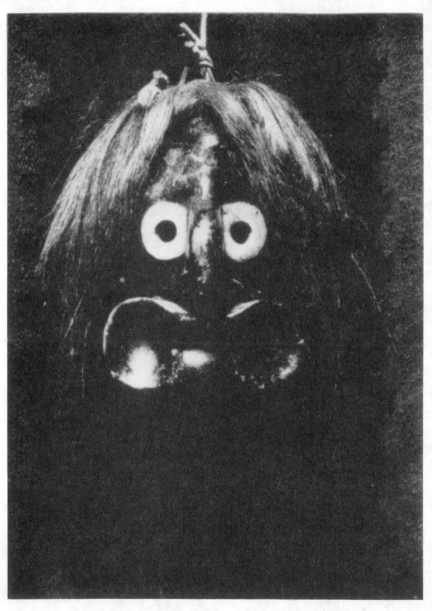

HADUI MASK OF THE FALSE FACE COMPANY.

VII

30. THE DUEL OF THE DREAM TEST BETWEEN UNCLE AND NEPHEW

There was a great long house built of poles and bark. This long house was in a secluded place where men were not accustomed to come, but there were sorcerers who knew its location, but shunned it, for there lived Shogo^{n}'gwā's and his nephew Djoñiaik. The nephew was young when the uncle assumed charge of him, and he had no real regard for the boy, for he had slain by sorcery all his near relatives, and knew that he must some day overcome the orenda (magic) that had accrued to the boy, or he himself would be undone.

Djoñiaik was carefully reared, for the uncle wished to make him suffer at the end and cry out his weakness, thereby more greatly enjoying the triumph over him.

When the boy had grown to the age just before he became eligible for his dream fast, the uncle said, "Now my nephew, the time has come when you should hunt for yourself without me. Go into the forest and bring me meat."

Thereupon Djoñiaik took his small bow and after a time found a partridge which he shot. Bringing it to the lodge of his uncle he presented it to the elder man. "Oh now, my nephew," said Shogo^{n}gwas, "what is the name of this thing?"

'Oh my uncle," replied the boy, "I have never known the name of this kind of a thing."

"Ho!" exclaimed the uncle, "How then do you expect to be able to eat it?"

The boy then was given the task of cleaning the bird for soup, and when it was ready the older man put it in a clay kettle and boiled it with a gruel of corn meal. Then he lifted out the meat and placed it with the fat gravy in a

bark bowl which he laid aside for himself. Taking another
bowl he filled it with the thin soup from the middle of the
kettle and handed it over the fire to the boy. The boy
reached from his seat, stretching his arms and finally
grasped the bowl, but as he did so the uncle pulled on the
bowl and the boy fell face forward into the fire, scorching
his chest and burning his hands. At this the uncle roared
and called him clumsy, asking moreover, "Where is your
soup? You have tried to put out the fire with it!"

With great gusto the uncle devoured the partridge, picking the bones clean and casting them into the fire. Djoñiaik
had nothing for his meal and was very hungry. Wearily
he wandered out into the thicket, coming at length to an
unfamiliar spot where there was a low mound, as if a
mud hut had fallen down and become overgrown. As he
looked at the spot he heard a sound, "Ketcuta, ketcuta!"
Peering more closely in the snow-covered moss he saw
the face of a tcis'gä (skull) looking at his with open
mouth.

"I am your uncle," said the skull. "Give me tobacco."

Djoñiaik obeyed, and when the skull had smoked a pipeful, it coughed and said, "I am your uncle, bewitched by
my brother who has stolen you in order to work vengeance
on you for the power you inherit from your relatives who
have been killed by sorcery. You must remember the
names of the animals you kill and the next one you shall find
will be a raccoon. Remember its name and when your
guardian asks you its name tell him 'raccoon'."

In time the boy went hunting again and finding a raccoon
shot it. Greatly excited he began to repeat the name raccoon over and over. "Raccoon, raccoon, raccoon, raccoon,"
he shouted as he bore it to his uncle's lodge. But so rapidly
was he running that he fell over the door-sill and sprawled
into the lodge.

"Oh now nephew, what have you this time?" inquired
the uncle, but so excited and chagrined was the boy that

he totally forgot the name. "Wa!" exclaimed the old man, "If you cannot speak the name of this thing you shall not eat of it. Dress it for me and I will cook it as a soup."

When the raccoon was cooked the old man skimmed off the fat and poured out some thin soup for Djoñiaik, who by this time was very hungry. Uncle and nephew sat on seats opposite each other with the lodge fire between. Passing over the bowl of soup the uncle gave a quick jerk as the boy grasped the rim and again pulled him into the fire.

"Oh nephew, I am sorry," said he, laughing, "I am always in a hurry." But Djoñiaik was sadly burned about the face and made no reply. With hungry eyes he watched his uncle stow away the uneaten portion of the raccoon. He had not a mouthful.

That afternoon he again visited his skeletal uncle and related all that had happened. He was thoroughly afraid now for his uncle was most ugly. But the skull, when it nad smoked, only advised him to remember the names of the animals killed. "Today, I believe, you will shoot a turkey. Remember the name and begin to use your power to retaliate," said the skull.

After watching quietly Djoñiaik saw a turkey,—a very large and fat turkey, which he shot. Tying its feet together he held it to his back by a burden strap and lugged it home, rushing into the lodge saying, "Turkey, turkey, turkey, turkey."

This time the uncle asked no questions, but with a frown watched his nephew pluck the turkey and prepare it.

"This time I shall prepare a roast of meat," said the boy. "I shall not make soup as my uncle does." So he cooked the turkey in a pot and when done he divided the meat in two portions, putting each in a bark bowl. "Now come eat, Uncle," said the boy handing the bowl over the fire to his uncle.

As the old man's hand grasped the bowl, Djoñiaik gave

it a quick pull, overbalancing his uncle and pulling him into the fire.

"Oh nephew!" exclaimed the uncle. "You have purposely abused me and burned my face and stomach. My hair is on fire. You have distressed me." But the boy said only, "Oh I was in such a hurry." And then he fell to eating the turkey, putting the uneaten portion on the shelf over his bed. This time the old man ate nothing.

The next morning very early the boy said, "I shall now arise and hunt game which comes to feed early in the morning." So saying he arose, dressed and took his bow and went out. The old man was awake and looked very angry.

So Djoñiaik went directly to the skull and gave it tobacco. When it had smoked it said, "You shall hunt today and shoot a deer, but when you go back to the lodge your uncle will say, 'It will be a cold night and I will gather large logs for a night fire.' He will awaken at midnight with a dream and you must hit him on the head to awaken him, when he will relate his desire, it being to barter meat for fat bear casings. You must prepare yourself by taking a grape vine and transforming it as desired." So instructed the boy went upon his hunt and killed a deer, bringing it home saying, "I have furnished a deer for the larder." That night after they had eaten of the deer, the old man looked very angry.

"This will be a very cold night, I think," said the old man. "I shall gather logs to burn during the night." And so saying he made a roaring fire and went to bed.

Cautiously the nephew arranged his buffalo skin coverlet so that he had a peep-hole through a worn spot. At midnight the uncle arose and walking on his knees to the fire began to utter a worried sound, "Eñh, enh, enh, enh!" Then he threw one of the burning logs upon Djoñiaik, his nephew. Immediately the boy leaped up, being awake, and threw the log back into the fireplace, at the same time crying, "What is your dream, my uncle?" and then tapping the old man on the head with a club.

"It has now ceased," answered the uncle, rubbing his head and becoming awake.

"The roof must be removed," said the uncle, meaning that he had dreamed that the two must engage in a duel of wits. "Tomorrow we must barter, and I shall give, and you, Oh nephew, shall repay me with that which I must not tell you, but which you must guess, and failing great calamity will befall us."

"That is very easy," answered the boy. "Go to sleep; in the morning I will be ready."

Morning came and the old man began to sing. "Yoh heh, yoh heh, yoh heh, I shall trade with my nephew Djoñiaik, and he shall give me my desire." So did he sing continually.

It was a song that only a sorcerer would sing and its sound traveled far, so much so that all the wizards heard it and said, "Shogoⁿ'gwā's is singing again and this time has chosen his own nephew as a victim." So they all came and perched about in the house, being invisible, to watch the duel of orendas (magic powers).

Djoñiaik was bidden sit at the end of the long house, and it was very long indeed, there being many abandoned fireplaces in it. Far at the end he sat on the far side of an old fire bed. His uncle began to sing again, and walked forward with a bark tray in which were pieces of meat. "I offer these to you," he said. "You shall give me what I am thinking about."

"Only give me a clue, uncle," begged the boy. "How can I divine what is in your mind?"

"Torture by fire awaits you if you guess not by midsun," sang the old man still holding out the meat, while the boy pretended to be thinking deeply.

"Oh, uncle," said the boy, "you desire raccoon meat."

"No, not raccoon meat. Oh nephew, you must divine my word."

"Oh uncle, you want turkey."

"No not turkey. Oh nephew, you must divine my word."

"Oh uncle, you want partridge."

"No not partridge. Oh nephew you must divine my word."

Again the boy sought to evade his uncle by exclaiming, "How can you expect me to guess your dream unless you give me some clue to your desire?"

Again the uncle fell to singing the charm song that conjures up flames, and suddenly they burst forth from the ground with a loud sound enveloping the poor nephew who wrestling with them, cried, "Oh uncle your desire is for the bear casings enclosed in deep fat."

"Niio'!" exclaimed the uncle, and the flames died down, whereupon Djoñiaik brought forth his grape stalk which he had conjured to look like the casings of a bear. Then was the uncle satisfied.

That afternoon the boy retired to the forest and sought his skeletal advisor, telling him all that had happened.

"Once more," said the skull, "your uncle will make a demand and all the circumstances will be similar. This time he will desire a bear's liver. Go to a log in the swamp, pluck a red tree fungus and rub it with your hands until it becomes a liver."

So instructed the boy was ready for his wizard uncle. As before the logs were gathered and a great fire made, and in the middle of the night the old man flung fire upon the boy again.

When the dialogue was over the boy found that once more a test was to come. "It is nothing," said he. "Go to sleep."

Morning came and the old wizard sang his charm song. The boy took his seat as before and when pressed by the flame he cried out, "You wish a liver of a bear, Oh uncle."

The uncle was not at all pleased with his nephew's power for he wished to consume him with fire, after the manner prescribed for torture, but he could not.

Reporting the event to the skull, the boy asked for further help. "Tonight you must dream, and when your guardian has struck you with a club to awaken you, you must crave the guessing of your word, which shall be one of the squashes that grow in a sand box under your uncle's bed. It is a great prize. Have no mercy but get what you demand."

That night the boy gathered firewood, remarking that he expected the night to be very cold and wanted to warm the lodge. The uncle only scowled.

Midnight came, and the invisible wizards and sorcerers were watching. Stealthily the boy arose, and creeping on his knees, he approached the fire, grasping a blazing log and throwing it upon his uncle, as sleeping persons do. Then he began to grunt, "Eñh, enh, enh, enh," as if in distress.

The uncle awoke, being severely scorched and his bed set afire. "Oh nephew," he called as he gave the boy a knock on the head to awaken him. "What do you wish?"

"It has now ceased," said the boy. "Oh uncle, I have dreamed that you and I must exchange gifts, and that you must give me what I desire."

"It shall so be," answered the uncle. "This is nothing."

The two then retired and early in the morning the boy awoke and took his seat. In a tray he had some turkey meat.

Commencing his song he called out, "I am trading a gift with Shogo^n"gwa's, my uncle. He shall give me in exchange what I most desire." So saying he sang the charm song that conjures flames from the earth.

The old man took his seat and when approached said, "I shall divine your word if you will give me a clue."

"Any clue would spoil the intention of the dream, uncle."

"Then tell me at once what you wish,—be quick about it!"

"To utter one word would be fatal to my desire."

"Then the word is deer meat."

"No not deer meat, uncle. Hurry for I shall sing."

"Then you wish moose meat."

"No not moose meat, uncle. Hurry or I shall sing."

"Then you wish my coonskin robe."

"No not your coonskin robe. I now commence to sing."

"Then you wish my otterskin robe," hastened the uncle, naming one of his prized possessions.

"No uncle, not your otterskin robe. I now sing."

With a burst of the conjurer's song, the boy began to sing, "Yoh heh, yoh heh, yoh heh. My uncle and I are exchanging. He shall give me what I most desire." As he sang his flames leaped from the ground, for Djoñiaik was now an adept in magic. Surrounding the uncle the flames began to singe him. With a shriek he leaped to the platform above his bed, but the flames followed, until he called out, "Oh nephew I yield!"

Descending he said, "You desire the squash beneath my bed," and the boy exclaimed, "It is so."

With great reluctance the old wizard opened the bed, lifting up the bottom boards like the top of a chest. Beneath in boxes of sand were vines with squashes growing upon them, though it was winter outside. Taking a look at the largest, the old man shut down the cover and exclaimed:

"Oh nephew, it is the custom to simulate what is desired in a dream. I shall now carve you from wood a squash that you may preserve as a charm."

"Only the real object desired shall satisfy me," answered the boy. "Must I sing again?" And he started his song which brought forth flames that enshrouded the old man, causing him to cry out, "Oh nephew, I yield!"

This time the boy obtained the squash and with it the injunction to take care of it, for it was a great prize.

Reporting the episode to the skull, the boy received further instruction. He was to dream again and was to demand as the satisfying word, his hidden sister who was concealed in a bark case beneath the wizard's bed. This was a great surprise to the boy, for he had not dreamed that he had a sister concealed, this being the treatment given children born with a caul. They were hidden by day and only allowed to go out by night.

"The wizard hopes to keep the child," said the skull. "It is his greatest prize and unless you are very firm he will cause you to err, thereby escaping your demand. Have no pity but push him to the uttermost with your demand."

Again the boy built the lodge fire and as midnight came, he crept from his coverings and crawled along the floor of the great cavernous lodge. Slowly creeping to the fire he seized a blazing log and with a cry flung it upon his sleeping uncle, at the same time grunting, "Enh, enh, enh, enh," as if in distress.

With a whack of his club the old man awakened the boy, who called out, "It has ceased," meaning the vision.

"Oh uncle," he said. "I have dreamed that you must give me something in exchange for the gift I shall offer you tomorrow."

"It shall be done," answered the uncle with a dark frown.

Morning came and with it the test. Long the old man sought to cause the boy to make one small slip in the custom but he failed. Mid-day came and as the sun beat down through the smoke hole the boy began his charm song, causing flames to arise as torture for the old wizard.

After much haggling the old man opened his bed once more and revealed a bark case beautifully decorated. He removed this and placed it on a mat, after which he opened the case and unwrapped a small woman, beautifully white, and perfect in form, though only as long as a man's arm.

"Oh nephew," said the uncle, "Now that you have seen

your sister, I will replace her and give you what is customary in such instances, a carved imitation. You will be greatly pleased with the doll I give you."

In reply the boy gave his charm song and again the magic flames circled about the uncle like a clinging garment. 'Oh nephew, I yield," he cried and handed over the case.

After much haggling the old man opened his bed once assured that success would come if he withstood one more test,—that of bodily torture by cold. "Your uncle will dream tonight and his word will be satisfied only by causing you to be divested of all clothing and tied to a bark toboggan and dragged ten times around the long house where you dwell. I know not that you will endure, for your magic is equal."

As predicted the old man dreamed that his nephew strip the next morning, though the weather was extremely cold. "I must drag you around the lodge ten times," said the uncle, but first I must bind you securely with thongs."

"It will be very easy," said the boy. "Really, it is nothing at all."

Emerging from the door the boy stood in the intense cold and stripped himself, throwing his garments back into the lodge. "Now I am ready," said he, and his uncle then bound him tightly with thongs, placing him on the bark toboggan.

After the first trip around the uncle called out, "Oh nephew, are you still alive?" And the boy answered, "Yes, uncle," in his loudest tones.

For a second time the uncle made a circuit of the long house, which was the longest in the world, and again called out, "Oh nephew, are you alive?" receiving an answer just a bit fainter, "Yes, uncle."

Each time around the uncle asked the same question and each time the answer was fainter until the ninth time his nephew's voice was scarcely audible. So he made another circuit, thinking as he made it, "This time he is frozen as stiff as an icicle."

So when he had completed his tenth round he spoke again, "Oh nephew, are you alive?" And to his great surprise the boy called in the most sprightly tones, "Yes uncle," whereupon he was released of the cords and entered the lodge.

All this the boy reported to the skull who said, "On this night you shall dream, and you shall demand that your wizard uncle submit to the same ordeal. Allow him no mercy, for if he gains in one point all is lost."

Midnight came and with it the episode of the dream demand. The old man weakly yielded and then both slept until morning. The test then began, but the old man begged, saying, "I am old and if you will allow me to retain my clothing you will be satisfied." But the nephew answered, "Oh no, uncle, I must be satisfied according to my desires. What you say has nothing to do with the event."

"Then do not bind me, for the cords will cut my flesh and this is not a part of the demand."

Nevertheless the boy bound his uncle and threw him on his toboggan. With the completion of each circuit he would ask his uncle if he were alive, and each time would be assured that he was. Upon finishing the ninth trip he again asked, "Uncle, are you alive?" but there was no reply and drawing the toboggan to the door he felt of his uncle and found him frozen as stiff as an icicle.

He thereupon, lifted the toboggan high, and his uncle was upon it. With a mighty fling he threw it afar and when it came down with a crash his uncle broke into bits like an image of ice.

Reporting the event to the skull he was praised for his endurance. "Now we shall all live again and those who have been overcome by magic will be set free," said the skull. "Cover me with a bear skin and when I call lift me from the ground." Soon he called and Djoñiaik grasped the skull and lifted it from the earth and with it the cramped body of the tcisga.   Rubbing it with his hands and anointing it he restored it to the form of a normal man.

"I am your uncle, restored," said the former skeleton. "Let us now search for your father and mother."   Together they set off and found another mound from which they conjured the skeletons of a man and a woman, and restored them by rubbing and by oil.

All with great joy returned to the long house where they attended to the little sister, Djoñiaik rubbing her as was his custom and restoring her to a full grown maiden.

Everyone was now happy, and the roosting wizards silently departed, leaving the great long house habitable for the restored family, and soon more men and women and children came to live in the long house and it became a dwelling where all were happy.

THE VAMPIRE SIRENS WHO WERE OVER-
COME BY THE BOY WHOSE UNCLE POS-
SESSED A MAGIC FLUTE.

There was a long bark lodge, alone by itself in a small
clearing. Here dwelt an elderly man and his nephew.
Hadno"sĕⁿ, the uncle, possessed a marvelous flute, which he
kept in his war bundle, wherein also were all his charms for
luck in warfare and in hunting. The flute possessed great
power, and it was the oracle most consulted by the old man.
Misfortune had befallen the people through the machinations of certain sorcerers, and the flute remained the only
potent charm left by which the old man might fortell events.

As the uncle grew older he began to worry about the
future, for he was reaching the age when men cease to go
on hunting excursions. Now his nephew, Hauñwaⁿ'dĕⁿ',
was at the age when it was considered that a boy is not yet
ready for the rigors of the chase. Therefore, the old
uncle was perplexed.

On a certain night the old man came home to the great
empty bark lodge and threw down a deer. "This is my last
hunt," he exclaimed. "My nephew, you must soon learn to
shoot."

"Oh I can shoot as well as any one," said the boy with
great assurance, and so the old man gave him his bow and
an arrow. "Shoot the spot where I have hit that stump
with an arrow," said the old man, and the boy taking the
big bow and long arrow, pulled the cord back and shot. His
arrow struck the very spot where his uncle had pointed
out an arrow mark. "Tcă', tcă'!" exclaimed the old man.
"You are now able to shoot. Tomorrow you may go hunting, but first wait, I will tell you what animal you will be
able to kill."

So saying the uncle took his flute from its bundle and
examined it. Then he blew a few notes of a charm song
upon it. In another moment the flute itself uttered notes

though nobody blew upon it. "This indicates that you will kill a deer," announced the uncle.

The next day Hauñwandeh went into the forest alone and shot a deer, which he brought home to his uncle. "This is good," said the uncle. "Now let me consult my flute again."

Once again he blew the notes of the charm song upon his flute, waited a moment and then heard it call out, "Two deer shall be killed tomorrow."

"Now, my nephew," said the uncle looking very grave, "I must tell you that while you must in the future hunt for both of us, you must never go south. Listen to what I say, never go south."

On the morrow the boy returned dragging two deer and threw them on the ground outside his uncle's doorway. Again the uncle expressed his satisfaction, and again he consulted his flute. "My nephew," he announced after listening to the oracle, "tomorrow you shall kill a deer and a fat bear. Again I warn you never to go south."

The boy that night had troubled dreams and through his mind the question was repeated over and over, "Why may I not go south, Oh why may I not go south?"

The hunting continued each day as before, but the boy was greatly troubled about his uncle's command. Nevertheless he obeyed until he saw that the lodge was well supplied with meat which hung in the smoke from every rafter, curing for winter's use. Then he thought that come what might to him he would go south, and if he died his uncle would have plenty to eat for a long time.

So resolved he went on his hunt, and by taking a circuitous route, he went from east to south. Soon he found the trail of an elk which he followed southward for a very long ways. Greatly fatigued by the chase he still kept up the pursuit, until he came to a little open place in the forest, where to his great surprise he saw a young woman sitting on a log at the side of the trail. She looked up at him with a bewitching smile and said, "Come sit on the log with me, you look tired."

Hauñwandeh looked at her, found her pleasing, and so went to the log and sat down, saying nothing. Soon the girl spoke again. "It is not customary," said she, "for young people to sit so far apart when they meet as we have done. Draw close to me and rest your head on my lap, for you are very tired."

The boy therefore sat closely to her and then placed his head in her lap. Thereupon the girl fell to stroking his hair and scratching his head, looking the while for wood lice. As she did this the boy began to feel sleepy and fearing something of evil might befall him tied one of his hairs to a root beneath the log, which act the girl did not notice. Then he fell into a deep sleep.

When the young woman saw that he was fully asleep she began to pat his body with her hand, and the boy shrunk in size with every pat until he was so small that the young woman placed him with ease in the basket she carried. Then she leaped into the air and flew away, as witches do. In a short time, however, she came to a halt and was slowly

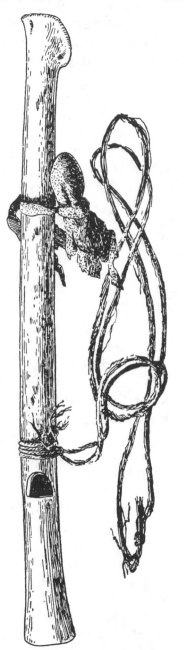

MAGIC WHISTLE.
This whistle, used in shamanistic ceremonies, is made from an eagle's wing-bone.

drawn back to the log from which she had started. The hair had stretched its limit and drew her back. She took the boy out of the basket and struck him with a small paddle and he became restored. "I will fix him next time," thought she.

Hauñwandeh was now in the power of the witch-girl and stayed all day with her, until he became sleepy again, when she stroked his head once more, putting him to sleep. Making him small by patting, she again placed him in her basket and flew through the air to a river bank. Taking him out she asked, "Do you know where you are?" Hoping to destroy her magic he answered, "Oh yes, I know where I am. This is the place where my uncle and I catch our fish." So she put him in her basket and flew to an island in a large lake. Taking him out she questioned him further, "Do you know this place?" Still hoping to deceive her he answered, "Oh this is the place where my uncle and I come with our canoe."

Angry that she could not take him to an unfamiliar spot the witch-girl replaced him in her basket and leaped high in the air, this time taking him to a far distant place. Descending she alighted on the edge of a great precipice, so deep that the tops of the trees below were only faintly visible. She gave a shriek and threw the basket over the cliff.

Now Hauñwandeh, being attacked by the powers of witchcraft, began to develop his own magic power, and when he went over the cliff and felt himself falling, he desired to fall as an autumn leaf, and so he fluttered down to the bottom without injury. He tumbled out of the basket and saw that he was in a deep hole in the earth and that there was no means of escape. Looking about him he saw the skeletons of numerous men, and not far away he saw two men who were alive but partially eaten.

They spoke to him. "Oh miserable youth," said they. "We are of the opinion that you have not long to live."

"How did you get here?" asked the boy.

"We met a young woman," said they, "who lured us to be friendly with her, and she stroked our hair, then took us in a basket and threw us down the cliff. A great bird comes and bites our bodies and we are being eaten and yet cannot die."

As they spoke, a gigantic bird flew by, and darting at the youth, took a large bit out of his arm. He looked at the wound and licked it, and it immediately healed.

* * * * *

When the uncle missed his nephew he became greatly distressed. Taking out his flute he looked at it and found that the mouth of it was stained with a smear of blood. "Agi'," he exclaimed. "My nephew has disobeyed and now is wounded."

* * * * *

The next day the big bird returned and took a mouthful from the boy's arm, but as before he placed the wound to his mouth and healed it by his own power.

That night the waiting uncle looked at his flute again and found it very bloody. "Agi'," he exclaimed, "some direful thing has happened and I shall never see my nephew again."

On the following day the bird swooped at him and tore his body cruelly, eating large chunks of it, but as before he healed himself.

As he lay pondering over his misery he heard a voice and looking up saw a little old woman. Very small was she and stooped over. "I have taken pity on you," she said. "I have a medicine for you. Take it and if in the morning you find a green sprig coming from your mouth, snatch it quickly, for it is a quickly growing tree. Pull up the plant that you find beneath your feet and put the green sprig into the hole. It will grow to the top of the cliff and you may escape. If you have strong power within you there can be no failure." So saying she handed the boy a small white root which he swallowed. Seeing this the little old woman vanished.

The next morning Hauñwandeh felt a pain in his stomach and soon he felt a scratching in his throat. Out came a green sprig which he snatched quickly and, pulling up a small withered plant he thrust the sprig into the hole and waited.

For a very long time the uncle awaited the return of his nephew, and mourned greatly. Not once did he leave the lodge but sat within with his face covered with the white ashes from the lodge fire. Each day a sound would be heard and a voice would call, "Hail Uncle, I have returned!" Leaping up with gladness the uncle would look out, but see only a scampering fox or mocking screech owl, or perhaps a wild goose. So he fell to answering all calls by saying, "Depart quickly, I know that you are deceiving me." So, in mourning he sat, covered with ashes and growing thinner and weaker every day.

Hauñwandeh watched the green sprig, and noticed that it had begun to grow. This pleased him greatly and he called all the bones in the valley saying: "I will gather you together in one pile. I will cause your resurrection and you shall escape with me for I have a growing tree which we may climb." So saying he gathered the bones in a pile and called quickly, "Hurry now, for you shall arise. Quickly, for the tree is growing. Hasten, for I am now thrusting a tree upon you, and you must arise before the tree falls upon you." Then he kicked over the tree and it fell, but before it touched the ground all the skeletons arose looking like men. The two partly eaten men recovered and said, "We are your relatives." Now two men who had been restored fell to quarreling, because each had taken the other's legs in the haste of arising, but the boy commanded them to be still and follow him up the tree. So all followed, and he further ordered all to look upward and not downward, for one look downward meant destruction. The tree was very tall and it took a long time to climb it, and when the company had climbed a long ways the two quarreling men looked down to see how far they had gone, and as they looked they turned to skeletons again and their bones rattled through the limbs of the tree and past the others who were climbing.

At length all reached the top and gathered about the edge of the cliff. Then the boy saw that the company looked very friendly, and he discovered two brothers among them. "I must go to the house of the young woman," he said to his brothers. "I leave this company in your care. I must overcome the evil magic of the great witches. When I have done this I shall return. Wait for me."

Hauñwandeh determined to have his revenge. He sought the house of the witches and went straight toward it. Reaching the door, he entered saying, "I have come."

Sitting in the lodge was the young woman who had bewitched him, and at the lodge fire was the mother, the great witch, and in the rear of the lodge were six daughters.

The mother looked up, saying, "Oh son-in-law, I dreamed you would come. My daughter is waiting for you."

That night the old witch became disturbed in her sleep and arose and flung herself in the fire, crying out a strange noise. Hauñwandeh grabbed the corn pounder and hit her on the head, saying, "Awake and tell me." So she awoke and said, "Oh son-in-law, I have dreamed that calamity will befall us unless you repair to the long lake and kill two white otters, and do it quickly, before the skin curtain of the lodge door stops swinging, from your out-going."

"That will be very easy," answered the youth. "Be at ease and I will soon return." So speaking he tied his long hairs together and made a string that reached from the door to the lake. This he tied to the skin curtain and kept it swinging as he ran to the lake.

"Otters come forth," he commanded, and one great white

otter leaped from the lake, but the youth killed it with a round white stone that he carried in his pouch. As he did this a wave arose and sped toward him bearing on its crest the other great white otter. As it leaped toward him he killed it as he had the first. Running back to the lodge he flung the bodies in, with a laugh, exclaiming, "Here are your otters."

"Where?" screamed the witch woman, leaping from her bed. "Here," he replied. "I shall now build the fire and skin them." He did this, saving the skins and throwing the carcasses into the fire. At this the witch woman screamed, "Oh, you have killed my brothers!" And the boy replied, "Did you not require this of me?" It was true, the otters were the witch woman's wizard brothers, and they were mighty in magic. The water in which they lived was magic water and when it touched the skin of a man the flesh was eaten off, as if scalded. But Hauñwandeh was harmed not at all. He was becoming a great wizard himself.

The following night the witch woman dreamed again and when awakened by her son-in-law, required that he immediately depart and kill a great eagle that dwelt in the top of a certain tall tree, and do so before the door curtain stopped swinging from his departure. Hauñwandeh obeyed and finding the tree, shot a strong arrow at the big bird, but though he used great force in drawing the bow, the arrow paused in mid-air and returned. The eagle's magic was too great. Again he shot an arrow, commanding it to kill the eagle, and the arrow obeyed, piercing the heart of the bird. It fell to his feet, and grabbing it in haste he ran to the lodge. With a laugh he flung it in the door saying, "Here is your third brother!" "Where?" shrieked the old witch, leaping from her bed. "Right here by the fire," answered Hauñwandeh. "I shall now skin it and burn its body.' When he had done this, the old witch was in a great rage. With all six daughters she was screaming and waving her blanket.

Hauñwandeh then beckoned to the young woman who had bewitched him. She looked frightened. "Come along," he commanded, "this is a bad place. We are going away."

Taking the young woman outside, he ordered her to look at the lodge, at the same time saying, "House become flint. House become heated red hot." The house obeyed and all the witches inside perished.

Then he took the young woman to the precipice and greeting the men he had rescued said, "This young woman is said to be my wife." So saying he tied her with bark cords and flung her over the cliff.

The entire company of restored men then followed Hauñwandeh, and he led them back to his uncle's lodge, calling from without, said, "Hail uncle, I have returned."

Again and again he called, and after a time he heard a voice answering, "Be away, be away from here! I shall not be deceived again by you animals!"

"I am your nephew," called the boy. "I have returned."

"Well, if you are my nephew thrust your hands through the hole in the curtain and grasp the door post," said the uncle.

The boy did as suggested and his uncle tied his arms very tightly, so that he was made prisoner. Then the uncle looked out and saw his nephew.

"Oh wait until I become cleaned," cried the uncle, brushing off the ashes and washing his blackened face.

So he cleansed himself and untied his nephew's arms. Then he invited all the restored relatives into the lodge for a great feast; so then Hauñwandeh told the story of his adventures; that is how we know about it.

32. YOUNGER BROTHER ELUDES HIS SISTER-IN-LAW BY CREATING OBSTACLES AND LIBERATES OLDER BROTHER.

Far from any settlement of Oñgwe Hoñwe', there was a lonely lodge wherein dwelt two brothers, one older than the other. Older Brother was the hunter and provided meat for the lodge, and Younger Brother cooked the food. All things went well until upon a certain day Older came home with no game. Younger carefully observed his clothing and found fresh blood stains upon it, thereby knowing that he had killed game.

Day by day the brother now returned without game of any kind, although his body and clothing proved by blood stains that he had been successful. Food in the lodge became scarce and Younger began to get very hungry, but Older seemed to be well fed. Younger watched him and noticed that he seemed to be thinking of something other than the matters about which he spoke. Inquiry revealed nothing of value, for Older would always say, "Oh my Younger Brother, you should not bother me."

The Older Brother went on another hunting trip, taking many accoutrements, as if for a long trip. Younger determined to follow him and spy upon his actions. Carefully tracking Older, Younger went down the trail until he came to a spring, where he noticed a small path concealed by leaves and branches. He determined to follow this. In a short time he saw a new lodge. It appeared to be very new for the bark had not yet fully dried, being still of the smell of the tree. Concealing himself in a clump of bushes he watched. Soon he heard two voices, one of them a woman's. The woman was ordering a man to do certain things and he was pleading to be set free. Soon a man came out of the lodge and went west. Younger then saw that it was his brother.

When Older had been gone for a time Younger stood up and walked toward the lodge, making a noise with his feet to attract attention. The woman heard the sound and came out of the house. She was young and very handsome and had a peculiar way of lifting her head and when she looked she seemed to draw her eyes together making an upright wrinkle between. Her eyes seemed yellow with bright spots in them.

Soon she observed Younger standing still on the path and smiled, calling him to her. He advanced to the lodge and she stepped inside, saying "Dadjoh," inviting him in. Younger entered and the young woman embraced him and placed her hand on his body, in greeting. Younger noticed that she had a hook on her hand attached to a long fish line and that she was endeavoring to fasten the hook into him. He fled from the lodge and ran down the trail, saying, "I will make ready and return." Younger now returned to his own lodge and awaited the coming of Older Brother.

After a long time Older returned and sat down by the fire. Younger looked at him a while, and noticed as usual, blood stains on his shirt. He observed something else.

At last Younger spoke. "My Older Brother," he said, "It is my opinion that you have a fishhook in your neck. You are held by a long line that goes out of the lodge. I shall now proceed to remove the hook."

Taking Older out of the lodge he removed the hook and fastened it to a thorn bush that stood on the edge of a cliff. "Oh now, my Older Brother, I must tell you that soon a woman, who is your wife, will pull on the line and when you do not return she will be after you. Such is my opinion. I also think that the woman is a sorceress and that she will endeavor to kill both of us. Now I have acquired strong magic and will save you. You must stand here and allow me to pat you into a small object which I will place in the hollow of an antler-tipped arrow-point. I will shoot this arrow into the sky. It will go a long ways and then fall to the ground. When you strike the ground become normal in size and run as fast as you can until you find a new lodge far to the east. There dwell until I come for you."

Now all happened as related by Younger and when the arrow was shot it made a path in the sky, and striking the earth, Older came out of the conical tip and ran east.

After the arrow's flight the sorceress pulled on the fish line, seeking to draw Older back to her, but the string held fast. So she followed the line until she came to the thorn bush. Then she saw what had happened and was very angry. Her first thought was to hunt for Younger, to whom she attributed the blame.

Younger ran as fast as he could, aided by his magic, but the sorceress was swifter than he and soon saw him before her. With a shrill cry she bore down upon him making a barking sound and yelling, "You cannot escape me, you cannot escape me."

Younger then disappeared around a big rock and took off his moccasins. "Run to the end of the world," he commanded, and then transformed himself into the likeness of an old stump.

On came the sorceress, following the moccasin tracks. She paused at the stump and then said, "Most truly this stump looks like a man, but I see his tracks going in a direction away from here." Thereupon she began her chase again yelling as was her custom, "You cannot escape me." After a long time she came to the end of the world and found a pair of moccasins. Her rage was terrible and she tore up the ground, saying, "He thinks, perhaps, that he has deceived me, but I will find him. He cannot escape me." She retraced her steps and came to the place where the stump had been but it had vanished, for Younger had been running away all this time. The sorceress followed his trail until she came into sight of him again, when she yelled, "You cannot escape me." When she was almost upon him he took a small round stone from his pocket and cast it upon the ground, at the same time running with all the speed his magic would give.

The stone became an immense escarpment, so high that the sorceress could not climb over it. She uttered exclamations in token of her disgust and began to run at the foot of the cliff but it went on without ceasing until she came to the end of the world, when she ran back to the place where she had started and then on to the other end of the world. Returning she began to push the cliff and then to beat it with her hands. Finally she ran into it trying to batter it down with her head but she crashed into the rock with such force that she fell down as if hit by a war club, and fainted. For a long time she lay still like a dead person, but finally revived. Looking about she spied a small white stone. "Tcisna!" she exclaimed, "Have I been overcome by so small a stone? I now perceive that the boy is a magician."

Again she began to run and soon again saw Younger running before her. "You cannot escape me," she called as she ran toward him, whereupon Younger took a handful of pigeon feathers from his pouch and cast them into the air, saying, "Do you become a great pigeon roost as if of long duration."

With this command the feathers became pigeons and they flew through the trees until all were filled. Beneath them the ground became deep with slime and into this the sorceress ran. She drew back for it was like a pitch bed to a beetle. In vain she tried to plow through, and then turned and ran along the edge until she reached the end of the world, and failing to break through she ran the other way, but found the slime made a track to the other end of the world. Returning to the middle spot she began to beat it with her head, but became smothered and fell down in a faint, as if dead.

After a long time she revived and found a pigeon feather on her nose. "Tcisna!" she exclaimed. "This boy is a magician. But he cannot escape me." So crying, she started the pursuit again and after a long time saw him ahead of her running very fast. When she was nearly upon him Younger stamped his foot into the ground and cried, "Become a deep hole." Then he ran on. The sorceress came to the hole but it was so wide and so deep that she could not cross it. She endeavored to run around it but could not find an end in either direction and finally returned to the starting point and endeavored to jump across, but she fell in with a loud noise and went to the bottom, knocking her head on a stone. Long she lay stunned and when she revived she looked about and saw only a moccasin track in the mud, laid across the path. "He is a magician, he thinks, but he cannot escape me," cried the sorceress, and began the chase once more.

Now after a time Younger came to a broad river where he saw a great number of people swimming about and racing in the water. He heard the sounds of the sorceress as she pursued him and exerting his magic said, "May the swimmer who is the greatest distance out in the river take on my appearance, whilst I become a tree stub." The angry sorceress reached the river and paused at the stub, and soon discovered the appearance of Younger far out in the river. In plunged the angry woman and soon came to the bather whom she saw was not her victim. With a cry she swam back to the shore to find the deceiving tree stub, but it had vanished leaving moccasin tracks in the direction it had taken.

Younger ran very fast this time for he was almost at the end of his tricks. When he was about discouraged, a strange old man with a broad back and a wide mouth appeared before him. "My nephew," said the old man. "My name is Toad. I will aid you in your escape. I understand that there is a woman who is pursuing you, and this is great trouble. Get on my back and bounce up and down. I will give a spring and throw you far up on a smooth hill. Climb as far as you can to the top."

Younger clambered on Toad's back which was very springy, and Toad arose with a leap throwing Younger far through the air and landing him on the surface of a slippery hill. He endeavored to climb the hill but reaching a very shiny spot fell into a groove and began to slip. Down, down he slipped with great rapidity until he slid with a cloud of dust into a big lodge where an old woman and her two daughters were boiling bear oil over the fireplace.

"Augh!" cried the old woman, "I guess somebody has fallen in our trap. Let us see what it is."

When the women saw Younger, the old woman asked, "What are you doing here?"

"Oh my aunt," exclaimed the distressed Younger. "I have been running away from a very evil witch. She is now pursuing me. I met an old man who threw me upon a slippery hillside and I slipped down where I am now sitting."

"Well, she is coming now," said the old woman. "You climb up on the platform over my bed and hide. I think I can overcome this witch."

Younger obeyed with alacrity, and soon heard the sorceress slide into the lodge, crying, "He cannot escape me!"

"What are you doing here?" asked the old woman.

"I am pursuing a very bad magician," answered the sorceress. "He has caused me much trouble. Have you seen him in this lodge?"

"Oh yes, my niece," answered the old woman. "I have him now. He is a great magician and went into this pot of bear oil."

Now the old woman possessed magic, and conjured the face of Younger into the bottom of the pot of oil.

The sorceress looked in, and, crying, "You cannot escape me now," leaped into the pot, going to the bottom. Now the oil was boiling and it killed her so that she could never return to life again. It was the end of her.

Then the old woman called Younger and said, "I have been waiting for you a long time. I notice that you are of our kind of people. You shall become my son-in-law, by taking my youngest daughter."

Younger looked at the girl and saw that she was most desirable. He had never seen a girl who was so much to his taste. So soon they were married.

Younger lived in the lodge with the women and he hunted for them, bringing in a great number of deer every day, which the women dried and smoked. After a year Younger's wife bore him two sons. They were precocious boys who learned to talk very early, also to play about.

It was not long before they were full grown and asked where their relatives lived. Younger, their father, answered that all had been killed by sorcery but their uncle, his own brother, whom he has rescued by sending him away in an arrow.

"It is well," said the boys. "We will go after him." So they set forth after their uncle. Long they traveled until in a strange country they found an old lodge and in it a lonely old man with a sore spot in his neck, which he was continually nursing.

"Our uncle," they called to him. "We two are your nephews and have come for you. Come with us. We have an aunt older than our mother. You can marry her."

So Older returned with his nephews and when he came to the lodge he found his brother Younger. Then he saw the woman who would become his wife. He liked her and they were soon married. All lived together and they had no more trouble with wizards or witches. Younger had too much power now, and everything otgont (evil) was afraid of him.

33. THE ISLAND OF THE CANNIBAL.

Ganondai'yeo lived with his aged grandparents in the depths of a great wood. The old people were always sad but Ganondai'yeo was never able to discover the cause and inquiry would only bring the injunction, "Never go west!" The boy obeyed and played happily in the forest to the north and the south and the east but shunned the dark woods to the west.

At length Ganondai'yeo began to reason upon the matter:

"Never go west," he said to himself. "Now why may not I go west? Is not west as good as east? Surely I am denied my rights and shall no longer submit. I am going to find out why the west is to be avoided."

Thus determined, he crept cautiously through the vine-bound underbrush and with caution advanced in a westerly direction. He kept on for some time and then, to his surprise, found himself on the borders of a large body of swift water. He looked across the broad expanse with admiration and wonder. Was this the sight his grandparents wished to deny him? "Oh the shameful rule that forbade him this!" he thought. While he was gazing at the scene and meditating upon it, he heard a sound behind him. A pleasant voice was saying:

"Hai', Hai'! Is it not a beautiful stream and wonderful too? Did you never see it before? Come, jump into my canoe and let us visit some of the inlets and islands that are found hereabouts. We will return in a short time and you will have seen sights worth talking about."

Ganondai'yeo was charmed with the words of the stranger, and following him, stepped into the canoe that lay on the sandy beach of a cove. The stranger gave the canoe a shove with his paddle and sent it shooting out from the shore. With swift even strokes he carried it far out from the land.

"We shall visit a beautiful island," said the stranger.

A short distance ahead Ganondai'yeo saw a small island in the center of which was a dense clump of trees. It lay near a very large island. Such a charming spot was it that he wondered if its inhabitants were men or ghosts.

Soon the canoe grated upon the sandy beach and, both jumping out, the stranger drew up the canoe.

"Now," said he, "look around and see what a fine place this is. Oh you will like it,—you will like it; I do!"

Ganondai'yeo walked up the shore toward a tall plant that bore flowers, (a mullen stalk). He stood viewing it for a few moments and then turning to follow his guide found that he had disappeared. He ran to the water to find the canoe but to his dismay found that it, too, had gone. Glancing up and over the lake he saw far in the distance the canoe and the stranger, and then he realized his situation.

Heavy hearted he dragged himself halfway around the island and then walking inland for a few rods sat down dejectedly on a fallen tree. Tears filled his eyes and he moaned bitterly, "I am a miserable creature."

While he thus sat lamenting his fate he heard a loud whisper, "Kechuta, kechuta!"

Starting up he looked around to discover the source of the sound but failing, sank back to his seat with a groan of pure misery.

Presently he heard the same sound, "Kechuta!"

It seemed to issue from the ground at his very feet. This time he was thoroughly frightened, and again he looked about to discover, perchance, who the speaker was, but as before he failed and flinging himself upon the log began to weep violently.

"Kechuta!" came the sound again and looking down at the ground at the end of the log he noticed a white glistening spot. Poking away the sod he saw first the hollow eye socket of a skull and then jaws full of white teeth.

"Kechuta!" said the skull and then Ganondai'yeo knew

that the thing wished to smoke. "Dig into the sod by that knot on the log and you will find my bag and pipe," so spoke the man-reduced-to-bones.

Marveling, the boy obeyed and soon pulled out a decayed pipe bag and a tobacco pouch. He packed the pipe bowl full of tobacco. Then picking up a hard round stick, the size of an arrow shaft he twisted it in his bow string, placed a pitted stone on one end and put the other end on the log. Pushing his bow backward and forward he twirled the stick with great rapidity. Soon a tiny spark ignited the wood dust and caught in a blaze on the shredded cedar bark. It was a laborious task but Ganondai'yeo at length had the pipe in smoking order. Leaning over he pried apart the jaws of Tcis'gä, as he had named the skeleton, and pushed the pipe stem between its teeth. Tcis'gä smoked with great diligence and exclaimed, "Agwas'wio', oh how good, how I enjoy it. I've not had a smoke in a great while. Oh I am glad you came to me! Now let me tell you a story, but first fill up this pipe again. There. Now, boy, this is an enchanted island. You are trapped, the same as I was and the same as many more have been. There is a man who lives here, there is a man who visits here and there is a man who hires men here. He who lives here is S'agowenot''a, a great sorcerer, he who visits here is Oñgwe Iās, an evil ogre. Both eat men. They ate me, they ate many others; they will eat you unless you listen closely. Before sunrise tomorrow, run to the beach where you landed and bury yourself in the sand only leaving one eye and an ear uncovered. Look and listen. No one has ever escaped; but you may if you obey me, and moreover you overcome the island's evil spell."

The boy solemnly promised obedience and after a restless night ran to the beach and buried himself in the sand. Soon he heard the sound of singing on the water. The song grew louder and Ganondai'yeo knew that the singer was nearing the beach. He heard the sound of the canoe as it shot up against the sand and knew that the singer had land-

ed. He listened closely to the song and then hummed it softly to himself. The sound of footsteps neared and turning his
eye he saw a man whose grim visage pronounced him a
man of terrible passion. Ganondai'yeo looked as well as he
could from his hole in the sand and knew that was Oñgwe
Iäs. At the feet of the ogre was a pack of dogs who
followed him up the incline.

As Oñgwe Iäs stepped upon the island Sagowanota sang
his magical song from his den in the grove.

When Oñgwe Iäs reached the top of the incline he
roared, "Well, where is my meal?"

"He cannot be found," came the answer. "Put your
eyes in the bushes,—send the dogs after him," roared
Oñgwe Iäs.

The search was fruitless and grumbling in rage the man
returned to his canoe, threw in his dogs and jumping in,
swept his paddle through the water and sped back to main-
land.

Ganondai'yeo jumped from his place of concealment and
rushed to the log where Tcis'gä lay. Breathlessly he told
what he had seen and heard and told how thankful he was
that he had escaped being eaten.

"Smoke, tobacco, I wish to smoke," whispered Tcĭs'gä,
dustily. So taking an ember from the fire he had started
Ganondai'yeo lit the pipe and shoved it between the teeth of
the skull. When it had finished smoking it said, "I am glad
that you have succeeded so well. It is an omen of good
fortune. Now listen. Make seven dolls from dry rotten
wood and make a small bow and arrow for each, then, place
each doll in the top of a tree. Conceal yourself in the sand
again and see what will happen.

Ganondai'yeo did as directed and the next day when
Oñgwe Iäs landed he grumbled loudly and vowed he would
find the boy for he was very hungry. He strode up the
beach and his dogs with noses close to the ground followed
the track of Ganondai'yeo as it circled the isle. Suddenly one

FIGURE OF DANCING WARRIOR

This figure carved from wood was used in shamanistic ceremonies.

dog with a yelp fell pierced with an arrow. Oñgwe Iās yelled in rage and his rage increased as one after another fell dead. Snatching up the body of each he threw it upon his shoulder and going back flung it into his canoe, and then paddled back across the lake.

Leaping from the sand Ganondai'yeo ran back to Tcis'gä and related his observations.

After Tcis'gä had been satisfied with tobacco he said to Ganondai'yeo:

"Now I will tell you more. Oñgwe Iās, always fearing death, leaves his heart in his lodge. It hangs suspended over a pot of water; likewise the hearts of the dogs. When he returns he will place the dogs' hearts back within their chests and as they beat the dogs will revive. He will then remove them and return to the island on the morrow to renew his search for you. Now listen closely. Bury yourself in the sand as before and as Oñgwe Iās approaches the shore sing the Sagowenota song. Oñgwe Iās will then rush up the shore, the dolls will shoot again and while Oñgwe Iās is obscured in the bushes jump into his canoe, go directly across the water and when you touch the shore you will find a path that leads to a lodge. Enter the lodge and destroy the hearts you find there. Then you may return to me."

The next morning Ganondai'yeo covered himself with sand and when he heard the song of Oñgwe Iās floating over the water he shouted back:

"I have caught a rabbit, rabbit, rabbit,
Soon I'll skin it, skin it, skin it!"

Oñgwe Iās stopped short in his song and listened. Then he shouted back:

"Ho-yo-ho! So you have him. So, I'll be there!"

From a mound in the center of the island came a voice. In pleading tones it cried:

"No, no! I did not call you. Do not come. Oh do not!"

"Oh no," came the mocking reply. "You cannot cheat me. You have found him and wish to eat him alone."

Landing, Oñgwe Iās ran toward the mound. Ganondai'-yeo jumped into the boat and with his swiftest, strongest stroke sent it gliding out over the lake. At length he reached the land. Leaping to the shore he ran up a path and burst through the curtain into a lodge. A young girl was refining bear oil by boiling it in a kettle. Without stopping to greet her Ganondai'yeo cried:

"Give me his heart!"

"No, no, do not touch it. It is his, it is his!" remonstrated the girl in terror.

There was the sound of foot steps outside. Oñgwe Iās had followed in some mysterious manner and was now at the door. Springing toward the back of the lodge, Ganondai'yeo grasped a large beating heart. Oñgwe Iās was pushing aside the curtain and now snarled in terrible rage as he saw the boy who should have been his victim holding his heart. With marvelous swiftness Ganondai'yeo flung the heart into the pot of boiling fat. The ogre tottered. His dogs began to yelp up the trail and as Ganondai'yeo glanced through the door between the curtain and the swaying body of Oñgwe Iās, and saw their dripping bodies, red eyes and froth laden fangs as they leaped toward their master, Oñgwe Iās trembled, and fell. Ganondai'yeo swept the seven dogs' hearts into the scalding liquid only a moment before the ogre crashed his head into the fire, breaking the pot of oil and spilling out the hearts. Oñgwe Iās was dead and seven dogs lay before the door.

The girl who during this terrible scene had cringed in one corner now rushed toward Ganondai'yeo with a glad cry.

"Oh my brother!" she cried. "You have rescued me. I am your sister who was captured. Oñgwe Iās kept me as his slave. Oh my brother, you have saved our family!"

Ganondai'yeo hardly knew what to make of these words

but looking down at the girl saw in her his lost sister, lost years ago. He rejoiced with her and then running back to the shore paddled swiftly to the Isle of Fears. Going up to the log he appeased his friend Tcĭs'gä with tobacco and told his story.

"Now," said Tcĭs'gä, "you have done well. You can be of great service to me if you will obey a few more instructions; for instance, shoot that fat bear over there and place her pelt over this little mound where I am. Scold that stump and make it move away so that you may cover the mound entirely. Then smoke!"

Ganondai'yeo was startled as he looked up and beheld an enormously fat bear asleep not ten steps from him. Fixing an arrow he shot and killed the beast and removed its hide. Walking up to the stump he shouted:

"What is the matter with you? Get out of my way or I will smash you. Go on now and with the help of a kick the stump jumped backward into a clump of bushes. Placing the skin over the mound Ganondai'yeo built a little fire and began to throw on tobacco to make the smoke fragrant.

The sun was hot and the oil fairly dripped from the skin into the ground.

Ganondai'yeo became impatient. "What is the trouble with you, Tcĭs'gä?" he called. Move lively. You are lazy. Hurry or I will leave. I cannot wait all day. Hurry or I will kick over this stump upon you."

There was a slight movement beneath the bear's skin.

"Hurry now," continued the boy, "or I will pull off the skin," and stooping down he gave it a fling. As he did so from the ground arose a company of men. All were quarreling. "You have my legs—my fingers—you have my hands—you have my feet—my ribs—my neck—where is my backbone—three ribs missing—oh someone has my whole body—didn't have time—made us hurry—too quick —short notice!" came the mingled cries from the strange swarm.

Before Ganondai'yeo was as queer a company of men as the sun has ever seen. Some had one long leg and one short one, some were hump-backed, some small-bodied and large-limbed, some had head on backward, some had no necks, some double the wonted length, and soon each man was a sight to behold. All were angry, and fighting, disappeared into the forest, all but one. It was Tcïs'gä. He stepped forward and took Ganondai'yeo by the hand and said,

"I am your brother, let us go home."

Hastening to the shore the two seated themselves in the canoe and paddled back to the lodge on the opposite shore. A meal awaited them and after eating it the boys built a great fire and burned the evil lodge.

That night the three slept in the open. The next morning the brothers and their sister tramped through the forest and found the old people mourning over the loss of Ganondai'yeo.

The old folk were exuberant with joy when they found that not only was Ganondai'yeo well and alive but also their other grandchildren.

The boys built a large lodge and made the days of the old people easy with soft beds, much meat and pleasant company.

Then the grandparents said, "We are old and wise but we know now that which we did not before: It is evil to forbid a boy of resource to do or go without a reason."

So here it ends, this ga-gah, this ancient story.

34. THE TWELVE BROTHERS AND THE WRAITH OF THE EVIL WARRIOR.

A Story of Shodje'asko[n'], a Mischief Maker.

Twelve brothers had planned a war expedition and singing their songs had started a war dance. Scarcely had they begun when a messenger came running towards them and related that Hadi'ĭŭsgōwa', the greatest warrior of the nation, was dying and wished the twelve brothers to officiate at his funeral. In respect to the man who far and wide had the name of being the most terrible and successful warrior in all the world the twelve brothers postponed their dance and hurried to minister to the dying warrior. He desired them to dress him, not in the customary funeral robes but in the full regalia of battle with his knife at his side and his tomahawk in his hand. His face he wished painted black on one side and red on the other, in token that he was the fiercest warrior in all the earth.

So when he died the twelve brothers prepared his body just as was directed and doubled him up in his shallow grave. When the funeral rites were over the brothers renewed their dance and on the next morning started off on their war expedition to the south.

Now in those days the Iroquois had trails that led from their villages to all parts of the world. At the distance of a day's journey on every trail was built a trail lodge, where travelers might find shelter, and so on for many days' journeys were built trail lodges. At the end of the first day's journey the twelve brothers came to the trail house and halted to prepare their evening meal. One of the men shot a deer and was dressing it when the oldest brother, the chief of the party, ordered the youngest to run to the spring after water. Grasping a bark bowl he obeyed and ran down the path to the spring and was bending over the water to dip, when he saw reflected in the ruddy sun-painted water the form of a warrior whose face was painted on one side red and on the other black. He gazed at the vision terrified by its import and then dropping his bowl rushed up the path and stammered out his frightful discovery. He had seen Hadiiusgowa, the warrior whom they had buried but the morning of that day. The chief looked at his young brother in amazement and then, dropping the deer ham that he was preparing, burst out into a loud derisive laugh. "If you are afraid of visions of dead men," he laughed, "how can I depend on you when live ones appear?" But the boy would not be laughed out of believing the evidence of his own eyes and so the second brother was sent to the spring. When he reached the pool he looked across the river and to his indescribable horror saw the dead warrior standing on the opposite bank, his face wrinkled into a fiendish grin. Back to the lodge he sped trembling from cheek to feet. A chorus of laughter greeted his story and the chief angrily declared that his younger brothers were endeavoring to frighten the party by their impossible tales. Then the third brother was sent and soon returned and with stiffened lips said that he had seen the figure of Haddiiusgowa standing in the middle of the stream. The fourth brother saw him standing on the rocks close to the shore, and the fifth saw him on the pebbly edge, and the sixth on the river's bank, the seventh half way to the spring, the eighth at the spring, the ninth advancing toward the trail, the tenth on the trail, the eleventh half way to the trail lodge, and then the chief, who had now ceased to scoff, when he looked up saw Hadiiusgowa in the clearing before the lodge. Hastily he commanded that all should enter the lodge, the youngest first and the rest according to their ages. When all had done so he fastened the door and lay down across the door-way. All except the two youngest suddenly became overcome with a stupor and fell into a deep sleep. The two youngest lay awake and listened to the efforts of the ghostly warrior to effect an entrance. Suddenly the door burst inward and with a yell the tchisga (ghost) swooped down upon the chief and scalping him brandished the scalp aloft and screeching, "Gowe! Gowe! Hadiiusgowa!" Jumping into the air he yelled a death cry and sped from sight, his cry growing fainter and fainter as he went. Returning shortly afterwards he scalped the next brother, returning at an interval to scalp one after another of the party. When the third oldest brother had been scalped and the tchisga had disappeared, his death cry echoing fainter and fainter as he sped further and further, the second youngest brother was overcome with a lethargy and fell into a deep sleep from which he never awoke, for the tchisga returned and killed him, as he had the ten others. The youngest then began to despair saying to himself, "I cannot escape even by running nor can I hide for Hadiiusgowa has power to discover me wherever I go, but even a tchisga may be deceived." So saying he placed some bloody deer meat on his head and pulled his bear skin cap tightly over his brow. Wrapping his blanket around his ears so as to leave no part of his body exposed he waited the coming of Hadiiusgowa. His skin at least was protected from the death touch of the tchisga and perhaps he would escape. Soon the wraith came screaming into the lodge crying, "I have slain eleven and now the twelfth shall go!" Grabbing a bunch of black hair that protruded from a robe of deer skin he haggled off a circular piece and with a demonic shriek flew into the air crying "Gowe! Gowe! Hadiiusgowa!"

The boy finding himself unhurt jumped to his feet with the exclamation, "I will follow the tchisga and outwit him yet!" So he ran out into the darkness.

The ghost soon discovered his error and the boy could hear his cries of rage in the distance. He approached rapidly screaming, "You cannot escape me, you cannot hide from me!" Each yell stole the strength from the muscles of the frightened boy who soon sank in dispair to the ground. The tchisga was coming and there seemed no escape. Feebly lifting his head the boy saw a hollow elm log and in a dazed way remembered that he had heard of hollow logs. Mustering all his strength he crawled in the log and none too soon for just as he had stowed himself within the protecting log the ghost struck it with the cry, "Now I have you!"

It is strange, but a ghost never can enter the space within a hollow log. Thus the tchisga cut a sharp stick which he thrust in the hole at one end hoping to spear the boy. But his victim was not an easy one for he caught the thrusts deftly and turned them aside. Finally realizing that he could not harm the boy in this manner he yelled, "I know where you sit and will kill you yet!" Then he commenced to chop a hole into the log where he judged his victim to be but when it had been made the boy had moved further in and escaped the thrusts of the spear. Another hole was made but all the prodding that the tchisga made had no effect upon the elusive boy. A third trial had no better result and finally the tchisga screamed, "The next hole will bring me success,—I cannot fail!" Then he fell to whacking the log until the raining blows sounded like the beating of a death drum. The hole was completed and the dispairing boy found that there were so many openings that he could not hope to escape. The tchisga prepared to grasp his victim and was on the point of uttering a yell of triumph when a little bird on a branch above began to twitter and the yell of victory turned to a groan of dispair. "Fortunate for you," he cried, "but woe to me!" Then he faded into the glow of the morning when ghosts cease their black works.

The boy was highly elated at his good fortune but lost no time in dancing over the matter. Instead he jumped to his feet and ran with all his speed to the village crying as he went, "Gowe, gowe!" His shrill cry awoke the villagers who hastened to the long house to listen to the distress news that someone was bringing. Dashing into the council the

boy related his story and when he had finished the village
sachem arose and said, "If this boy's tale is true we are all
threatened with the ghostly-warrior. Now we know why
arrows never killed him,—he was a wizard. We must
kill him before he kills us. We must burn his body. First
then let four swift runners go to the first day trail house
and see if conditions are as reported and in the meantime
we will prepare to kill the ghost." The warriors hurried to
obey instructions and after the runners had departed a company built a little cabin from large logs over the grave of
the wizard and others gathered piles of logs for fuel. It
was toward sun-set when the runners returned and reported
that things were just as the youngest brother had told. The
grave was then dug into and a foot below the surface a
sharpened pole was discovered and to it were fastened
eleven scalps still bleeding and a small circle of bear skin.
Below this was found the body of the witch-warrior steaming with sweat, his face and hands slimy with blood and
his weapon still dripping red. The boy's words were confirmed. A warrior lifted the terrible form from the bark
upon which it rested and brought it into the cabin. The
head sachem then addressed it. "You were a great warrior
in life," he said, "and we know that we never appreciated
you. We now wish to make a great ceremony and have
made a lodge for you where all may see you. So stay here
and let us honor you." So saying the chief backed out of
the cabin and fastened the door. Heavy logs were piled
over the structure and then a fire ignited that soon enveloped the whole mass. The flames soon ate their way into
the burial lodge and filled it with a mass of burning coals.
Logs were piled on higher and higher in order that they
might press down the witch and give him no chance to
escape. Suddenly a voice from the blazing coals sounded
forth. With one long drawn wild scream it said, "I will
kill you all, I am escaping despite you." But a log falling
pinned down the wizard who fell into his grave pit now

white with heat. His head burst and when the steam was cleared away a screech owl was seen flying up from it. The warriors made a frantic effort to kill it but the intense heat prevented them and so it soared away into the night screaming defiance at its pursuers.

In this manner was the wizard-warrior killed but his spirit still hovers over the land and wherever the screech owl lingers there is the evil spirit brooding mischief.

GENERAL NOTES.—In this legend we have several interesting ethnological allusions. We are told of "trail houses," which were erected at intervals along the trails throughout the Iroquois country, and in which food and other necessities were left by travelers who had used the shelter. Inquiry brought out the fact that these public hospices were common in the old days and were frequently built in response to dreams. We are also given a glimpse of the burial rites of warriors, and told that the corpse was properly painted and then doubled up in its grave. We are again given an account of the magical qualities of a hollow log, which a ghost cannot enter. Here, also, we are told that a wizard's head when burned bursts and sends forth screech-owls,—birds of ill omen to the red man as to us of today.

35. THE CANNIBAL AND HIS NEPHEW.

De'o'niot was Oñgwe Iās, a man eater. He had developed his man-flesh appetite early in his childhood because his mother had associated with witches. He lived in a hidden place far away from other human habitations. The only human creature who came near him and was not eaten was his nephew who lived on the other side of the partition that divided his long bark house. The cannibal was fond of his nephew and did not wish to come into close contact with him, lest his appetite for flesh become too strong a temptation and leave him without a companion. Thus it was he divided his house and satisfied himself with the sound of the youth's voice, for each hunted their game separately and rarely saw each other.

One day as the nephew was sitting on his doorstep, he saw a beautiful woman approaching. She advanced and sat down by his side.

"I would like to marry you," she said after a moment's pause.

"I would like to marry you also," was the answer, and then he added, "but you would not be my wife long because my uncle would eat you."

"Oh then you had better watch that he does not eat you. If he does not I am satisfied he will not take me," replied the woman.

"Well, if you are determined after what I have told you, I cannot say further but take you." Leading her into the lodge he continued, "My uncle will call from his room for someone to bring him my bow or axe with which to slay some animal. Do not answer him but keep very silent and do not venture from the lodge to satisfy his wants. Obey my instructions for I am going on a hunting journey."

Empty handed and hungry De'o'niot returned from his hunting excursion. Going into his apartment he flung himself upon the floor to rest, then starting up, he called, "Hurry, bring me my hatchet, Oh quick, I need it immediately to kill this beast!"

Forgetting all that her husband had told her the bride picked up a hatchet and a bow and ran around the lodge to the opposite door.

When the nephew returned he found his wife missing. The only trace of her was her skirt that lay on the floor.

"Ho!" he exclaimed, "De'o'niot has feasted on my woman and thrown her skirt to me as a reminder." Then calling to his uncle he asked, "Oh uncle, how did you discover my woman?"

'Because I knew that it was not your breathing but a breath much faster that I heard over the partition," was the reply.

The next day another woman came with a proposal of marriage. At first refusing her, and then accepting her on the condition that she would quietly remain in his room and heed not the entreaties of De'o'niot, he married her, but when he returned from his hunting, she, like the first, had formed the repast of his uncle, who as before flung her dress over the partition. In like manner another wife came and was eaten.

Finally a married woman came weeping through the woods and begged De'o'niot to protect her.

'Protect you!" the man-eater roared, "O ho! I would be more apt to eat you. That is my business,—eating people!"

"Oh protect me!" pleaded the woman, "for my husband is a ferocious giant and is now pursuing me!"

"So truly if that is the case you had better go into my nephew's room where I cannot reach you and stay there while I watch for that man of yours."

Presently in the distance De'o'niot saw a giant striding through the underbrush.

"Ho, ho!" he exclaimed to himself, "That woman is the

first one I ever saw and liked, so I am truly glad to do her a service in destroying her man-giant."

With a whoop the giant pounced upon De'o'niot. "Where is my wife?" he bellowed.

De'o'niot did not answer but grasped the giant's throat and after a frightful struggle twisted his neck.

"I am greatly obliged to you," he called to the woman. "Such an amount of flesh will keep me from hunger for many days."

When the nephew returned he found the new wife awaiting him and after some questioning he accepted her.

"That is right!" called the uncle over the partition, "don't worry, she is a good woman. I will not eat her."

'Wife," he said, "I believe that we must depart from these regions for I fear that my uncle will become so hungry that he will forget his love for us."

Soon afterward the uncle from his chamber shouted:

"Oh my children, do not leave. You fear my appetite but I promise you that I will never harm you."

The nephew (however), would not believe these promises, but thought his uncle only shaming. In order to discuss the matter further he awoke his wife in the middle of the night and in whispers talked with her, how best to escape.

'Boy, you are going away tomorrow!" exclaimed a voice from over the partition.

"No, no, uncle," answered the nephew. "Go to sleep and do not dream such things."

"Ah, you cannot deceive De'o'niot," replied the uncle. "I know you are going away tomorrow and when you go, go west, for you have relatives there. If ever danger threatens call my name and I will be on hand to save you. Distance does not stop my promise. Call me anywhere and I will come."

At dawn the next day the couple drank from the spring that filled a basin on one side of the room and ran out of the other. Then, packing up a bundle of food, they turned their backs on the morning and journeyed to the west.

At nightfall they saw in the distance a stream of water that reflected the light of the moon in a most peculiar way, and coming up to it they found that its strange gleam resulted from its frozen surface. The creek did not appear wide and the couple decided that it could be jumped easily. Running back a short distance each dashed forward and attempted to leap across, but great was their surprise and chagrin when they landed on the ice in the middle of the stream, and greater was their dismay when they began to slide forward. The creek ran down a steep incline and with great rapidity the two slipped downward over its surface into the uncertain light. In a moment, however, they saw that they were headed directly for a great lodge into which the stream flowed. In desperation they clutched at the ice and endeavored to hold back but vain was their effort, and in a few moments they had plunged into the lodge and into the midst of a dozen howling warriors armed with war clubs.

Surrounding them, the warriors began to brandish their clubs. Death seemed certain. The couple trembled and believed that death has surely come. Suddenly the wife started boldly up and shouted:

"De'o'niot, hagesa!" she cried.

The warriors fell back with cries of dismay at the sound of the magical name.

In the distance came a signal call, then came a song. It was the battle song of De'o'niot. The warriors huddled in the corners of the lodge quaking with fear. The words of the song became distinct as De'o'niot drew nearer.

The couple looked out and saw the man-eater sliding down the incline holding in his arms a kettle, a bowl and a spoon.

"I will stay here with my meat," he shouted as he burst into the lodge. "You had better go on to the village. Your parents and people are there. Now leave me here and go on."

The two gladly hurried from the house and toward morning came to a village when both found friends and relatives.

After the nephew and his wife had lived in their new home for a year, one by one the children of the settlement began mysteriously to disappear.

"My uncle surely must be in this vicinity," reflected the nephew, "I will go on a hunt for him."

So the nephew started out and after a time of journeying saw De'o'niot leaning over the bank of a creek groaning in agony.

"Oh uncle!" exclaimed the nephew, "what troubles you?"

"Oh nephew," came the groaning reply, "I have eaten many children and am very sick. My belly is hurt with pain as if by claws clutching inside."

"Cheer up uncle, I can cure you. Only obey my instructions."

The nephew made a soup of fish bones and skins and fed it to his uncle. He continued this treatment for three days, until De'o'niot had disgorged. By this time he was ravenous and begged for food and new clothing, for his old rags were very foul. The nephew bade him strip and plunge in the water and bathe himself. Then, after giving him some new clothing he fed him on a little corn pudding, gradually increasing the allowance at each meal and each time moving the camp nearer the village.

"You must now learn to cook, uncle," said the nephew, "then you will forget your unnatural appetite. God made men above all creatures, uncle, and gave them great skill. Men are not made to devour one another, or for beasts to devour, but beasts are food for men. So now, promise never to touch the meat of mankind again."

"Aye, never more will I eat of human flesh or the raw

flesh of any creature but only fruits and roots and cooked meat!"

So the nephew brought him into the village and introduced him as his uncle from afar. And the uncle grew so fond of this nephew's wife's cooking that he married a woman to have a cook for himself.

36. A YOUTH'S DOUBLE ABUSES HIS SISTER.

There was a lodge in the forest where very few people ever came, and there dwelt a young man and his sister. The youth was unlike other persons for one half of his head had hair of a reddish cast, while the other side was black.

He used to leave his sister in the lodge and go away on long hunting trips. On one occasion the young woman, his sister, saw, so she thought, her brother coming down the path to the lodge. "I thought you just went away to hunt," said the sister. "Oh, I thought I would come back," said he.

Then he sat down on the bed with the sister and embraced her and acted as a lover. The sister reproached him and said that she was very angry. But again he endeavored to fondle her in a familiar way, but again was repulsed. This time he went away.

The next day the brother returned and found his sister very angry. She would scarcely speak to him, though hitherto she had talked a great deal.

"My sister," said he. "I am at loss to know why you treat me thus. It is not your custom."

"Oh you ought to know that you have abused me," said the girl.

"I never abused you. What are you talking about?" he said.

"Oh you know that you embraced me in an improper way yesterday," said the sister.

"I was not here yesterday," asserted the youth. "I believe that my friend who resembles me in every respect has been here."

"You have given a poor excuse," replied his sister. "I hope your actions will not continue."

Soon the brother went away again, stating that he would be absent three days. In a short time the sister saw, as she thought, a figure looking like her brother skulking in the underbrush. His shirt and leggings were the same as her brother's and his hair was the same. So then she knew that her brother had returned for mischief. Soon he entered the lodge and embraced her, and this time in anger she tore his cheeks with her nails and sent him away.

In three days the brother returned with a deer, but his sister would not speak to him. Said he, "My sister, I perceive that you are angry at me. Has my friend been here?"

It was some time before the sister replied, and then she wept, saying, "My brother, you have abused me and I scratched your face. I perceive that it is still torn by my finger nails."

"Oh, my face," laughed the brother. "My face was torn by thorns as I hunted deer. If you scratched my friend that is the reason I am scratched. Whatever happens to either one of us happens to the other." But the sister would not believe this.

Again the brother went on a hunting trip, and again the familiar figure returned. This time the sister tore his hunting shirt from the throat down to the waist line. Moreover she threw a ladle of hot bear grease on the shirt. This caused his quick departure.

Returning in due time the brother brought in his game and threw it down. Again the sister was angry and finally accused him. Pointing to his grease-smeared torn shirt she said that this was evidence enough.

"Oh my sister," explained the brother. "I tore my shirt on a broken limb as I climbed a tree after a raccoon. In making soup from bear meat I spilled it on my shirt." Still the sister refused to believe him.

"Oh my sister," said the brother, in distressed tones. "I am greatly saddened to think you will not believe me. My friend looks exactly as I do, and whatever happens to him happens to me. I shall now be compelled to find my friend and bring him to you and when I do I shall be compelled to kill him before you for his evil designs upon you. If you would believe me nothing evil would befall us, but I now think I myself shall die."

The sister said nothing for she would not believe her brother.

The brother now began to pile up dried meat and to repair the lodge. He then went out into the forest without his bow and arrows, and in a short time returned with another man exactly resembling him, and whose clothing was spotted and torn in a similar way. Leading him to the lodge fire he began to scold him in an angry manner. "You have betrayed me and abused my sister," he said. "Now is the time for you to die." Taking out an arrow from a quiver he cast it into the heart of his double and killed him. The sister saw her assailant fall to the floor, and then looked up as she heard her brother give a war cry and fall as dead with blood streaming from a wound in his chest over his heart.

37. MURDERED DOUBLE SPEAKS THROUGH FIRE.

(Second Part of a Youth's Double.)

After lying as dead for a time the youth's inherent magic began to bring about a restoration of life. Soon he sat up and looked at his sister. Then he spoke.

"Oh my sister," he said. "The mother of my friend will shortly come for him, believing him married to you. We must dispose of my friend's body and when the woman comes we must act as if we were husband and wife."

The youth now removed the stones of the fireplace and dug a deep hole beneath. In this he buried the body of his slain friend, smoothed the earth and restored the ring of stones. He now rekindled the fire, and all trace of the murder was wiped away.

After a while footsteps were heard and the door was flung back. A witch woman looked into the lodge, and seeing someone that resembled her son standing closely to a young woman, the witch said, "I now perceive that I have a daughter-in-law."

Thereupon the fire began to flicker and a voice came clearly from it, saying, "My friend has killed me, my friend has killed me."

"Wu'!" exclaimed the witch mother, "What words is your fire speaking?"

"Oh, my mother, pay no attention to the fire," said the youth. "The fire thus speaks because I scrape the blood from my arrows into it." So saying he scraped an arrow into the fire and it spoke as before, "My friend has killed me."

The witch was disturbed and requested her pretended son to return to his maternal lodge bringing his wife with him. The youth now told his sister that the simulation of married life must be above suspicion, and then together all three went to the lodge of the witch.

As they sat down the pet owl of the lodge began to hoot. "The stranger has taken to wife his younger sister." The old woman looked up and asked what the meaning of this omen might be, whereupon the youth answered, "It is because you have not fed the owl. I now give it meat." The owl was then satisfied and continued to speak its accustomed notes.

That night the youth slept with his sister. As he entered the sleeping apartment the owl screamed as before, "It is not this one; this one takes to wife his younger sister."

The youth called out, "Give no heed to this owl, he is hungry," and he flung it more meat. Nevertheless the witch woman was suspicious and resolved to watch the couple.

During the night she spied through the curtain covering the bed, but the boy and his sister were simulating sleep, though arranged in an affectionate attitude. The old witch then placed her hand in the bed and under the covers, touching the couple, and she was then satisfied that the two were married.

Early in the morning the youth whispered to his sister that they must make their escape or the witch would discover the truth and kill them. Together the two went out of the lodge and the youth taking out his medicine pouch thrust his hand into it and took out a small dog which he tapped with a red rod. The dog grew in size with every tap until it was large enough to carry a human being. Placing his sister on the dog, the youth said, "Go forward and let nothing turn you aside. The dog will carry you to the lodge where is our refuge."

The dog ran forward but after a long tedious journey the sister dismounted to rest, and seeing a pretty bird fluttering just before her, began to chase it. It finally flew out of sight and when she returned to find the dog it had disappeared. She then remembered her brother's warning and stumbled forward hoping to find relief.

Meanwhile the brother ran on to the refuge but when he reached the lodge he found that his sister had not come. Some one was coming, however, for he heard footsteps. He looked and saw the witch approaching. "Where is she?" cried the witch, "Where is my daughter-in-law?" The youth was perplexed, but answered, "She is coming, you must have passed them."

"I cannot rest," said the witch, "for your pet owls continually say, 'It is another and she is his sister.'"

The youth now perceived that he must escape the witch and so he asked her where she was going. "To your lodge," she called as she sped onward over the trail.

The youth hurried forward over a shorter trail and reached the lodge before the witch. "Where is my daughter-in-law?" yelled the old woman as she entered the lodge.

"She has returned to the other lodge," answered the youth.

"It is another one," sang the fireplace, and then added, "My friend has killed me and taken his younger sister to wife."

"I must meet my wife," said the youth as he hurried away. He knew that he must now make his escape.

The witch was now thoroughly suspicious and dug into the fireplace. Soon she discovered her son and saw that indeed he had been killed. Burying him in another place she ran to her own lodge and took her witch charms, invoking them to give her power. To make herself mighty she drank the oil of hickory nuts. To test her power she smote a hickory tree but her blows only loosened all the bark. Drinking more oil she struck the tree again, reducing it to splinters. Now feeling confident she transformed herself into a Niă"gwahē and started in pursuit of the youth, crying, "You cannot escape me."

When the youth found himself closely pressed he threw

out a handful of pigeon feathers ordering them to become a monster flock of pigeons and to make the ground beneath them impassable. Immediately pigeons flew thickly in the air and covered the ground with an impassable slime in which the witch wallowed until exhausted, when she swooned. When she recovered the youth was far away and only a few pigeon feathers could be seen on the ground.

Again she caught sight of him and cried out as is the custom for the Niä"gwahē beast, "You cannot escape me." This time the youth cast a white stone in the path and commanded that it become an impassable cliff that stretched from ocean to ocean. Against this the witch batted her head until she swooned. Awakening she saw only a small quartz pebble and in anger arose again in pursuit, crying as she caught up to him, "You cannot escape me."

The youth was now sorely pressed but in running along the trail he saw an old man. "I am your uncle," said the old man. "Run onward to your mother's lodge, and meanwhile I will protect you." The youth ran on and the old uncle caused a vast field of sharpened posts to spring up, making a terrible barrier to the onrushing Niä"gwahē.

The youth passed another old man who called out to him, "I am your uncle. Run onward to your mother's lodge, and meanwhile I will protect you." This was reassuring, for just then the witch came into view and cried, "You cannot escape me." Then the witch monster ran directly into a net-like entanglement and with wild rage floundered about until it had freed itself.

Meanwhile the youth was speeding forward. Soon he saw a handsome lodge before him and into this he ran. There he found his sister and the dog, an older woman, a younger woman and another youth.

"Protect me," cried the pursued youth looking at the inmates of the lodge. "Niä"gwahē pursues me."

"I am your mother, my son," said the oldest woman. "I will save you from trouble."

Taking up a pot of boiling bear's oil she waited until the witch beast had thrust its head into the lodge when she threw the oil full in the creature's face. It gave a great snort and fell down dead.

The mother came up to the youth, saying, "Here is your older brother and older sister. Your younger sister and your dog came here and found me. We are all now safe and are reunited, so now all is well and I am thankful."

38. THE VAMPIRE CORPSE.[1]

An old man had a house far back in the woods, a long ways from any village. It stood in the midst of a good hunting ground. The old man always welcomed any hunting party and provided them with all the utensils necessary for curing their meats and tanning their pelts. It seemed however, that the place was haunted by an evil spirit that delighted to inflict those who tarried there with very bad dreams, and sometimes it killed them by sucking out their blood like a weasel.

One time, so it is said, a man and his wife and child went to this hunting ground and went to the lodge of Taiiani Gowa, the old man of the solitudes, to ask for shelter. Now when he called there was no answer and so he entered and found Taiiani Gowa dead in a bark coffin. This coffin had been prepared long before and Taiiani Gowa having a premonition of coming death had crawled in his box and died; so the man said.

Now it was nightfall and the man lay down beside his wife and baby to pass the night. Toward the hour of midnight the woman was awakened by a sound of gnawing,— cautiously she looked about and sliding out her hand on the floor felt a warm pool of blood. Quickly she realized what had occurred. The old man was dead but his evil spirit was making him conform to its vampire appetite. It was chewing off the face of her husband. But she did not scream, instead she said carefully, "Husband, our child wishes water, you are too sleepy to care for her while I go for some, so I will take her with me, give her a drink and soon return." With these words she arose and went out carrying a bowl with her. She ran to the spring, dropped the bowl and then ran toward home as fast as her strength gave her ability for running. "Unless I hasten," she

---

1 Related by Edward Cornplanter, and later by George D. Jimerson.

thought, "the tcĭs'gä will overtake and devour me. I heard
him go back to his coffin, but his hunger will soon return
and he will come for us, and finding us missing, will pursue
us. Oh my baby, we must hurry!"

An echo of a loud cry sounded through the silent forest
and the woman caught the words, "She has deceived me!"
Then she knew that the tcĭs'gä had started on her track.
She heard him at the spring, so she used all her speed to
escape him, but presently she heard a growling close behind
her and heard him exclaim, "Ah you cannot escape me!"
Unloosening her skirt she flung it on a swinging branch
and hurrying on, hear the tcĭs'gä crying, "Ah now I have
you!" Then he tore the garment into shreds and found out
his mistake. So then he ran screaming on. When he had
neared her again she threw her blanket upon a log and ran
on. The tcĭs'gä stopped and whooped because he was very
angry. Then he chewed up the blanket but finding no blood
rushed on after his victim, only to be delayed again and
again by the same trick. After a time she had stripped herself and her baby of all their clothing and she was nearly
exhausted, with the tcĭs'gä close upon her; then she heard
the sound of drumming across a little valley and crying
"Gowen'" she ran on. The sentinel outside the long house
heard her cry and gathering a number of warriors about
him, ran at full speed toward the cry of distress. Each
warrior bore a flaming torch the lights of which confused
the pursuing tcĭs'gä and gave hope to the woman. Throwing their robes about her the warriors carried her to the long
house where after reviving her from her faint, they heard
her story. Then said the chief, "If her story is true we must
keep the lights burning and dance till morning for the
tcĭs'gä may return and kill us all; on the morrow we will
send a party to examine the lodge of Taiiani Gowa and find
out what the trouble is." So the dance continued all night
and in the morning a party headed by the chief went to the
lodge of Taiiani Gowa and found the dead man in his coffin

and the husband with his face chewed clean to the skull. Then the chief stepped to the side of the coffin and said, "We have come to make a great ceremony. We will bind up your box and then have our ceremony." The warriors bound up the coffin with their strongest ropes and piled it high with brush and logs. Then a torch was applied and the coffin was surrounded by flames. The old man could not escape although he threatened terrible results for he could not pass outside of the flames. So his head burst and a white rabbit ran forth into the underbrush, eluding all the arrows of the warriors and escaping. Then did the people prove that Tiaiiani Gowa was a wizard and discover the form of his evil spirit. Likewise they knew why his guests became sick. He was a bad spirit.

TALES OF TALKING ANIMALS

VIII

39. THE MAN WHO EXHALED FIRE— HIS DOGS AND THE WOLVES[1]

Now this is great.

A man had a dog and was always kind to it and the dog loved the man. Now this man would smoke tobacco after he had eaten his evening meal. Smoke issued from his mouth and sparks of fire flew from his pipe. The dog noticed this.

The man was a hunter and had large stores of meat hung up on poles and stored in his lodge. This was fortunate for the man because game was now very scarce. The wolves about were ravenous. They came from great distances toward the lodge of the hunter because they smelled his meat. The hunter's dog saw them and asked them what they intended to do. They answered that they were hungry and intended to kill the hunter and eat his meat. They also advised the dog to keep away for they surely would kill his brother (the man) and also him if he interfered or warned his master. This worried the good dog and he thought some time how he could save his brother. So he spoke and said, "You can never kill my brother. He is too great a wizard. He has the greatest charms on earth. He eats fire and blows it from his mouth with clouds of smoke. Beware, I tell you,—do not attempt to injure him, for if you do he will torture you in the flames. You will be unable to escape for the smell of his fire travels a great distance and is great magic. If you do not believe me come and look after the evening meal and see for yourselves."

Then did the wolves laugh and say, "You are somewhat of a liar but we will come and see."

The dog was very angry then.

---

1 Related by Edward Cornplanter, 1905.

When evening came the wolves gathered around the hunter's lodge and watched him eat his meal. When he had finished they saw him take a brand of flaming fire and put it to his face. Then he waved the flame in front of his face and it disappeared. Then smoke in volumes issued from his mouth because the fire must have entered his stomach and be burning. Sparks flew in the wind and they smelled the smoke of the fire. They had never seen such a performance before and were frightened. So they did not dare attack the man at night. They ran back in the forest and hid. The next day the dog went and found them. Then the wolves said, "We can not kill your brother, he is too great a conjurer. His power is too much for us to fight. We are glad you told us."

Now this was all right. The dog did not tell his master but defended him with his wits. If one is kind to a dog he will never know how many times the dog will save him from danger and death. That is all.

40. THE TURTLE'S WAR PARTY.[1]

Turtles have never done anything wonderful since the foundation of the world. This is what a discontented turtle thought. "Now it is for me to show myself a leader of warriors and thus bring glory to the turtles."

Thus the turtle set about to devise a song by which he should call volunteers together. After a prolonged study he composed a tune and chose the words of a stirring war song, crawled into his canoe and paddled down the river, singing as he went.

A wolf running along the shore lifted his head and pricked his ears as he heard this odd song floating down the river, and listening, caught its import. When the turtle came near he began to yelp.

"I am a famous warrior and will volunteer," he shouted.

The turtle grounded his canoe and crawled up the bank to inspect his would-be recruit.

"Well, what can you do, wolf?" said he.

"Oh ho! I can run," said the wolf and then started off at a furious pace and returning asked what impression he had made.

"Now it seems to me," answered the turtle as he started to turn around, "you would be very apt to desert me when I most needed your support, so I say good-bye."

Going back to his canoe he tumbled in and paddled down the stream, once more singing.

A fox barked and waving his brush signalled the singing turtle.

"I will be your follower for I am a cunning warrior," said the fox.

Pushing the canoe ashore the turtle flopped out and ambled up to the fox.

"Now warrior," said he, "show me your excellence."

---

1 Related by Chief Cornplanter, 1904.

The fox gave a sudden spring and was out of sight before the turtle could turn to look, then bounding back asked if he were not skillful indeed.

"Your feet may be swift," replied the turtle, "but I see no signs of a warrior in you," and pushing his way over the pebbles he reseated himself in his canoe. Paddling out into midstream he resumed his singing and after some time was hailed again. Landing he found a new volunteer in the form of a skunk.

"Well now what can you do," said the turtle looking at the handsome creature before him.

Without moving from his tracks the skunk gave a satisfactory demonstration of his ability, to the turtle's great delight.

"Jump in, Sě'no', two brave fellows as we can collect a most formidable party," said the turtle, and he changed the words of his song as he paddled.

A rattlesnake next offered his services and when he had shaken his rattles and shown his fangs, was accepted.

"Tumble in," said the turtle, "and we will sing until another warrior as brave as we is added to our party." So all sang, as they coursed down the stream.

The song attracted a hedgehog, and wishing to become a warrior too, he shouted from the shore.

"Well, what can you do?" inquired the turtle as the canoe neared the bank.

"I can shoot my arrows," said the hedgehog, and mounting a stump shook himself until his quills flew in all directions.

"You are my warrior," said the turtle as he shoved his canoe to a convenient embarking point.

When the hedgehog had climbed over the side of the canoe and the war party had paddled off from the shore, the turtle swelled proud in his skill and sang a mighty war song defying all foes.

The party councilled together and decided to make their

first attack upon a human settlement. Reaching a short distance below they secreted their canoe and crawled stealthily through the bushes and grass to a lodge not far from the river. It was evening and the party resolved to take their positions of attack and await the coming of dawn. The skunk lay at the back door, the hedgehog at the wood pile, the snake coiled in the kindling barrel and the turtle hid beneath the rocks of the spring and morning found them ready to fight.

A woman pushed aside the curtain of the lodge door and stepped out of doors. The skunk was on the alert and shot her full at her face. The woman with a groan fell upon him and beat his head flat with her fists. Another woman, hearing the commotion rushed out and standing at the wood pile to watch her distressed sister received a sudden shock. The hedgehog ran between her legs and filled them full of his sharp barbed quills. With a scream the woman dealt her assailant a death blow with a billet of wood and ran screaming into the house. Soon, out came another woman bearing a basket which she set down in the kindling barrel as she paused to look at the dead bodies of the hedgehog and the skunk. Through the splints she saw the coils of a snake. She picked up a heavy stone and flung it into the barrel and killed the snake before he had had a chance to strike.

A man now emerged from the lodge laughing, "Ha, ha! Women are always in trouble, Hoh ho!" Laughing at the discomfort of his wife and sisters he ran down the spring path and sank his clay kettle beneath the surface of the spring. This was now the turtle's opportunity and with a furious leap he fastened his jaws in the man's leg. The man endeavored to suppress a howl as he felt the sudden pain and tried to beat off his enemy, but the turtle's jaw was set and his back was armored.

"Oh get off," begged the man doing his best to conceal his suffering, but the turtle only bit deeper.

Loudly the man cried and then began to threaten to kill the turtle. "I will drag you into the fire," he said. This so frightened the turtle that he began to waver with fear but gathering up courage determined to escape without crying for quarter, so he said, "Hurry then, put me in the fire, it is my natural home and I am lonesome, hurry now!"

The man groaned and cried in desperation, "The river for you, I will drown you!"

The turtle pleaded most earnestly to be spared that fate but the man was resolute and limping to the river he thrust in his leg. The turtle gripped until he bit through the leg bone, then relaxing his jaws, he swam rapidly under the water and crawled out in a sheltered spot.

"Agi̇́!" exclaimed the man as he crawled to his lodge, "I am glad he is drowned."

The turtle found his canoe but was unable to push it back up the stream against the swift current. Discouraged, he sank it and swam back to land where he lay lamenting his failures, then he turned on his back as if dead and gave himself up to grief. Grief gave place to meditation and at last he righted himself and crawled away saying:

"No, I am not a great chief, but I am a turtle and am satisfied, for the glory of turtles is that the earth and all creation rests upon the back of one. That is good enough."

41. THE RACE OF THE TURTLE AND THE BEAVER.

There was a turtle who lived in a deep hole in a stream. He lingered there and it was a favorite spot for his fishing. On the shore there was a swampy place where he hid himself when not in the stream.

One day it grew very cold and the turtle felt very sleepy. He looked about for a soft spot in the mud and found one beneath some tall sheltering rushes. "Here I will sleep," said he. So saying he slept.

When he opened his eyes there was a vast expanse of water over his head. Everything had changed and all the rushes had vanished. He threw off the mud blanket that covered him and ambled out on the floor of his resting place. "Iik," he exclaimed. "Something has happened. Some magician has taken liberties with my home." So saying he swam to the surface of the water.

Instead of the little stream with its neighboring swamp he saw a big lake. As far as he could see there was a lake. He looked about and saw an island in the lake and to it he swam. It was covered with sticks, and when he crawled upon it there was a hollow sound within, which frightened Turtle and caused him to slip quietly off and conceal himself.

Soon he saw a dark form emerge from the water beneath the island and rise to the surface.

Craftily Turtle raised his head and called. "Who are you?" Then he submerged quickly.

There was a whistling answer, a slap of the water and a voice said. "I am Beaver. Who are you?"

"So that is the case," thought Turtle. "So someone has stolen my fishing place." He was very angry and swam to the shore where he saw all kinds of branches broken up by cutting.

Soon he heard someone say, "Get out of my way."

Turtle looked up and saw Beaver dragging a branch.

"One would think," answered Turtle that it should be I who said 'get out of my way'."

"Well, what right have you here?" asked Beaver.

"This is my home," said Turtle. "I have lived here a long time."

"Ho! ho! ho!" laughed Beaver. "If this is your home, where is your house? Now I say this is my home, for there is my house." He pointed to the thing that Turtle had thought an island.

"How did you get here?" asked Turtle.

"I came here and built a dam, made this lake, and now I have a house here."

"I came here long ago," said Turtle and built a fishing hole. My abiding place is in the swamp. You, Oh Beaver, have no right to spoil my home. It is my intention to break down your dam and restore my home."

"Well," said Beaver, "that would not do us any good for I would build another and others of my tribe would catch you and gnaw your head off."

"How shall we settle this thing?" asked Turtle.

"We will see who can stay under water longest," said Turtle.

"No, that would be too easy for me," said Beaver. "I could sleep a year under water. I was going to ask that as a test myself. I propose that we run a race."

Turtle was vexed, for he did not wish Beaver to win, and so he did not insist upon the under water test. He was also crafty. So he said:

"Whoever wins the race shall stay here; whoso loses shall depart. First we shall have a trial of racing, and then the race will begin."

So they both came abreast in the water and started to swim. Soon Turtle called Beaver back. "Now we will begin again," said he, with a wicked gleam in his black beady eye.

As they were about to start, Turtle said, "I will purposely lag behind. When I pinch your tail then we will both start swimming."

Soon Turtle bit Beaver's tail and both started swimming, but crafty Turtle hung onto Beaver and was dragged through the water until within sight of shore, when he bit harder than ever.

Beaver gave a big grunt and whistled, "So you are there behind me? Well, I will win yet!"

Turtle bit again, this time harder than ever, making Beaver squeal with pain. "I'll fix you for this," he called, and flopped his tail over his head. Turtle hung on, and when he felt himself over Beaver's head he let go and continued to speed through the air like a flying squirrel. Far upon the shore he landed, way ahead of Beaver.

"I have won this race," he called back defiantly. "You must go away from here; this is my fishing pond."

Thereupon, Beaver was greatly vexed, and swam away to nurse his sore tail. Turtle had outwitted him.

42. THE WOLF AND THE RACCOON AND HOW THE BIRDS WERE PAINTED.

There was a wolf, T'hǎ'hyoñ'nǐ', a friend of the birds. He always helped the birds and told them where to find food. Now Djoagǎ', the raccoon disliked Tah'yoni and when he met him one day he made insulting remarks. Tah'yonǐ' became angry and snapped at Djoaga. The raccoon rolled over on his back and with teeth and claws was on the defensive. Tah'yonǐ' then did not want to fight. The raccoon did not wish to fight, moreover. So when the wolf turned his head Djoagǎ ran up a tree where he could insult Tah'yonǐ' without danger. A wolf cannot climb a tree. It was night now. So the wolf sat beneath the tree and quarreled with the raccoon. He sang:

"Djoaga, Djoaga! Diotion so go ge se da o!
Djoaga, Djoaga! Diotion so go ge se da o!"

The raccoon replied:

"Tah'yonǐ, Tah'yonǐ! Diotion so go ge se da o!
Tah'yonǐ, Tah'yonǐ! Diotion so go ge se da o!"

So back and forth they sang alternately all night. Towards morning the raccoon discovered that his enemy below was strangely silent. He did not respond to his insults, neither did he sing his threats. So Djoaga sang again and listening heard no response. "He is asleep," he thought. "I will climb down and see." Djoaga descended cautiously and looked at the wolf. True he was asleep. "Now I have you to advantage," said Djoaga softly. Then he squatted his haunches and covered Tah'yonǐ's eyes with pitch and clay. When he had done this he ran off thinking that he had done a great trick. Then he laughed. "Tah'yonǐ' went to sleep," he chuckled. "It is better not to sleep if you wish to get the best of a fight." After that he ran off into the woods to relate his joke.

Now then the wolf was very tired and did not awaken until noon. It was dark to him and he could not open his eyes. There seemed to be a dried plaster sealing them over. This frightened Tah'yonï'. Then he howled. He called the birds. So first came the tree tappers. Tah'yonï' said, "Remove the plaster from my eyes and I will reward you with whatever you may ask." So now then the birds began to eat the plaster from his eyelids and after a while he was able to see. Then he was very grateful to the birds, so he asked them what they desired most and they answered that they would like to be painted. So he painted the birds. Some he striped, some he spotted and some he mottled. He painted birds, blue, red, black, white, green, yellow, and all the colors. The birds were very glad then that they had helped the wolf for now they were handsome to look upon. Thus came there to be different colored birds so it is said by the ga-gä (legends). So it ends, the tale.

43. THE CHIPMUNK'S STRIPES.

There was a hungry bear. He could find nothing to eat. At length he caught a chipmunk and held it a prisoner. After a while he intended to eat it. Now the bear was about to eat the chipmunk when the little animal begged that it might be allowed to sing his death chant and dance his last dance. So the bear let him free for a time but watched him closely. Now the chipmunk sang this song:

> Si! Si! Oyade agadiangwa! Sa hi hi hi hi!
> (Si! Si! Hole I wish for! Sa hi hi hi hi!)

Now he sang this over and over as he danced over the leaf mold of the forest. After some time he felt a soft spot and thought a hole might be beneath. He gave a jump and sank in but the bear was watching and as he disappeared down the hole he grabbed the chipmunk by the neck and drew his four claws over its length. This hurt the chipmunk and tore his skin. After that scabs formed and when they came off the chipmunk had stripes on his back. He was glad that he had escaped. Now it is said that so came the stripes of the chipmunk. So it ends.

44. THE RABBIT SONG.

There was a certain woman who was accustomed to ridiculing Gwaio, the rabbit. She called him Honishogwadusshe. Usually she called him Hegowa (gallops). One day Gwaio was running by this woman's house. She saw him and came out to deride him for she always thought rabbits queer animals. When she saw him she sang a song. This is what she sang:

He'gowa, He'gowa! Ne"ho ni'shogwadase oi' daĕ'!
(Gallops, Gallops! There growing all around, hair is!)

Now this made Gwaio embarrassed and he hastened to escape from the sound of the song. He ran very far but soon saw the woman again singing as before.

"Gallops, Gallops, with hair circling round!"

Then he ran fast again and when he thought that he had escaped he heard the woman singing again,

"Gallops, Gallops, with hair circling round!"

This made him angry and he was mystified to know how the woman could be ever before him singing her song when he had passed her twice. So he ran again and when he thought himself safe again he saw her before him singing as before,

"Gallops, Gallops, with hair circling round!"

Again he ran and hearing her sing once more fell exhausted at her feet tortured by the song and laughter of the merciless woman. He said, "O woman, you must be a great witch to be ever before me when I pass you."

Then the woman laughed and said, "O rabbit you must be a great fool not to know that I have not moved and that you have been running around in a circle. When you ran up to me I sang the song,

" 'Gallops, Gallops, with hair circling round'!"

Now the old people say that when you see a rabbit and wish to kill it to remain still and make ready to shoot. He will come again round a circle and you can kill him. This thing was learned from this legend. Now when you hunt rabbits sing this song when you see one and soon he will appear again for he runs in circles and returns to the same spot in which you saw him first. So now all.

45. THE RABBIT GAMBLER.

In old times there was a rabbit,—Osīda Hodaweo, that was his name. Now Osīda was a gambler and was continually winning games. He had a deadly enemy, Sēno,—that was his name, a skunk. Now this Sēno loved two sisters. He never gambled but always had plenty to eat. Osīda, also loved the same two sisters. He gambled and had stores of goods. So Osīda was the choice of the women but his grandmother said that they would be fickle and would desert him when his luck changed. Then Osīda laughed at the old woman.

His wives were always faithful and cooked good food. Each morning he returned from his gambling. Then he sang a song:

"One Djagwehee! Deiogwaie do-no!
One Djagwehee! Deiogwaie do-no!
Now I am coming home; all night I have gambled!
Now I am coming home; all night I have gambled!"

Then his wives hearing his song in the distance would run out on the trail to greet him. They would sing a song:

"Osida-a-a-a Hada-weo! Dondae!
Osida-a-a-a Hada-weo! Dondae!
Feet Earrings! He is returning!
Feet Earrings! He is returning!"

So it happened this way continuously. Then it changed. One morning he sang his song but his wives did not come to greet him. He did not hear their song. He thought that it was strange. But he kept singing. He had no goods with him. For a long time now he had brought nothing home. His luck had changed. Therefore he wished his wives to come and cheer him but they did not come. He continued to sing until he stood outside the lodge door. He paused and listened but heard no sound within. He thought that was strange. He entered the lodge and it was empty.

No one was within. There was a hot meal ready for him
and he sat down and ate. He was absent minded and did
not see what he was eating. After a time he heard singing
in the air above the lodge. He heard the words:

> "Ionegattha sago no sothetstsowa Haiasho!
> Ionegattha sago no sothetatsowa Hayasho!"

These were the words he heard and then he voided his
meal.[1] He ran out of the lodge, and above the trees overhead he saw his wives paddling a canoe through the air.
They were not descending. Osīda was sick at stomach but
he ran to catch them. They paddled fast and he did not
succeed in getting near them for some time. At last he was
at the side of the canoe which the women were paddling
over the ground. He leaped into the canoe but the women
leaped out and hopped away into the bush lands. Osīda
chased them but lost sight of his runaway wives.

Now Sēno heard a noise above his burrow and sticking
his head from the door saw the women whom he loved running. "Kwe!" he cried, "what is your haste?"

"We are running away from Osīda," they replied.

"My lodge will be a safe refuge," he answered with a
smile, and beckoned them in. So they entered.

Osīda spied their tracks in the mud and stalked them
to a burrow. He was about to run into the hole without
looking when a hairy tail of some animal was pushed against
his very face. He had no warning and was drenched with
Sēno's fetid water. He fell back and cried loudly for he
was greatly in distress. By and by his grandmother came
to him. She said something to him, but Osīda did not
laugh. He went home with his grandmother.

---

[1] Because he realized that he was scatophagous.

46. THE RACCOON AND THE CRABS.

There was a raccoon who was fond of crabs. It was his custom to catch the crabs when they swam out from under a rock in the water. After a time the crabs learned how he caught them and when he came near the water they would hide under a flat rock and not come out until a sentinel told them that the raccoon had gone. The raccoon thought it strange that the crabs had grown so wary and resolved to play a trick. He crept to the bank of the brook and lay upon his back pretending to be dead. After some time the crabs crawled out to the bank and looked carefully at the "dead" raccoon. Then the chief of the crabs, Hasanowane Odji'eg'dă, was his name, notified all the crab people to come out and see their dead enemy. Now when they had all assembled the chief said, "He is dead, let us all rejoice. He who destroyed us is himself at last destroyed. So let us rejoice and show our gladness by a dance." So they danced and this was the song:

Do sa gwe Do sa gwe ga no ho tci do
(Chorus) ie ie ie ie ie ie ie ie!

Soon one of the crabs said, "Are you sure that he is dead?" And the chief answered, "Go pinch him and see." So the crab went and pinched him and the raccoon did not move, so he answered, "Yes, he is dead." Then they danced again and after a time a crab asked of the chief, "Are you sure he is dead?" And the chief answered, "Go and see, then tell us." So the crab went up and crawled down the raccoon's throat. When he came out he answered, "Yes, he is dead there is evidence inside." Then the crabs danced again but after a time a crab asked of the chief, "Are you sure that he is dead?" And the chief answered, "Go and see for yourself, then report to me." So the crab crawled up and pinched the raccoon's heart. This made the raccoon very angry and he said to himself, "Now is my time to feast, I have waited too long." So he leaped up and began devouring the crabs and he ate until his belly was gorged. Then he laughed and thought himself a great trickster. Now that is how the raccoon outwitted the crabs. It is said that it is not safe to rejoice at the downfall of an enemy lest he rise again and devour those that thought they danced at his funeral.

47. THE CRAB'S EYES.

Now a crab slept so long that his eyes dried up. When he awoke he did not know where he was. He could not open his eyes because they had dried up in his head. So he strained for a long time. He crawled along endeavoring to find his way to water. As he crawled he kept striving. After a time he came across an obstruction. So he sang this song:

> A-di-na-ote sa-hi ga-i'
> De-sa-si-no gwa-do-nio!
> What kind of a standing tree
> With crooked legs here?

And the tree answered, "I am the oak!"

"Oh! Oh!" cried the crab, "How far I am from water!"

Now he crawled along straining his eyes and singing his song. He asked every tree whose crooked legs he ran against but they answered, maple or beech, and he was discouraged. After a time a tree said, "rock elm." Then he was encouraged and said, "Water must be near at hand!" So he kept along striving and singing and when he heard a tree call out "willow" he was exultant. He strained still harder and when he struck water the paste over his eyes melted and so intense was he that his eyes shot out of his head and waved about. Now this was convenient for he could see better than he had ever before. So he decided to keep them out where he could adjust them as he wished. Now the old people have said that this was the way the crab got his eyes and it may be true. So it ends.

48. HOW THE SQUIRREL GAVE A BLANKET TO HIS WARRIOR, ROBBED THE WOODCHUCK OF HIS TAIL AND THE FROG OF HIS TEETH.[1]

There was a time when animals and birds were very large. So, also, trees were more lofty and rivers broader. This was long ago.

Now, in those days there was a great chief of the squirrels, and he was very wise. It was his custom to go stealthily through the forest and watch his people as they worked or sported.

One autumn morning as he lay concealed by the leaves on the limb of a giant oak, he heard a chattering voice call from a hemlock. It was the voice of a squirrel.

"All the autumn days I have been gathering nuts," said the squirrel in an aggrieved tone, "and yet day by day my store is growing smaller. Who is stealing my hoard? Truly some culprit lurks here and is robbing me of my winter's food that I have patiently stored in that stump!"

Up from a hole in the hillside popped Tēdo', the woodchuck. From the dark scummy swamp water a big frog lifted its green head.

"How unfortunate!" said the woodchuck, "Some thief must be lurking here."

"Yes, I too think it strange," croaked the big frog, "Surely some thief must be hidden here."

Then in a chorus both poured out their sympathy to the indignant squirrel.

The squirrel chief seated on the oak limb listened attentively and then nodding his head spoke thus to himself. "True, indeed, thieves are not far away. I think this sympathy betokens knaves."

At night the chief hid in a branch that overhung the stump that the squirrel had pointed out.

---

1 From Mrs. Aurelia Miller.

When the sun had gone in his western door and darkness had obscured the earth, from a hole in the hillside a brown head cautiously emerged and after peering slyly around the woodchuck crept from his burrow, swung his tail jauntily and trotted down his path to the swamp. A green backed frog pushed his way from a high tufted hummock of grass through the black water of the swamp toward the hillside. But he made no froggish splash, no gurgling trill, no croak but swam in silence. Reaching the bank he sneaked his way up the path to the stump beneath the squirrel's hemlock where a furry brown bulk was rumaging.

"Kwe!" exclaimed the frog in a startled note.

"Kwe!" came the hollow reply, and Tedo, the woodchuck, withdrew his head to see who had discovered him but finding it to be only Skoak, the frog, he resumed his work of pilfering the squirrel's store.

"Iis kho, and you too," he said in a muffled voice as with bulging cheeks he hurried back to his hole.

Now the frog in those days had sharp gnawing teeth like a beaver's and when he entered the hollow stump he tested the nuts to find what variety he would choose. He had taken hickory nuts before but now chose to take chestnuts.

From the limb over the stump store house a shrill cry sounded.

"Thief found!" came the alarm, and the woodchuck and the frog buried their ears in their booty to shut out the sound.

On the following day the squirrel chief called a council of all the animals, for in those days the squirrel was a famous animal and mightier than a wolf.

"Thieves have been found," said he. "I call a council to pronounce judgement."

Every animal from the neighborhood was present except the frog and the woodchuck.

A delegation was sent to examine the houses of these

absent two and after some time returned with the most guilty pair ever brought to council for judgement.

Said the squirrel chief. "I saw you steal the squirrel's nuts, the delegation found them in your houses, therefore, you shall be punished. You, the woodchuck, shall have your tail removed to humble your pride, and you the frog shall have your teeth taken from your mouth that you may not be further tempted to steal another's store. You the squirrel have been too careless. Henceforth build your storehouse high and in order to protect yourself from offenders that might attack you, I give you this blanket to stretch from leg to leg so that you may skim the air like a leaf."

A wolf snapped off the woodchuck's tail and a heron extracted the frog's teeth and so punished the guilty knaves in sight of all.

So now all these things came to pass; all frogs were afterwards hatched without teeth, all woodchucks had bobbed tails and all the descendents of the squirrel had blankets fastened to their legs and bellies and made a tribe of their own. Moreover, since that time all frogs have been afraid of long-billed birds and all woodchucks are afraid of wolves but some squirrels have blankets and can skim the air like leaves.

49. THE CHICKADEE'S SONG.[1]

Djikdjunkwa was a lonely chickadee. She was very sad and sat on the limb of a tree singing a sorrowful tune. Then she flew to another tree and listened for an answering call.

A wolf passing by heard her crying song and tears came in his eyes. "Let me be your helper?" he asked.

"What kind of food do you eat, good friend?" asked she.

"Raw meat, raw meat," exclaimed the wolf, seeking to lure the Chickadee to him.

But Chickadee screamed a fluttering note and flew away. Soon again she sang her song.

"I am so lonesome, I am looking for somebody to marry me."

"A crow flying over listened and was moved to help the distressed little bird.

"Oh poor Chickadee," said Crow. "I would like to marry you."

"What would you feed my young ones?" asked the Chickadee.

"Ripe dead meat," answered the crow, whereupon Chickadee flew away and hid herself in a low bush, until the crow had flown away. Then she returned to a tree and sang again:

"Dji-he, dji-he, dji-i-he, I am so lonely that I would like to marry. Dji-he, dji-he, dji-i-he."

Soon she heard an answering call and saw a bird like herself. He flew toward her and said, "I am the one and we will marry now."

---

1 Cornplanter says, "Some girls sing this song and boys know what they mean."

50. THE BIRD WOMAN.[1]

Sitting mournfully on the edge of her nest was a heart-broken Gonadjodjo, (Chewink). Her husband had been blown away on the breath of a storm and the bird mother was left alone to care for her hungry brood.

All day long she had waited for her mate to return but, alas, he seemed to have forgotten her. Disconsolate, she listened to her children's cries. When she would fly to find their food they would shiver with cold and when she nestled them under her wings they would scream for bugs and seeds and berries. Something must be done or her callow nestlings would perish. So with a sad heart she began to sing in melancholy note.

Fluttering upon the stump of a fallen tree she sang and an owl within a hollow stub nearby poked out his head and said, "Oh may I not be your helper and care for your nest?"

"Alas!" sighed Gonadjodjo in great distress, "it would never do for my young birds would die when they heard you."

The owl drew back into his hole and Gonadjodjo sang again.

From another hollow tree came an answering call. "May I not be your helper?" screeched a night hawk.

"Ah, what yould you say to comfort them?" said Ganojojo.

"I would say Hai", hai", hai", hai"!"

"Oh no, no!" cried Ganodjodjo, "they would scream the worse."

Flying to an open spot she sang again and a crow poking among the weeds paused and lifted his head as he heard the song. Then, with all compassion he said, "Oh, Ganodjodjo, I would like to help you."

---

[1] Related by Chief Cornplanter, 1905.

"Then what would you say to soothe my children?" sighed the unhappy bird.

"Ga! ga! ga! ga!" replied the crow, but Ganodjodjo cried in terror that his harsh hoarse voice was far too hoarse for her little ones, so, the crow croaked and strode on.

Winging her way to the top of a dead tree Ganodjodjo sang again her plaintive song. There was a whirr of wings and a bluejay alighted on the branch beside her.

"I will help you gladly," said he.

"Well," said the hapless Ganodjodjo shyly, for she was impressed with the gay bird at her side, "what would you say to my children?"

"In my softest voice I would say, "Di", di", di", di", di", di", di", skil'lŭm, skil'lŭm!""

The sharp shrill cry of the bluejay made Ganodjodjo's ears ache and fluttering to the ground half fainting she fell in a mouldering pile of leaves. Plaintively she sang her song again. The leaves on the ground a distance away began to tremble and rustle and then there was a faint sound of "tci'-wii', tci'-wii'!" The disconsolate bird stopped short, and darting to the spot found her own lost mate.

"I have been stunned and bruised," he said, "and only awoke when you called."

She plucked him a red berry for medicine and then together they flew to their nest, he with unsteady wings but she in strong and happy flight.

51. THE PARTRIDGE'S SONG.

Now there was a partridge[1] woman who had a large family. She had a house under a big log and her house was hidden by plants. A good many people (animals) tried to find the partridge's house because they wanted to eat her eggs or her children. Now one morning her children were all asleep and she was running about eating worms and seeds. At this time she smelled an enemy so she was alarmed for her children's safety. Now then she sang a song to awaken them:

> Djut-gan-nio, djut-gan-nio! Ho-sho-ga-he shoda-die-ə!
> Ya-ha-ne sho-da-ges! Ia-ha-ne sho-da-ges!

which meant that the skunk was prowling about and would soon find them if they did not scurry away. After a time they heard their mother's song and ran into the bushes and she hid them in a safe place.

Now this is the partridge song and it is a good thing to sing it when you see or smell an enemy about a partridge's house. It is good luck.

---

1 **Partridge** in Seneca is Deyenego.sda′sden′, meaning, Her two wings are large.

TALES OF GIANTS, PYGMIES AND MONSTER BEARS

IX

52. A TALE OF THE DJOGEON OR PYGMIES

There was a young man named Snow who lived with his parents along the bank of a river. He played about the door yard every day and sometimes swam in the river. When he was very young he obeyed everything his father told him and refrained from going toward the south, where he had been forbidden to venture.

One morning he took his bow and arrows and began to hunt cedar waxwings. It was spring time and there were many of these birds on the tall trees. Just as he was about to shoot, the birds flew to the south and so kept on flying up the bed of a smaller stream, emptying into the river. As Snow chased the birds he noticed that the walls of the stream grew higher and higher until they were very high and close together at the top. It became very dark and Snow became confused and could not tell where to walk, for the rocks began to get more and more jagged. So he sat down on a large stone, feeling very miserable.

Suddenly he heard a stone strike the ground at his feet. He looked about in the gloom and then heard another strike. The next time the stone struck him on the forehead between the eyes and Snow fell over like a dead person.

After a long time he heard voices speaking. The discussion was about him and he heard a voice say, "Now we have him." He resolved to keep his eyes shut and wait for a good opportunity to escape. Soon he heard foot falls about him; they were very light like a small child's. Then more came about him and soon he heard the sound of drumming. Presently small voices began to sing and the singing continued for a long time.

Snow understood every word and remembered the songs. Finally he made up his mind that there was nothing malign about the intentions of the beings that moved about him and he opened his eyes.

All about him were pygmies,—little people,—dressed just like Indians. There was a shout when he opened his eyes and he was told to rise and be seated. He could now see clearly by aid of a fire on the slaty bottom of the creek.

At length one of the little people spoke, asking him if he had tobacco. Snow searched through his hunting pouch and found a small quantity which he gave the chief. This caused an expression of great pleasure.

The chief of the little people now spoke. "You have come to our home," said he. "We sent for you in order that we might teach you our ways. You are to stay here until you have learned our customs."

Snow lived with the little people and became versed in all their arts. He was told that when the Djogeon were in need of tobacco they would be heard singing, and then the Indians must throw tobacco into the gulches where the sound emanated. Sometimes drumming would be heard instead of singing, and this also indicated the need of tobacco. The little people would also be pleased to have finger nail parings in order to give them certain human powers. Snow was told about the different tribes of Djogeon and about the stone throwers. Some Djogeon had power over the fruits and plants and even the health of people. They had some valuable hunting charms which they would bestow if man would guard their potency by appropriate ceremonies. All this Snow learned.

The time came for him to depart, and the Djogeon gave him presents, telling him their purposes and magical attributes. Snow now departed and returned to his people, who had grown very old. They scarcely knew him because of his long absence, which seemed to him only a few days.

Snow now called together his friends and taught them the ceremonies and the songs of the little people, and these ceremonies have come down to this day. They must be performed in the dark.

After that time the people began to see Djogeon in various places, but they felt safe, knowing how to appease them.

53. BEYOND-THE-RAPIDS AND THE STONE GIANT.

Skŭn'niwŭndi[1] was a great fighter. His name as a warrior was famous everywhere and he was called the greatest war chief in the world. Skŭnniwŭn'di was a great name.

Skŭnniwŭn'di was passing along the bank of a river one time when he heard his name called out, "Kwe Skŭn niwŭn'di," some voice was saying. "You are the best fighter in the world,—you are the best fighter in the world." Skŭnniwŭn'di looked up and saw across the river a terrible Genonsgwä, a stonish giant, a female giant. So he answered, "Kwe! What do you want?"

"I want to fight with you," she answered.

Skŭnniwŭn'di never had fought with a stonish giant but he answered, "All right, come over!"

Now at this place on the river there was a deep hole above the ripples and there was a ford at the ripples. Now the Genonsgwä walked into the hole and was a long time crossing over under the water. Skŭnniwŭn'di thought he would cross over on the ripples and he was in a great hurry and forgot his tomahawk. Now he stood on the opposite side when the stonish woman appeared.

"Kwe!" she cried, "where are you?"

"Right where I was before," answered Skŭnniwŭn'di.

"That is strange," she replied, "for here is your little weapon."

"Oh I was passing this place some time ago and dropped it," he explained.

"Oh what a tiny thing to fight with," she laughed. "How do you ever expect to fight with it!" She licked it with her tongue and then said, "It is no good, see me smash it on this rock!" Then she hit the rock and to her surprise

---

1 Meaning Beyond-the-Rapids.

the rock split asunder.[2] She did not realize that it was her saliva that made the tomahawk strong medicine.

"Ho ho!" she exclaimed, "are all your weapons so effective on stone?"

"That little weapon is nothing," said Skŭnniwŭn'di, "I have a knife here that will cut stone by drawing it over it."

"Let me see it," begged the giantess.

The man threw it across the stream. The stonish woman picked it up and drew it across her lips moistening it with her saliva. This is the custom of the giants when they wish to use anything and they do not know that it makes power. Taking the knife she drew it over a flint and the flint was cut. She rubbed its edge on her coat and it was slit. Then she threw back the axe and the knife now possessed with a wonderful power and Skŭnniwŭn'di exultant asked her to hurry and commence the fight.

"No," said the giantess, "Your medicine is too strong. You are truly the greatest warrior of the earth. I will go."

When the stone giantess left Skŭnniwŭn'di she ran out to a river and followed it as it flowed until she came to a house where a man, woman and child were sitting around a fire inside. She unfastened her stone coat and entered. After greeting them she said, "I am fleeing from my husband who seeks to kill me. Only be my friends and I will give you something." The people were kind and told her that she could stay, but even so, they were afraid of her. So she sat and swung the hammock in which lay the baby daughter. She began to sing without realizing that her song would offend the parents:

> "Oh what a tender morsel,
> How I would love to eat you!"

The father remonstrated and implored her not to destroy

---

2 This episode is identical with that recorded by Barbeau in a Huron myth.

their child. Then the giantess was sorry and asked forgiveness.

The next morning she went out into the woods and killed two deer and a bear and brought them back for her hosts.

After a number of days she said, "I hear my husband coming. You can save me. Cut six basswood poles as tall as a man and when we fight and he throws me down thrust them one by one into his back and you will kill him. Then I will repay you."

The great stone giant came making a roar like a whirlwind, "Who-whoa-hoh-hoh-hoh!" and the giantess whispered, "Be ready and do your best. Do not be afraid."

The man hid behind the big rocks and saw the female giant and her husband rush upon each other. They fought very hard and the stone broke when they hurled each other against them.

"The world is small, you could not escape me," the giant thundered as he flung his wife upon her back and made ready to kill her. Then the man ran out and thrust the sharpened poles into the giant and they came out of his mouth.

"Oh, oh!" he cried, "I am killed, I am gone!" and he fell over dead.

The giantess was glad and rewarded her friend with a small patch of skin. "This skin is covered with the hairs of all animals," she said, "and when you wish to kill a beast remove a hair and blow it on the wind. The animal will appear and you will be able to kill it."

So the giantess went away and the man kept his great game charm and was thought a most successful hunter, and no one knew how he got animals when no one else could; but one day a boy saw him blow a hair and a beaver came. Then he hit it with a club and chopped off its tail.

54. THE ANIMATED FINGER.[1]

There was a boy named Skunniwundi who was a hunter. It was a time when there was a great famine and game was very scarce. The people were starving. Skunniwundi thought he would find out why there was no game. Long he had been warned not to go north, but north he went.

When he had traveled a long ways he saw something moving in the rocks ahead of him. Concealing himself in a hole he watched. Soon he saw two stone coated women approaching. They were looking for food. Then did Skunniwundi know that the stone giants were eating all the game, thus making the famine.

After a while Skunniwundi noticed that one of the women took something out of a bag and placed it on the palm of her hand. As she did this she exclaimed, "Ghaah!" and commenced to walk directly toward him. At this he began to run toward a creek hoping to cross it but they were too swift for him. Hoping to secape he ran into a clump of tall trees and climbed one. The women followed his tracks to the tree and then began to look around for him. Not once did they think of looking up, for their necks would not bend. If they tried they would crack off. Failing to find him one of the giant women put her hand in her pocket and took out something again which she placed on the palm of her hand. Skunniwundi looked down and saw that it was a human finger and that it was standing up pointing at him. "Where is he?" asked the woman and the finger wriggled and pointed. This puzzled the women and Skunniwundi felt that he was secure. Soon he began to think that this finger would be a helpful possession and began to consider how he could obtain it.

The women continued at the foot of the tree and finally discovered Skunniwundi's hatchet and arrows which he had

1 Related May, 1906, by George Jameson, Tahadondeh, Cattaraugus Seneca.

left on the ground at the foot of the tree. One woman picked them up and began to lick them, smelling for blood.

Skunniwundi now saw that all was lost unless he hastened. So with a quick slide he came down the tree and seized the finger. With a bound he jumped into the water, but as he heard the giant women follow him he turned back under water and stood on the spot where he had dived off. The women came out of the water on the opposite shore and were greatly surprised. So they plunged in the water after him and when their heads were under Skunniwundi swam across and stood on the opposite shore. He could swim very fast now that he had the finger. When the women came out of the water they saw him where they had stood but a moment before, and were again surprised. They plunged in again and this time Skunniwundi ran very rapidly to escape them. Soon he heard the women crying, "Oh give us back the finger. We promise not to eat you."

Skunniwundi now was filled with power and kept asking the finger where the giant women were, and by going in another direction he escaped them until he came near to his own settlement, which lay across a stream of very cold water. In he plunged and swam across.

When he arrived on the other shore, toward the village he saw a herd of deer. Fixing his bow he shot and the arrow went through seven deer killing them all. He then ran on toward the village. He showed his uncle the finger and told the people to go for the game, but they returned in fright saying that there were sounds of giants on the other side of the stream.

Skunniwundi and his uncle then went to the river and saw the giant women on the other side. "Oh Skunniwundi, give back the finger," cried the women. "We will not molest you any more."

"Give it to them," said the uncle. "They will be friends with us if we appease them."

Skunniwundi then took the finger and held it way out

over the water and the giant women leaned over from the cliff on the other side and just as they were about to grasp the finger Skunniwundi drew back his hand and the women were overbalanced and fell in the river, falling head first. Down they went to the bottom, and the river froze as hard as stone, killing the stone coated women.

After that time, Skunniwundi had the finger for a hunting charm and he supplied game for the village.

55. THE STONE GIANT'S BATTLE.[1]

The stone giants had conquered all the tribes of the north and had grown tired of such easy combats.

So they came toward the south and heard of the fame of the Six Nations and right away desired to fight with them. In order to present a formidable force they sent messengers back to their own north country with orders to bring back a fresh party of warriors. These crossed the north ocean and coming to the Niagara river made a path of rocks across it and walked over without even wetting the soles of their moccasins.

Now the Six Nations knew all these things because Gwä gwä having seen them flew up to the clouds and told the sun and the sun told Soñgwayadï"sä'ë', the Great Ruler. Then Soñgwayadï"sä'ë' instructed Gwä gwä to nip off a grass-hopper's big leg and dangle it from the sky over a village while screaming his cry. So Gwä gwä obeyed.

An old man was crossing a clearing. In the air above him he heard what seemed a death cry and looking upward he saw a human leg writhing as it bled from the clouds. The old man dropped his head down and away from the sight and walked on pondering over the wonder, and he never knew that it was only Gwä gwä with a grass-hopper's big leg. The old man lay down to sleep and as he slept he dreamed the interpretation of the sign and knew that the stone giants were coming.

On the following day the old man took two friends and hid on the summit of a high mountain. For two days the men camped there listening to the war songs of the on-marching foe, and at evening on the second day they saw the vast war party of giants march into sight far down the valley and pitch camp on the shores of a lake. Then a

1 Related January, 1905, by Aurelia Jones Miller, Cattaraugus Seneca.

spirit came out of a tree and revealed to the men that the Creator had planned to save them. He instructed them to choose a messenger from among themselves and dispatch him for a few more people to witness the battle with the giants.

Accordingly, a runner was sent to the village and a small party was guided back to the mountain top, where all found shelter beneath a great rock.

A terrible storm burst from the sky—He"no^n roared from the heavens and sent down his fire upon the camp of stone giants. Then the earth trembled and the mountains on either side of the valley slid down upon the giants below.

It seemed that all were killed.

56. THE BOY AND THE FALSE FACE.[1]

There was a certain tribe that had been almost exterminated by a hostile people in the west. The western warriors would swoop down on the settlements on the Lake (Ontario) and carry off many captives and scalps.

Now there was a boy who had no settled home. His parents were dead and his grandmother also. He was a wanderer and showed no special ability in anything.

Now this boy was named No'gwăgwă and he began to have dreams. He dreamed that a great false face came to him and said, "You must lead a war party beyond the Mississippi." Then again he had a dream and the false face said, "You must lead a war party beyond the Mississippi. You must hold a war dance and gather your warriors."

Now again he dreamed that the false face came to him in his sleep and said, "You must lead a war party across the Mississippi. You must hold a war dance and gather your warriors. Go in a fleet of canoes." Now moreover he dreamed again that the false face said, "You must lead a war party beyond the Mississippi. You must hold a dance and gather your warriors. Go in a fleet of canoes. Sit in the first canoe but do not allow anyone to pass the middle for I will be in the front of the first canoe and give your expedition success. You can not fail."

Now when the poor boy had heard the false face speak four times he believed his dream and proclaimed himself a war-chief. Then all the people laughed. Now he notified all the boys of the village that he was a chief and would lead a party against the hostile nation in the west. Now many of the boys came and danced. The Nogwagwa said, "I have a power and can not fail. I have a magic friend." After a while the people ceased to scoff and all the men

---

[1] Related by George (Dondeh) Jemerson. This legend shows the use of a large false face as a war-bundle charm.

joined his party. Now there were many canoes and No-gwagwa sat in the middle of the first canoe and would not allow anyone to pass by him. Now after seven days they reached the country of the enemy. The warriors wondered when the "friend" was to appear and could not believe that he sat in the prow of the first canoe. Now the enemy appeared and immediately there rose into view in the prow of the first canoe a gigantic false face. Now he was the mark of the enemy and they shot at him. He had a great shield and caught all the arrows and no one was killed but when Nogwagwa's party shot their arrows they killed many people. Then the party disembarked and pursued the enemy far inland. The giant false face and Nogwagwa led the party and they killed the entire tribe of men and took their scalps. Then the false face disappeared and Nogwagwa led the party home. After that the boy, Nogwagwa, was his name, was a great chief and he was an influential man. So it is said this day that orphan boys without homes may become great chiefs.

57. HOW A BOY OUTWITTED A NIA"GWAHE.

Great sickness had killed many men and Sondowĕk'owa, the beast of Death, had touched the father and mother of two children, who lived far back in a place in the forest away from the villages. The children, a boy and a little girl, were left alone to care for themselves.

The baby sister was swinging in a grapevine hammock one morning, when from over the hill came floating a song. The boy glanced out from the lodge and saw an old woman hobbling down hill and crooning as she went. He did not like the sounds in her song and turned uneasily back to his work.

Presently the old woman came up to the little girl and croaking an unfamiliar song held out a little bark bowl of pudding, inviting her to accept it. The child looked up and held out her hands to take it when her brother rushed out and forbade her.

"The woman is a witch," he whispered to his sister. "If you eat her food it will charm you away!"

The old creature heard this exposure of her true self and fled vowing to return the next day. True to her promise, she came again and held out a delicious looking pudding on the top of which was a singing mocking-bird. The boy ran out from the lodge and stoned the old woman away and in anger she pointed her fingers toward him and screamed, "It does not matter for I will come again!"

The next day she returned and again was driven away by stones. She then departed with the same threatening words. But on one day she exclaimed, "Oh why do you not accept my beautiful gift! Do so now for I am hungry and wish to eat you. Oh, Oh—!"

The boy was frightened by her frank avowal but determined to be rid of the old witch and so drove her away once more.

"Tomorrow I will enter the lodge and eat her before your very eyes. Now remember my promise!" She screamed as she trampled back through the trees.

The boy was aroused and resolved to use every power to save his sister and himself, so that night he carved two dolls from chunks of rotten wood and placed them upright against the walls. Taking his sister he uttered certain magic words and made her very small. He placed her within a horn arrow-tip and then shot the arrow through the smoke hole. Leaping magically after the shaft, he followed and picking up the arrow followed the trail in the darkness.

The next morning the witch came again this time taking the form of a nīa"gwahē. She tore down the hill and pawed before the lodge door.

"I have come, Oh I have come!" she said. "You cannot escape me now for I am nīa"gwahē!"

"Oh please stay away, we are afraid," wailed two tremulous voices inside. "Spare us for we are young. Oh choose some older ones!"

"Oh no!" snorted the witch, "I have been hungering too long for you two," and bursting into the lodge prepared to seize the baby girl. She then was disappointed when she saw no trace of the children.

"I am nīa"gwahē!" she screamed, "no one can escape me!"

"Dogĕs! Is that very true?" asked small voices on opposite sides of the lodge.

The witch-beast looked about, and then seeing the wooden dolls trampled down the entire lodge. Then, running in an ever increasing circle she found the boy's tracks and following them with furious speed she screamed, "I am nīa"gwahē, no one can escape me!"

A short distance behind him the boy heard her voice and unable to withstand her speed he planned to outwit her by changing his form. He took the guise of an old man. He kicked off his moccasins and bade them run on and make tracks to the end of the earth or until a hole appeared in the soles. Standing with his arrow fixed he gazed upward at an old robin's nest that stuck upon a dead branch.

The witch-beast came crashing through the bushes.

"Kwē!" she screamed.

"Cii!" whispered the boy, "do you not see I am watching for game? Agē! I have been waiting three years for the bird to perch back on its nest and now you have warned it away with your yells. Oh now you must stay and help me kill it for I am very hungry."

"Oh nonsense!" exclaimed the beast. "I am hungry too. Tell me now old man, did you see a boy running by here?"

"Cii!" whispered the boy, "you will frighten my bird. Go away. See those tracks? Follow them and leave me to my bird!"

The nīa"gwahē struck the trail and followed the tracks of the moccasins through the forests and swamps and when many days had been spent she came to a log and on it were two moccasins with holes in the soles and no tracks beyond or around save those she had followed.

"Agī!" screamed the beast, overwhelmed with chagrin. "He has deceived me. Now I know he was the old man who gazed at the old nest and sent me away! Oh he shall not escape me for I am nīa"gwahē!"

In the meantime the boy had been running as fast as his legs and his magic would bear him but after a time he heard a far away call. "I am nīa"gwahē, he cannot escape!"

"Oh uncle," said the boy as he caught sight of an old spider, "help me to escape, a nīa"gwahē is pursuing me to eat my sister and me."

"I am your friend," said the old spider as he unrolled a net and spread it over the ground in all directions. Away sped the boy and soon the witch-beast came bounding into sight. Seeing her victim's tracks, she rushed squarely into the net and became badly entangled. Very furiously she wrestled with the snare endeavoring to become disentangled and when at last she did the boy was far away.

In an evil temper at the delay the witch-beast snorted wildly as she ran to the north, in which direction the boy had gone.

"I am nīa"gwahē, you cannot escape me," she screeched as she ran and the fleeing boy hearing her boast ran faster than ever, until he saw a boy with a basket of pigeon feathers, he stopped.

"Save me!" he cried, "give me your basket!" and snatching it from the owner he scattered the feathers to the winds crying, "Be pigeons and stop witches!"

Instantly the feathers were transformed into myriads of pigeons who flying in clouds, sent down a kind of rain that covered the ground for miles around with a slime so deep and slippery that no creature could wade through it.

Nīa"gwahē rushed into the slime and sinking into the depths wallowed and struggled until almost exhausted. Finally she was able to get back to its border and ran madly onward. "I am nīa"gwahē, no one can escape me!" she called, for it was her magic to say these words.

The boy heard her voice and holding fast to the precious arrow, in which his sister was hidden, he hurried toward a false face man whom he saw dancing about a tree.

"Oh grandfather!" he cried, "save me. Nīa"gwahē is after me!"

The false face held out his hand for tobacco and the boy gave him some. Then he pointed his hand toward a large cliff from which smoke issued.

The boy darted forward, and after him, close pursuing, was the witch. The false face halted the creature and demanded tobacco, but the witch being in the form of a nīa"gwahē could not give it unless she became her human self. This she knew meant delay, but the false face was insistent and then she was forced to shake off the beast form and give the tribute. It is woe to those who deny the false faces, and she knew it.   Then she resumed her beast shape and galloped onward.

The boy ran toward a rock and when he saw a small hole he entered and then crawled into a spacious cavern.   A woman within was boiling bear's oil.

"Save me!" cried the boy as the nïa"gwahē snorted at the entrance and forced in its head.

The beast struggled.   It was trapped.   The woman lifted her pot of boiling oil and threw it upon the face of the witch-beast.   A man forced out its carcass with a club and shot arrows into a black spot on its feet.

"I am your mother," said the woman.

"I am your father," said the man, "we were rescued from death by the false faces."

"And I am your daughter," said a voice as the boy uncapped his arrow, "and my brother has saved me!"

58. NIA"GWAHE THE MAMMOTH BEAR.[1]

In the olden times in the valley of the Dociowĕh lived a newly married couple. Their lodge was far back by the big rocks and when danger threatened they hid in the caves. After a time there came to the young wife two baby boys. When the twins were five weeks old the mother died. The father was at first dumb with grief for his heart was very heavy. Then looking up toward the heavens he sang, "I see a hemlock tree. It has but two branches. The tree is twisted in the hurricane and is broken midway. The two remaining branches on the stub are thrashing in the gale. The tree is I. My wife is broken from me and my children are in the storm! Let me burn tobacco, the wind will cease; let me burn tobacco and my sorrow heals. It gives me thought!"

The dead mother had not lain long on her bed of spruce boughs when the hungry babes began to cry. A sudden thought came to the father. He cut down two strings of deer meat and flung them into the mortar. Grasping the pestle he pounded the meat into a powder and soaking it in hot water fed the liquid to his children. For several months they were nourished with this and they grew lusty and fat. When the corn was ripe, "in the milk," the father scraped the kernels from the cob and pounded them in his mortar, mixed the paste with water, skimmed off the gruel and cooked with venison broth, and thus made a new food upon which the children thrived. When they were a year old they ate the same food that their father did and grew tall and strong.

The years went by and they grew vigorous and lithe and became expert runners often keeping pace with the swiftest of the tribe. At the age of fifteen one of them ran a race with a deer and falling exhausted died. And the

---

1 Related by George D. Jimerson (Tahadondeh), June, 1903, at the Silverheels' homestead, Cattaraugus Reservation.

father sorrowed again and became melancholy. After the death of his brother the other seemed to double in strength of body and mind. His name was Hahyennoweh meaning the Swift Runner. In this son the father took great pride for it was his sole remaining "branch." Thus he instructed him in every art known to the hunter and warrior.

Hahyennoweh was a skilled bowman but as he developed greater speed in running he came to believe the bow and arrow coward's weapons.

"A fight to death and face to face is the only fitting way," he said.

With this idea in his mind and a sharp flint in his belt, he broke his bows and snapped his arrows. Then when he wished to slay an animal he would pursue it and when it fell exhausted he would wait until it recovered its breath and strength, slit its throat and carry it home. Bear, deer, elk, moose and buffalo all fell victims of his speed.

Like every brave and skillful man he loved to boast of his power, and no one ever made a statement of their skill lest he exclaimed, "Ho, that is nothing! I am braver than that for I am the most skillful of all the tribe!"

The father began to worry about this fault of his son's, for it was a serious one. His entire conversation was self praise, which while excusable when indulged in occasionally, was unpardonable when continued forever. Wishing to warn him the father spoke to the boastful young warrior. "Son, I am your father, hear me!" he said. "You must not brag or boast yourself hereafter!"

But the son merely laughed and replied, "Father, I do not. I speak truth!"

"But, my son," the father entreated, "the animals will hear you,—will hear your boasting and out of revenge will slay you."

"No, I think not, father," he replied, "for no animal can outrun me, not a beast in all this forest."

"Son!" the father spoke gravely, "think wisely and hold

your tongue. The winds will steal your words for mischief
and the magically endowed animals will know it. Then, my
son,—then I shall lose you!"

"Father," replied the son, "I shall ever boast if speaking truth is boasting!"

The father continued his warnings but Hahyennoweh
only laughed and bounded back into the forest.

One evening Hahyennoweh came home after an exciting
race and began again to boast his prowess. Sadly the
father looked at him, and said sorrowfully, "Son, again I
bid you to cease your boasting. Evil will befall you for
I feel it." But the son was asleep.

A knock sounded at the door and the father pushed aside
the bear skin curtain saying, "Dahdjoh!" "Gahdjih!" said
a voice and the father went out. A stranger stepped from
a shadow.

"I have come," said he, "to tell you that the animals
have heard your son's voice. They have heard his auda-
cious voice and his unseemly boasting. They have felt his
knife and died. They have chosen me and I have come to
him. I have come to tell him he must race me. I am the
chosen one to race him from the sun-rise to the sun-set.
We race the way the sun goes. If I win, then I shall kill
him. If I lose then he shall slay me. Tell him he must
meet me at the windfall."

Awaking, the son heard the voices outside and when the
father pushed aside the curtain to re-enter he began to
question him. The father's brow was wrinkled, his cheek
had a gray color. He had sorrow in his voice.

He spoke "My son, you are all I have and you have
loudly boasted about running swiftly. Did you not hear
my advising words of caution? Did you not hear my
entreaties? Nia"gwahē has been here and spoken to me.
You have heard our talk together. You will be hurt by
him. Hahyennoweh! My only son I believe that you will
perish!"

Hahyennoweh smiled, and then laughed at his father saying, "Nia"gwahē is an old and foolish creature. So it is only he who makes this challenge! Chisnah! He should know that I am the champion of runners. Father, tell me more particularly about him, I would like to know how to feel afraid, but what you have said does not make me afraid."

Turning, the father answered, "Nia"gwahē is a mighty conjurer. He can change his form to suit him any time he wishes. He has never once been beaten in a race. Now you had better go to sleep and let me think about it and when I am done I shall awaken you." So the son drew his blanket over his head and went back to his dreaming.

Seizing the pestle, the father pounded parched corn and maple sugar together and moistening the meal molded it into a cake and put it into a rawhide bag. After awhile he awakened his son for he had been thinking as he had worked.

"Son, awake!" he said. "I have been thinking and now I will advise you. The small humming bird is the swiftest of all the feathers and Nia"gwahē has never had a race with him. In your cap I am going to put two feathers from the humming bird's breast; they are a race charm."

The father did not want to sleep that night but sat and threw pinches of oyankkwaoweh, the sacred tobacco, on a small fire to calm his fears and give him power with medicine spirits.

Before the sunrise the son awoke and going down the trail to the creek took his morning plunge and returned to eat his venison. Finishing his meal, he shook his father's hand and said, "Oneh, now I am going." His limbs felt strong and elastic for he had rubbed them well with plenty of oil. As he ran he thought he would like to test his jumping power,—just for luck,—and nearing the windfall, judged its breadth seven times his length. Increasing his speed he gave a great leap and cleared it. "Ho!" said he, "I am ready for any race in the world and ready for Nia"gwahē, the beast-conjurer. My legs move of their own accord and my feathers give me power. Now where is this old thing that gives me a challenge?"

Just as he spoke there was a loud snort, and looking up he saw the monster.

The sun was about to go under the rim of the sky, over Onondasdaht, the big hill. Hahyennoweh spoke, "Shall we race now? I am ready, it is sunrise!" But Nia"gwahē did not answer. He simply blew wind through his nose and started running.

The monster's path was toward a swamp and Hahyennoweh followed after. The great beast ran very fast through clumps of bushes, just as easily as the son ran over grass. Saplings, stumps and trees fell before the big animal. For about five miles the son labored through the muck and tangles, and then seeing that these obstacles were too much for his style of running, concluded that it would not be wise to follow much longer through the swamp-land. He, therefore, decided to return to the starting point and take his route over the high ridge that curved for miles around the big swamp. Toward noon, when he had circled it, and had run miles beyond, he saw Nia"gwahē far in the distance. Increasing his speed he soon reached the animal with the exclamation, "Ho-hoh, I am up to you!" But the mammoth bear only replied, "Ungh wooh!" The son saw that the Nia"gwahē was very tired and as he ran beside him he said, "Kway Nia"gwahē! Adekoni, it is time for eating!" But the beast with heavy breathing kept on running. Hahyennoweh, the Swift Runner, paused in the race, and sitting down on a stone, took a swallow of water and slowly chewed a handful of parched corn and sugar. He rested for a while after his meal and then after a swim in the brook, near by, he started on his race again.

When the sun was mid-way from the high heavens to its setting, the son caught up to the beast again. "Ho-hoh,

I am up to you, old opossum!" he said, but the huge animal was too tired even to grunt. A stream of water poured from his body leaving in his tracks a muddy streak and his big sides bulged within and without.

Again Hahyennoweh sat down and rested, for besides the giving of rest it made greater excitement. Taking up the race again the son ran over the path made by the monster. On and on he sped but Nia"gwahē was nowhere within range. The path that he had made was a line that ran beyond the eye's reach. He increased his speed but even then Nia"gwahē was not to be discovered. Then he began to get frightened and wondered if the monster called into play his magic powers. It seemed so for though Swift Runner ran his swiftest the beast seemed to run still swifter. But he did not despair but kept on his journey, hopeful that his charms would be strong. After a-while, far in the distance, was a small speck that grew larger as Hahyennoweh ran toward it. That made him run faster and after some time he overtook the magic monster. It was nearly dark when Hahyennoweh caught up to the beast and it was none too soon for the race was almost over. He was very tired but as courageous and boastful as ever, so Hahwennoweh said, "Ho hoh, I'm up to you again! You are no runner! Who said you could run, you have been flattered. You are an ugly old woman to be flattered. You run just like a lame old woman. You have forgotten how to run. No you never knew how to run at all. Just let me show you how to run. I'll never let you catch me as I have you. Oh you are very slow like a three-legged turtle. Now see me run!"

The young warrior ran ahead with very great speed over the plain until he saw the sun hang low and red over the hills. Then looking back, he saw a small speck. Two thoughts came into his mind. The first that he should go back and kill the beast, as the sun sank below the hills, and the second that perhaps the monster was shaming and would speed ahead should he retrace his steps. But in a moment he laughed at this second thought and was not afraid. Running back he saw that the Nia"gwahē had fallen, unable longer to stand the strain of the contest. His panting was so great that he blew up leaves and sticks high in the air and bent the saplings about him.

The sun disappeared and the evening star shone bright in the sky. It was twilight and Hahyennoweh stood looking at the fallen big meat before him. He grasped the small blow gun from his back and fixed a small sharpened arrow. He aimed for a dark spot on the left front foot of the animal. He shot and the heaving sides no longer took in wind. The beast died where he fell.

It was getting dark and the Swift Runner was tired by his race, so he lay down beneath a high tree and went to sleep.

THE RETURN.

When he awoke the next morning he found himself wondering what could be on the road through the swamp,— the route chosen by the Nia"gwahē. "Surely it must be some mischief," he thought, "or he would not have been so maddened when I ran on the ridge. I think the monster grew so slow was because he was mad. I must explore the swamp and find the evil."

The huge beast in his mad race had beaten a good path through the swamp, which the son proceeded to follow. After a journey of ten miles he made a discovery. The footprints of a hostile people, the marks of the enemy's moccasins, were fresh in the path. Hahyennoweh advanced with caution and as it grew dark he saw ahead of him two fires. Hidden in the underbrush were temporary shelters erected by a hostile war party. Home was but five miles distant and the son crept noiselessly past the encampment and sped toward his father's lodge. In the moonlight he saw a deer with very large legs. He looked still closer. The

deer had men's legs and wore leather leggings! The truth
flashed upon his mind. Two of the enemy were recon-
noitering and were planning an attack before the sunrise!

Entering the lodge he greeted his father and gave him
the beast's tusk, the big tooth that sticks out. The father
received it without a comment and continued his smoking.
Then very loudly the son exclaimed, "I've seen a deer. I
am going to out-run him. I am going now to race him!"
Then in a lower tone he added, "I will return soon, father,
and tell you of my adventure, but wait."

Grasping a stone axe he ran out in search of the strange
deer. At length he espied it back of the lodge, peering in
at his father. Creeping up with stealth the son struck the
strange animal a crushing blow between the shoulders, the
hatchet sank deep and the forequarters of the deer dropped
to the earth without a sound. Quickly snatching the skin
he wrapped it around the hind quarters and led them struggling into the lodge.

"Well father here is the deer of which I told you! Let
us skin him and see what is inside! Unwrapping the skin
he revealed the captive, who, nearly smothered, was too
feeble to further resist. Hahyennoweh flung him into a
corner and began to ply him with questions. "How many
of you are there in the swamp? Why came you to kill my
people? Where is your party hidden? What chief sent
you? Who is your leader? Are any other tribesmen with
you?" These and other questions he asked him. Bidding
the captive lead the way Hahyennoweh advanced toward
the enemy's camp and reached it about midnight. He lashed
the captive to a tree and stopped his mouth. The sleeping
warriors were not aware of danger and never moved as
they slept. Lifting high his hatchet Hahyennoweh struck
the sleepers. Forty-two times he struck and each time killed
an enemy and the captive bound against the tree saw it all.
"Ha"dĕgaiiwio'!" he exclaimed as the last sleeper was
struck and then turning to the terrified man bound to the

tree he said "Iīs newa, now you!" He lifted his tomahawk but paused as he was about to strike then lifting it
again let it fall with a blow the shook the tree. But it had
not touched the man, the blow was not aimed at him, but
instead it cut the thongs and set the captive free. "Now go
with all your speed and tell your tribe not to send war
parties against us again for we have strong medicine and
cannot be harmed." The captive thought so.

That night as the son sat at the fire in the lodge with
his father stretching the scalps on hoops he told the story
of his great race but not in a boastful way. His great deeds
had made it necessary for him to boast no longer, for if he
should men would laugh and say, "Hoh, you did better than
that once!" So never after did he boast but took a good
woman who had asked him to marry her.

In after years he told the story of the race again, that
the tribe might not forget it, but his grandchildren were un-
believing. "Show us the spot and the bones and then we
will glory in our grandfather," they said laughing. So, undaunted, the old man whose name was changed to Nia"gwa-
hēgowa, (Mighty Magical Bear), in recognition of his great
race, took his grandchildren on the journey and showed
them the place where the beast had fallen. They dug into
the soft soil and found the hugh bones and the jaw where
he had broken out the tusk.

The Indian story teller adds: "White man find bones
right where the Nia"gwahē fell long after, to this day. Put
them in big musees, so story real true I guess!"

59. THE BOY AND THE NIA″GWAHE.

The Five Nations had waged a war with the Snake People who lived in caves (the Cherokee). The Five Nations became exhausted. Both began to see that the cause was not worth such a loss of life, and so a treaty of peace was made. Each party promised to send warriors, women and families to settle with the other, and thus, by mutual adoptions and inter-marriage weave a bond of friendship.

The day arrived for the mutual emigrations, and patiently the Five Nations awaited the coming of their visitors, but none came, nor could news be obtained of their own party. A messenger was dispatched but he never returned. More were sent but, likewise, they never came back to report. At last the chiefs called a council to devise means to get to the land of their former enemies and learn how the party and the messengers had fared. A new messenger was chosen from the bravest of the warriors and a short distance behind a watcher followed. For two days all was well, but on the third the watcher looking ahead on the trail saw the messenger crawling laboriously along. Running toward him he found him wounded, stripped of all clothing and bleeding from tusk wounds and heavy bruises.

Nīa″gwahē!" whispered the man hoarsely, and fell dead.

The runner dashed down the trail crying, "Gowĕ′! Gowĕ′!"

A council was hastily called and the fate of the messenger discussed.

"Agē! So it is Nīa″gwahē who has been destroying our people and not our allies," said the chief. "Truly now, some one must be found who is able and willing to destroy the evil. A brave one must he be for he will battle with the most powerful of all beast magic. He who grasps this white wampum belt shall be the chosen man and he shall have the belt 'on his body'."

The chief circled the council, holding the belt before every man but no one moved or lifted a hand.

"What!" said the chief, "are real men cowards! Has no one a heart and mind and arm strong enough to take this belt!"

Standing in the doorway of the council house was a boy, awkward in figure and uneven of feature. His parents were dead and his home was with his grandparents. He was accounted of a lowly family and as of foolish mind. The chief wished to make a laugh to break the seriousness of the situation and so called out, "Why not try Tedo'!" The chief did not smile although the entire assembly laughed, but holding the beautiful belt out to the boy said, "Are you Oñgwĕhoweh?"

The boy grasped the belt and threw it over his shoulder.

"Do you know what you have done?" asked the chief solemnly.

The boy nodded his head and clasping the wampum ran from the council to his grandmother's lodge.

"Oh grandmother!" he cried, "I have taken the belt to kill the nīa"gwahē, he who blocks trail to our new 'friend'."

"What, you!" exclaimed the grandmother. "Why you are nothing but a ragged simpleton!"

"Well hurry then, and prepare my owĭs'hä," said the boy, "for I am to kill nīa"gwahē and need food for my journey."

The old woman pounded the parched corn and mixed it with maple sugar.

"Now be off," she said, "you and your dog!"

The boy started down the path talking to his dog. "I will not yield, I will demand yielding," he said. "I will not be pursued, I will pursue, I will not see failure, I will succeed."

For two days he journeyed down the trail that led to the allies' country. At dawn on the third day there was a wild trampling in the forest and from the thicket rushed the nī"gwahē. The dog rushed forward with a yelp but the great beast merely opened his jaws and drew in a breath and with it the dog flew down his throat.

Picking up a stump, the boy dashed forward, yelling, "I am after you, you cannot escape me!"

Now it happens that these words are the very ones used by a nīa"gwahē when it pursues its prey, and such a charm have these words, that, as the beast repeats them, animals and men become weak and fall down as victims of the creature's cunning. When this nīa"gwahē heard its own cry flung back in its face, it was surprised. Its own words were turned into its own ears. Then the great beast turned and fled.

"Ha, ha!" laughed the boy, "you cannot escape me!"

All day the nīa"gwahē fled from the boy who pursued it crying shriller and sharper, "I am after you, you cannot escape me!"

The sun began to set and the boy sat down on a log to eat his owĭs'hä with a little water, but when he opened his pouch he found his food a mass of wriggling maggots.

"Agē!" he exclaimed, "this does not discourage me," and leaping from his seat, he took up the chase again, following closely upon the heels of the nīa"gwahē. "Oho'!" he cried, "You are the one for whom I am looking! Very soon I will kill you."

The sun went under the hills and the black night came.

"Agē, I am tired now, nīa"gwahē, and must rest," he said, "but I will kill you as soon as I get time."

The beast trembled and ran on a short distance in the vain hope of escape but returning put his nose to the boy's ear.

"Kwē!" he whispered, "Are you asleep?"

"No, not yet," replied the boy with a yawn.

"Well then," continued the beast, "I wish to tell you that I know I am defeated, but oh spare me, I beg of you, spare me! Have mercy and do not kill and I will flee from the land of men and hide in the icy north, never more to disturb or devour men."

"Ho ho! this is your trick," laughed the boy, with a sneer. "No mercy for you, you deserve only death. Hold up your foot and show me the spot!"

"Oh no, no, no," begged the nīa"gwahē plaintively. "Let me live and as a pledge of my truthfulness I will give you my teeth."

The boy debated with himself and then asked, "What profit are teeth?"

"My teeth are my magic," answered the creature, "and my magic is his who holds my teeth."

"Well now," said the boy slowly, "if your teeth will bring fortune to men I will accept them, but if ever you visit again the haunts of men, remember that I am the mightiest of wizards!"

With many groans the beast shed his teeth, crying, "All my magic strength and power are his who holds these teeth."

The boy threw them in his pouch and bade the monster depart forever. The boy rested for some time and then ran with all speed to the land of the allies. He called a council and told his story.

"We thought your nation had destroyed our ·people whom we sent to you," said the chief of the allies at the close of the boy's speech.

"We also thought the same of you," answered the boy.

The boy departed for his own village and held a great council, telling all he had seen, heard and done. The people were astonished beyond measure and cried, "Oh, tell us how you became powerful! What are your charm medicines?"

"This," said the boy, "I grasped the white belt, I went and would not be pursued, neither would I fear."

"But all thought you a fool," said the people.

"Perhaps I am," answered the boy, "if silence and observation mean I am only dull. But I only thought I would hold my mouth until my ears filled up."

Then all the people shouted and called him a great chief.

Thus were the nations saved, so was the trail established and so was the nīa"gwahē slain.

Now this is true and medicine men (Hotci'no'gä) have the teeth to this day and use them for magic.

TRADITIONS

EMILY TALLCHIEF.

An informant on traditions and a leader among the Christian Seneca. Mrs. Tallchief was the great grand-daughter of the famous Chief Cornplanter. She was a member of the Wolf Clan.

Photo by E. C. Winnegar.

X.

SENECA BELIEF IN WITCHCRAFT

It will be remembered that one of the first major tests of the authority of the State of New York over the Seneca Indians occurred in 1821 when Thomas Jemmy, a Buffalo Creek Indian, was indicted in a state court for the murder of a witch. Jemmy had been chosen executioner of the witch, after the order of tribal law, but his action aroused the attention of the neighboring whites who took court action against him.

Jemmy was defended by Red Jacket whose speech in defense of the accused man is a classic of Indian oratory. The trial resulted in the claim that state courts had no jurisdiction over the internal affairs of Indian tribes, and Jemmy was acquitted.

This incident serves to call attention to the very general belief of the Seneca Indians in witchcraft. Indeed not only did the Indians believe in it, but many of the neighboring whites. There are many white rural communities today where belief in witches is current, and one has only to visit the rural settlements about Reading, Pa., or read the accounts of investigations reported in the *Journal of American Folk·Lore*, to find how prevalent among the whites of today is the belief in witches.

Red Jacket was somewhat familiar with history. In his defense he said, "Go to Salem, and there find a record of hundreds persecuted and scores slain for the same crime that has brought down the arm of vengeance upon the (guilty) woman. . . . What crime has this man committed more than the rulers of your own people, in carrying out in a summary way the laws of his people and ·your people, and the laws of his God and your God. . . . ?"

This belief in witches and sorcerers has not been entirely

eradicated among the state Indians to this day. All the older Indians have witch stories to tell, and some of them have had personal experience with witchcraft. It is not considered good form to talk about witches, for if one reveals too much knowledge he is apt, himself, to be accused of the evil art. It matters not whether the Indian is a christian or non-christian as far as witchcraft is concerned. Both christians and followers of Handsome Lake express a belief in it.

It is customary for the Indians to call all manner of sorcerers, "witches." Both sexes are implied, and it is to be doubted that an Indian would recognize the term wizard, though for the sake of consistent English I have employed the term throughout this work. To the Seneca all "otgont" charm holders are witches and capable of witchcraft. An Indian will seldom mention anything about witches to white people for fear of ridicule, but they admit that some white people know much about the sinister art. The Tonawanda Indians, for example, know of a white doctor who is capable of diagnosing the symptoms of witch poisoning, and he has a great reputation for curing bewitched patients.

An understanding of the Seneca belief in witchcraft is essential for an understanding of Seneca folk-lore, and not only folk-lore but the psychology of the group.

Certainly, all through the folk-lore of the Seneca, one will find a steady belief in the ability of "powered" persons to transform themselves into any sort of creature desired, particularly the form of some chosen animal. One of the most common methods is to have a collection of animal pelts into which the person may enter and assume the character of the beast, but retaining human intelligence. Most frequently in modern times the witch is reputed to be able to become an owl, a dog or a big snake.

To guard against witches many Indians buy witch powder from witch doctors. By using this properly the witch is kept away from the person and his household.

In case of uncertainty the witch doctor goes into a trance and prescribes the proper remedy. Sometimes a person is bewitched by a spirit or by a charm that he has failed to pacify. The charm then causes bad dreams, wounds, broken bones and even death in the family unless satisfied by the proper ceremony.

60. CONTENTS OF A CHARM HOLDER'S BUNDLE.

Edward Cornplanter stated that a complete bundle of charms (godä'ĕsniyus'ta'kwa), should contain the following articles: (a) Scales of the great horned serpent or some of its blood; (b) round white stone given possessor by a pygmy; (c) claws of the death panther or fire beast; (d) feathers of dewat'yowais, or exploding bird; (e) castor of white beaver; (f) otnä'yont, or sharp bone; (g) gane'ont-wŭt, or corn bug; (h) small mummified hand; (i) hair of dagwanoeient, or flying head of the wind; (j) bones or bone powder of the Niä"gwahē or monster bear; (k) small flute or whistle from an eagles' wing bone; (l) anti-witch powder; (m) bag of sacred tobacco; (n) claws or teeth of various wild animals; (o) a small mortar and pestle; (p) a small war club; (q) a small bow and arrow; (r) miniature bowls and spoons of wood; (s) a small wooden doll; (t) clairvoyant eye-oil. These objects are called otcinä'ke^n"dä'.

Individuals also had other charms, as different kinds of stones or wooden tablets that they scraped into a powder as "medicine."

By consulting his bundle a charm holder could tell how to overcome a sorcerer's influence, or determine what spirit had been offended and needed propitiation.

Each bundle was "sung for" in an appropriate ceremony of the charm-holders' society.

61. CONTENTS OF A WITCH BUNDLE.[1]

In a witch bundle found in an abandoned house of an old witch, the following articles were found:

1 bundle containing miniature weapons and utensils.

1 bundle containing dolls made of some soft brown wood.

1 package of small sacks from animal hearts.

1 ball of fine cord or thread.

1 box of dried snake blood.

1 bottle of eye oil.

1 package of hair of different shades.

1 bundle containing packages of various powders.

1 box containing a collection of various greases.

1 package containing smaller parcels of nail parings.

1 package of many wrappings containing a smaller inner package, with wet blood, and containing a small sharp bone.

1 dried human finger.

Collection of snake skins.

The witch is also reputed to have had a black calf skin, and a big dog skin. She was capable of transforming herself and much of the time lived in a small round pond as the wife of a monster black-snake. When she finally died and was buried a witch light, gahai", was seen over the pond.

---

1 From notes supplied by Everett R. Burmaster.

62. OVERCOMING A WITCH.[1]

A strong man began to feel sick and could not tell what troubled him. He took all kinds of medicine and went to three doctors but he grew steadily worse. After a while he could work no more and went to the home of a friend for help. His friend told him to stay with him until he recovered.

He was given a room on the far side of the house and as it had only one window it could be easily darkened. He was very weak and could eat only one meal a day. This caused him to stay in bed most of the time. After a while his friend said: "I am going to go to Newtown after a witch doctor who has just come from Tonawanda." So he went after the witch doctor.

The witch doctor made a poultice and placed it on the sick man's abdomen. He covered the poultice with rags and moss. The poultice was very hot and appeared to be drawing something out of the patient. Pretty soon, the witch doctor yelled, "Now is the time," and grabbed the poultice and ran to the kitchen stove where he threw the contents of the poultice into the ash pan. Then he stirred into the poultice and pulled out a small sharp bone with a white hair wound around it.

Everybody examined the bone, and finally the witch doctor said, "It is my opinion that Widow — is bewitching you."

"Why, she calls here every day to see how he is," said the woman of the house.

The witch doctor told her to watch for the witch and notice what she did when she came next time. The sick man did not sleep that night but covered his face and began to talk to himself. He was now becoming a "witch" him-

---

1 Related by Fred Kennedy, 1903.

self. In his hand he held the witch bone with the hair around it.

The next morning an old woman left her cabin on a hill and started down into the valley and up another hill to visit the sick man. Suddenly he began to talk. "Here she comes," he said. "She is now leaving her house. Now she is down by the well. Now she is on the road. Now she is crossing the bridge. Now she is at the gate. Now she is walking up the path. Now she is by the apple tree. Now she is at the door." As he said this there was a rap-rap-rap outside and the housewife opened the door, and there stood the old woman.

The old woman looked worried. "I couldn't sleep last night," she said. "I worried too much about Bill, besides I think I have lost something." Then she went in to see the sick man. He had his head covered but yelled out, "You're the one; you leave me alone after this or I will kill you."

The old woman pretended she didn't know what he was talking about and soon went out.

That night the sick man talked to the bone. He wound one of his own hairs about it and then threw it at the wall, saying, "You go back to her and stick in her heart."

Everybody in the house heard the bone fly through the wall, for it went "ping!" Then the sick man went to sleep.

The next morning the old witch didn't come so the people went to her house and it was locked. Someone climbed in a window and found her dead in bed. They turned back the quilts and found the sharp bone driven into her heart. Nobody felt sorry but said, "It served her right; she had no business witching people."

63. THE SCORNED WITCH WOMAN.[1]

There was a beautiful young woman, the daughter of a witch. When the old witch died her husband wanted to burn up her bundles of witch poisons, because he was a Christian, but the beautiful daughter said, "Father, let us keep this bundle; you never can tell what might happen if we should destroy it." So she hid the bundle.

Now, there was a handsome young fellow living in the neighborhood and he came to the house once or twice to see her father. The young woman determined to get this young man so she made witch medicine and put it in his cider when he visited the house the next time. It was night and when the young man went out to go home she went out the back door and followed him. Pretty soon she coughed and he looked around. Then she called him and he asked her what she wanted. She asked him to sit down on a log by the road. They stayed there quite a while. After a while the girl said, "Why don't we two get married?" The young fellow replied, "What is the use?" Then he went home.

Now he had just secretly married another girl from Cold Spring and he went to her house. Pretty soon she said, "You have been somewhere. You have been visiting some other woman." She then scolded him.

He felt very bad for he loved his bride, but he felt that he could not help having made the mistake of calling on the man who was his friend. He never thought about the girl because he did not like her. He therefore made up his mind that he had been witched.

He felt very bad the next day and wanted some more cider, but the man who had it lived a long way past his friend's house. Nevertheless he tried to go past the house to the one further on, but all the while he felt something pulling him back. In a moment he yielded and returned to

---

1   Related by Laura M. Doctor, of the Tonawanda reservation.

the house, where the beautiful young woman let him in at the back door. He drank some cider, and called for more. This was the young woman's chance and she put in a double portion of love powder. His mind changed quickly and he began to sing love songs. After a while the girl said to her father, "We two are going to get married." The father didn't know what to say . He should have been glad, because the young fellow helped him draw wood in winter. But he had heard that his friend had another woman. He therefore said nothing, but looked worried.

After a while the young man went out again and as before the young woman followed him and they sat down on the same log as the previous night. It was dark and the girl kissed him and held onto him. After a while he said, "I am going home, I really don't love you. I am married to Fidelia."

At this the young girl became very angry and said, "You had better leave her and come to live with me. If you don't I will bewitch you and make you sorry."

"How can you witch me?" asked the young fellow.

"I never will tell you," said she, "but I will make you so sorry that you will wish you were dead."

The young fellow then left her and went home to his own wife. As before she scolded him roundly and accused him of unfaithfulness, but he said nothing. He was a good provider and worked hard.

In a few days the young fellow began to be sick. He had sharp pains all over his body. He kept at work, however, and though he was tempted to visit his friend and get cider he kept away. Day by day he grew weaker and at night it seemed as if some one were scraping his body. Each day he grew thinner until he could work no more.

After thinking over the matter he decided to call in a witch doctor. This he did and the doctor advised him to visit a certain swamp near the creek and watch from across the water what was happening. That night he went down the hill and crouched back of a dead tree, at the same time keeping a sharp eye on the swamp across the stream. It was moonlight and he could observe everything in detail, for the stream was not wide. Soon he saw something swinging in the wind near an elm tree. He looked more closely and saw that it was a large bark doll suspended by a long string. Soon the moon shone full upon it and as he looked he saw the beautiful young witch woman come through the grass. She paused beneath the tree and saluted the doll, calling it by the young fellow's name. She took out a knife and began to scrape it, to reduce its size, and as she did this the young fellow began to feel a sinking feeling as if he were shriveling up. The girl kept talking and laughing at the doll, saying, "You are tied up now. Well when the string rots you will fall and die. Meanwhile I will scrape you and eat your body." Then when she had said this, she took out some sharp thorns and stuck them in different parts of the doll, and the young man yelled right out it hurt him so. Thereupon the young woman laughed and said, "Aha, I can hear you groan way here."

After this the young fellow went home and was sick all night. The next day he resolved to do what the witch doctor had told him, but he was as yet too weak to perform the ceremony. As he lay thinking about his misfortune he heard a footfall outside and then a rap. His wife went to the door and there stood the young woman. "I have brought him some nice soup," she said. "I hear he is very sick."

She entered and went over to the young fellow. He hid his face and said, "Go away, I know what you are doing to me. You have poisoned me. I am sending for a crow today."

The girl laughed and said, "What are you sending for a crow for?"

"You will soon find out," he said.

That afternoon the witch doctor came and asked, "Well

has she been here? If she has I can go ahead with the plan; I have brought the crow."

So the young fellow took the crow and cut out its heart at the same time saying, "I bestow upon you the name of ———," the name of the young woman.

The witch doctor and he then went into the back shed and made a model of a kettle-hanging frame. They put it on the dirt floor of the shed and then put a long splinter through the heart. They lighted another splinter and passed it under the heart several times, scorching it.

The next day the young woman came to the house again. This time she was crying very hard. She came in and said, "Now look what you did to me." She opened her waist and showed her breast. It was burned and blistered.

The young fellow then said, "You let me alone and quit witching me or I will burn your heart right out of you. You made me do wrong. I've got a good woman."

Then the young woman said, "I'll quit; you are too strong for me." After that the young fellow got well.

After that the young woman never witched anybody, but was a good friend to the young fellow's wife and took care of her babies.

64.   CATCHING A WITCH BUNDLE.[1]

One night three men came to the house of a man named William and asked him to go with them to a place on the Four-mile Level. It seemed that a man by the name of Jesse ———— had been having very bad luck and had lost one child after another by some strange disease. William was reminded of this and asked by one of the men, a Tonawanda witch doctor, to assist in the hunt for the mysterious source of death. He consented and went along with the party.

Reaching the desired spot the witch doctor took a forked stick and held it by the long forked ends, one in either hand. He walked forward and when he pointed the stick in a certain direction the stick would glow. He kept following the glow until he reached an old stump way in the heart of the bush lot. The three men followed him silently. When he touched the stump the forked stick seemed on fire and bent down and touched the ground between two roots. "This is where we must dig," said the witch doctor.

One of the men carried a spade and dug as directed. Very soon he struck a stone, after which the witch doctor assumed charge of the digging. A lantern was lighted and as the earth was scraped away the investigators found a cubical slate box with a cover over it, made from thick slabs from the creek bottom. The witch doctor lifted the cover and looked in. "It is there," he whispered, placing some white powder on the top of the box.

The party now went back to Jesse's house and dug a hole at the corner of the woodshed. In this the witch doctor placed a five-gallon crock. Over this he placed a large piece of silk, weighted at the corners so that it stretched taut, like a drumhead over the mouth of the crock. He then made a little fire and cast medicine powder into it, at the same time talking and commanding the witch bundle to

———
1   Related by William Parker, Cattaragus reservation, 1904.

come from its slate box through the air into the crock. After a while there was a ball of fire flying through the air and it came down and went through the silk without burning it.

"Now we have it," said the witch doctor. "We can open it now." So they opened it and found a bundle of rags all saturated with fresh human blood. In the middle of the bundle they found a sharp bone called otnä'yont, and it was red with blood. It was the bone that had been drinking the blood of Jesse's children. The witch doctor then took the bone and took care of it. After that there was no more sickness and the last child got well. It seems that these sharp bones must be taken care of and if neglected they will eat the blood of children until some one finds the bundle and takes care of it.

65. WITCH WITH A DOG TRANSFORMATION.[1]

A sick woman with a wasting disease noticed that every night something would peek in her window. Her husband could find no evidence of this until one night after a snow storm he found the tracks of a large dog outside the window. Following the tracks to the road he saw that they became human footprints and were lost in the other tracks at the side of the road.

The next morning among the friends that called upon the sick woman was an old lady who lived near the creek in a small house. She was a widow and lived alone. This old lady asked about the sick woman in such a peculiar manner that the husband grew suspicious. After the old woman left the sick woman began to feel much worse.

That night she screamed, "She is looking at me!" And the husband going outside saw as before dog tracks running down to the road. He watched and soon some men came by and he asked them if they had seen a large dog. The men said they had; one had just ran down the road toward the creek. Morning came and the husband determined to investigate further. He crossed the road and walked down the other side until he came to the Esther ——— place. He noticed that a large dog had run along the fence and had leaped over it. On the other side there were human footprints going to the house.

Morning came and the old woman called again inquiring about the health of the sick woman. This time the husband said, "If you don't stop witching my wife I will fix you." The old lady asked him what he meant and said that she was not a witch.

The husband then resolved to watch in the wood-shed all night, if need be, and to catch the dog looking into the window. He got some blankets to keep himself warm and waited with his rifle. After a while he heard a sniffing sound and presently heard something walking around the house. Cautiously he looked out and saw the dog with its paws on the window-sill of his wife's room. Fire was coming out of the dog's eyes. The husband now ran out and chased the dog which ran down the road. There were many people on the road, for it was moonlight and it was sleighing time. They saw him chasing the dog. It ran to the fence and jumped over. As it poised in mid air over the fence the man fired his gun. There was a yelp and the people saw something shoot through the air and jump into the window of the cabin. The people watched this and looked over the fence but there was no mark or track on the snow, except some dog hair. Three days later the people went to the house and found the old woman dead on her bed with a bullet in her heart. There was dog hair on the window where she had dived through. It was sure then that she had been a witch. The sick woman recovered.

66. WITCH STEALS CHILDREN'S HEARTS.[1]

There was an old woman who always helped with children's funerals, and would sit up all night while the tired parents slept. She would lock the door and stay with the dead children. Everybody thought she was a nice old woman until one time a woman walking by her house saw a witch light fly out of her chimney and go into the graveyard. "Hoh," she said to herself, "I guess old lady E—— must be a witch."

Soon thereafter another child died and the old lady came as usual to help with the funeral. That night she sat up with the corpse but this time the woman who had suspected the old lady told her husband Gus to watch her through a window.

Gus found a place outside where he could see into the room. At midnight the old lady took a knife and cut the heart out of the child and then ran out of the house while everybody else slept. She went to her own house and shortly turned into a ball of fire and flew out of the chimney. The light went to an old cemetery where there were many sunken graves. Gus followed, though he was frightened. He saw the old woman put something into a hole in a grave hollow and say, "There, I have got you another. Now you are my friend and will have to show me where I can get money."

Soon the light soared overhead again and went back into the old lady's chimney.

The next morning Gus went to the father of the dead child and told him what he had heard and seen. The father was very mad but after examining the child could find no marks where the heart had been taken out. The old witch had healed the cut. So then they went to the cemetery and found the grave. Digging down where they saw the hole

1 Related by Aurelia Jones Miller, 1905.

they came to a corpse and it was all covered with blood and had a child's heart in its mouth, gnawing at it. The men poured kerosene from a lantern in the hole and set it afire. Then they went to the old lady's house and found bloody rags on the table, but she was not there having gone back to the house for the funeral. The father of the dead child then ran home and found the old lady there.

"You are an old witch," he stormed. "Now I know why you have been going to children's funerals. You must confess now or I will kill you." He grabbed her by the hair and swung her around. She burst out crying and said, "Yes, I now confess. I took children's hearts to give to my friend. This friend gives me luck and I would starve without her."

"You go home and quit this business," said the father.

The old lady went home and after the child was buried the family called in a witch doctor and they made a charm against the witch woman, and soon she died.

67. HOTCIWAHO. (HAMMER IN HIS BELT.)

This was near a river. There lived Hotciwaho an old man. His house was apart from all others and his grandson lived with him. Now this Hotciwaho wore women's clothes and beneath his skirt he wore a hammer (mallet), and he would hide by the springs back of the rocks and kill children when they came for water. He would strike them on their heads when they stooped over to dip. Their bodies would be found at the spring by the people who after a time found so many that they thought some subtle poison must haunt the places where they drew their water. Now this Hotciwaho would always go to the house where they were mourning over the death of the child and he would weep. Now the people never saw the tears fall from his eyes but they were always wet when he moaned over the child and said, 'Hagiä"!' He did not truly cry but before entering wiped his saliva over his cheeks and eyes so as to appear grieving. This was his trick.

Now why did he kill people? He was lazy and loved good food. Now at funerals the bereaved always provided a feast and afterwards the death feast and the mourners could take away a portion of the soup, bread and cakes. This is why he killed children. He wanted the food.

Now such a man when he does a wrong many times thinks it no offence. The grandson thought this all wrong and being afraid that he too would be killed stole his grandfather's hammer and struck him a blow on the head and killed him. So he died in the same way.

68. HOW AMERICA WAS DISCOVERED.

HANDSOME LAKE'S STORY.

According to Chief Cornplanter, Handsome Lake taught that America was discovered in the manner here related.

A great queen had among her servants a young minister. Upon a certain occasion she requested him to dust some books that she had hidden in an old chest. Now when the young man reached the bottom of the chest he found a wonderful book which he opened and read. It told that the white men had killed the son of the Creator and it said, moreover, that he had promised to return in three days and then again forty but that he never did. All his followers then began to despair but some said, "He surely will come again some time." When the young preacher read this book he was worried because he had discovered that he had been deceived and that his Lord was not on earth and had not returned when he promised. So he went to some of the chief preachers and asked them about the matter and they answered that he had better seek the Lord himself and find if he were not on the earth now. So he prepared to find the Lord and the next day when he looked out into the river he saw a beautiful island and marveled that he had never noticed it before. As he continued to look he saw a castle built of gold in the midst of the island and he marveled that he had not seen the castle before. Then he thought that so beautiful a palace on so beautiful an isle must surely be the abode of the son of the Creator. Immediately he went to the wise men and told them what he had seen and they wondered greatly and answered that it must indeed be the house of the Lord. So together they went to the river and when they came to it they found that it was spanned by a bridge of gold. Then one of the preachers fell down and prayed a long time and arising to cross the bridge turned back because he was afraid to meet his Lord. Then the other crossed the bridge and knelt down upon the grass and prayed but he became afraid to go near the house. So the young man went boldly over to attend to the business at hand and walking up to the door knocked. A handsome man welcomed him into a room and bade him be of ease. "I wanted you," he said. "You are bright young man; those old fools will not suit me for they would be afraid to listen to me. Listen to me, young man, and you will be rich. Across the ocean there is a great country of which you have never heard. The people there are virtuous, they have no evil habits or appetites but are honest and single-minded. A great reward is yours if you enter into my plans and carry them out. Here are five things. Carry them over to the people across the ocean and never shall you want for wealth, position or power. Take these cards, this money, this fiddle, this whiskey and this blood corruption and give them all to the people across the water. The cards will make them gamble away their goods and idle away their time, the money will make them dishonest and covetous, the fiddle will make them dance with women and their lower natures will command them, the whiskey will excite their minds to evil doing and turn their minds, and the blood corruption will eat their strength and rot their bones."

The young man thought this a good bargain and promised to do as the man had commanded him. He left the palace and when he had stepped over the bridge it was gone, likewise the golden palace and also the island. Now he wondered if he had seen the Lord but he did not tell the great ministers of his bargain because they might try to forstall him. So he looked about and at length found Columbus to whom he told the whole story. So Columbus fitted out some boats and sailed out into the ocean to find the land on the other side. When he had sailed for many days on the water the sailors said that unless Columbus turned about and went home they would behead him but

he asked for another day and on that day land was seen
and that land was America. Then they turned around and
going back reported what they had discovered. Soon a great
flock of ships came over the ocean and white men came
swarming into the country bringing with them cards,
money, fiddles, whiskey and blood corruption.

Now the man who had appeared in the gold palace was
the devil and when afterward he saw what his words had
done he said that he had made a great mistake and even
he lamented that his evil had been so enormous.

69. ORIGIN OF THE CHARM HOLDERS' MEDICINE SOCIETY.[1]

There was in old times a young chief who was a hunter of great cunning, but though he killed many animals he never took advantage of their positions. He never shot a swimming deer or a doe with a fawn, he never killed an animal fatigued by a long run nor took one unawares. Before the hunt he always threw tobacco and made a ceremony to ask permission to kill game. Nor was he ever ungrateful to the animals of the woods who had been his friends for so many years. The flesh that was useless he left for the wolves and birds, calling to them as he left it: "Come, my friends, I have made a feast for you." Likewise when he took honey from a tree he left a portion for the bears and when he had his corn harvested he left open ears in the field for the crows, that they might not steal the corn sprouts at the next planting. He fed the fish and water animals with entrails and offal. No ruthless hunter was he but thoughtful. He threw tobacco for the animals in the woods and water and made incense for them with the oyeñkwaoñ'we', the sacred tobacco, and "threw it" even for the trees. He was a well loved chief for he remembered his friends and gave them meat. All the animals were his friends and all his people were loyal to him. All this was because he was good and he was known as the "protector of the birds and beasts." So he was called. It is supposed that his own name was His-hand-is-red.

The southwest country is a land of mysteries. There are many unknown things in the mountains there and also in the waters. The wildest people have always lived there and some were very wise and made different things. When, many years ago, the Oñgwe' hoñwe', (Iroquois) began to make excursions to this distant country they encountered

---

1 Related by Chief E. Cornplanter.

THE RESTORATION OF RED HAND.

In this drawing the animals whom Red Hand had befriended are shown anxiously awaiting his revivification by use of the sacrificial medicine made from the "life sparks" of their companions. The Bear is shown raising him to his feet.

many nations that were friendly and more that were hostile. The Iroquois used to like to go in this country for there they learned new things and found new plants and new kinds of corn and beans and when they would fight and destroy a tribe they would carry away curiously-made things and some captives back to their own country.

While one of these exploring parties was in the far southwest looking for war and new things, a band of very savage people attacked them. The young chief, the friend of the animals, was with the party, and, being separated from the rest of his party, was struck down by a tomahawk blow. The enemy cut a circle around his scalplock and tore it off. He could not fight strong because he was tired and very hungry from the long journey, so he was killed. The enemy knew him because he had been a brave fighter and killed a good many of their people in former battles so they were glad when they killed him and prized his scalp. Now he lay dead in a thicket and none of his warriors knew where he was but the enemy showed them his scalp. So they knew that he was dead but they did not kill all the Iroquois.

Black night came and alone upon the red and yellow leaves the chief lay dead and his blood was clotted upon the leaves where it had spilled. The night birds scented the blood and hovered over the body, the owl and the whippoorwill flew above it and O'sh'ä'dä'geä', the Dew Eagle, swooped down from the regions over the clouds. "He seems to be a friend," they said, "who can this man be?" A wolf sniffed the air and thought he smelled food. Skulking through the trees he came upon the body, dead and scalped. His nose was upon the clotted blood and he liked blood. Then he looked into the face of the dead man and leapt back with a long yelping howl,—the dead man was the friend of the wolves and the animals and birds. His howl was a signal call and brought all the animals of the big woods and the birds dropped down around him. All the medicine animals came,—the bear, the deer, the fox, the beaver, the otter, the turtle and the big horned deer (moose). Now the birds around him were the owl, the whippoorwill, the crow, the buzzard, the swift hawk, the eagle, the snipe, the white heron and also the great chief of all birds, Oshadahgeah, who is the eagle who flies in the world of our Creator above the clouds. These are all the great medicine people and they came in council about their killed friend. Then they said, "He must not be lost to us. We must restore him to life again." Then a bird said, "He is our friend, he always fed us. We cannot allow our friend to die. We must restore him." Then the Wolf came up to the body and said, "Here is our friend, he always gave us food in time of famine. We called him our father, now we are orphans. It is our duty to give him life again. Let each one of us look in our medicine packets and take out the most potent ingredient. Then let us compound a medicine and give it." Then the Owl said, "A living man must have a scalp."

So the animals made a wonderful medicine and in its preparation some gave their own lives and mixed them with the medicine roots. Now when the medicine was made all of it was contained in the bowl of an acorn. So they poured it down the throat of the man and the Bear feeling over the body found a warm spot over his heart. Then the Bear hugged him close in his hairy arms and kept him warm. The Crow had flown away for the scalp but could not find it, then the White Heron went but while flying over a bean field thought herself hungry and stopped to eat and when filled was too heavy to rise again. Then the Pigeon Hawk, the swiftest of the birds, said that he would go and surely find it. By this time the enemy had become aware that the animals were holding a council over their friend whom they had slain and so they carefully guarded the scalp which they stretched upon a hoop and swung on a thong over the smoke hole of a lodge. The Pigeon Hawk, impatient at delay shot upward into the air and flying in wide circles discovered the scalp dangling over the fire drying in the hot smoke. Hovering over the lodge for a moment he dropped down and snatching the scalp shot back upwards into the clouds, faster and further than the arrows that pursued him swift from the strong bows of the angered enemy. Back he flew, his speed undiminished by his long flight, and placed the scalp in the midst of the council. It was smoky and dried and would not fit the head of the man. Then Big Crow (buzzard) emptied his stomach on it to clean it of smoke and make it stick fast and O'sh'ä'dä'geä' plucked a feather from his wing and dipped it in the pool of dew that rests in the hollow on his back and sprinkled the water upon it. The dew came down in round drops and refreshed the dry scalp as it does a withered leaf. The man had begun faintly to breathe when the animals placed the scalp back in his head and they saw that truly he would revive. Then the man felt a warm liquid trickling down his throat and with his eyes yet shut he began to talk the language of the birds and animals. And they sang a wonderful song and he listened and remembered every word of the song. This song the animals told him was the charm song of the medicine animals and they told him that when he wished the favor of the great medicine people and when he felt grateful, to make a ceremony and sing the song. So also they told him that they had a dance and a dance song and they told him that they would teach him the dance. So they danced and some shook rattles made of the squashes (gourds) and though his eyes were closed he saw the dance and he knew all the tunes. Then the animals told him to form a company of his friends and upon certain occasions to sing and dance the ceremony, Hadī"dōs, for it was a great power and called all the medicine animals together and when the people were sick they would devise a medicine for them. Now they said that he must not fail to perform the ceremony and throw tobacco for them. Now the name of the society was Hadi"dos. Then the chief asked the medicine people what the ingredients of the medicine were and they promised to tell him. At a time the animals should choose they would notify him by the medicine song. Now he could not receive the secret because he had been married. Only hoyahdiwadoh (virgin men) may receive the first knowledge of mysteries. Now the chief greatly wished for the medicine for he thought it would be a great charm and a cure for the wounds received in war. After a time the chief was lifted to his feet by the hand of the bear and then he recovered his full life and when he opened his eyes he found himself alone in the midst of a circle of tracks. He made his way back to his people and related his adventure. He gathered his warriors together and in a secret place sang the medicine song of the animals, the Hadi"dos. So they sang the song and each had a song and they danced.

After some time the chiefs decided to send another war party against the enemy in the southwest to punish the hostile people who were attacking them. Then the friend of the birds and animals said, "It is well that we destroy them for they are not a reasonable people," and so he went with his party.

Now after a certain number of days the party stopped in an opening in the forest to replenish their stock of food. Now the place where they stopped was grassy and a good place for camp. Now a short distance away, a half day's journey, was a deer lick and near it a clear spring and a brook that ran from it and to this place all the animals came to drink. The party wanted fresh meat and so dispatched two young men, hoyahdiwadoh, to the lick for game. As they approached it they heard the sound of a distant song and drawing near to the lick they sat down on the bank over the spring and listened to the song. It was a most wonderful song and floated through the air to them. At a distance away the animals came and drank but so entranced were they by the music that they killed none. Through the entire night they sat listening to the song, and listening they learned sections of the song. In the morning they returned to the camp and reported what they had heard to their chief. Then said the chief, "That song is for the good of the medicine. You must find the source of the song and discover the medicine that will make us powerful in war and cure all our ills. You must purge yourselves and go again on the morrow." So the young men did as directed and went again to the spring and threw tobacco upon its surface. As night came on they listened and again heard the great song and it was lounder and more distinct than before. Then they heard a voice singing from the air and telling them the story of their lives and they marveled greatly. The song grew louder and as they listened they discovered that it emanated from the summit of a mountain. So they returned in the morning and reported to their chief and sang to him parts of the song. Then he said, "You must cleanse yourselves again and this time do not return until you have the medicine, the song and the magic." So the young men cleansed themselves again and went to the spring and as the thick night came on they heard the singing voices clear and loud, ringing from the mountain top. Then said one of the young men, "Let us follow the sound to its source," and they started in the darkness. After a time they stumbled upon a windfall, a place where the trees had been blown down in a tangled mass. It was a difficult place to pass in the darkness for they were often entrapped in the branches but they persevered and it seemed that some one were leading them. Beings seemed to be all about them yet they could not see them for it was dark. After they had extricated themselves from the windfall they went into a morass where their footsteps were guided by the unseen medicine animals. Now the journey was a very tedious one and they could see nothing. They approached a gulf and one said, "Let us go up and down the gulf and try to cross it," and they did and crossed one gulf. Soon they came to another where they heard the roaring of a cataract and the rushing of waters. It was a terrifying place and one of the young men was almost afraid. They descended the slope and came to a swift river and its waters were very cold but they plunged in and would have been lost if someone unseen had not guided them. So they crossed over and on the other side was a steep mountain which they must ascend but could not because it was too steep. Then one of the young men said, "Let us wait here awhile and rest ourselves for we may need our strength for greater dangers." So he said. But the other said, "I am rested, we must go onward somehow." When he had so spoken a light came flying over and sang for them to follow it. So they followed the winged light and ascended the mountain and they were helped. The winged light kept singing, "Follow me, follow me, follow me!" And they were safe when they followed and were not afraid. Now the singing, flying beacon was the whippoorwill. He led them. After a time the light disappeared but they struggled up the mountain side unaided by its guidance. The way became very stony and it seemed that no one were helping them now and then they wished that their unseen friends would help them, so they made a prayer and threw sacred tobacco on the path. Then the light came again and it was brighter, it glowed like the morning and the way was lighted up. The singing continued all this while and they were nearing its source and they reached the top of the mountain. They looked about for they heard the song near at hand but there was no one there. Then looked about and saw nothing but a great stalk of corn springing from a flat rock. Its four roots stretched in the four directions, north, east, south and west. The roots lay that way. They listened and discovered that the music emanated from the cornstalk. It was wonderful. The corn was a mystically magic plant and life was within it. Then the winged light sang for them to cut the root and take a piece for medicine. So they made a tobacco offering and cut the root. As they did red blood like human blood flowed out from the cut and then the wound immediately healed. Then did the unseen speaker say, "This root is a great medicine, and now we will reveal the secret of the medicine. So the voices told them the composition of the medicine that had healed the chief and instructed them how to use it. They taught the young men the Gano'ta', the medicine song, that would make the medicine strong and preserve it. They said that unless the song were sung the medicine would become weak and the animals would become angry because of the neglect of the ceremonies that honored their medicine. Therefore, the holders of the medicine must sing the all-night song for it. And they told them all the laws of the medicine and the singing light guided them back to the spring and it was morning then. The young men returned to their chief and told him the full story of their experiences and he was glad for he said, "The medicine will heal all wounds."

It was true, the medicine healed the cuts and wounds made by arrows and knives and not one of the Iroquois was killed in their battle with the enemy. When they returned home the chief organized the lodges of the medicine and the medicine people of the Hadi"dos and the Niga'ni'gă'a' were called the Hono^n"tci'no^n"gä. The medicine was called the niga'nigă'a', (little dose) because its dose was so small. So started the Hono^n"tci'no^n"gä.

70. ORIGIN OF THE FALSE FACE COMPANY

THE STONE GIANTS.[1]

There were different things in the olden days, strange happenings, strange animals and birds, and strange people. It seems that they do not live any more, so men only half believe the tales of them now.

The stone giants are a kind of men-being that are now gone. What we have heard about them I will tell.

There was once a far north country where a race of giants dwelt. They were very tall and bony. It was cold in that north country and the giants lived on fish and raw flesh. When the summer came to that region there was dry sand upon the ground and the giants, it is supposed, taught their children to rub it on their bodies every day until the blood came out where the skin was worn through. After awhile the skin became hard and calloused, like a woman's hand when the harvest is over. Each year the young rubbed their bodies with the sand, until when they had grown to be men, it was hard like rawhide and the sand stuck in and made them look like men of stone. This is what some wise men thought, but others said stone giants were born that way.

As time went on these giants grew more ferocious and warlike. They became tired of the flesh of beasts and fish and yearned for the flesh of men. Then they sallied forth to the lands south of them and captured Indians and devoured their flesh, tearing it from their living bodies. All the nations and tribes of Indians feared them, for no arrow would pierce their hard stony coats. Thus, secure in their armors of callous and sand, no season was too cold for them, no journey too long and no tribe strong enough to overwhelm them. They became more and more boastful

---

1 Related by Aurelia Jones Miller, Seneca, 1905.

and arrogant until they even laughed at the warnings of the Great Ruler, the Good Minded, and hallooed up to the skies mocking words. "We are as great as the Great Ruler," they said. "We have created ourselves!"

When the Confederacy of the five brother nations was young, these terrible stone giants crossed the river of rapids and swept down upon the scattered settlements of the Five Nations. By day they hid in caves and at night they came forth in the darkness and captured men, women and children, rending their bodies apart and chewing up their flesh and bones. When they pointed their fingers at men they fell down dead.

The medicine men cried to the Good Minded Spirit until it seemed that prayer was only like hollow talking in one's throat. The giants kept on with their raids and feasted undisturbed. No dark place was secure from their eyes, they penetrated the deepest shadows and found the hiding places of those who fled from them. Villages were destroyed and abandoned, councils were not held, for sachems and chieftains were the victims for the flesh-of-men feasts of the giants. The boldest warriors shot their strongest arrows from their strongest bows upon these invaders, but though the arrow shafts were strong and tipped with the toughest of flint, when they struck the stone-coated giants, the arrows broke and the flints snapped and the giants gathered up the warriors and shredded their meat from their bones with their sharp teeth.

At last the Good Ruler saw that men would become exterminated unless he intervened. Thus, he commanded the Holder of the Heavens to descend from the sky and use his strategy to destroy the entire race of stone giants. Accordingly, the Holder of the Heavens dropped from the place above the clouds, and hiding in a deep forest, took the form of a stone giant and went among the band. Awed by his display of power, his wonderful feats and his marvelous strength they proclaimed the new comer the great chief of all the stone giants. In honor of his installation the Holder of the Heavens swung his huge war club high over his head and roared ferociously, "Now is the time to destroy these puny men, and have a great feast such as never before!" Leading forth the mighty tribe he planned to attack the stronghold of the Onondagas. Arriving at the foot of the great hill on whose summit was the stockade where the Onondagas had assembled, he bade the giants hide in the caves in the hills or make burrows and there hide. They were to await the dawn when they would commence the assault. Having instructed them the Holder of the Heavens went up the fort hill on a pretense and then gave the whole earth a mighty shake. So mighty was the shaking that the rocks broke from their beds and fell in masses over one another and the earth slid down making new hills and valleys. The caves all collapsed and the crouching stone giants were crushed to bits. You could see bones once in caves among the Onondagas. All but one was killed and he, with a terrible yell, rushed forth and fled with the speed of a being impelled by the Evil Minded to the Allegheny mountains, where, finding a cave, he hid so long in the darkness that he became the Genonsgwa, a new creature to terrify men-being.

THE GENONSGWA.[1]

The Genonsgwa was a monster terrible for his anger and fierceness. But one spot on his entire being was vulnerable and that was a certain spot on the bottom of his foot. The Holder of the Heavens did not pursue this solitary fugitive, but rested content in the fact that the race of stone giants was destroyed and that this one survivor would not be particularly harmful when his fury subsided and his terror gave way.

For many years the Genonsgwa lived in the mountains,

---

[1] This portion of the legend was related by George D. Jimerson.

or, sallying forth on long journeys, made new abodes where for a time he dwelt. Sometimes in fits of rage he would rush from his cavern in the rocks and hurl stones into the rivers until he had made a waterfall, the booming of whose waters made noises like the voices of the Hi"nos, and then in his madness, he would call up to the father of thunders, and he, looking down, would become enraged at the insolent Genonsgwa and fling his fires down upon his cave retreats in the mountains. Then when the earth shook with the rumbling of thunders, reminding Genonsgwa of the awful day when the Holder of the Heavens shook down the rocks, he would crawl far back into the rocks and the listener miles away might hear his voice as he moaned and pleaded and quarreled with the powers that threatened his life.

As the years went by, Genonsgwa became more human and his spirit was quelled, but yet those who sought him found no mercy for he was the last of the stone giants. No one could see him, so terrible was his visage and so strong was his magic.

Now at this time a hunter lost his direction in a strange forest and though he traveled far and sought with vision keen the trail that should lead him out, he failed. A terrific hail storm broke from the heavens and snapped the branches and ripped off the leaves of the trees and beat down the underbrush and the hunter was bruised and dazed by the tumult of the storm. All day he wandered, wading blindly through marshes or stumbling through windfalls, wounded and bleeding. The hail like sharp flints still rained from the skies and the thunders still rumbled their threats and the hunter feared the anger of the heavens. A great rock like a deep shadow loomed up dark against the trees and the hunter hurried to it and found a great cavern for a shelter. When the leaves had been carried into a corner by the wind he made himself a bed and slept.

The rock shook and the hunter awoke and thought the great turtle moving from his moorings. A rhythmic roaring filled his mind with fear. A voice cried out, "You are in my lodge without permission! Who was it that bid you enter! Do you not know that I kill everybody!"

The voice was terrifying and hurt the hunter's ears like thunder when it is very close. Then again it spoke. "Oh warrior, see by my eye-light the bones of people who have sought me to kill me,—they are a yellow powder! Listen! I know you came without intent of evil and therefore you shall not suffer. I am the last of the kind of men that were here before men came here, so harken, for I have seen the earth in its making. When the turtle's back was small I lived here. My brothers are all departed but their spirits still are living. They are in the forest's depths and live within the trees. Only you must dream and you shall see their faces. Some are monsters, some are human, some are like the beasts,—but dream and see them. Then go forth and carve their faces on the basswood that speaks when you approach. It is my voice speaking. Be wise and learn my secrets, how disease is healed, how man and beast and plant have the same great kind of life, how man and beast and plant may talk together and learn each other's mission. Go and live with the trees and birds and beasts and fish and learn to honor them as your own brothers. I will be with you always in your learning. Go now and carve the faces that you see in your dreaming and carry back the faces to your people, and you and those that see them shall organize a society to preserve my teaching. Moreover, that posterity may not forget me and these words I speak within the mother turtle's shell, I bid you collect many turtles and make rattles of their shells and when the company of faces shall shake them, let all who know my wisdom and remember you and your adventure and me and who I am."

For a long time the hunter meditated upon the wisdom of the giant within the cave and when the wisdom was imbedded in his mind he lay down and slept again and had visions of strange things. When he awoke he found himself lying at the foot of an enormous basswood tree that as he looked at it it transformed itself into a great face like one he had seen in his dreams.

THE FALSE FACE.

Unfolding from the trunk of the basswood, the great face stared out at the spellbound hunter and opening wide its wide protruding lips began to speak. He told of his wonderful eyesight, its blazing eyes could see behind the moon and stars. His power could summon the storms or push aside the clouds for the sunshine. He knew all the virtues of roots and herbs, he knew all the diseases and knew how to apply the remedies of herbs and roots. He was familiar with all the poisons and could send them through the air and cure the sick. He could breathe health or sickness. His power was mighty and could bring luck in battles. Evil and poison and death fled when he looked, and good health and life came in its stead. He told of the basswood and said that its soft wood was filled with medicine and life. It contained the life of the wind and the life of the sunshine, and thus being good, was the wood for the false-faces that the hunter must carve.

Long the hunter listened to the words of the giant false-face and then he wandered far into the forest until the trees began to speak. Then he knew that there were trees there in which were the spirits of the beings of which he had dreamed and that the Genonsgwa was speaking. He knew that now his task of carving must begin and that the dream-beings, the voices, the birds and the animals that he saw must be represented in the basswood masks that he must make. And so he began, and for a score of years he continued his carving. He lived among the animals and trees and learned all that they could tell, becoming so attached to the things of life that men call beneath them, that he wished forever to stay and be as a brother to the animals and trees. But a day came when the giant's voice spoke from a basswood tree and bade him return to his kinsman. The hunter who had entered the forest young now was old. He was filled with knowledge and mysteries and was wiser than all men living. Gathering up the many faces that he had carved he made them into one big bundle and lifted it upon his broad shoulders and found the trail that led from the forest to the villages of his people. Of strange appearance and of gigantic proportions, he entered the council hall of his nation and calling a chosen few together told the story of his adventure and related the laws of the order of which he was the delegated founder.

THE FALSE FACE SOCIETY.[1]

The society, known as the False Face Company, was to be a most secret one and only for a qualified number. Its object was to benefit, protect and help all living things of earth. Its meetings were to be held only when the moon was away and when there was no light in the night. The hunter taught the chosen band a new dance and a new song and beat time with a large turtle shell as he sang. He explained the meanings of the masks and distributed them among the band, telling each person his special duty to the new society. He explained the relation of mankind to the rest of nature and enjoined all to use every influence to protect all living nature. In return for this kindness he promised that a great power should come upon them, the power of the spirits of the Genonsgwa, and how they should become great medicine men, whose power should be over the spirits of the elements. He unfolded and conducted the band through all the elaborate ceremonies that had been taught him in the forest by the animals and trees and spirits of the Genonsgwa. The Company was to have

---

1 Related by Edward Cornplanter.

no outward sign and members were to recognize one another only by having sat together in a ceremony.

So deeply was the assembled company impressed by the hunter's words that the new society at once became a strong and well united organization and other lodges spread rapidly through all the nations of the Iroquois and the False Face Company became one of the greatest factors for good that the people had ever known. They drove all the witches away and cured all the sickness of the people.

THE MASK-MAKING CEREMONY.

The masks are carved from living basswood trees and are thereby supposed to contain a portion of the life or spirit of the tree. In making these masks the Iroquois select the basswood not alone for its absorbent quality which is supposed to "draw out" disease, but for its remedial values as well. In solution a tea of its bark will cure a cold and relieve spasmodic affections. Its astringent sap is applied to relieve wounds and bruises, while the mask itself is supposed to be of signal importance in the relief of corruptive diseases.

In the ceremonies attending the making of a living mask, the tree is visited for three days. At the dawn of the first day the leaders of the False Face Society gather around the tree and smoke the sacred tobacco into the roots and throughout the branches to their topmost. As the smoke "lifts to the sunrise" songs of incantation are sung and the tree is asked to consent to share its heart with whomsoever the sacred gift is to be sent. At sunrise the ceremony is repeated and the next day continued in the same manner until the three days' propitiation chant is completed and then the axe is lifted to the tree. If at the first stroke of the axe the tree remain firm and unbending it has consented to lend its heart. An outline of the face is then drawn on the bark and cut into the tree to a depth of about six inches.

After thanking the tree this block is gouged out to be carved into the desired shape during a final song and dance that concluded the ceremony.

GENERAL NOTES.—This account of the stone giants or stone coats, Gĕⁿnoⁿ''sgwa', has been compiled from the accounts of several informants. There appears to be some confusion as to the origin of the stone coats as well as a disagreement as to the origin of the false faces. In one widely accepted account the Hadui false faces were the whirlwind spirits; in this account the last survivor of the stone giants is the founder of the False Face Company. In 1903 I was given a wooden mask covered with sand and pebbles and having a large flint arrowhead in the center of the forehead. The Cattaraugus Seneca woman who gave it to me stated that it was a secret mask and represented the stone giant. There appears, therefore, to be a ceremonial connection between the stone giants and the false faces.

71. THE ORIGIN OF THE LONG HOUSE.[1]

Chief Big Kittle relates the following story of the origin of the League of the Five Nations.

Where the Mohawk river empties into the Hudson in ancient times there was a Mohawk village. The people there were fierce and warlike and were continually sending out war parties against other settlements and returning would bring back long strings of scalps to number the lives they had destroyed. But sometimes they left their own scalps behind and never returned. They loved warfare better than all other things and were happy when their hands were slimy with blood. They boasted that they would eat up all other nations and so they continued to go against other tribes and fight with them.

Now among the Mohawks was a chief named Dekǎnǎwǐ'da, a very wise man, and he was very sad of heart because his people loved war too well. So he spoke in council and implored them to desist lest they perish altogether but the young warriors would not hear him and laughed at his words but he did not cease to warn them until at last dispairing of moving them by ordinary means he turned his face to the west and wept as he journeyed onward and away from his people. At length he reached a lake whose shores were fringed with bushes, and being tired he lay down to rest. Presently, as he lay meditating, he heard the soft spattering of water sliding from a skillful paddle and peering out from his hiding place he saw in the red light of sunset a man leaning over his canoe and dipping into the shallow water with a basket. When he raised it up it was full of shells, the shells of the periwinkles that live in shallow pools. The man pushed his canoe toward the shore and sat down on the beach where he kindled a

1 Related by Delos B. Kittle, Jan., 1905, at Newtown, Cattaraugus reservation.

fire. Then he began to string his shells and finishing a
string would touch the shells and talk. Then, as if satisfied, he would lay it down and make another until he had a
large number. Dekaniwida watched the strange proceeding
with wonder. The sun had long since set but Dekanawida
still watched the man with the shell strings sitting in the
flickering light of the fire that shadowed the bushes and
shimmered over the lake.

After some deliberation he called out, "Kwē, I am a
friend!" and stepping out upon the sand stood before the
man with the shells. "I am Dekanawida," he said, "and
come from the Mohawk."

"I am Haio'wĕnt'ha of the Onondaga," came the reply.

The Dekanawida inquired about the shell strings for he
was very curious to know their import and Haio'wĕnt'ha
answered, "They are the rules of life and laws of good
government. This all white string is a sign of truth, peace
and good will, this black string is a sign of hatred, of war
and of a bad heart, the string with the alternate beads, black
and white, is a sign that peace should exist between the
nations. This string with white on either end and black in
the middle is a sign that wars must end and peace declared."
And so Haiowentha lifted his strings and read the laws.

Then said Dekanawida, "You are my friend indeed, and
the friend of all nations.—Our people are weak from war-
ring and weak from being warred upon. We who speak one
tongue should combine against the Hadiondas instead of
helping them by killing one another but my people are
weary of my advising and would not hear me."

"I, too, am of the same mind," said Haiowentha, "but
Tatodaho slew all my brothers and drove me away. So I
came to the lakes and have made the laws that should govern men and nations. I believe that we should be as
brothers in a family instead of enemies."

"Then come with me," said Dekanawida, "and together

let us go back to my people and explain the rules and laws."

So when they had returned Dekanawida called a council of all the chiefs and warriors and the women and Haiowentha set forth the plan he had devised. The words had a marvelous effect. The people were astonished at the wisdom of the strange chief from the Onondaga and when he had finished his exposition the chiefs promised obedience to his laws. They delegated Dekanawida to go with him to the Oneida and council with them, then to go onward to Onondaga and win over the arrogant erratic Tatodaho, the tyrannical chief of the Onondaga. Thus it was that together they went to the Oneida country and won over their great chief and made the people promise to support the proposed league. Then the Oneida chief went with Haiowentha to the Cayugas and told them how by supporting the league they might preserve themselves against the fury of Tatodaho. So when the Cayuga had promised allegiance Dekanawida turned his face toward Onondaga and with his comrades went before Tatodaho. Now when Tatodaho learned how three nations had combined against him he became very angry and ran into the forest where he gnawed at his fingers and ate grass and leaves. His evil thoughts became serpents and sprouted from his skull and waving in a tangled mass hissed out venom. But Dekanawida did not fear him and once more asked him to give his consent to a league of peace and friendship but he was still wild until Haiowentha combed the snakes from his head and told him that he should be the head chief of the confederacy and govern it according to the laws that Haiowentha had made. Then he recovered from his madness and asked why the Seneca had not been visited for the Seneca outnumbered all the other nations and were fearless warriors. "If their jealousy is aroused," he said, "they will eat us."

Then the delegations visited the Seneca and the other

nations to the west but only the Seneca would consider the proposal. The other nations were exceedingly jealous.

Thus a peace pact was made and the Long House built and Dekanawida was the builder but Haiowentha was its designer.

Now moreover the first council of Haiowentha and Dekanawida was in a place now called Albany at the mouth of a small stream that empties into the Hudson.

The great council belt of the Five Nations. Each square represents a nation and the heart in the center represents the Onondaga.

72. DEAD TIMBER, A TRADITION OF ALBANY.[1]

There was a time of wars. The white men were angry
with the Indians and organized an expedition against them.
The Mohawk had done something and the white men were
going up the Hudson river to fight them.

Now an Indian family lived in Ganonoh (Manhattan
island), and the father said to the boy, "Take this *oshoe*
and run up to our people and do not stop until you warn
them that the white soldiers are coming." So the boy ran
and when he had found a canoe he crossed over the river
and ran again. Now when he thought that he was near the
Mohawk river he gave a cry "goweh! goweh! goweh!" and
at intervals he continued to cry, "goweh!"

After a time a Mohawk chief in the woods heard the
cry "goweh" and ran out to see who was coming and when
he saw the boy he said "follow me," and ran to the village
where he called a council. Here the boy told how a party
had been sent against them and how his father had sent
him to warn them just as the soldiers were leaving and
how for more than two days he had kept in advance of the
white men. The chiefs listened attentively and then ordered
everyone to hide what they could not carry for they would
burn the village before the soldiers arrived. So the chiefs
set fire to all the houses and took the people to a safe
retreat further up the river. Now when the women and
children were safe the warriors selected five of their swiftest runners and sent them back to discover where the
enemy was. Stealthily they made their way through the
underbrush and found the white men encamped near the
burned village. So the runners went back and the warriors
followed them. Some men were walking around the camp
but a few arrows prevented them from giving an alarm.
The white men were sleeping on beds of leaves wrapped

---

1 Related by Delos Big Kittle.

in blankets. Their arms were not at their sides but stacked up in piles like bean poles. The warriors surrounded the camp, gave the cry, *"baha a a a ah!"* and dashed upon the sleeping men and killed them all before they could reach their arms. So the Mohawk were not punished. They built a new village. Now the next spring the trees all died for a great distance around the place where the soldiers had been killed and there was a big dead woods there and to this day we call it *Dyohadai* (Dead Timber), but the white men call it Albany.

APPENDIX

XI

APPENDIX

A. ORIGIN OF THE WORLD.

RELATED BY ESQUIRE JOHNSON AND RECORDED BY MRS. LAURA M. WRIGHT.[1]

Many moons ago, there was a vast expanse of water, seemingly boundless in extent. Above it was the great blue arch of air, but no signs of anything solid or tangible. High above the lofty blue expanse of the clear sky was an unseen floating island, sufficiently firm to allow trees to grow upon it, and there men-beings were. There was one great Chief who gave the law to all the Ongweh or beings on the Island. In the center of the Island there grew a tree so tall that no one of the beings who lived there could see its top. On its branches, flowers and fruit hung all the year around, for there was no summer or winter there, or day or night.

The beings who lived on the Island used to come often to the tree and eat the fruit and smell the sweet perfume of its flowers. On one occasion the Chief desired that the tree might be pulled up. After some time one of the people volunteered to pull it up. He was very strong and after one or two efforts he succeeded in uprooting it. The Great Chief was called to look at the great pit which was to be seen where the tree had stood. As he and his wife stood looking down, he saw a little light very far down, down in the pit. As his wife stood looking intently, gazing at the pit by the side of her husband, he suddenly pushed her in. She fell down, down, until her husband lost sight of her entirely

---

1 From the original notes of Laura M. Wright, the missionary to the Seneca, 1835-1887. The manuscript bears the date 1876.

and forever. On the great expanse of water below there were sporting an innumerable number of water fowl, and in the water there were a variety of amphibious animals such as beaver, otter, muskrats, etc. One of the fowls looked up and saw the woman coming slowly down—and immediately gave the alarm. One wiser than the rest said: "What shall we do? She will be killed. We must get some *oehdah* (dirt) for her to stand on." They all looked anxiously about. The muskrat told them that he had seen *oehdah* far down below the bottom of the water and he could bring some up. The turtle offered his shell for a support and the muskrat commenced diving. After several ineffectual attempts he succeeded in bringing up a small lump of earth and put it on the turtle's back, which immediately commenced to increase in dimensions, and as it grew in size, the turtle spread out more and more to support the woman. The fowls began to fly upward to meet the woman who they perceived was much exhausted. They received her on their wings and landed her safely on the turtle's shell. The woman soon recovered and looked around her much surprised at her new companions. She soon began to wander over the Island as it seemed to her. At stated periods she went around it and soon noticed that it took her a longer time to make its circuit, so she concluded that it was growing larger all the time. As the time passed away the ogweh woman became quite reconciled to her new home and then she gave birth to a daughter to whom she devoted all her time, and forgot her old friends in the love she felt for her child. The daughter grew very fast and was very obedient to her mother. In time the mother gave up going around the Island at regular intervals and sent her daughter to perform the duty, who ran around the Island much interested and delighted with the task. Wonderful to relate, to the great surprise and sorrow of the woman the daughter gave birth to twin boys and immediately died. The mother was greatly distressed at the loss of her daughter and after mourning over her some time, she made a grave for her in the soft rich earth, of which the Island was composed, and buried her. She took the boys in her arms and told them they should not suffer for she would take care of them. The children grew rapidly to manhood, and were very strong and active. The woman used often to go to the grave of her daughter and watched it very carefully. At length she perceived something growing in two hills over the bosom of her daughter. After a while she commanded the eldest to repair to the grave. She said, "You must take charge of what you find there. See that nothing is lost." When he came to the grave he found the two hills his grandmother had seen. From one, corn was growing, and from the other beans, which he carefully picked and brought to his grandmother, who said to him, "Take good care of them that those of whom you may hereafter say, 'they are my descendents' may eat of it, for you are of the earth and must live from what grows out of the earth." He carefully preserved and planted the corn and beans, and at harvest there was a great increase and then he began to eat the fruit of his labor. As yet there was no other plant or grass on the Island. Having seen the great value of what he had planted, he was suddenly inspired with a desire to see other things grow and he spoke authoritatively and said, "Let grass grow and cover the surface of the Island." Immediately grass began to spring up looking green and fresh, and it made everything look beautiful. He then commanded the willow to grow and many kinds of plants and trees which bore fruit, and the appearance of the Island was much improved. Then his grandmother said to him with a very solemn and impressive manner: "*Now* you must go and seek your father until you find him, and when you see him you must ask him to give you Power." Pointing to the east, she said, "He lives in this direction. You must keep on until you reach the limits of the Island, and then upon the waters until you come to a high mountain, which rises out of the water which you must climb to the summit. There you will see a wonderful being sitting on the highest peak. You need not be afraid of him. He will not hurt you. You must obey him in everything. You must say to him, 'I am your son, I have come to ask you to give me Power.' He will say to you 'I never saw you before. I do not know you. But if you are my son, then take that stone and throw it up very high.'" The stone his father pointed at was a very large rock which covered a good deal of ground, but the son did not hesitate, he took it up as though it had been a pebble, and threw it up very high, and when it came down it broke into a great many pieces which rolled down the mountain. The wonderful being seemed much pleased and said, "I am now satisfied that you are my son, and I will give you the power you want." Suddenly a great roaring wind began to blow, and a very bright light followed so that he could see his father very plainly as he sat on top of the mountain. Then there was a loud noise and fire fell and great streams of water rushed by him. After a little there was a calm. Then his father said to him, "With *these* you will have power to perform *anything* you wish to undertake." He then gave him a bag which he charged him not to open till he got to his Island home. Receiving the bag he laid it upon his shoulders and turned toward home. At first the bag seemed quite light and easy to carry, but he noticed that it grew heavier as he carried it along, and as he drew near the Island, its weight seemed almost insupportable, and when he came within a bound of the shore, he came very near losing it. He took one step upon the land and down upon the earth the bag fell. He could not take a second step. The mouth of the bag opened as it fell and there came out birds of every kind and color. They flew into the woods and lighted on the branches of the trees and opened their throats and poured forth the richest and sweetest songs, and while the birds sung and flew from tree to tree the quadrupeds came out of the bag. They sprang upon the grass and into the woods. The deer and bear, the porcupine, rabbits and foxes each soon found their natural places,—all in perfect harmony, roamed over the Island together.

When the younger brother saw how successful his brother had been in producing useful and beautiful things, he was filled with jealousy and envy amounting to hatred, and began to devise plans to thwart him in his good work, by trying to spoil some things he had made and he thought he would kill him if he could find means to do it. So he commenced questioning his brother, "What do you think would most likely be fatal to your life?" He replied, "I think the leaves of the cattail flag might kill me if I should be pierced by them." So the younger brother got a bunch of the leaves, and thrust them at him hoping to pierce him, but the leaves only bent and did not hurt him at all.

Then he asked him again, "What do you fear most of all things?" He replied, "I am afraid of deer's horns, they are so sharp and hard." Then the younger brother went into the woods and found a cast-off horn with which he chased his brother into the woods trying to hit him with it. At last the older brother turned to the younger and said, "Now you must stop your bad work. See how you have spoiled the fruit of the crab-apple tree. Taste of its juice. You must not go on spoiling things in this way. If you do not stop, I shall punish you. I will shut you up in darkness beneath the ground with some of the animals who don't like light, as the mole and the hedgehog. These hands will not destroy you, but I will put you where you can not do mischief.

"Your dominions shall be in the darkness beneath the surface of the ground for I shall make light." Then turning and addressing the birds and quadrupeds he told them of his plan. Some of them objected but the great majority were greatly pleased.

So the tree of light was created and from it sprang

beautiful flowers. In its light, the older brother went forth and made the hills and valleys and into the valleys he poured out the water of his mouth and it formed the rivers and creeks, and the waters flowed into the deep valleys and made lakes. Then he created the stars and the moon and to the moon he gave the task of marking the months and the years. Then he made a new light and hung it on the neck of a being and he called the new light Gaa' gwaa' and instructed its bearer to run his course daily in the heavens over the earth. "You shall go each day and perform this duty so long as I will it," said the older brother. "I will notify you when I wish you to go no longer."

The moon and the stars shone in the heavens when the sun had finished his day's run and all things were perfected. He now dug up the tree of light and looking into the pool of water in which the stump had grown he saw the reflection of his own face and thereupon conceived the idea of creating Ongwe and made them, both a man and a woman. He blessed them and gave them dominion over all things and recapitulated all he had prepared for them and how he had created good things.

"I give you all that exists upon the face of the earth," he said, "all which the earth grows and maintains, the birds that fill the air and the fish in the water. You two are united aht tgea nigaa and from you future generations shall succeed."

B. THE WYANDOT CREATION MYTH (Extract).

Collected by C. M. Barbeau.

"The people lived beyond." They were Wyandots. Word was sent out that the chief's only daughter was very sick; and that all the doctors had in vain tried to cure her disease. A specially appointed messenger brought back a very old doctor that lived far away from the rest of the people. When he saw the chief's daughter he told the people, at once, that they must dig around the roots of a wild apple tree that was growing just a little way out from the chief's lodge. Many of the people at once began their digging all around the tree. The old doctor instructed them to bring the chief's daughter, and place her under the tree as near the edge of the hole (that they were digging) as thy could, "for," he said, "if you dig down into the roots of the tree, you will find something that will cure her disease." He added that as soon as she would see this object she would know it; and being near enough she could stretch her hand out and take it at once.

So they brought the girl and placed her at the edge of the hole that they had dug around the tree. They went on digging with great might. As soon as a party of the diggers became tired, another stepped into the hole and carried on the work. When they had placed the girl at the edge of the hole, a party of the diggers had stepped out; and before another could replace it the people were startled by a terrific roar that seemed to come nearer and nearer. They were all looking and wondering whence it had come. They soon discovered that all the ground around the tree was dropping downwards. Then they saw the tree falling down through the hole; the sick girl being pulled down with it, entangled in its branches. The world underneath, into which the tree fell, was a broad sheet of water about which no land was to be seen. On the water were swimming around a pair of great white birds with long crooked necks: I suppose they were swans. They heard a peal of thunder as the tree was falling down; this was the first peal of thunder ever heard on those waters. Both of them glanced upwards and saw the woman falling down. One of them said to the other:—"What a strange creature it is that is falling down from above. I know that she can not be borne up by the water; we must swim close together and hold her upon our backs." So they did, and the woman fell gently upon their backs and rested there. Then, as they swam along, they turned their long necks around and looked at the woman; they said to each other:—"What a beautiful creature it is; but what shall we do; we can not always swim this way and hold her up. What shall we do?" The other replied:—"I think we must go and see the Big Turtle. He will call a council of all the animals to decide upon what is to be done with the creature." So they swam away, found the Big Turtle, and showed him the woman that was resting upon their backs. Then the turtle had to decide as to what was to be done. A "moccasin" (ra''cu', i.e., a messenger) was sent around to call the animals to a big council. They came at once, and were all in a great wonder. For a long time they looked with awe at the wonderful creature. Finally the Turtle told them that they must come to a decision as to what should be done regarding this creature; that they could not let her die as—"she must have been sent to them for some good; that since she had thus come to them, it was evident that their duty was to find some place for her to live." The swans came forward and spoke of the tree that they had seen falling first. Then some one else got up and said that if the place could be known where this tree had fallen into the water, some of the divers might go down and get just a little bit of the earth that must be clinging to its roots. The Big Turtle found the idea a good one and advised that if the swans could show the very place where the tree had fallen, some one else should go down and get a little of the dirt clinging to its roots; that an island could be made with it for the woman to rest upon, even if he himself (the Turtle) had to hold the island upon his back. The swans told the animals that they could find that very place; they turned around, and swam with the woman upon their backs. The other animals followed until they came to the place where they had seen the tree and the woman falling. There they stopped. The Turtle called upon the otter, the best diver, for him to go down into the water and bring back some of the dirt clinging to the roots of the tree. The otter at once dived down. As he had been for some time out of sight the other animals began to speculate as to whether he was going to come back. By and by, they saw him coming back through the water. Upon reaching the surface he was so completely exhausted that he opened his mouth to gasp a breath and went down again,—dead. Then the muskrat was appointed to dive down. He remained still longer under the water. The same fate as the otter's befell him. Then the beaver and a number of other animals tried and failed in the same day until so many had been lost that way that the Turtle said he would not call upon any other to dive down. He suggested, however, that somebody should volunteer to do so. They remained in expectation for a little while. Finally, away out to one side, a little old ugly toad (těno''skwaoyę) spoke up and said that he would try. The other animals looked at each other, laughing and jeering at the presumption of this little toad. The Big Turtle, however, acceded to her suggestion, acknowledging that she might perhaps accomplish what the others had failed to do. So she took a long breath and down she went. The others all gathered around and watched her as she went away down out of sight into the clear waters. For a long time they looked downwards with the expectation of seeing her coming back. But she remained so long in the water that the others began to whisper to each other that she would not come back. For a long time they remained in expectation. At the end they saw a bubble of water coming up towards the surface of the water. They could not see the toad as yet. The Turtle said:—"She must be coming. I will swim right over the spot where the bubble came up; and if the toad comes back we shall hold her up." So it was done. A little while later the toad appeared away down in the water. Some of the animals said:—"She must have some earth as she has been gone so much longer than the others." Then the toad emerged from the surface of the water, just by the Big Turtle. Just as she reached the surface she opened her mouth and spat out a few grains of earth that fell upon the edge of the shell of the Big Turtle. Then she gave one gasp and fell back dead. As soon as those grains of earth had fallen upon the edge of the Big Turtle's shell, the Little Turtle came forward and began spreading it and rubbing it around the edge of the Big Turtle's shell. While she was so doing an island began to grow around the shell of the Big Turtle. The animals were looking at it while it was growing. After it had grown into a place large enough for the woman to rest upon, the two white swans swam to its edge and the woman stepped off on to it.

NOTE.—Recited by B. N. O. Walker, Chief Clerk at the Quapaw U. S. Agency, Wyandotte, Oklahoma. Mr. Walker, now about 40 years of age, is a descendant of Wyandot ancestors, on one side, and of European ancestors on the other. His first European ancestor was made prisoner by the Wyandots in Virginia, when a child. Mr. Walker is a thoroughly reliable informant who has often-times heard this myth, as well as others, repeated by his Aunt Kitty Greyeyes, a thoroughbred Wyandot, who was living with his family. Kitty Greyeyes was possessed of a good knowledge of both English and Wyandot, and she had learned this myth in Wyandot. Kitty Greyeyes died at B. N. O. Walker's father's home, when he, himself, (B. N. O. W.), was about 22 years of age. Mr. B. N. O. Walker has heard this myth many times when between the age of 11 and 19. He states that his Aunt Kitty, who, by the way, was a Canadian Wyandot from Anderdon, Ontario, had learnt those stories from her Aunt Hunt, who spoke Wyandot almost exclusively. "Aunt Hunt seems to have been the story-teller of the family." (Barbeau, "Huron and Wyandot Mythology," XXXIX, 6-17.)

C. AN INTERVIEW WITH "ESQ." JOHNSON BY MRS. ASHER WRIGHT.[1]

Esquire Johnson does not recollect the name of the man who first gave the name Nan-do-wah-gaah[2] and then went to where they lived and said to them, "You are O-non-dah-ge-gaah,"[3] and then he went to another place and said to the residents, "You are Ga-nyah-ge-o-noh,"[4] and then he came to where he called them O-ne-yut-gaah,[5] then again to another place and said "You are Que-yu-gwe-o-noh";[6] five nations, for the Tuscaroras were then at the South. This was long before the confederacy of the Iroquois, and the Tuscaroras did not return until after the Revolutionary war.

The Mohawks have 5 achems,[7] The Onondagas, he thinks have 4, also the Oneidas and Cayugas four each, the Senecas have 4 also and two war chiefs, the other tribes had no war chiefs.

Sha-dye-na-waho,[8] Nis-ha-nye-yant,[9] Gah-nya-gaeh,[10] Shah-de-gao-yes,[11] Sho-guh-jis-wa,[12] Ga-no-ga-ih-da-wit, De-yo-ne-ho-gaah-wah,[13] were Seneca Sachems.

The Long House was first opened at Onondaga[14]; the Senecas also had a long house.[15] When anything occurred

---

1 Copied *verbatim et literatim* from the manuscript notes of Mrs. Asher Wright, who interviewed Johnson in 1870.
2 The Seneca.
3 The Onondaga.
4 The Mohawk.
5 The Oneida.
6 The Cayuga.
7 Johnson's estimate is wrong, the number of sachems being as follows: the Mohawks, 9; the Oneidas, 9; the Onondagas, 14; the Cayugas, 10; the Senecas, 8; making the Council of 50. Note that while he says that the Senecas have only four he gives the names of seven. There were eight and he names all but Ga-ne-o-di-yo, Handsome Lake. He may have withheld this name on account of prejudice against him, for Ga-ne-o-di-yo at this time was in disrepute on account of his assumption of the role of prophet of "The New Religion."
8 The Helper.
9 Falling Day.
10 Great Forehead.
11 Level Heavens.
12 Hair Burned Off.
13 Open Door. (This sachemship was once held by Gen. Ely S. Parker.)
14 The Confederate or League of the Five Nations Capitol or Long House.
15 The national Long House of the Seneca.

to render a council necessary, any trusty young man might be sent as a runner to the other tribes to call them together.

When they came together the evening before the council they sang a song (In Seneca Wa-a-non-dah ga-ya-soh,) and in the morning one man sang a different song as they were going to start, i.e. the volunteers to revenge the murder or whatever the injury was.

In the council some leading chief would state the business and ask, what shall we do? A few of the chiefs would tell their views and then leading men of influence would say, We will do so and so, and the multitude would acquiesce and the council would break up.

In case of making peace between the Senecas, or the Iroquois, and the Cherokees, e.g., two messengers would be dispatched by the party desiring peace. They would be called before the enemies' council and introduced by the chief and then would deliver their message. If their proposals for peace were accepted they would agree to bury the whole list of grievances (bury the hatchet, Dyo-an-jo-gut,) so that they should not come up in sight again. If they refused the terms they would send the ambassadors back again to convey their refusal to the people and the war would continue.

The Quapaw war was long before the Cherokee war. This last was the last Indian war carried on by the Six Nations with the other Indians. Jak Snow's widow was a Cherokee and Gah-no-syoot Hay-a-soo-oh who died at Allegany, but Johnson never heard that Blue Eyes was a Cherokee.

The office of the Ga-yah-gwaah-doh was to give notice of the death of a sachem and the convocation of the general council to mourn for the dead and to raise up some one in his place, and at such convocations all the subordinate vacancies would be filled by the "raising" of chiefs and the elections of new ones.

In the election of new chiefs the women of the family

in which the vacancy occurred having the name of the office in her keeping could confer it on any one of the family (always on the female side), whom she should regard as the most reliable. It was always the province of the female head of the household to settle such questions although she consulted the whole household as to their judgment of the fitness or unfitness of any candidate. In like manner she could also depose (knock the horns off), for any dereliction of duty. After the election etc. the act would be confirmed (Da-ye-a-wit ha-di-yaas-gwah), by the relations and then by the council. These rules applied to all ranks even to the Ho-ya-neh-gowaak of the Grand Council.

Johnson says that 72 years ago[16] last spring, he with many others, was invited over from Canada by the chiefs and that he was 20 years old at this time and he says at that time the Indians had an idol over at Cornplanter's made of wood and ornamented with feathers around which they sung and danced and called it GOD. He had seen the idol but not the dancing around it. He says that Cornplanter's son threw it into the river (corroborating the story I have heard before). He says that he never knew of any other such idol. But he says that the women very commonly made little images, made in conformity to their dreams. (They consider all remarkable dreams as revelations from the spirit world.) And not alone the dolls, but images of any other object they might be impressed by in a dream, they considered them to be their gods, considered them as their protectors, etc. Some of them, not all of them, used to dance before them as objects of worship. (He does not know that the women ever received from the Catholics any images of the Virgin, but he has often seen gold or silver crucifixes among them used simply as ornaments.)

The Indians did not all believe that their New Years and other feasts were ordained of God. Johnson says that when he was about ten years old he saw some of the dis-

---

16   This was probably in 1798.

gusting things connected with the New Years and he asked his grandfather if God appointed that institution. The old man said *No*. And from that time Johnson did not believe in them and hence when the gospel came his mind was open to conviction and he embraced it. He says they had the New Years from time immemorial, but the dog burning, he thinks, was added to it not very long ago in consequence of somebody's dreams. The Big Feather and Green Corn dances he thinks were of equal antiquity with the New Years. He thinks all other observances comparatively modern, dreamed out and agreed upon and then proclaimed to the people as being God's ordinances.

He adds to the smoke of the tobacco to propitiate the pigeons when they took their young, the offering of payment to the old ones,—a brass kettle or other little dish full of ot-go-ah,[17] brooches, and various other things which the man who raised the smoke would deposit on the ground before he put the tobacco on the fire, and he says that they left the kettle there when they left home, considering it a real payment to the pigeons, etc. (The prayers are the same as related by Oliver Silverheels.)

He says that anciently they had a law that if a man died his widow should mourn a whole year, she should clothe herself in rags, keep her head covered with rags, never wash her face or hands, never to go anywhere except at night weeping to the grave. (The same rules applied in case it was her child that died. It was the general law of mourning.) The chiefs at last forbade these customs, as being too hard, often resulting in the death of the mourners before the year was up, and they appointed that the mourning should last only ten days, at the end of which they should hold the funeral feast (Ho-non-di-aak-hoh-ga-ya-soh), and during these ten days they should abstain from all ordinary business; a chief, e.g. could not meet in council or attend any public business till the ten days were over.

---

[17] Wampum.

At the funeral feast the chief or other person would proclaim the removal of the disabilities.

Johnson says that a long time ago squashes were found growing wild. He says that he has seen them and that they were quite unpalatable, but the Indians used to boil and eat them. He says that in their ancient wars with the Southern Indians they brought back squashes that were sweet and palatable and beans which grow wild in the South, calico colored, and which were very good, and he thinks the white folks have never used them. Also the o-yah-gwa-oweh they brought from the south where it grows wild, also the various kinds of corn, black, red and squaw corn they brought from the prairie country south where they found it growing wild. All these things they found on their war expeditions and brought them here and planted them and thus they abound here, but he does not know where they first found the potato.

STONE GIANTS.

He says the old people used to tell the story that after God had made the world and man and animals he was one day walking around and he saw a strange people coming towards him, clothed with stone and he asked them who they were and who created them. They replied that they were free and independent and that they had no creator, that they were their own masters. He then said, "Where are you going?" They said, "We are going to find men that we may devour them." He said, "You must not go. Very likely if you do they will kill you." But the more he forbid them the more they were determined to go. So he went away and blackened his face with coal and took him a basswood club three or four inches through and came around in front of them and fell upon them and killed all but two who fled and he came around again and having washed off the black met them in the place where he first saw them, and said, "What is the matter with you that you flee so?" They

answered, "They have been killing us, and we only are left."
He said, "That is what I told you," though he had done it
himself. He said then, "You must go away and leave mankind alone. You must keep away from and never come
nigh them again."

THE THUNDER GOD.

He also at another time saw the Hih-noh coming
towards him and did not know him for he had not created
him and he said to him, Who are you? Who created you?
And whom do you own as your lord? He answered no
one. Then he said What do you think of men? He replied
Oh they are my grandchildren and if you wish me to do
anything I can do it, (or I am ready to do it.) GOD said
to him, What can you do. Oh he said I can wash the
earth, &c. And so the Indians, when it thunders think that
Hih-noh is washing the earth again and they call him
Grandfather because he told GOD that they were his
grandchildren.

ANOTHER STORY, OR FABLE, THE THUNDERER.

In ancient times there was a war party got up to go
against the southwestern Indians. There were four or
five men and there was a poor friendless boy, an orphan,
and he came to one of these men and found him painted
and ready for the expedition. He painted himself, and
the man befriended him and sent him to where there was
a company of men, who seeing him painted enquired the
object and said to him, that man is your friend? He said
yes and they said we will go with you. There were five in
the party besides this boy whose name was Shot-do-gas, in
allusion to his filthy miserable condition. They came
together near Smoke's Creek (near Buffalo) and there they
made a bark canoe and then started up the lake. They
came after several nights to Ga-yah-hah-geh (Clear Land),
and there while the moon was yet high and it was quite

light, they became sleepy, and the leader said Let us stop here. So they ran in among the cattail flags and tied a lot of them together on each side of the canoe and fastened it to them, so as to have it lie still. (Noe-oh-gwah ga-ya-soh, cattail flag.) So they slept in the canoe. After a little while the leader awoke and thought he saw evidence that they were in motion, and putting his hand over the side of the canoe, felt the rush of water, and aroused his companions, saying Wake up! The canoe is running swiftly. Another put his hand on the other side of the canoe, and said Yes we are going rapidly! They could not tell the cause of the motion, but the canoe kept on. They lay in it mostly asleep and when they awaked they found themselves at Green Bay, and the canoe kept on, and they finally landed at Chicago, at daylight, having come from Cleveland in one night. They took the canoe into the bushes and hid it and got ready their breakfast and ate it and about noon they found a trail leading off into the country and they started on that trail and they went till night and camped and started again the next morning, and till perhaps 5 p. m., they saw a man coming. They stopped beside the trail till he came up. He said the chief sent me on this trail saying you will meet men coming. Tell them to come on with you. They went on a great way for he had run very fast and at length they came to a house. Beside the door there was something tied and concealed, and he said to them you must not look upon this. Something will happen to whosoever looks upon it. (It was a She-wah, a sable.) They went into the house, no one of them having looked upon the forbidden object. They found the house full of people who made room for them, and all men, women and children saluted them kindly. The chief said to his family We are in a hard case we have nothing for these guests to eat. They can not eat our food. You must provide for them of such kind of food as they can eat. Four of them then went out and presently it began to thunder. Then these men began to realize their situation. They had come into Hih-noh's house. The whole household were his family, although in form and speech they seemed to be human beings. These four soon returned bringing with them green corn, beans, squashes, etc., for their guests. The women cooked these things for them and they ate. They soon discovered that the Hih-noh family lived upon serpents,—that whenever they discovered a snake they shot down a bolt upon him, and carried him home for food, and that it was this that made the old man say We are in a hard case because our guests cannot eat our food. They remained there a long time living together. At length the old man said to them, Pretty soon you will see something coming in the air from the North. We have tried to kill it but we cannot do it. You can do it for us. They then all went out and soon there was a wind from the North and they saw something flying towards them. It seemed to be a man entirely naked of a yellow color, without wings or any means of flying, and yet it flew swiftly towards them. Shot-da-gas said, "Shoot it with an arrow," and he shot, and he shot and the arrow fell below and he shot again but over-shot it. By the time his third arrow was ready it had come directly over-head, and he shot and pierced him through the body, so that he fell but a little way off. The Hih-noh family were greatly rejoiced and poured forth many thanks upon him for his exploit.

Afterwards Hih-noh said, Yonder is another thing which we cannot kill, and he led them a long way till they came to a monstrous big whitewood tree, and from a large limb projecting from near the top there was a creature sitting and Hih-noh said Shoot that, and Shot-de-gas drew his bow and shot it through the body. It crawled along the limb and finally fell, (bum!) and was stone dead. It proved to be a monstrous porcupine with quills as large as one's finger, which the Hih-noh family had tried in vain to kill.

They staid a long time, when at last Hih-noh said, they

are about to take you home, but let Shot-do-gas remain with us, we will take care of him. Shot-do-gas was willing and his friend gave his consent. They went out and saw a very big Mortar, (gä-ne-gah-tah,) and Hih-noh called them to it. Shot-do-gas climbed into it and there he was killed, but Hih-noh restored him to life and he also became a hih-noh. Then the five men were about to start, and all at once there commenced a terrible thunder storm and Hih-noh said now take them home, and suddenly they were taken up on the backs of as many men and carried along with the storm and down at Smoke's Creek where they started. They then washed off their paint and started to go home, but they found the trail grown up with bushes; they kept on to where there was a bark shanty, it had been rebuilt,— to the council house, it was gone, every(thing) was changed they kept on and at last met a man whom they did not know, he asked them where and whither they were going, they replied we went from here and have come home, he said wait and I will go and tell the people. He found the chief and told him here are men whom I never saw before, saying that they have come home. The chief gave the call implying important business,—the people rushed together into the council house, the man told what he had seen, the chief said to him go call these men, they came, no one knew them and they knew no one. The chief asked the leader of the party for his name, we may perhaps remember that, he would not tell his own name but the rest of the party told it and each others names, but nobody recollected them. Then said the chief there is a very old woman living yonder, go call her, if so be she can recollect them. She came and they told her their names and that one of the party named Shot-do-gas had remained behind. She recollected the leaving of the party a long, long time ago, and recalled their names, and said that when they went away, there was a poor miserable little boy, on that account called Shot-do-gas, who left with them. It proved that one of these men was elder brother of this old woman, and he returned in all the freshness of youth, as when he left, while his younger sister had become a superannuated old woman. All the rest of the people had grown up since they left and therefore did not know them. She, the sole survivor of her generation, was the only one to recognize them and remove the unbelief of those that did not believe that they had ever gone from this region of country.

D. EMBLEMATIC TREES IN IROQUOIAN MYTHOLOGY.[1]

By Arthur C. Parker.

A student of Iroquoian folklore, ceremony or history will note the many striking instances in which sacred or symbolic trees are mentioned. One finds allusions to such trees not only in the myths and traditions which have long been known to literature and in the speeches of Iroquois chiefs when met in council with the French and English colonists, but also in the more recently discovered wampum codes and in the rituals of the folk-cults.

There are many references to the "tree of peace" in the colonial documents on Indian relations. Colden in his Five Nations, for example, quotes the reply of the Mohawk chief to Lord Effingham in July, 1684. The Mohawk agree to the peace propositions and their spokesman says: "We now plant a Tree who's tops will reach the Sun, and its Branches spread far abroad, so that it shall be seen afar off; & we shall shelter ourselves under it, and live in Peace, without molestation." (Gives two Beavers).[2]

In a footnote Colden says that the Five Nations always express peace under the metaphor of a tree. Indeed in the speech, a part of which is quoted above, the Peace tree is mentioned several times.

In Garangula's reply to De la Barre, as recorded by Lahontan are other references to the "tree." In his "harangue" Garangula said:

"We fell upon the Illinese and the Oumamis, because they cut down the Trees of Peace—." "The Tsonontouans, Gayogouans, Onnotagues, Onnoyoutes, and Agnies declare that they interred the Axe at Cataracuoy, in the Presence

---

1 First published in *American Anthropologist*, Oct.-Dec., 1912.
2 Colden, History of the Five Nations, reprint, p. 58, New York, 1866.

of your Predecessor, in the very Center of the Fort; and
planted the Tree of Peace in the same place; 'twas then stip-
ulated that the Fort should be us'd as a Place of Retreat for
Merchants, and not as a Refuge for Soldiers . . . You

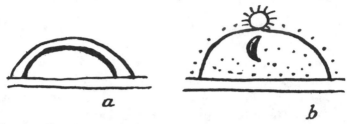

Fig. 1.—The pictograph of the sky-dome in the Walam Olum. *a* is
interpreted "At all times above the earth." *b*, "He made them [sun
and moon] all to move evenly."

ought to take Care that so great a number of Militial Men
as we now see . . . do not stifle and choak the Tree of
Peace. . . . it must needs be of pernicious Consequences
to stop its Growth and hinder it to shade both your Country
and ours with its Leaves."[3]

The above examples are only a few of many that might
be quoted to show how commonly the Iroquois mentioned
the peace tree. There are also references to the tree which
was uprooted "to afford a cavity in which to bury all weapons of war," the tree being replanted as a memorial.

In the Iroquoian myth, whether Cherokee, Huron,
Wyandot, Seneca or Mohawk, the "tree of the upper-
world" is mentioned, though the character of the tree differs
according to the tribe and sometimes according to the myth-
teller.

Before the formation of the lower or earth-world the
Wyandot tell of the upper or sky-world and of the "Big
Chief" whose daughter became strangely ill.[4] The chief
instructs his daughter to "dig up the wild apple tree; what
will cure her she can pluck from among its roots." David

3 Lahontan, Voyages, Vol I, p 42. London, 1735.
4 Connelly, W. E., Wyandot Folk Lore, Topeka, 1899.

Boyle[5] wondered why the apple tree was called "wild," but that the narrator meant wild-apple and not wild apple is shown by the fact that the Seneca in some versions called the tree the crab-apple. The native apple tree with its small fruit was intended by the Indian myth teller who knew also of the cultivated apple and took the simplest way to differentiate the two.

With the Seneca this tree is described more fully. In manuscript left by Mrs. Asher Wright, the aged missionary to the Seneca, I find the cosmologic myth as related to her by Esquire Johnson, a Seneca, in 1870. Mrs. Wright and her husband understood the Seneca language perfectly and published a mission magazine as early as 1838 in that tongue. Her translation of Johnson's myth should therefore be considered authentic. She wrote: "—there was a vast expanse of water—. Above it was the great blue arch of air but no signs of anything solid—. In the clear sky was an unseen floating island sufficiently firm to allow trees to grow upon it, and there were men-beings there. There was one great chief there who gave the law to all the Ongweh or beings on the island. In the center of the island there grew a tree so tall that no one of the beings who lived there could see its top. On its branches flowers and fruit hung all the year round. The beings who lived on the island used to come to the tree and eat the fruit and smell the sweet perfume of the flowers. On one occasion the chief desired that the tree be pulled up. The Great Chief was called to look at the great pit which was to be seen where the tree had stood." The story continues with the usual description of how the sky-mother was pushed into the hole in the sky and fell upon the wings of the waterfowl who placed her on the turtle's back. After this mention of the celestial tree in the same manuscript is the story of the central world-tree. After the birth of the

---

5 Archaeological Report of Ontario, 1905. Boyle, David; The Iroquois, p. 147.

twins, Light One and Toad-like (or dark) one, the Light
One, also known as Good Minded, noticing that there was
no light, created the "tree of light." This was a great tree
having at its topmost branch a great ball of light. At this
time the sun had not been created. It is significant as will
appear later that the Good Minded made his tree of light
one that brought forth flowers from every branch. After
he had gone on experimenting and improving the earth
"he made a new light and hung it on the neck of a being
and he called the new light Gaa-gwaa(gä"gwā) and instructed its bearer to run his course daily in the heavens."
Shortly after he is said to have "dug up the tree of light
and looking into the pool of water in which the stump
(trunk) had grown he saw the reflection of his own face
and thereupon conceived the idea of creating Ongwe and
made them both a man and a woman."

The central world-tree is found also in Delaware mythology, though as far as I discover it is not called the tree
of light. The *Journal*[6] of Dankers and Slyter records the
story of creation as heard from the Lenape of New Jersey
in 1679. All things came from a tortoise, the Indians told
them. "It had brought forth the world and in the middle
of its back had sprung a tree upon whose branches men
had grown."[7] This relation between men and the tree is
interesting in comparison with the Iroquois myth as it is
also as the central world-tree. Both Lenape and the Iroquois ideas are symbolic and those who delight in flights
of imagination might draw much from both.

The Seneca world-tree is described elsewhere in my
notes as a tree whose branches pierce the sky and whose
roots run down into the under-ground waters of the under-
world. This tree is mentioned in various ceremonial rites

---

[6] Journal of a Voyage to New York in 1679-80, by Jasper Dankers
and Peter Slyter. Translated in Vol I, Trans. L. I. Hist. Soc. 1867.

[7] With the New England Indians the idea was held that men were
found by Glooskape in a hole made by an arrow which he had shot
into an ash tree.

of the Iroquois. With the False Face Company, Hadĭgo$^{n''}$săsho$^{n''}$o^n, for example, the Great Face, chief of all the False Faces, is said to be the invisible giant that guards the world-tree (gaindowo′ně′). He rubs his turtle shell

Fig. 2.—A false face leader rubbing his rattle on a stump. Drawn from a photograph.

rattle upon it to obtain its power and this he imparts to all the visible false faces worn by the Company. In visible token of this belief the members of the Company rub their turtle rattles on pine tree trunks, believing that they become filled with both the earth and the sky-power thereby. In this use of the turtle shell rattle there is perhaps a recognition of the connection between the turtle and the world-tree that grows upon the primal turtle's back.

In the prologue of the Wampum Code of the Five Nations Confederacy we again find references to a symbolic "great tree." In the code of Dekānăwĭ'dă and with the Five Nations' confederate lords (rodiyā'nĕr) "I plant the Tree of the Great Peace. I plant it in your territory, Adōdar'ho' and the Onondaga nation, in the territory of you who are Firekeepers.

"I name the tree the Tree of the Great Long Leaves. Under the shade of this Tree of Peace we spread the soft feathery down of the globe thistle, there beneath the spreading branches of the Tree of Peace."

In the second "law" of the code the four roots of the "tree" are described and the law-giver says, "If any individual or any nation outside the Five Nations shall obey the laws of the Great Peace and make known their disposition to the Lords of the Confederacy, they may trace the Roots to the Tree and if their minds are clean and obedient—they shall be welcome to take shelter beneath the Tree of the Long Leaves.

"We place in the top of the Tree of the Long Leaves an Eagle who is able to see afar;—he will warn the people."

In another place is the following: "I Dekānăwĭ'dă, and the union lords now uproot the tallest pine tree and into the cavity thereby made we cast all weapons of war. Into the depths of the earth, down into the deep under-earth currents of water flowing to unknown regions we cast all the weapons of strife. We bury them from sight and we plant again the tree. Thus shall the Great Peace, Kayĕ"narhe'-kowa, be established."

These laws and figures of speech are very evidently those which the Iroquois speakers had in mind when addressing "peace councils" with the whites.

Symbolic trees appear not only in Iroquois history,

mythology and folk beliefs but also in their decorative art. The numerous decorative forms of trees embroidered in moose hair and porcupine quills by the eastern Algonquins and by the Huron and the Iroquois appear to be attempts to

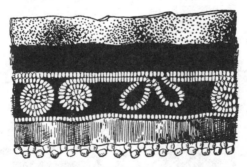

Fig. 3.—Portion of legging strip. The inward curving design at the top sometimes symbolizes sleep or death. (Specimens collected for the New York State Museum by M. R. Harrington.)

represent the world-tree and the celestial tree, in some cases with its "all manner of fruits and flowers." Many, if not most, of the modern descendants of the old time Indian, who copy these old designs have forgotten their meanings and some have even invented new explanations. A few of the more conservative, however, remember even yet the true meaning of their designs and from such much of interest has been learned.

In examining examples of Iroquois decorative art one is immediately impressed with the repeated use of a pattern consisting of a semi-circle resting upon two parallel horizontal lines having at the top two divergent curved lines each springing from the same point and curving outward, like the end of a split dandelion stalk, (See fig. 4b.) This design or symbol, with the Iroquois represents the celestial tree growing from the top of the sky, or more properly, from the bottom of the "above-sky-world" (gä'oñyä'gĕ"). The two parallel lines represent the earth. This symbol is found with the same meaning among the Delaware. In the Walum Olum[8] parallel semi-circles represent the sky-dome, though single semi-circles appear. Two parallel horizontal lines, likewise, represent the earth. (See fig. 1, a.)

With the Iroquois the sky-dome and earth symbols are employed as pattern designs for decorating clothing. Near-

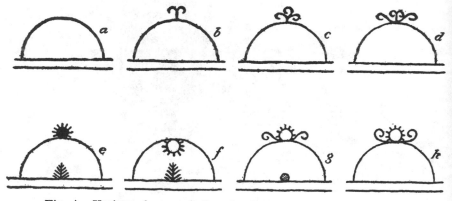

Fig. 4.—Various forms of the sky-dome symbol as employed in Iroquois moose-hair and quill embroidery.

ly always these symbols are associated with the celestial-tree symbol, though sometimes this is employed alone. These patterns appear embroidered in moose hair, porcupine quills and beads as borders for leggins, skirts, breechclouts and moccasins. (See fig. 5.) Occasionally the pattern

8 Brinton: Lenape and their Legends, p. 170. Phila., 1885.

is found on head-bands and hair ornaments. In some cases, especially in examples of silver work and beaded articles it seems evident that the decoartor has not the meaning of his pattern in mind. This is true of some of the more modern attempts to use it.

These outward curving designs, beside being symbols of the celestial tree have a secondary meaning, that of life, living and light. Curving inward upon themselves they sometimes represent sleep and death. Fig. 3 shows this design on a leggin strip. In fig. 4 h we have it used in conjunction with a sleeping sun. The Onondaga call the double curve design oĕⁿ"shă', tendril.

In this connection it may be well to note that the "horns" wampum when placed upon a dead civil chief's body is curved inward, the two ends touching and forming the outline of a circle or heart. When the condoling ceremonial chief finishes his address and is about to lift the strands of wampum from the corpse to hand it to the successor he turns the wampum-string so that the ends point outward and away from each other. These particular symbols while being those of death and life respectively are regarded as horn and not tree symbols. The wampum so employed "the horns," onă'gasho"ă, and alludes to the symbolic title of the civil chief (roya'ner).

The celestial-tree symbol appears also as a trefoil. The third tendril or branch unfolds from the center of the tree. (See fig. 4 c.) A fourth branch is often used and then appears as a double tree. (See fig. 4 d.) In 4, e the night-sun is represented over the world-tree and in meaning this sign is found to be the same as 4, h. In fig. 4, f the day-sun is represented as shining at zenith above the world-tree. In 4, g the sun-above-the-sky is awake and roosting in the celestial-tree. All of these designs are found on borders of Iroquois garments some of which are shown in plate 1.

Another important modification of the sky-dome and celestial-tree combination is that which represents the sky-dome with the celestial-tree upon it and the earth-tree within the dome below and resting upon a long intersection of an oval (possibly the turtle) and sending its long leaves or branches upward to the sky-arch.

Sometimes the design is used as the motif of a rosette or other balanced design. Morgan figured several and the Report of the Director of the State Museum of New York for 1907 shows a picture of Red Jacket's pipe pouch ornamented with such a pattern. There the ends of the tendrils are split and represented as conventional flowers. In other instances the motif is built upward upon itself as shown in figure 6. The first "tree" in this figure is copied from Lafitau[9] and the others from Mohawk moccasin toes.

With the Iroquois the celestial-tree symbol is generally represented by this anies-like figure. The *earth-tree,* on the other hand, is less highly conventionalized. With the Iroquois as with many other tribes in the forest area in North America, the Ojibwa for example, the ordinary tree sign is commonly used,—that depicting the upward slanting branches of the balsam fir. Figure 7 shows the Ojibwa pictograph which is interpreted as "the big tree in the middle of the earth." The terminal buds on the conventionalized trees of the Huron moose hair embroidery type resemble in form this balsam fir symbol. The Huron indeed call the bud "balsam fir."[10] The method of slanting the hair to form the design creates the resemblance and causes the confusion, in all probability. Used alone the "bud" would be a tree if placed in proper position but as ordinarily used by the Huron at the extremity of an embroidered branch, it seems paradoxical to find a tree on the small end of one of its branches. This is discussed more fully hereinafter.

Figure 4, e, and f show the Iroquois "middle-of-the-

9 Lafitau, Moeurs des Savvages Ameriquains, Tome II, plate 3, page 43, Paris, 1724.
10 See Speck, F. G., Huron Moose Hair Embroidery, Amer. Anthropologist, N. S., Vol. 13, no. 1, p 1.

world-tree" as used in conjunction with the sky-dome and sun symbols.

Another, and more elaborate, form of the "tree" as it appears in Iroquoian decorative art is a flowering plant or

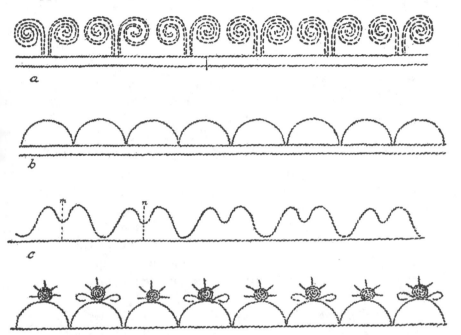

Fig. 5.—Borders embroidered in moose-hair on deerskin garments. (Seneca specimens in the New York State Museum.) *a* is the "two curve" pattern common in Iroquoian decoration. *b* represents a series of "sky-domes" resting upon the earth, the two parallel horizontal lines. *c* represents a series of the "trees" of Iroquois symbolism. The unit of the design is indicated by *m-n*. *d* shows a series of suns and celestial trees resting on the sky-dome.

tree having conventionalized leaves (generally, "long leaves"), branches, buds, tendrils and flowers. See plate 2. In this plate (9) is shown the flowering tree as embroidered in porcupine quills on an Iroquois pouch collected by Lewis H. Morgan, and now in the New York State Museum. It will be perceived that here the diverging curved lines play a conspicuous part in the make-up of the tree.

Like all Iroquois symbolic trees of the purely conventional type the tree is exactly balanced on each side of the central line that represents the trunk or stalk.

With the Huron these trees are, likewise, used as an adornment for bags and other things where a comparatively large surface is afforded. Dr. Speck illustrates one of these trees in the article on moose hair embroidery previously cited, and gives the Huron interpretation for the various parts of the tree. With the Huron, it is most interesting to note, the topmost flower is called not a flower but a star, thus suggesting some dim recollection of the "tree of light."

The Confederated Iroquois made similar trees, though they interpret some of the parts differently. With them the significance of the tree is recognized. Mr. Hewitt describes the tree in his Onondaga creation myth.[11] His informants in relating the myth said: "And there beside the lodge stands the tree that is called Tooth (Ono"djă'). Moreover, the blossoms this standing tree bears cause the world to be light, making it light for men-beings dwelling there." This agrees with the Seneca version previously cited in this article.

The "Tree of Peace" symbolically planted by Dekănă-wĭ'dă, as has been noted was called the "Tree of the Great Long Leaves." It will be observed that the "tree of light" in nearly every case where leaves are shown at all has long sword-like leaves. This is true among the Huron in their older patterns, as among the Iroquois. The Huron, however, now call these long leaves "dead branches" and the unopened flowers "balsam fir."[12] The Huron, as with most of the Iroquois, have likely forgotten or confused the true names of the elements of their designs. These designs, with the Huron at least, seem to have undergone some change due to the necessity for trade purposes of working

---

11 Hewitt, Iroquois Cosmology, Part I, p. 151; 21 An. Rept. Bur. Am. Eth., Washington, 1903.
12 Speck, op. cit.

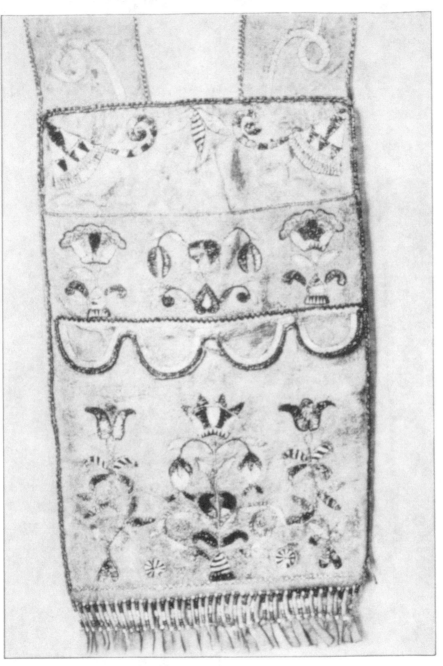

Embroidered pouch made by the Seneca before 1850. Note tree and floral designs. Specimen in New York State Museum. Scale x½.

their patterns in outline and quickly. It is most important to observe, however, that oftentimes when the object of
using a symbol is primarily for decorative purposes, the
Indian artist or needle-worker gives parts of the design
"pattern names," often at entire variance with the real

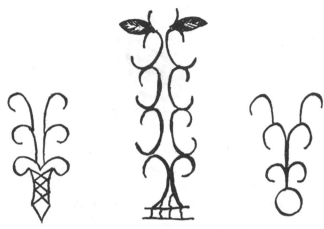

Fig. 6.—Various forms of the celestial tree. Here the unit is super-
posed to form the tree.

meaning of the part but based upon real or fancied resemblance. With the Huron with whom the decorative element
is now of primary importance this seems to have been the
case. Indeed, Dr. Speck does not say that the parts of the
designs which he illustrates are symbols though he does
give the names which the Huron told him. The Huron are
very likely making "trees of light" and do not know it, in
this respect being similar to their Iroquois brethren. The
designs are worked, as some of my Indian informants say,
"because they are Indian" and likewise because they have
become accustomed to them and because there seems nothing more appropriate to invent.

This instance suggests how with change of environment
myths, symbols and ceremonial rites may lose their meaning
and yet preserve their outward form.

The two-curve motif in Indian art is widely distributed throughout America. In many instances it seems to have meanings similar to that given it by the Iroquois, though

Fig. 7.—"The big tree in the middle of the earth." From the Ojibwa *Midéwiwin.*

there are other instances where it has not. It is sometimes used with a few simple additions to represent the face of the thunderbird or even the human face, at least the eyes and nose. In a more elaborate form it is found in the Fejérvary Codex as a tree symbol though a variation of the form in the Vienna codex makes the cross-section of a vase.

It is not strange that the simple outline should be found almost universally. It is one of those simple conceptions in art that would occur to any people independently. Many things in nature suggest it. It is not its outline, however, so much as its use as a definite symbol and its combination with others that gives it interest to the writer.

The world-tree with its long leaves and luminous flowers is worthy of more detailed consideration. It seems to have been a deeply imbedded concept with the certain branches of the Algonquin stock and of the Iroquois, affecting not only their mythology and ceremonial language but also their decorative art. Whether the idea has a deeper and more primitive meaning than here suggested the author does not pretend to **know.**

E. THE SOCIETY THAT GUARDS THE MYSTIC POTENCE.

Among the Seneca Indians for many years the most important ceremonial society has been and now is the organization called Neh Ho-noh-chi-noh-gah (Ne' Hono^n'tci'no^n''gä'), commonly called the "Secret Medicine Society," and as often the "Little Water Company."

This society (hoĕnnidio^n'got) is instituted primarily to preserve the mystice potence or orenda (meaning magical power) supposed to be inherent in the medicine called the niga'ni'gä'ă' (meaning small dose), and to preserve the methods of administering it.

Of the several native societies that have survived among the Seneca, none remains more exclusive, more secret or so rigorously adheres to its ancient forms. No organization among the Seneca is so well knit together and not one is so united in its purpose. Its members and officers are among the most conservative and best respected men of their communities, and they preserve the rites of the order with great fidelity. Harmony prevails for discord of any kind would be at variance with the very fundamental teachings of the order. No organization among the Senecas to-day is so mysterious, nor does any other possess the means of enforcing so rigorously its laws. The Honohtcinohgah is without doubt a society of great antiquity; few Iroquois societies, perhaps, are more so. One authority has contended that it is a tribal branch of an organization found everywhere among Indians throughout the continent and produced arguments to support the theory, but an examination of its traditions and ritual would lead to the opinion that it is purely Iroquoian.

In order to understand the organization it is first necessary to understand the legend of its origin when many otherwise obscure allusions will be made apparent. This is given in 69, under Traditions, page 386.

NEH NIGAHNIGAHAH.

The charm medicine is known as the niga'ni'gă'a' and each member possesses a certain amount of it. The secret of compounding the niga'ni'gă'a' rested with only one man in a tribe, who, according to the teachings of the society, would be apprised of approaching death and given time to transmit the knowledge to a successor whom he should choose. According to the traditions of the Honohtcinohgah the secret holder always foreknew the hour of his death and frequently referred to it in lodge meetings.

The "small dose" medicine is composed of the brains of various mammals, birds, fish and other animals and the pollen and roots of various plants, trees and vegetables. These ingredients are compounded and pulverized with certain other substances as squash seeds, corn roots, etc., and constitute the base of the niganigaah.

That this medicine actually possesses chemical properties that react on human tissue was proven by Dr. J. H. Salisbury, an eminent physician and a former State chemist, who according to Mrs. H. M. Converse analyzed and experimented with a small quantity that he had secured from a member of the society.

The medicine itself is of a yellowish hue and when opened in the dark sometimes appears luminous, probably from the organic phosphorus that it contains. The utmost caution is employed by the members of the Honohtcinohgäh to preserve the medicine from exposure to the air in unsafe places and from contaminating influences. It is held in a small skin bag[1] and wrapped in many coverings of cloth and skin and finally enclosed in a bark, wood or tin case to keep it free from moisture, disease and dirt.

---

[1] The wrapping must not be from the skin of any "medicine animal."

Among the Seneca of modern times John Patterson was the last of the holders of the secret and the secret of the precise method of compounding the medicine died with him, he in some way having failed to instruct a successor. The members thus doubly guard their medicine and are loath to use it except in cases of extreme necessity for when it is exhausted not only will they be unable to secure more but by a legend when the medicine is gone the Senecas will forever lose their identity as Indians.

METHOD OF ADMINISTERING THE CHARMED MEDICINE.

A person who wishes to have the medicine given him for the cure of a wound, broken bone or specific disease, must purge himself and for three days must abstain from the use of salt or grease. His food must be the flesh of white birds or animals and only the white portions. The system of the patient is then ready to receive the medicine. The medicine man comes to his lodge and an assistant searches the house for anything that might destroy the "life" of the medicine such as household animals, vermin, decayed meat, blood, soiled garments, etc. These things removed from the house, the patient is screened off and the guard patrols the premises warning away all infected or obnoxious persons. An attendant who has previously been dispatched to a clear running stream enters with a bowl of water that has been dipped from the crest of the ripples as they "sang their way down the water-road." Not to antagonize the forces in the water, it was dipped the way the current ran, down stream, and not upward against it.

Everything now being in readiness the medicine man takes a basket of tobacco and as he repeats the ancient formula he casts pinches of the tobacco into the flames that the sacred smoke may lift his words to the Great Spirit. The water is then poured out in a cup and the medicine packet opened. With a miniature ladle that holds as much of the powder as can be held on the tip of the blade of a small penknife, the medicine man dips three times from the medicine and drops the powder on the surface of the water in three spots, the points of a triangle. If the medicine floats the omen is good, if it clouds the water the results are considered doubtful and if it sinks death may be predicted with a degree of certainty and the medicine is thrown away. In the case of severe cuts or contusions and broken bones the medicated water is sprinkled upon the affected part and an amount is taken internally. A medicine song is then chanted by the "doctor" who accompanies himself with a gourd rattle. After the ceremony of healing, the people of the house partake of a feast of fruit, and the medicine man departs with his fee, a pinch of sacred tobacco. The following description of the lodge ceremony from the lips of a Seneca will not be out of place. The story is related exactly as it came from the tongue of the interpreter.

Jesse Hill speaking: "Mother scraped off basswood bark, soaked it in water and wrapped it around my leg. Next day we sent for the medicine man. He came at sun set and sent to the creek for fresh water to be dipped where the current was swift, with a pail not against the current. Poured some in a tea cup and pulled out the medicine bag. Opened it with a charmed shovel not much larger than a pin. Dipped three times. Cup of water. Floated. Go up or down. Understood it was good medicine. Took some in his mouth and sprayed it on my leg. Told mother to put a curtain around my bed so no one could see me. If anyone saw any part of my body, medicine would do no good. Soon came dark. All the animals were put out. Took tin pail and made fire. Put in center of room and all sat around in silence. Medicine man made prayer. Scattered tobacco mother had prepared over fire. Took rattle made of gourd and chanted medicine song loud and louder. Half hour pain had gone. Boiled different fruits together till soft. Put kettle where all could help out with little dipper. Left two doses of medicine. Eat nothing but white things. White of egg of chicken had white feathers and eat chicken if white. Five or six days spoke things. All certain took pain away."

THE MEDICINE LODGE RITUAL.

The Honohtcinohgah "sits," that is, holds lodge meetings, four times each year; in mid-winter, when the moon Nïsha proclaims the new year, when the deer sheds its hair, when the strawberries are ripe and when corn is in the milk. At these ceremonies each member brings his or her medicine to be sung for and if unable to be present sends it by messenger.

Only members know the exact place and time of meeting. At the entrance of the medicine lodge, a private house of a member chosen for the ceremony, a guard is stationed who scrutinized each person who attempts to pass within. Across the door within is placed a heavy bench "manned" by several stalwart youths who, should a person not entitled to see the interior of the lodge appear, would throw their weight against the bench and force the door shut leaving the unfortunate intruder to the mercy of the outside guards and incoming members.

Each member entering the lodge has with him his medicine, a quantity of tobacco, a pipe and perhaps a rattle although most of the lodge rattles are in the keeping of Honondiont or officers. As the members enter the room they deposit their contribution of tobacco in a husk basket placed for the purpose on a table at one side and then put their medicine packets beside the basket of the sacred herb.

The ceremony proper commences about 11 P. M. in the summer and in winter an hour earlier and lasts until nearly daybreak. The feast makers enter the lodge several hours previous to the ceremony and cook the food for the feast and prepare the strawberry wine.

The seats in the lodge are arranged around the sides of the room leaving the center of the room open.

When all is in readiness a Honondiont takes a basket of sacred tobacco, oyĕñkwa oñweh, and, as he chants the opening ceremony he casts the sacred herb into the smouldering coals. The lights are all burning and the members are in their seats, the only exception being the feast makers whose duties require their attention at the fireplace.

From the manuscript notes of Mrs. Harriet Maxwell Converse, I find the following translation of the "Line Around the Fire Ceremony."

THE LINE AROUND THE FIRE CEREMONY.

The Singer, (to the members): "This is the line around the fire ceremony. Now I have asked blessings and made prayer."
The Singer sprinkles sacred tobacco on the fire.

(The Singer speaks to the invisible powers):
"Now I give you incense,
You, the Great Darkness!
You, our great grand parents, here to night,—
We offer you incense!
We assemble at certain times in the year
That this may be done.
(We trust that all believe in this medicine,
For all are invited to partake of this medicine.)
(Now one has resigned. We ask you to let him off in a friendly manner. Give him good luck and take care that his friends remain in faithful!)
Now we offer you this incense!
Some have had ill luck
Endeavoring to give a human being.
We hope you will take hold
And help your grandchildren,
Nor be discouraged in us!
Now we act as we offer you incense!
You love it the most of all offerings!
With it you will hear us better
And not tire of our talking,
But love us with all power
Beyond all treasures
Or spreading you words through the air!

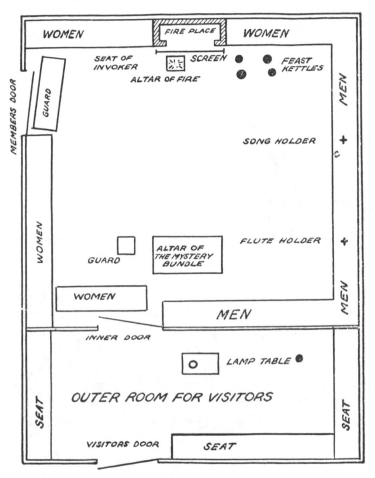

WOMEN   FIRE PLACE   WOMEN

MEMBERS DOOR

GUARD

SEAT OF INVOKER   SCREEN   FEAST KETTLES

ALTAR OF FIRE

MEN

SONG HOLDER

WOMEN

GUARD   ALTAR OF THE MYSTERY BUNDLE   FLUTE HOLDER

MEN

WOMEN

MEN

INNER DOOR

LAMP TABLE

SEAT

OUTER ROOM FOR VISITORS

SEAT

VISITORS DOOR   SEAT

ARRANGEMENT
OF THE
LITTLE WATER LODGE

This diagram shows the arrangement of the lodge room of the
Little Water Company, sometimes also called the Medicine Society,
the Guards of the Mystic Potence and the Night Song Company.

All men traveling under the great heavens,
You have invited, your grandchildren and all nations!
    Oh you that make the noise,
You the great Thunderer!
Your grandchildren wish to thank you!
All your grandchildren have asked me
To offer this incense upon the mountain to you!

(Speaking to the Great Spirit, Sho-gwa-yah-dih-sah-oh):
    Oh you the Manager of All Things!
We ask you to help us,
To help us make this medicine strong!
You are the Creator,
The Most High,
The Best Friend of men!
We ask you to help us!
We implore your favor!
    I have spoken.[1]

After the tobacco throwing ceremony the keeper of the
rattles gives each person in the circle a large gourd rattle
and then the lights are extinguished leaving the assembly
in total darkness. The watcher of the medicine uncovers
the bundles exposing contents to the air and as he does so
a faint glow like a luminous cloud, according to the elect,
hovers over the table and disappears. The leader or holder
of the song gives a signal with his rattle calling the assem-
by to order and then begins to beat his rattle. The people
shake their rattles in regular beats until all are in unison
when the holder of the song commences the song, which is
taken up by the company. "And such a song it is! It is a
composition of nature's sounds and thrills the very fiber
of those who hear it. It transports one from the lodge
back into the dark mysterious stone-age forest and in its
wierd wild cadences it tells of the origin of the society, of
the hunter in the far south country and how when he was
killed by the enemy the animals to whom he had always
been a friend restored him to life. It tells of his pilgrimage

---

[1] Recorded literally as translated by Wm. Jones.

over plain and mountain, over river an dlake, ever following the call of the night bird and the beckoning of the winged light. It is an opera of nature's people that is unsurpassed."

The first song requires one hour for singing. Lights are then turned up and the feast maker passes the kettle of sweetened strawberry juice and afterward the calumet from which all draw a puff of the sacred incense. Then comes an interval of rest in which the members smoke sacred tobacco and discuss lodge matters. The medicine is covered before the lights are turned up.

With a chug of his resonant gourd rattle the leader calls the people together for the second song which is wilder and more savage in character. The whippoorwill's call is heard at intervals and again the call of the crows who tell of a feast to come. The whippoorwill song is one that is most beautiful but it is played on the flute only at rare intervals and then it is so short that it excites an almost painful yearning to hear it again but there is art in this savage opera and its performers never tire of it because it is wonderful even to them. During the singing every person in the circle must sing and shake his rattle; to pause is considered an evil thing. It is no small physical effort to shake a long necked gourd a hundred and fifty times a minute for sixty minutes without cessation. This I soon discovered when as a novitiate of the society I was placed between a medicine woman and man and given an extra heavy rattle. Every now and then a hand from one or the other side would stretch forth from the inky blackness and touch my arm to see if I were faithful and sometimes a moist ear would press against my face to discover if I were singing and listening a moment to my attempts, would draw back. The song in parts is pitched very high and it is a marvel that male voices can reach it. At times the chief singers seem to employ ventriloquism for they throw their voices about the room in a manner that is startling to the novice. At the close of the song lights are turned up and the berry water and calumet are passed again and a longer period of rest is allowed. There are two other sections of the song-ritual with rest intervals that bring the close of the song close to daybreak. The feast makers pass the berry water and pipe again and then imitating the cries of the crow, the ho-non-di-ont pass the bear or boar's head on a platter and members tear off a mouthful each with their teeth imitating the caw of a crow as they do so. After the head is eaten each member brings forth his pail and places it before the fireplace for the feast maker to fill with the alloted portion of o-no"-kwa or hulled corn soup. When the pails are filled one by one the company disperses into the gray light or dawn and the medicine ceremony is over. At the close of the last song each one takes his packet of medicine and secretes it about his person.

The medicine song according to the ritual of the society is necessary to preserve the virtue of the medicine. It is an appreciation of the founder of the order and a thanksgiving to the host of living things that have given their life-power that the medicine might be. The spirits of these creatures hover about the medicine which they will not desert as long as the holder remains faithful to the conditions that they saw fit to impose when it was given to the founder. The psychic influence of the animals and plants is the important part of the medicine and when the medicine is opened in the dark they are present in a shadowy form that is said to sometimes become faintly luminous and visible. Members are said frequently to see these spirit forms, and sometimes not individual members only but the entire company simultaneously,—but I am now trenching on a subject of which I am asked not to speak. There are marvels and mysteries connected with the ceremonies of the Honotcinohgah, suffice to say, that white men will never know, nor would believe if told. The Indian has some sacred mysteries that will die with him.

Some one has suggested that Indian songs are not stable

but vary from time to time, but this idea is at once dispelled when we see a company of fifty young men and old chanting the same song without a discord from night till morning. The song is uniformly the same and probably has varied but slightly since it originated. It is still intact with none of its parts missing, although the words are archaic and some not understood.

The medicine men teach that if a charm packet is not sung for at least once in a year the spirits will become restless and finally angry and bring all manner of ill luck upon its possessor. The spirits of the animals and plants that gave their lives for the medicine will not tolerate neglect and will relentlessly punish the negligent holder and many instances are cited to prove that neglect brings misfortune. The medicine will bring about accidents that will cause sprains, severe bruises and broken bones and finally death. I know of several persons, myself, who becoming Christians, have neglected their medicine. Whether the belief is true or not, some have certainly met with repeated accidents. In every Seneca settlement the story is the same and individuals are pointed out who having neglected their medicine have become injured or maimed for life. Should some member of a family die leaving his medicine its orenda will compel the person who should take the dead one's place to respect its desires. I will relate one instance. When John Patterson the last holder of the secret died he left his medicine in the loft of his house. His son, a well educated man of wide business experience, one of the shrewdest men of the Seneca and a person seemingly free of superstition, thought that he would allow the medicine of his father to remain idle. He wished to have nothing to do with the old fashioned heathenish customs of his father. Indeed he did not take interest enough in the medicine to look for it. Several medicine sittings passed by and the man began to suffer strange accidents. One evening as he msat with his family on the veranda of his home (a modern dwelling such as is found in any modern town), the members say that he heard the medicine song floating in the air above him. He was startled and each of the family was frightened. The singing continued until at length it grew faint and ceased. Upon several occasions the family and visitors heard the song issuing from the air. Mr. Patterson sent for the leader of the lower medicine lodge, William Nephew, who asked where the medicine was hidden. No one knew but after a search it was discovered. Mr. Nephew ordered that a feast should be made and the rites performed. Then was the modern educated Indian forced to join the lodge and take his father's seat. This story, of which I have given but the bare outline, is commonly known among the Senecas, Mr. M. R. Harrington, of the American Indian Museum, being perfectly familiar with the facts of the case which he took pains to learn while staying at the Patterson home. Howsoever this may be explained it is nevertheless considered one of the mysteries of the medicine and the instance is not a solitary one.

Few white people have ever been allowed in a medicine lodge and when they have been they have not seen to witness the ceremony in full. I know of only four who ever become members, holding the medicine: Joseph Keppler, the publisher, and Mrs. Harriet Maxwell Converse, George K. Staples, and George L. Tucker, with all of whom I have sat in the medicine lodge.

BIBLIOGRAPHY

BIBLIOGRAPHY

WORKS CONSULTED IN EDITING THIS COMPILLATION.

Barbeau, C. M.
: *Wyandot Tales*, Jour. Amer. Folk Lore, Vol. 28, (1915), p. 83-95.
Huron and Wyandot Mythology, Dept. Mines, Canada, No. 80.

Beauchamp, W. M.
: *Iroquois Trails*, Fayetteville, N. Y., 1897.
Iroquois Folk-Lore, Onondaga Co. Hist. Soc., Syracuse, 1922.

Boaz, F.
: *Mythology and Folk Lore of the N. A. Indians*, Jour. Am. Folk-Lore, Vol. 27, 375.

Hewitt, J. N. B.
: *Iroquois Cosmology*, 21 An. Rept. Bur. American Ethnology.

Hewitt and Curtin
: *Seneca Myths, Fiction and Folk-Tales*, 32 An. Rept. Bur. Amer. Ethnology.

Leland, C. G.
: *Algonquin Legends*.

Lowie, R. L.
: *Test Theme in N. A. Folk-Lore*, Jour. Am. Folk-Lore, Vol. 21, 97-148.

Mooney, James
: *Myths of the Cherokee*, 19 An. Rept. Bur. Amer. Ethnology.

Radin, Paul
: *Literary Aspects of N. A. Mythology*, Bulletin 16, Canadian Department of Mines.
Religion of the N. A. Indians, Jour. Amer. Folk-Lore, Vol. 27, 335.

Reichard, Gladys A.
: *Literary Types and Dissemination of Myths*, Jour. Amer. Folk-Lore, Vol. 34, 269-307.

Skinner, Alanson
: *Central Algonkian Folk-Lore*, Jour. Am. Folk-Lore, Vol. 27, 97-100.
Menomini Folk Lore, Anthrop. Papers, Amer. Mus. Nat. Hist., Vol. XIII, 1915.

Waterman, T. T.
: *Explanatory Elements in the Folk Tales of the N. A. Indians*, Jour. Am. Folk-Lore, 38, 1.

INDEX